I0808322

TITLES IN THE SERIES

Airpower Reborn: The Strategic Concepts of John Warden and John Boyd

The Bridge to Airpower: Logistics Support for Royal Flying Corps Operations on the Western Front, 1914–18

Airpower Applied: U.S., NATO, and Israeli Combat Experience

The Origins of American Strategic Bombing Theory

Beyond the Beach: The Allied Air War against France

"The Man Who Took the Rap": Sir Robert Brooke-Popham and the Fall of Singapore

Flight Risk: The Coalition's Air Advisory Mission in Afghanistan, 2005–2015

Winning Armageddon: Curtis LeMay and Strategic Air Command, 1948–1957

Rear Admiral Herbert V. Wiley: A Career in Airships and Battleships

From Kites to Cold War: The Evolution of Manned Airborne Reconnaissance

Airpower over Gallipoli, 1915–1916

The History of Military Aviation

PAUL J. SPRINGER, EDITOR

This series is designed to explore previously ignored facets of the history of airpower. It includes a wide variety of disciplinary approaches, scholarly perspectives, and argumentative styles. Its fundamental goal is to analyze the past, present, and potential future utility of airpower and to enhance our understanding of the changing roles played by aerial assets in the formulation and execution of national military strategies. It encompasses the incredibly diverse roles played by airpower, which include but are not limited to efforts to achieve air superiority; strategic attack; intelligence, surveillance, and reconnaissance missions; airlift operations; close-air support; and more. Of course, airpower does not exist in a vacuum. There are myriad terrestrial support operations required to make airpower functional, and examinations of these missions is also a goal of this series.

In less than a century, airpower developed from flights measured in minutes to the ability to circumnavigate the globe without landing. Airpower has become the military tool of choice for rapid responses to enemy activity, the primary deterrent to aggression by peer competitors, and a key enabler to military missions on the land and sea. This series provides an opportunity to examine many of the key issues associated with its usage in the past and present, and to influence its development for the future.

SELLING SCHWEINFURT

TARGETING, ASSESSMENT, AND MARKETING IN THE AIR CAMPAIGN AGAINST GERMAN INDUSTRY

BRIAN D. VLAUN

NAVAL INSTITUTE PRESS
Annapolis, Maryland

Naval Institute Press
291 Wood Road
Annapolis, MD 21402

Library of Congress Cataloging-in-Publication Data
Names: Vlaun, Brian D., author.
Title: Selling Schweinfurt : targeting, assessment, and marketing in the air campaign against German industry / Brian D. Vlaun.
Other titles: Targeting, assessment, and marketing in the air campaign against German industry
Description: Annapolis, Maryland : Naval Institute Press, [2020] | Series: History of military aviation | Includes bibliographical references and index.
Identifiers: LCCN 2020016789 (print) | LCCN 2020016790 (ebook) | ISBN 9781682475362 (hardback) | ISBN 9781682474679 (ebook) | ISBN 9781682474679 (epub)
Subjects: LCSH: Operation Pointblank, 1943–1944. | World War, 1939–1945—Aerial operations, American. | United States. Army Air Forces. Air Force, 8th. | United States. Army Air Forces—History—World War, 1939–1945. | Great Britain. Royal Air Force—History—World War, 1939–1945. | World War, 1939–1945—Military intelligence. | Bombing, Aerial—Germany—History—20th century.
Classification: LCC D790 .V56 2020 (print) | LCC D790 (ebook) | DDC 940.54/49730943—dc23
LC record available at https://lccn.loc.gov/2020016789
LC ebook record available at https://lccn.loc.gov/2020016790

♾ This paper meets the requirements of ANSI/NISO z39.48-1992 (Permanence of Paper).
Printed in the United States of America.

28 27 26 25 24 23 22 21 20 9 8 7 6 5 4 3 2 1
First printing

To the extraordinary and talented men and women who comprise the various organizations of America's air intelligence enterprise.

Intelligence. Reprinted from 3rd Bombardment Division, "Combat Crew Handbook," War Department, Maxwell AFB, AL: AFHRA, 10 May 1944

CONTENTS

ILLUSTRATIONS

ACKNOWLEDGMENTS

I wish to extend my sincere gratitude to Dr. Stephen Chiabotti, professor emeritus and former director of Air University's PhD program at the School of Advanced Air and Space Studies, without whom this book would not have been possible. Also, I wish to thank Dr. Mark Conversino and Dr. Paul Gelpi for their thoughtful feedback and encouragement.

For assistance with this project's core research, I owe my wholehearted thanks to Ms. Tammy Horton and Ms. Maranda Gilmore of the Air Force Historical Research Agency at Maxwell Air Force Base and to Ms. Terry Kiss and Ms. Yvonne Kincaid of the Air Force Historical Support Office at Joint Base Anacostia-Bolling.

As with all works of history, especially those that examine human or organizational behavior, this study is unavoidably influenced by the author's perspectives and inclinations. Although I have made a conscious effort to guard against such biases, any remaining errors of fact, omission, or interpretation are entirely my own. Finally, the conclusions and opinions expressed in this book do not reflect the official position of the U.S. Government, the Department of Defense, or the United States Air Force.

INTRODUCTION

> The formulation of bombing policy is a fairly complex subject. It demands the combination of a massive flow of intelligence, with a feeling for changing bombing capabilities, and the changing sequence of war strategy and timing, in its broadest sense. The fact that this intellectual process related directly to violent acts of war gave to it, at the time, extraordinary point and vitality.
>
> —WALT ROSTOW, ENEMY OBJECTIVES UNIT[1]

> What we all want is results. I am certain that neither you nor anybody else in Washington wants it better than we in the field, and I am certain also that nobody is trying harder to accomplish a high level of bombing accuracy than we are. Let us continue, therefore, to report our bombing as we see it here.
>
> —MAJ. GEN. IRA EAKER TO MAJ. GEN. BARNEY GILES, 15 SEPTEMBER 1943[2]

By the time of the German surrender on V-E Day, 8 May 1945, Allied air forces had dropped a combined total of almost 2.7 million tons of bombs on Germany, 83 percent of which fell after 1 January 1944.[3] Along with Gen. Dwight D. Eisenhower's return to Europe as supreme allied commander and the realignment of strategic bombers under his command at the start of 1944, the focus of the air campaign shifted—at least in its stated purpose—to support his invasion forces for Operation Overlord.[4] The battle for air superiority turned decisively after Jimmy Doolittle famously unleashed VIII Fighter

Command following an order from Gen. Henry H. "Hap" Arnold to "destroy the Enemy Air Force wherever you find them, in the air, on the ground, and in the factories."[5] When the winter weather finally cleared the week of 20–26 February 1944—later known as "Big Week"—Eighth Air Force culminated Operation Argument, nearly exhausting its planned targets against German aircraft production.[6]

Big Week occurred barely a month into Lt. Gen. Carl A. Spaatz's command of all U.S. bombers in Europe. Along with Lt. Gen. Ira Eaker's seasoned staff from Eighth Air Force, Spaatz inherited immense pressure from Washington. Despite his two most vexing factors—winter weather and targeting diversions—he knew he needed to show he was adhering to General Arnold's target preferences as best he could.[7] He needed to improve both the tempo and results of the air campaign as it reached its final stages. Both the cross-Channel invasion and the future of the Army Air Forces potentially depended on airpower's demonstrated success.

Spaatz's first month had not gone well. Preempting criticism, he reported to Arnold on 5 February 1944 that in January, "only 51 percent of the efforts of Eighth Air Force, 4 percent of the efforts of the Fifteenth Air Force, and 91 percent of the efforts of the RAF [Royal Air Force] Bomber Command were directed against Pointblank targets."[8] Spaatz knew this was a problem, because Pointblank *was* the air campaign, which his boss and the air proponents in Washington viewed as synonymous with independent strategic bombing. Much of the diverted U.S. bomb-tonnage in January had gone to targets that aimed to keep Londoners safe and protect the build-up of land forces in England.[9] These targets may have served valid political and operational aims, but they would not force Germany to capitulate. The air plan's success hinged on bottleneck targets such as ball-bearing production, so exactly as Arnold's intelligence staff had recommended the preceding November, Spaatz returned to attacking Schweinfurt's ball-bearing factories as soon as he felt he could.

Enjoying "unlimited visibility," a massive force of thirteen combat wings launched on 24 February, from which 235 bombers aimed for the "undamaged and repaired buildings" among the several ball-bearing factories; twenty fighter groups escorted the operation, including two groups of P-51s and two more of P-38s that stayed with the bombers all the way through the target area.[10] This first effort against Schweinfurt in 1944 boasted great promise. Intelligence analysts from Eighth Air Force immediately set to the task of evaluating postraid results, and they initially emphasized the positive: "It is believed that all formations bombed near the assigned M.P.I. [mean point of impact]."[11] Perhaps the bombers had finally dealt a decisive blow against a brilliantly selected target to bring German industry to a screeching halt and Adolf Hitler to the negotiating table. In any case, this is what Arnold's analysts in Washington hoped to hear.

Not every bomber crew had aimed upon its assigned target, but the crews were universally triumphant during their postflight interrogations. The 351st Group, for example, confessed to their group's S-2 (intelligence officer) that they had shifted their aiming point to the Deutsche Star factory, located on the far southwest corner of the target area, because smoke from previous groups blocked their assigned target. The S-2 supported the crews' claims, arguing that a preliminary review showed "generally good" results, including "hits on the Deutsche Star buildings."[12] The 379th Group's S-2 had nothing but positive remarks in his narrative. He claimed that "both the lead and low group dropped their bombs directly on the briefed target" and that "the strike photos show the result to be very good."[13] Lead bombardiers from two other groups reported favorable results as well, including "good bomb strikes at the aiming point."[14] From the bomber crews' own words and their unit intelligence officers' reports, one might have expected follow-up bomb damage assessments (BDA), as crafted by a unit dedicated solely to this purpose, to have shown considerable target destruction from the nearly five thousand bombs aimed at Schweinfurt that day.

A closer investigation, however optimistic, revealed that the bombing had not been particularly efficient and may have been too little, too late. Reviewing the strike photographs, interpreters at the Allies' Central Interpretation Unit (CIU) concluded that "three of the four main factories of the Schweinfurt ball-bearing industry were hit." However, all the photos showed was that two factories had received a few more than a dozen impacts, the Deutsche Star factory showed a single hit, and the fourth factory went completely unscathed.[15] CIU interpreters also noted from the strike photographs that "external repairs to the more important buildings damaged previously were virtually complete."[16] This raid had found the ball-bearing production industry fully recharged, so the factories may have been back in production for weeks. Unfortunately, there was no way for Spaatz to know this ahead of time, because photoreconnaissance and interpretation units had been so consumed with other objectives that the CIU interpreters had not issued any updates on Schweinfurt since October—not even one of their typical repair and reconstruction reports.[17]

A few weeks later, CIU interpreters reviewed images from a new photoreconnaissance pass. The damage appeared to be far more impressive than initially reported; perhaps the follow-on area attack that night by the British bomber command had complemented the U.S. effort. The CIU concluded that there were actually five plants, not four, and four of them "had been affected . . . all fairly severely."[18] Depending on who provided the analysis, when they provided it, and what sources they had used, the postraid reports varied considerably.

After only six more weeks, Spaatz's first report card was due. It arrived on General Arnold's desk in the form of a semiannual assessment—a rollup of the air campaign's progress—produced by the air staff intelligence chief, Brig. Gen. Thomas White. White's report noted that new raids over the first quarter of 1944 had left the Axis with just 65 percent of its ball-bearing output compared to pre-August 1943 numbers, but White struggled to reconcile the apparent bombing success with an observation that the seventeen total attacks by U.S. bombers on ball-bearing factories (in addition to those aimed on the city area by the RAF) had not yet caused any actual reduction in German matériel "as a direct result of bearing shortages."[19] In other words, given the considerable weight of effort and cost to the U.S. bomber force of these highly contested raids, there was no quantifiable impact to the German war effort, except perhaps an apparent commensurate "reduction in requirements resulting from bomb damage to aircraft and other industries."[20] Unsurprisingly, lower production of German aircraft required fewer ball bearings.

However, rather than concede that evidence suggested that the ball-bearing target was more of a slow leak than a particularly insightful or decisive industrial bottleneck, White insisted that "continuation of attacks will seriously reduce German war production in 1944."[21] Cumulative results of the seventeen previous attacks had not made a difference, yet Arnold was led to believe, and he accepted, that the bombing effort and target selection had been on the right track with just six more weeks until the planned cross-Channel invasion. The idea emanating from Washington was unambiguous and unrelenting: keep at it.

Why were there so many attacks against the same types of targets and industries if there had been no demonstrable result on the German war effort? What might a closer look at the intelligence behind the air plan reveal? Who were the air intelligence analysts, and what role had they played in target selection and their commanders' perceptions of the war effort? The answers to these questions lie partly outside the story often told, within a deeper investigation of the sources and plans of the target nomination and assessment processes, and, most of all, in the minds of the teams of analysts who produced and briefed their reports.

As Phillip Meilinger argues in his treatment of the air campaign over Germany, "Targeting was the key to everything, and intelligence was essential to conduct that function; analysis was then needed to ensure the targets were indeed the correct ones, which in turn required more intelligence. It was an iterative and complex process."[22] Meilinger traced the accomplishments and inevitable shortcomings of the newly formed, competitive, and underequipped intelligence organizations as they aided the judgment of Allied commanders and planners.[23] These intelligence organizations, as he noted, were prone to "counting things, mistaking that practice for evaluation and measurement," "mirror-imaging" U.S. industry, and building analyses on a foundation devoid of "the requisite experience and methodologies."[24] Meilinger's insights reveal a host of questions requiring exploration if we hope to learn how and why these organizations behaved as they did and what impact they had on the air campaign.

For example, if air intelligence organizations preferred quantitative methods, why was that so, and what was the source of their methodologies? Why were some organizations prone to mirror-imaging? Meilinger concludes that "a skeptic could argue that a history of air strategy is a history of the search for the single, perfect target."[25] It may just be, however, that the most critical impediment to determining and destroying the elusive perfect target—if there is such a target—is the human bias in our own analysts and commanders as much as it is the enemy's wily resistance. Maybe it was these biases—not blind faith or incorrigible orders—that drove Spaatz to continue to press home ineffective attacks on ball-bearing production in 1944.

A common theme of airpower histories is that the combined bomber offensive was the proving ground for a postwar independent air force. Regardless of whether the U.S. Army Air Forces (USAAF or AAF) could perform to the hype of its interwar doctrine, Allied commanders based their differing approaches to victory in Europe on their differing views of independent airpower. Airpower proponents boasted of a quick-victory option that they believed was well suited to the limitations of the political will, manpower pool, and military-industrial complex of the United States. However, the war department's airmen lacked an intelligence apparatus with the industrial information and analytical experience necessary to select targets and assess results.

Against this backdrop, AAF leaders leveraged the air campaign against Germany as a platform to fight for organizational independence. The AAF grew in size and global presence as General Arnold purposefully sprinkled his Air Corps Tactical School (ACTS) graduates into key leadership positions at home and abroad to guide the AAF's fight per his direction. Arnold and his AAF leadership whipped up an air intelligence enterprise from several sources on short order, and they relied upon the British to reinforce their untested strategic-bombing doctrine. Whether the air campaign would precede a credible threat of a ground invasion, achieve the limited and supporting objective of air superiority, or even win the war outright, success might be measured in terms of quicker victory with more lives preserved, fewer forces mobilized, and less economic disruption. These were the U.S. hopes for the combined bomber offensive against Germany.

The AAF's burgeoning community of air intelligence experts, led initially by pilots temporarily assigned to intelligence duty, sought to prove that air intelligence demanded unique specialization, information requirements, and air-mindedness. These analysts fought not only for responsibilities, authorities, and resources independent from Army intelligence, but also for recognition as a valuable and separate enterprise from the pilot corps within the AAF. Roots of these organizational interests took hold by the fall of 1942 and blossomed to shape the air campaign as Eighth Air Force bloomed from "6 officers and no planes in February 1942 to 185,000 [Airmen] and 4,000 planes by December 1943."[26]

Air commanders pressed their staffs for decision-quality assessments and photographic evidence to support their arguments and project the air campaign's progress. They needed informed targeting plans and objective postraid reports. They needed an air intelligence enterprise to mature quickly out of interwar neglect. What they received was the collision of organizational interests and leadership personalities that shaped Ira Eaker's command of Eighth Air Force in 1943, the tumultuous air campaign over Germany, and the path of the postwar Air Force.

Beneath this history and behind the iconic commanders of World War II lies the network of academics, industrialists, lawyers, and wartime civilian-turned-military officers who shaped the targeting decisions and air campaign assessments. These planners and analysts were undoubtedly patriotic, honorable, and talented. But they were human; they brought with them their own experiences, inclinations, and postwar expectations. This book argues that various air intelligence organizations vied for influence in ways that stimulated quarrels rather than understanding among commanders. Air intelligence organizations may have sold their own agendas as they navigated the war's complex political landscape and generated reports that widened existing fissures in the chain of command. Of course, the iconic generals were busy selling their own ideas, so the interaction of analysts' and commanders' perspectives—sometimes conflicting and sometimes coincident—may have shaped the progress and potential of the air campaign.

Unwinding the bureaucratic tensions behind the air campaign's most contentious plans and battles, comparative analysis of actual intelligence assessments at the tactical (squadron/group), operational (Eighth Air Force), and strategic levels (war department, Joint Intelligence Committee, and combined chiefs of staff) reveals an air intelligence enterprise that swelled in both stature and influence as the early phase of the air campaign progressed. While air commanders struggled to pursue their aims against unanticipated operational realities, resource limitations, and enemy actions, the air intelligence organizations often pursued aims of their own.

ONE

THE AAF AT WAR FOR A BOMBER

One thing was apparent: whoever was running the Air Corps at that time, it wasn't the Chief of the Air Corps.

—MAJ. GEN. LAURENCE S. KUTER[1]

The U.S. experience in the closing days of World War I featured promising aerial attacks on troop concentrations, including rear echelon forces, rail yards, and other lines of communication, while the British had even managed some disruption of German industry—though mostly from workers' "lost sleep because of night raids" and never with enough consistency to achieve "cumulative results."[2] Early airmen, who augured the independent role of airpower, focused on developing this offensive potential. For these ambitious airmen, the locus of many important debates was the Air Corps Tactical School.

ACTS Shapes the Air Campaign

ACTS was born out of a concession by the war department general staff (at the time meaning only the Army) after the Army adopted the air service as one of its combatant arms in 1920.[3] The official purpose of ACTS was to standardize education for air service officers, who were initially only field-grade pilots with at least a year of aviation service, to prepare them for command and staff positions; its spirited cadre also developed "the tactics and techniques of the Air Service."[4] As the Air Corps' premier training institution, ACTS took on the unofficial role of professing airpower thought among its enthusiasts and inculcating those who would listen. Its instructors and students were competitively selected and continued to be predominantly pilots. Token numbers of faculty and students from other branches and services joined after 1925, adding to the school's credibility and its collective knowledge base.[5]

An air of innovation infused the school's hallways with a sense of quasi-intellectualism and empirical experimentation via twice-per-week training flights.[6] ACTS instructors were intrepid, air-minded, and strong-willed. These men were not career scientists, engineers, or economists. They were the country's foremost birdmen, capturing and teaching air doctrine and tactics; some of their ideas were proven, but most were forward-thinking. Their conclusions-turned-dogma often derived from excessive extrapolation or downright speculation, unconfirmed by the rigorous application of the scientific method. Factions of cadre were locked in a continual struggle to break from Army service culture, though their steps were necessarily incremental since the school still had to meet the war department's purposes. For example, air-minded cadre succeeded in purging the stable management course from the curriculum in 1923, but courses on infantry and field artillery remained until the school closed.[7] The ACTS motto, adopted in 1929, was *Proficimus More Irritenti*—"We Make Progress Unhindered by Custom."[8] In some ways, the motto was more of a desire than a reality, because Army customs died hard.

To Air Corps leadership and the ACTS instructors who busily promulgated interwar air doctrine, the B-17 became the long-awaited sine qua non for heavy bombardment aviation, capable of attack directly against enemy vital centers.[9] The B-17's longer range, bigger payload, and higher employment altitude than previous bombers, greater speed than contemporary enemy fighters, and defensive air-to-air firepower gave it the promise of lethality and invincibility.[10] To the Army and the Navy, the B-17 was a budgetary threat—a grand aluminum pawn that fueled bureaucratic tensions. The B-17 was a contentious manifestation of independent airpower.

With a fervor that would later draw much scholarly criticism, interwar ACTS instructors developed doctrine to support their expectations for the B-17 and an independent air campaign.[11] They pushed away from Army conceptions of offensive airpower as aerial extensions of artillery. It was an uphill battle. Army field

Photo 1-1. ACTS planes on the line.
Reprinted from AFHSO collection, 9 October 1931

regulations dating back to 1923 limited the scope of potential bombing objectives to "those vital to the functioning of the enemy's line of communications and supply," until called upon "to render the greatest assistance possible to the main attack" of decisive ground operations.[12] As the war department general staff saw it, bombing was a supporting function of ground operations—nothing more.

ACTS cadre sparred outside the war department as well. In fact, they tilted with the Navy by developing tactics and formalizing training for intercepts at sea during the interwar period. With unbridled confidence, the school produced exercise bombardment tables that assumed a 50-percent chance of sinking any ship up to 500 feet by 90 feet by dropping 4,300-pound bombs from an altitude of 8,000 feet; and with even greater optimism, "one hit on a carrier will put it OUT for airplane operations" (emphasis in original).[13] These were bold assertions. They were untested in combat conditions and undoubtedly provocative to the sea service.[14]

While there had been persistent daylight between ACTS instructors and both the U.S. Army and Navy on bombing theory during the interwar years, the RAF experience faded steadily toward compromise with the Royal Army. Although the RAF had secured its independence as an air force in 1918, its internal doctrine was not so secure. The predominant mode of thought throughout the 1920s, as espoused by Air Chief Marshal Sir Hugh Trenchard (as chief of the air staff), centered on defeating enemy morale through independent bombing.[15] However, by the mid-1930s, wing commander J. C. Slessor steered RAF viewpoints toward support of land operations while he was posted as a lecturer at the British Army Staff College.[16] Slessor notably advocated for air interdiction and the tactical role of bombardment as he argued to target "fighting troops and supply," which meant cutting off ground troops from their lifelines.[17] Both interwar Army doctrine and Slessor's theory assumed that the primary role of airpower was to support ground operations and that only ground operations could be decisive in war.

ACTS cadre refuted those assumptions, but they struggled with their limited influence. The opportunity to shape war department policy came in connection to the general staff's war plans division, which used ACTS (via the office of the chief of Air Corps) as a coordinating office. This role did not afford ACTS cadre any direct authority, so only through their professional credibility and skilled argument would their inputs be accepted.

A 1935 update to Army Training Regulation 440-15 (*Fundamental Principles for the Employment of Air Service*) provided one such opportunity. The Army conceded in its new regulatory framework that an air force could conduct "independent operations," but air objectives were still subordinated to the "territorial or tactical command."[18] This meant a theater ground commander, if assigned, would have sole authority for an air force's target selection.[19] For ACTS instructors, this compromise was problematic. They thought the best use of airpower was "to select targets whose destruction would disrupt the entire fabric of an enemy's economy" or collapse the enemy's "industrial web"—a concept that controversially surpassed even the primacy of air superiority within the school's walls.[20]

Optimistic assumptions about the bomber's offensive potential seemed to couple with similar attitudes about its defensive advantages as well. The "bomber mafia" among ACTS cadre insisted that "the bombers will always get through"—an assumption that diminished the school's emphasis on fighter escort.[21] Why should an air force, whose massed formations of bombers would be impervious to aerial attack by enemy fighters, waste effort or resources developing its own fighters or even planning to bomb enemy airfields if the key to victory was in attacking the enemy economy? ACTS cadre may have foreseen a potential need for detailed air intelligence in order to "defeat the enemy air defense force," as one instructor argued, but controversy about bomber invincibility seemed to stall the impetus.[22]

Unrestrained confidence in the heavy bomber at ACTS was remarkable given the instructors' limited experience; they didn't even have a B-17 while they were writing doctrine for it. As Brig. Gen. Haywood "Possum" Hansell later reflected about his time teaching at ACTS, "Because we lacked the airplanes themselves, we had a tendency to build our doctrine around the drawing board designs and the expected performance of aircraft still in the design stage."[23] If one thing was certain of ACTS, shortfalls in realistic data about bombing performance and potential air threats did not appear to inhibit bombing doctrine development.

Bombing doctrine, however hastily assembled, would necessitate information about potential targets. Without support from the Army staff, the targeting intelligence problem fell to an ACTS instructor: Maj. Muir S. "Santy" Fairchild. Major Fairchild had gained credibility flying night bombing missions in World War I and was among the first Distinguished Flying Cross recipients for his pan-American flight with then-captain Ira Eaker.[24] Major Fairchild compensated for what he lacked in information and support with brains and ingenuity. He has been credited with pulling together the conceptual pieces necessary for strategic bombing, ultimately justifying both expanded B-17 procurement as well as AAF use of the Norden bombsight, as he argued: "If it could be established that the destruction of a reasonable number of industrial targets might have disastrous consequences, it might be then possible to design and construct the required aircraft, bomb-sights, bombs, navigational aids and air armament, conduct the necessary training, and, finally, calculate the force required based on expected accuracy on the strength of enemy opposition."[25]

To support his claims, Major Fairchild recognized the need for intelligence data, but he was unable to obtain information about foreign industry. Because interwar Army doctrine pigeonholed heavy bombers into tactical and coastal defense missions, ACTS instructors were prohibited from conducting "independent school examination of the economies of foreign countries," which was to be the exclusive domain of the war department's military intelligence division.[26] Instead, Fairchild settled on a surrogate. As director of the school's department of air tactics and strategy, he initiated a vulnerability study based upon U.S. industry, from which he concluded, not so profoundly, that the U.S. "economy is highly specialized."[27]

Fairchild extended this logic much further. High specialization meant less redundancy, interdependence among industries, and geographic concentration; all of this amounted to vulnerability and the possibility of bottlenecks that could collapse a whole economy—not unlike the "economic dominoes" that had toppled the United States and its Western industrialized partners into the Great Depression.[28] With these features in mind, Fairchild supposed if airplanes could cause the collapse of a nation's modern industrial economy, its national will would follow.

Emerging bombing doctrine would require not only industrial intelligence for target selection, but also an enterprise for pre- and poststrike reconnaissance. To meet this need, ACTS instructors took incremental steps away from Army tradition and guided the school's curriculum toward the views of the air service's future leaders. From an instructional standpoint, significant curriculum emphasis fell simply on map reading and chart creation.

While advanced application of these skills would be useful to both observation and bomber pilots, longstanding Army traditions imparted ground-centric viewpoints into the course material. For example, many of the exercises in the 1935 "Maps and Photographs" course surveyed topography of Gettysburg and Fort Leavenworth.[29] In other cases, aerial photography appeared as an adjunct to ground-centric methods rather than as a deliberate and systematic tool for airpower assessment. The aerial photograph was "nothing more than a machine-made, but man-interpreted, substitute for maps or for visual reconnaissance," one course text declared.[30] Of eight reasons listed in course material for employment of aerial photography, the top two were "substitute for maps" and "furnish details on existing maps," while "allow detailed study of projected bombardment subject" and "confirm efficacy of artillery or bombardment operations" graced the very bottom of the list.[31] Aerial photography had entered the ACTS curriculum as a shortcut or an improvement to old methods but fell short of promulgating new intelligence requirements necessary to support strategic bombing theory.

As Fairchild and the other ACTS instructors saw it, photographic interpretation duties pertained to a select few trained intelligence personnel, at either the corps level or higher headquarters, far from the theater of operations. "We should find such personnel in the GHQ [General Headquarters] Air Force G-2 [Intelligence] Section," a course text suggested.[32] Otherwise, anyone—trained or not—who could get their hands on a photo might put it to their use, including commanders who desired to back their claims with "irrefutable evidence."[33] "The Bombardment Group Commander is certainly able and willing to interpret photos of destruction wreaked by his bombers," the text added.[34] In its infancy, the course left awkward contradictions of photo interpretation as a highly technical skill yet one with appeal and purpose to anyone with access to a decent reconnaissance photo. ACTS instructors seemed to grasp that BDA might serve more than one purpose; but given their broader doctrinal pursuits, they shaped their course material more toward the ways that poststrike images might demonstrate an attack's success to an external audience than to stimulate objective analysis for an internal one. In the course material, a dangerous sentiment germinated: a marketing role of air intelligence might be more important than learning.

Technology for bombing doctrine depended upon more than bombers; it also depended on the bombs. Both ACTS and the Army Command and General Staff College played an interwar role in evaluating effectiveness of the bombs themselves. While testing at both institutions was somewhat narrow in scope, both contributed to a general sense that the sizes and types of existing bombs were adequate for future bombing missions. The Army had little incentive to pursue aerial bombs as a tradeoff to other armament programs (especially tanks), while ACTS might have risked making the whole future bomber endeavor seem too expensive. The ACTS curriculum pushed the idea that small, well-aimed bombs were superior to large bombs that narrowly missed. After comparing tests with one-hundred- and three-hundred-pound bombs against brick and stone structures, one report concluded, "A direct hit with even a small bomb is immeasurably superior to near hits with considerably larger bombs."[35] Aiming accuracy, it seemed, was a better investment than larger destructive force.

A class taught at ACTS in the 1938–39 academic year by Capt. Laurence Kuter argued a similar theme: as a "principle of Bombardment Tactics: Never use a larger bomb than required. Attack more targets or get a better probability of hitting with a proper size bomb."[36] Kuter went on to argue, as if stating a proven maxim, "The use of too large a bomb is *obviously* bad practice, *obviously* uneconomical of force and *obviously* can accomplish the desired degree of destruction and unessential obliteration at the objective."[37] This methodology did not consider the possibility that unseen or unstudied attributes of the target (such as underground pipes or electrical cables) might be worthy of adding a little extra destructive force. Kuter's confidence in the accuracy and destructive force of small bombs as well as available intelligence of potential targets led him to conclude that given a bomber's limited payload, more bombs carried meant that more targets could be destroyed. A more conservative approach to these assumptions—in addition to the difficulty of reaching a heavily defended target with massed bombers—might lead to an opposite conclusion: erring on the side of dropping bigger bombs the first time might help to achieve the raid's destructive goals without having to fight all the way back to the target just to try again. Every repeated raid in an air campaign would have the opportunity cost of attacking another target.

Kuter also offered enthusiastic appraisals of bombs dropped in earlier air campaigns. He argued, for example, that "we have seen proved conclusively that a 100-pound bomb has the necessary power and effect to destroy buildings," including "the heavy factory type."[38] Kuter's observations were not unique to ACTS. A chart produced at the Army Command and General Staff College during the same academic year claimed that one-hundred-pound bombs were the preferred munition for buildings of "all types of construction except sky-scrapers."[39] It was clear that Air Corps officers sought to find the right balance between bomb sizes and bomb loads to offer the best chance to secure hits and achieve the desired damage. It was also clear that they had picked instances where small bombs had landed in ideal placement, and they had lacked a rigorous method for evaluating damage to building contents.

The school's speculative yet dogmatic views on strategic bombing—based upon drawing-board characteristics of the B-17, promotional aims of aerial photography, projection of domestic industries, and ideas that small bombs had sufficient accuracy and destructiveness for industrial targets—set the AAF up with a cascade of unacknowledged assumptions. However, ACTS was a school of junior and mid-level officers charged with flying, teaching, and experimenting however they could with the limited resources they had. These officers held a small

Photo 1-2. 100 lb. Mark III demolition bomb in place for firing. This example of a bomb test shows the weapon in ideal placement in a building that is clearly already damaged.
Reprinted from Kiel, Capt. E. C. Kiel, "Attack Weapons and Equipment," Air Corps Tactical School, Maxwell AFB, AL: AFHRA, 1934–1935

flame of airpower advocacy against a strong wind of long-established views of land- and sea-centric warfare. While ACTS cadre drafted and debated airpower doctrine at Maxwell Field, they lacked the information and tools necessary to validate their bombing theory. They were neither responsible for nor empowered to determine air intelligence policy or training requirements for the Air Corps. That battle occurred in Washington.

The Custody Dispute for Air Intelligence

The struggle over Army control of air intelligence policy—what information would be collected, by whom, and for what purpose—had come to a head with the creation of a GHQ Air Force staff in 1935, because the air arm needed information to support its interwar bombing doctrine. As Air Corps leadership sought to extract itself from the Army, GHQ Air Forces (then the Air Corps' warfighting headquarters) sought "additional autonomy in air intelligence, both for following foreign technical developments and for planning air operations beyond the lines of, and before the employment of, Army surface forces."[40] This ambition met with little success, which explains why not only ACTS, but also the air war planners were left to fend for themselves.

War department intelligence bureaucracy did not cope well with the idea of its air arm getting out in front of the ground forces and driving new intelligence requirements, much less the underlying assumption that it might be appropriate for air staff planners to select military objectives for an independent air campaign. By extension, any steps to shift either human resources or office duties from war department staff to Air Corps staff were unconscionable. Without cooperation from the G-2, initial efforts by Gen. Oscar Westover (former ACTS commandant and then chief of the Air Corps) to grow the Air Corps' organic air intelligence capability so saturated his nascent information division with collection requirements that they had no time for analysis. According to an unpublished study, "In April 1936, the Chief of the Information Division reported that his current Air Intelligence Section of one officer, one stenographer, one clerk, and one librarian working part time, could do little more than file intelligence reports."[41] Even a request to add five civilians was turned down. There were not enough people to go around, and many of those who were available were not up to the task.

The plans division, typically loaded with hard-charging aircrew, could not get the data they needed from the information division, so they attempted to procure it themselves. This practice served to marginalize the tiny intelligence section to one of its primary customers and created redundant work for the comparably understaffed plans division. When chief of plans Maj. W. R. Weaver made a habit of complaining that the Air Corps staff "lacked a ready digest of air intelligence subjects and had failed to secure professionally qualified personnel to evaluate and properly disseminate the information," he was moved into the chief of information position, meaning he inherited the problem himself.[42] Unfortunately, the lack of air intelligence was a much bigger problem than one major could solve.

As the AAF built up its case for divorce from the Army, air intelligence was caught in the middle. Brigadier General Sherman Miles, acting Army assistant chief of staff G-2, vehemently stiff-armed AAF attempts to mold their own intelligence service capable of collection and analysis adequate for strategic bombing.[43] The options for the subordinated A-2—to either steer G-2 toward a thorough acceptance of air intelligence requirements or take on responsibility for all aspects of air intelligence itself—reflected the same broader struggles of the newly dubbed Army Air Forces as a subordinate service to the Army. An air force capable of conducting independent planning and analysis might side-step the war department to offer independent advice to their shared civilian masters, and that advice might seek to preclude a ground campaign.[44]

Despite this context, Arnold was not pleased with his A-2's progress or the quality of his staff's intelligence products. For example, Arnold credited a visit with Charles Lindbergh with giving him "the most accurate picture of the Luftwaffe, its equipment, leaders, apparent plans, training methods, and present defects that I had so far received."[45] He knew his service had an intelligence problem, and it was going to take a battle within the war department to fix it. First, however, he decided to get a sense of events in England.

Airmen who rise to command positions with considerable influence often launch their meteoric ascents by showing talent in opportune moments—perhaps when tested under pressure or challenged to solve an intractable problem for higher-ups. Major (later General) Charles P. Cabell was one such airman.[46] Cabell proved his mettle in Panama as an Air Corps pursuit pilot and then as a flying training instructor at Randolph Field. He'd attended the requisite schools, graduating from ACTS at Maxwell, followed by the Army Command and General Staff College at Leavenworth. Finally, he found himself assigned to Wright Field, working in the Air Corps photographic laboratory.[47] He was there flying test sorties for the Air Corps matériel division and sorting through research and development requirements—mostly driven by the ground combat arms—for low-altitude reconnaissance when the call came. Air Corps higher-ups in Washington, the same gentlemen who were engaged in fiery debate with the war department over intelligence requirements, had sent for him.

Cabell stepped nervously into General Arnold's office in January 1941. Arnold intended to send a team of observers to England to report on findings from the British war experience. Direct U.S. support to the war effort seemed increasingly probable, and there was still time to adopt practices and adjust procurement plans based upon RAF lessons learned—or at least to be informed by them. Officially, Cabell was a junior member on a team of five (including two brigadier generals), so he was charged only with the narrow scope of a photography study. Nevertheless, Arnold was boiling with frustration over Air Corps intelligence shortcomings and his ongoing battles with G-2, so he was not taking risks that anyone on this team might miss the mark or misunderstand their responsibility. Cabell disdainfully recalled Arnold's gruff demeanor: "The way he literally backed me up against the wall, shook his finger at me and charged me with all the past ills of photography made me think I was faced with a mad man."[48] Arnold was serious. Cabell would soon be well outside the comfort of his previous experiences, helping to jump-start an intelligence apparatus neglected for more than two decades. On 25 January 1941, he departed New York harbor aboard SS *Excambion*, expecting to take a cursory sampling of RAF photography posts while cautiously avoiding being an imposition under wartime conditions.

What Cabell found during his two-month excursion to the United Kingdom seemed to him a mature air intelligence enterprise, managed from the Air Ministry on down by affable personalities who were eager to adopt a mentorship role to the Americans, *especially* under desperate wartime conditions. Cabell delved into their personnel practices and organizational processes with a keen eye as to how his observations might be incorporated into the AAF. He was so impressed, in fact, that his reports often failed to offer constructive criticism or to project potential downsides.

Cabell noted the Air Ministry's direct advocacy for aerial photography in stark contrast to the office of the chief of Air Corps, where little interest existed beyond Arnold himself. The first recommendation on Cabell's final trip report was to establish "an effective agency to formulate photographic policies and to coordinate research, development, procurement, organization, training, and methods of aerial photography," adding boldly, "The nucleus for this agency is already in existence in the Training and Operations Division of the Office of the Chief of Air Corps."[49] Cabell felt that if the cause for his trip was important enough to have General Arnold's personal attention, then it should probably have a place on his staff. Arnold clearly agreed. Cabell was transferred to Washington upon his return to the very office he recommended.[50]

During his trip, Cabell also visited the CIU at Wembley (which was then in the process of moving to Medmenham), the Photographic Reconnaissance Unit One (PRU-1) at Benson, the PRU-3 at Oakington, the Air Ministry Intelligence

Directorate at Farnborough, and various camera and film corporations. Cabell was startled by the revelation of British photo interpretation in comparison to the Americans' complete lack of attention to this field. He reported on specific details of CIU operations down to minutiae that Americans might mimic, such as their shift rotations and the amount of photograph analysis expected per photo interpreter per day, yet he was particularly awestruck by the skill and attributes he witnessed in those conducting the assessments. He later reflected that interpreters needed much more than just good eyesight. "Wide associations of memory and imagination were the essentials," Cabell wrote. "The interpreter with the eye could measure the dimensions of an object seen on a photograph, but only one familiar with the functions of a suspicious object, could relate the measurements to that specific function."[51] He had witnessed that a tuned combination of aptitude, training, and experience seemed to produce far more than "casual study by the average individual."[52] The Air Corps was well behind in developing such processes and certainly had not attracted or trained comparable talent.

Among the few concerns Cabell did note regarding British intelligence practices was an unusual degree of dissemination control on the most valuable assessments. Third-phase interpretation reports—the ones offering greatest promise for their damage assessment value—covering "such factors as enemy airdromes or oil refining systems" received only a "very limited distribution."[53] The Americans would have to find the right balance of security and need to know, but it seemed to Cabell that the British erred on the side of secrecy, sending their reports only to those whom they felt most needed them.

Among Cabell's observations spanning several of his detailed reports, five in particular shaped the Air Corps perspective most. First, Cabell noted the British had a "dependence of Intelligence upon these photographs for so much of their information," but he did not question this peculiarity.[54] Rather, he was motivated by the apparent disparity from his own air force to push harder for a similar apparatus. He also lacked the experience at this stage of his career to recognize the scarcity of fusion in British analyses with other intelligence sources. In one of his reports, he parroted from CIU leadership that "information of all kinds must be available to the interpreter so that he can compare the detail he obtains from any one sortie with that information obtained of the same area from all sources."[55] It was a prescient observation that might have had merit if it was actually followed in practice or helped him to refrain from concluding that a properly resourced photo interpreter could singlehandedly "produce the information required."[56] In reality, incorporation of other intelligence sources by Medmenham was quite limited at the time of Cabell's visit. For example, prisoner reports were notoriously unreliable or intentionally deceptive, so photographs might be used to verify accuracy of the information or the integrity of the source, though even this was rare.[57]

Second, Cabell noted increasing British reliance on night photography to evaluate bombing accuracy and damage assessment. RAF advancements in night photography complemented their penchant for night area bombing, but their distrust of this method of BDA persisted. Despite the employment of a camera on every bomber, Cabell was told it was not "feasible to rely on the photograph taken by the bombing plane to give results suitable for damage assessment."[58] At best, strike photos from bombers might show roughly the bombs' points of impact but not the results. Night photography presented myriad challenges with photo-flash bombs (flare-sized charges manually dropped by the radio operator to illuminate the ground), enemy search lights, shutter speed and timing, in addition to altitude and angle limitations.[59] The British had pushed technology to the limits, but they also partnered closely with industry to work through these challenges and many others. This direct collaboration with industry was another area where the Americans were well behind, and this shortcoming was partly Cabell's fault, given his previous assignment at Wright Field. The RAF was working through most of these challenges and using modified Spitfires from PRU-3 (which was assigned to Bomber Command) to take the poststrike bomb damage photos, with a setup of three cameras able to maximize coverage with simultaneous photos.[60] Clearly, the British were working hard to get the most from the photographs, but these photographs could only show so much.

Third, CIU leadership hinted at the awkward relationship between the regular officers and the academics in uniform. RAF leadership understood the advantage, in Cabell's words, of "building the organization around individuals who know how to handle and read aerial photos, but are not bound by the World War conception of interpretation."[61] Members of the Women's Auxiliary Air Force (WAAF) and others brought into the war effort during World War II were unaffected by the RAF's early interwar decisions or stale thinking and brought with them diversity of thought and skills. A question for Cabell was whether such an approach could work for the AAF. In spite of the AAF's rebellious behavior, it was still very much part of the war department and remained tied to its traditions. Though the idea of putting free-thinking academics and business leaders into uniform was not entirely new to the U.S. wartime experience, this approach for the AAF had potential merit along with some unintended consequences (discussed in later chapters).

Fourth, Cabell also picked up from CIU leadership its near-obsession with productivity and rapid distribution of information. On the one hand, speed was paramount. He noted, "The production side of an interpretation unit must be as efficient as a business concern."[62] This type of bureaucratic behavior—placing a premium on speed over quality—could result in routines that stifle innovation or overlook relationships between assessments, potential downsides that Cabell did not note. On the other hand, Medmenham leaders valued collaboration as much as possible without compromising timeliness. "As many opinions as time allows must be obtained on areas covered," proposed Cabell, noting it would be the responsibility of a duty interpretation officer to combine others' assessments into a single final report.[63] This construct not only broadened the scope of opinions cast into the final assessment but also fostered competition among interpreters to provide assessments they thought would make the final report.

Finally, of the photographic reconnaissance units, Cabell was fascinated by "the free hand which the Unit Commander has had almost from the beginning in developing his own methods of operation and in altering his aircraft" as well as picking his own personnel.[64] This level of autonomy and trust afforded a commander below the general officer ranks was startling, especially since it all added up to an unusual degree of motivation on the part of every member of the unit to make the mission successful.

No sooner had Cabell returned and submitted his observations to Arnold than the air intelligence battle began heating up. With Cabell's reports offering ample fuel for the AAF, the controversy ignited when the office of the chief of Air Corps, intelligence division, produced a ten-page study on 31 March 1941. The report boldly suggested an air campaign had "certain lines of action, involving specific air tasks, as a framework for the compilation of air intelligence, upon which ultimate decision rests."[65] Beneath all of the jargon, the report was blasphemous and insubordinate to Army intelligence. The study, with its exhaustive sketch of air intelligence requirements necessary for an air campaign, was groundbreaking in both its ingenuity and its departure from Army conventions.

For example, the report sought collection of information such as basic elements necessary to sustain the German population; the sources, transportation, storage, and distribution of German imports and exports; "inter-connection between systems," transmission, and effects of breakdown of the electrical power system; transportation vulnerabilities and mechanisms to "isolate vital industries, factories, or areas"; a comprehensive list of information about "essential materials and commodities," both strategic and "non-strategic but contributing to economic strength or weakness"; and studies of essential industries, including information such as sources, transportation and storage, manufacturing or processing plants, and "essential activities to which [each] industry and its products are necessary or valuable."[66] The report also justified collecting intelligence for objectives required to neutralize an opponent's air force (whether or not plans called for a ground offensive) as well as requirements to defend and supply potential air bases.[67] Most disturbing to the Army was the not-so-subtle hint that seemed to link independent air assessments to decisive airpower.

Miles, in his capacity as the acting Army G-2, found this comprehensive review to be particularly insubordinate because the study omitted any references to the division of responsibility between the A-2 and its higher-echelon G-2.[68] Miles did acknowledge the basic framework as helpful, but he felt it impermissible that the A-2 might go about pursuing independent collection or otherwise avoiding direct consultation with the war plans division. Miles also argued that the A-2 was officially charged to provide only "technical evaluation of information transmitted to them" by the G-2, whereas the military intelligence division was "charged with the compilation of air intelligence, as well as that pertaining to other component parts of the Army, for the purpose of formulation of comprehensive military estimates."[69] If the A-2 needed something, it would have to get it from the G-2.

In protest, Miles appealed directly to Army chief of staff Gen. George C. Marshall, advocating actions to put the A-2 back in its place. He cited an implied arrangement from a two-year-old memo directed by the secretary of war as Army Regulation 10–15 (published in August 1936), which charged the military intelligence division "with those duties of the War Department General Staff which relate to the collection, evaluation and dissemination of military information."[70] Miles' interpretation was that air intelligence was a subset of military intelligence, for which he was responsible. He had managed to reject the AAF's purpose by anchoring his argument to published guidance that did not keep up with recent, although ambiguous, changes in warfighting doctrine.

For the G-2, an even deeper issue hinged on the authority to determine campaign objectives and whether it was appropriate for the air staff to evaluate targets at its own discretion. Offering a first rebuttal was an airman sitting serendipitously in the seat as acting assistant chief of staff, war plans division, Brig. Gen. Joseph R. McNarney. He downplayed Miles' concerns with a patronizing tone, suggesting the office of chief of air service intelligence division was merely "determining the objectives for which objective folders should be prepared."[71] Miles fumed back: "The selection of military objectives rests with the High Command, based on comprehensive estimates of the situation drawn from General Staff Intelligence," adding that "the Air Corps' 'objective folders' are really just compilations of technical information on targets which may or may not be designated as objectives."[72] Neither side challenged the idea that compiling objective folders subdivided down to specific targets for pilots' use was an appropriate duty for the highest level of Air Corps headquarters.[73] However, General Arnold himself knew that intelligence information such as "the size, location, general characteristics, special distinguishing marks, the type of construction, and other details necessary for bombing operations . . . did not exist in the United States."[74] Advocacy had to come from the top.

With nothing to lose, Brig. Gen. George Brett, in one of his last acts as chief of the Air Corps (before Arnold assumed the position in a new consolidated role), retorted with a more congenial tone and subtle nuance:

> There is no question that the selection of military objectives, including Air Force objectives, rests with the High Command. But estimates of the situation upon which the decisions of the High Command are based should include not only the M.I.D. estimate of the broad enemy situation resulting from a large accumulation of experience and records, but also the technical intelligence pertaining to air operations, including the evaluation thereof by Air Corps specialists. While it would be disastrous to have divided responsibility in integrating the mass of intelligence on which decisions for the operations of the Army as a whole are to be based, it would also be disastrous to omit from that mass of intelligence

> detailed and technical air intelligence prepared by persons primarily responsible for air operations. Such air intelligence includes not only objective folders and target information but also a comprehensive and detailed analysis of the effects of air attack against military, industrial, and economic objectives.[75]

Brett introduced two facets of the argument previously either missed or otherwise unacknowledged by Miles. The first was the airman's view that air intelligence could only be accomplished by specialists who understood the application of airpower. The argument was a hard sell, because Brett was trying to convince a confident expert that his entire staff (minus the airmen) lacked the acumen and aptitude for thinking about potential targets in a new way. Miles possessed neither the humility nor the self-reflection to accept that argument. The second of Brett's arguments foretold of challenges to come: that the assessment of air attacks was also an air intelligence function and should be left to those who understood airpower. Only airmen could write the report card on the performance of other airmen.

The weight of Arnold's air branch, with its rapid growth but slow maturity, manifested itself through cracking and splintering the functions of the war department staff. Those at the top of the burgeoning air intelligence community began to see themselves as different than their war department counterparts, with different perspectives, technical skills, and responsibilities to support independent air operations. War department leadership, at this point, perceived no such distinction. To them, the air arm comprised Army officers whose specialized training made them no different than officers of other Army branches.

Arnold, appointed a member of the joint chiefs by the same order that had created the AAF, settled the matter for the contemporary conglomeration of personalities. Arnold made it clear that timeliness and adequacy were the overriding imperatives for air intelligence. In his view, A-2 reserved the right to obtain information from any source available *to* the G-2, not just *from* the G-2, and whenever "time is a determining factor," the AAF would perform its own collection.[76] To an airman, of course, time was always a determining factor. Arnold also knew that Miles did not think like an airman.

Further, Arnold insisted that air intelligence could be adequate only if "interpreted, evaluated, and disseminated by trained air force officers," and duplication could be minimized by "the elimination of unnecessary steps."[77] To

Arnold, the G-2's hand in air intelligence *was* the most unnecessary step. Without waiting for Army Chief of Staff Gen. George C. Marshall or Secretary of War Henry Stimson's approval, he had just cut the G-2 out of the loop and set about the creation of his air intelligence organization, which, in his words, "had no recourse but to go to other sources for its information."[78] As the AAF set about slowly building up its air intelligence enterprise, lack of cooperation from the highest levels of the military intelligence division inhibited the flow of resources that might have been available to the A-2. The G-2's almost pathological fear of duplication would deprive not just the war department's planners but also the most senior members of U.S. government the value of alternative viewpoints along the way.

Spaatz's Team: Underresourced and Overstretched

Plans to expand the intelligence division continued in July 1941 during Brig. Gen. Carl Spaatz's short stint as Arnold's chief of the air staff. He took on the task with the same relentless vigor and keen foresight he would later apply to operational challenges. He cautioned that existing AAF plans for only eight hundred intelligence personnel in 1942 would be the absolute minimum, adding ominously: "In the event of an emergency being declared in the near future . . . the Intelligence Division and, of course, the Army Air Forces would be greatly embarrassed by not having the machinery functioning to produce the required number of personnel for Intelligence duties."[79] He also secured $1.5 million to convert office space to a twenty-four-hour-a-day war room, which he proclaimed as "the absolute heart-and-soul of up-to-the-minute information, serving as the basis for the war in planning and immediate Air operations."[80] Not until a warfighter-minded commander like Spaatz had skin in the game would air intelligence have its growth spurt.

The combination of Arnold's bureaucratic ascendency, Spaatz's operational vision, and Cabell's insightful trip reports set off a chain of events leading to a concerted effort by the Air Corps to catch up with RAF's air intelligence. While Cabell spent the next two and a half years under Arnold's wing implementing his observations via various air staff positions (culminating as chief of Arnold's advisory council), other AAF officers would follow up with the British. The key was to figure out how many steps of the RAF's intelligence evolution they could skip and to adopt methods that would work for the AAF, both militarily and culturally.

While the Americans were learning from British intelligence, the British were frustrated by their own bombing doctrine. In August 1941, Mr. D. M. Butt submitted his famous (and eponymous) report, then assessing Bomber Command's night attacks: "Of those aircraft recorded as attacking their target, only one in three got within five miles," and when navigating through conditions of thick haze or a new moon, the appalling ratio had fallen to "only one in fifteen."[81] This statistician's review of photographic evidence confirmed that crew reports differed dramatically from reality; the startling result drew Prime Minister Winston Churchill's ire and stirred institutional soul-searching for the RAF.[82] It would have to figure out how to survive in daylight, bomb more accurately at night, or shift its approach to targeting. Otherwise, any reasonable offensive contribution of British airpower was doomed.

Air Chief Marshal Charles Portal, then chief of the air staff, pushed all of his chips in "to improve the accuracy of our night bombing," which was, as he saw it, "perhaps the greatest of the operational problems confronting us."[83] Bomber Command's operations research "boffins" (British slang for civilian scientists supporting RAF efforts in World War II) set to developing radio and radar technologies to assist with night navigation and blind bombing while crew training and tactics evolved.[84] Meanwhile, British air intelligence organizations gnashed over competing ideas about what best to attack with the inevitably reduced accuracy of bombing at night.

Major David W. Hutchison was the next to cross the Atlantic to observe British air intelligence for the AAF, this time focused on training, morale, and procurement priorities in preparation for a potential North Africa campaign. In October 1941, Hutchison spent some time observing the CIU's training program, which was by then firmly established at Medmenham. He noted the formal courses were four weeks long, comprised twenty-five to thirty students, and consisted of primary skills, notably "studying photographs and learning to identify military objects."[85] The course included real-world intelligence photographs and was followed with a secondary phase during which students reported to an operational section of the CIU until their on-the-job training was deemed complete by the respective section chief. CIU leadership was closely involved in the selection of students as well as the training, and instructors were hand-picked from among the best qualified. While the CIU clearly had an effective program for spinning up its novices, Hutchison ascertained that "selection of the student is far more important than the training the student receives."[86] He recommended that the AAF immediately stand up a photo interpretation school and leverage the RAF's willingness to send liaisons to the United States to help.

Hutchison noticed other stark contrasts between the AAF and RAF upon his visits to the RAF photography school at Farnborough and various other RAF stations. First, he observed that British manpower shortfalls had driven the RAF to fill noncombat technical jobs with WAAFs as well as with those "physically unfit or too old for the active Army service."[87] This practice was not yet familiar in the U.S. military.[88] At the RAF photography school, he noted that "as a whole the girls make better students and equally as good laboratory personnel as the men," despite their relative lack of experience.[89] Hutchison's observations presaged service by American women in the European theater. General Arnold was impressed by the dozen British WAAFs working for Maj. Gen. Ira Eaker when he visited in June 1942, but it was not until the following month, when General Eisenhower replaced a resistant Gen. James Chaney as theater commander, that American women received advocacy to assume such roles as in England.[90]

Hutchison found the morale at RAF stations to be equally intriguing. RAF officers still surged on a jolt of enthusiasm from the battle of Britain, but they lacked almost every source of entertainment except alcohol. "It is amusing to see how much pilots drink, knowing they are leaving on operations the next morning," Hutchison observed, before recommending that "proper recreation facilities such as pool tables, card rooms, game rooms, and motion pictures would attract the officers from the tap rooms."[91] On the positive side, he concluded that the American Air Forces were "far ahead of the RAF in providing entertainment and recreation for its men," but the consequence was that the Americans had come to expect it.[92] Cultures seemed to diverge not just between the two Allied air services, but also between the pilots and other officers within each service. For example, as one intelligence analyst who served on the Air Corps staff during this period noted, "There began to be a cleavage between 'first class' citizens who wore wings and 'second class' citizens who did not."[93] The prevailing attitude among the aviators was not quick to accept other professions as equals, whether in the air or on the ground.

Both Cabell's and Hutchison's visits were essential to the AAF's wartime formulation of air intelligence. Cabell had the necessary credibility at the right time to maneuver in both the senior AAF leadership and RAF intelligence circles. In many ways, however, the relationships both Cabell and Hutchison built through their humility and gratitude paid more to the AAF than the details of their observations. They had learned of the need for efficient and autonomous assessment organizations, but they also discovered that the AAF would need to find the right people, give them the right training, and provide the right environment for them—and the air campaign—to be successful.

In the meantime, those in Arnold's meager air intelligence section struggled to keep up, and their turnover hampered continuity. The acting section chief, Maj. Bartlett Beaman, submitted a frustrated progress report just a week prior to Pearl Harbor: "It has been absolutely impossible to complete even the highest priority projects within the limit of time requested," he wrote, due to both shortages in qualified personnel as well as workspace.[94] Most of his subunits were tied up in administrative tasks and unable to provide overview summaries for quick digestion by the planners who depended upon them, much less perform any in-depth analysis. The handful of civilians assigned to the section were undertrained and served only as clerks, but they were dedicated. They logged ninety-one hours of overtime in just one month trying to keep up.[95]

Pearl Harbor to Ploesti

Regardless of whether the Army Air Forces or its air intelligence capacity was ready, the 7 December 1941 sunrise surprise by the Japanese on Pearl Harbor silenced the doves and finally pushed the United States into World War II. Over the next two days, Japan's follow-on attacks all but obliterated the offensive power of the Far East Air Force in the Philippines, leaving the remnants of U.S. forces little choice but to withdraw to Australia.[96] Americans were stunned by a catastrophe that later led to numerous conflicting reports, inquiries, and a congressional investigation into intelligence failures and allegations of dereliction of duty up to the highest levels of the Navy and Army.[97]

With the U.S. Navy caught off guard at Pearl Harbor, the Army had been in hibernation, and this presented an opportunity for the AAF: "The Army would require about two and a half years after Mobilization Day to create, equip, train ground forces," noted Major Hansell, then a member of the air war plans division (AWPD). "The Air Forces, on the other hand, could move much more quickly due to the fact that they were already well along in mobilization as a result of President [Franklin] Roosevelt's decision to expand American aviation" in addition to Lend-Lease.[98] Since air forces could bed down overseas operations in a matter of several months, if the United States was to increase its forward role in Europe quickly, it would have to untether at least some of its air forces from any ground schemes of maneuver.[99]

Roosevelt knew this gambit was the best chance of keeping the conflict away from American soil. The air plan component (known as AWPD-1) of the victory plan called for "6,680 heavy bombers, 3,740 very heavy bombers, and 13,038 replacements" along with a force of 2,050,000 airmen.[100] The services, including the AAF, would get what they had asked for, although the charge to mobilize was an especially generous boon to the AAF.

Pearl Harbor may have been an unconscionable slap to the face of the American psyche, but it was a firm Anglo-American handshake that tugged U.S. strategy into the war. With grandiose media fanfare, the British prime minister's delegation arrived in Washington on 22 December 1941 for the Arcadia conference and a first opportunity to bring wartime political leaders and service chiefs together. Winston Churchill pressured Roosevelt to accept the British version of "Germany first" by way of a campaign in Northern Africa, but the meeting otherwise validated the ideas both sides tentatively arranged months earlier in a combined U.S.-British staff conference known as ABC-1.[101] Without committing to detailed timelines, ABC-1 had specified "a sustained air offensive against German military power" along with "defensive measures to protect the Western Hemisphere and the United Kingdom; maintenance of strong positions in the Near East, India, and Far East; and protection of sea communications."[102] This language reflected a compromise that allowed the United States to commit some ground forces to boost Allied morale prior to 1943, reduce near-term pressure on British forces, and preserve British access to the Suez Canal (a controversial concession by the Americans).[103] Another remarkable inclusion in ABC-1 was a declaration that "forces will be built up for an eventual land offensive."[104] No matter what strategic bombing might achieve in the war, the inherent design for U.S. participation in a ground invasion had been part of the plan well prior to dropping the first American bomb across the English Channel.

The Pacific was not the operational priority, but combat-ready reinforcements were necessary to contain the Japanese and defend Allied interests.[105] For the AAF, this meant shipping capacity and commensurate naval escort would be stretched thin with simultaneous requirements to transport troops and equipment to Africa and the Pacific.[106] Agreements at Arcadia gave the AAF the green light to join the RAF in attacking Germany, but the Allied shipping situation delayed hopes to get a bombing campaign under way from the United Kingdom for six more months. The clock was ticking for the airmen who hoped to defeat Germany with an air campaign.

SPAATZ GOES TO WAR

When Carl "Tooey" Spaatz assumed command of the newly activated Eighth Air Force on 5 May 1942, his immediate concern was to fill the gaps on his staff with capable cronies. A calm, deliberative, and confident leader, Spaatz prized trust and aptitude in his subordinates over recent military experience. He sought those whom he knew had proven leadership and business acumen from private life. Historian David Mets notes: "Spaatz seemed quite ready to accept people, even to recruit them, from civilian occupations to take care of staff functions related to their former work."[107] As a commander, Spaatz was renowned for his keen attention to operational particulars and for delegating administrative tasks; he was self-aware of this tendency, and it shaped the way he built his team. "Just out of civilian clothes . . . They were all close personal friends of General Spaatz," later reflected Richard D'Oyly Hughes, a former British army officer and eventual lead Eighth Air Force planner who had spent the interwar period enthusiastically scrutinizing German industry and culture before settling down with an American woman whom he had met on a cruise ship.[108] Of Spaatz's original team of planners, Hughes added, "None of them ever made an operational war plan before in their lives, none of them had had the opportunity to study the problems involved, and a more scared and nervous bunch of officers, I have seldom seen."[109] Hughes lacked nothing in self-assuredness or ambition, and he wanted a part of the action.

New agencies had emerged in Washington, including the Office of Strategic Services. With prescient insight, Hughes observed, "There was great competition between these agencies rapidly to build and expand their respective empires . . . and each expressed a very strong interest in getting into the 'strategic bombing advisory business.'"[110] Hughes rose to the occasion when one of Spaatz's cronies stumbled into his office looking for help putting together the details of Spaatz's initial bombing plans. By Hughes' own account, he drafted the plan himself, ended up personally briefing Spaatz and General Marshall, then soon afterward landed in London with a promotion to lieutenant colonel as Spaatz's lead target planner.[111] Spaatz may have assembled his team of planners by the summer of 1942, but they did not choose the AAF's first target in the European theater of operations.

The AAF launched its first deliberate attack across the Mediterranean on the evening of 11–12 June 1942, albeit via a task force led by Col. Harry Halverson rather than the Eighth Air Force. General Arnold picked the target himself when the original plan to attack Japan from China fell through, which began Arnold's titanic trend of operational interference from Washington.[112] Other accounts suggest grand strategy was at play since destruction of the Romanian oil refineries at Ploesti—the primary fuel source for the Axis—offered "the promise of maximum aid to the USSR in its struggle for survival" on the Eastern front.[113]

By all accounts, the sprawling Ploesti refineries should have been an easy target, but the attack resulted in utter failure with no real damage. The AAF's intelligence division, relying on an unconfirmed Navy intelligence report, related a single "oil depot at Ploesti was destroyed, one bomb fell in the woods, another hit a railroad station, while several fell on [the Black Sea Port of] Constanta without doing much damage."[114] Weather had obscured the intended impact points, the formation of thirteen bombers released weapons based solely on an unreliable time over target, and a disorganized egress plan resulted in aircraft scattered around the Middle East.[115] "Probably the most favorable aspect of the raid," quipped the AAF's historians, "was the impression the big [B-24] bombers produced on the intensely interested citizens of Ankara."[116] It was a disappointing start for U.S. bombers and certainly for those who sought to forward their strategic bombing theory.

The mission could be viewed as a success only from the standpoint that the AAF had attempted its first action derived from its plan to interrupt German industry. But there was not yet an AAF intelligence apparatus or collateral agreement in place in theater to provide detailed analysis of the results. If the AAF bomber forces were to improve on this first effort, they could not just do more of the same; they would need new organizations, training, and systematic approaches to contribute to the technological innovation and the unprecedented boost of resources that followed. Arnold first focused internally.

A School of Apprehension

Even the few hours of inadequate intelligence training conducted at ACTS were lost when the school was temporarily suspended in June 1940. The school's would-be students and experienced instructors were needed to fill field and staff positions as the air service ballooned.[117] The AAF needed to build a professional air intelligence corps quickly, and it needed officers—about two thousand of them in three years—who understood intelligence challenges and requirements unique to the air service.[118] Unfortunately, the official air intelligence training program stumbled over a rocky start. A task as straightforward as finding a location reflected the impetuous planning style then typical of Arnold and his staff.[119] The training program moved from Bolling Field in Washington, DC, to the University of Maryland's College Park campus, and then to Harrisburg, Pennsylvania, all within the first three months. The location-jockeying robbed its initial cadre of the opportunity to iron out administrative and logistical challenges before the first crop of students arrived. The air staff's intelligence division had inexplicably failed to consider details such as facility requirements, construction timelines, faculty travel, and course curriculum.[120]

This fledgling school put its graduates on a path to form a new air intelligence career field in the AAF. The professional identity of these air intelligence officers was shaped by how they were selected, how they were trained, and what was expected of them after they graduated. Though these three factors were not static throughout the war, the school bred cohorts of officers with different training experiences and expectations of their military service.

The air staff's personnel procurement division retained authority for student admissions and initially patterned its selection criteria after the RAF. Colonel E. F. Koenig, the school's first commandant, included a detailed discussion of student quality in his final report: "The first class sent here represented, with very few exceptions, a most unusual and most competent group of individuals. . . . they were all men of affairs, intensely patriotic, and unfailing in their devotion to duty."[121] They were a mix of intellectual and eccentric gentlemen, but at an average age of forty-one, they were not young by comparison with typical Army junior officers.[122] Maturity could be an asset, except that many of the older intelligence officers "found difficulty in understanding the feelings and attitudes of the younger crewmembers," as noted in an unpublished report.[123] A small minority mirrored the RAF's penchant for architects, engineers, and scientists who would follow on to photographic intelligence, but the preponderance of AAF recruits were attorneys, bankers, business executives, and teachers.[124] This latter group would specialize in combat intelligence, meaning most would follow on as group or squadron S-2s who dealt most closely with aircrew. The second class, Koenig remarked, "showed a marked deterioration."[125] The third improved after Koenig complained up the chain of command about student quality, but the fourth was abysmal. Students began to arrive with an inflated sense of entitlement and a negative attitude about the training. Some poor performers even expected to continue on to foreign service despite failing out, while others clearly did not even want to be there.[126] Later classes tended to be less selective, less educated, and much younger as the pool of highly educated and experienced eligibles dried up.

Coordination for total class sizes, specialized training allotments, and student placement after graduation was poor. Class size at Harrisburg swung between seventy-seven and nine hundred, reflecting haphazard planning and communication between the AAF Air Intelligence School (AAFAIS), the Technical Training Command, the air staff, and combat headquarters.[127] As the demand for air intelligence officers by VIII Bomber Command began to exceed the output at Harrisburg, officers were shipped from officer training school in Miami directly to Eighth Air Force in England to receive training there.[128] This placed an even greater burden on those in theater and dropped standardization across the career field completely.

The school's full schedule of academic instruction and military drill brushed aside other necessary ingredients of a professional military corps. As Carl von Clausewitz professed, "No matter how much one may be inclined to take the most sophisticated view of war, it would be a serious mistake to underrate professional pride (*esprit de corps*)."[129] Morale was not just undervalued in the early days at AAFAIS; it was nonexistent. Even the hardest working and highest quality instructors were routinely passed over for promotion. Top graduates who had stayed on as instructors found this especially grating "while their classmates basking in the spotlight in Washington have gained one and sometimes two grades." Those fortunate few in Washington were enjoying a slower pace of temporary duty, either studying or helping out the understaffed intelligence service with menial tasks while awaiting their numbered air forces to stand up and ship overseas.[130] The disparity in duty expectations was considerable.

Meanwhile, instructors at Harrisburg received promises to rotate into combat theaters, yet many remained on the staff.[131] The school's leadership at that time did little to encourage social bonds, develop unit cohesion, or inspire a sense of professional pride among intelligence officers. Guidance promulgated to both students and faculty maintained that social activities were superfluous. "This is a serious school," published the first commandant, "engaged in the grim business of preparing officers for battle."[132] Not until the school failed a higher headquarters inspection did the third commandant improve "unsatisfactory" officers' mess conditions and establish an officers' club.[133]

Perhaps the school's greatest flaw in its early days was to pull the top graduates directly onto the faculty before they gained any real-world experience.[134] This policy was especially problematic since most of the original faculty had lacked military experience as well. The result was to undercut the school's credibility to its own students while it robbed the combat theaters of the most promising graduates. One example was 1st Lt. Eugene McGuckin Jr., an immensely popular Princeton-educated industrial engineer who could "play football at a pace that wore down everyone's endurance but his own."[135] He undoubtedly was a charismatic and talented officer. However, instead of pushing him to thrive in combat (perhaps to bring him back later), the school tapped him to teach such material as "recent information on Photo Intelligence and Air Support Operations," even though he had no experience with either.[136]

A COURSE OF CONTRADICTIONS

Challenges with student selection, the training environment, and postgraduation expectations were many, and the quality of training during the school's early days fared no better. The school's curriculum evolved during its brief tenure, but most improvements came too late to impact graduates bound for the European theater. The school's initial charge from General Marshall was to "instruct and train students in interpretation of aerial photographs and kindred subjects allied to the subject of Air intelligence," but the balance favored the latter at Harrisburg; none of the first class received specialized photo intelligence training, and even by the third class, 262 students generalized in combat intelligence, while only 52 specialized in photo intelligence.[137]

Squadron- and group-level intelligence training conducted at the school in 1942 reflected the broader AAF struggles for independence from the Army as well as the primacy of pilots in the service. The school's official texts were shamelessly informal and awkwardly oriented toward cramming basic military knowledge into civilians. The school's material professed to its own students, "In view of the extreme youthfulness of our flying personnel and the admitted respect which young and active men have for age and success, it is advisable to choose the intelligence officer from among those men over thirty, who have made their mark in life in other fields of endeavor and thereby deserve and command respect and consideration."[138] This passage reveals the brazen demands for primacy by the AAF's aircrew and the challenges confronted by anyone outside the flying community who attempted to exercise a position of authority at the unit level. Since respect and credibility in the AAF derived from proof of aptitude and prowess in flight, the officer responsible for interrogating bomber crews had to establish respect in other ways. As incoming students tended to be younger and less experienced, they were ever more set up for failure in their duties to follow.

The school also demanded of its intelligence officers that they be more than merely a little enthusiastic about aviation and stay up-to-date as tactics changed. The effective intelligence officer "is always mingling with pilots and trying to get their point of view; he never misses a chance to fly in an airplane," whereas one "who is not familiar with the latest developments in the art of warfare, particularly of aerial combat, is a menace to his command."[139] There was no middle ground. Of course, the AAF's need for intelligence officers who understood air tactics and possessed airminded approaches to their profession had underwritten the argument behind the school's existence. However, the attitude evident in the text takes the argument so far as to undercut professional pride in themselves as intelligence officers. The more subservient they would be to aircrew, the less objective their assessments might be.

This expectation of a subservient mentality especially pervaded the intelligence officer's role in damage assessment. Postmission analysis began with intelligence officers questioning aircrew about the mission. The school's textbook for training squadron S-2s (the unit intelligence officer) defined this process as *interrogation*: "The extracting from a crew on its return from a mission of the maximum amount of reliable information . . . then transmitted to a higher authority, and thence downward to other units, in order that all flying personnel may derive the maximum benefit from the experiences from any particular crew on any given mission."[140]

The intelligence officer played the role of a compassionate filter. Despite the charge to obtain information "promptly, completely, and accurately," the intelligence officer was to be conscientious and considerate of combat crews.[141] "It is the announced policy of the Army Air Forces that combat crews returning from a mission shall not be harassed by being required to render complicated written reports," commanded the text. "At times, it may seem like a cruel task to quiz pilots and crews just returning from a dangerous mission, exhausted, tired, hungry, and thirsty."[142] But it was necessary to get information to higher headquarters as soon as possible, and that meant getting it out of the aircrew while it was still fresh in their often shell-shocked minds. The course text clearly reinforced the preferences of aircrew to be treated with special attention and portrayed the intelligence officers' work as tricky but mundane. Nevertheless, the intelligence officer was prized less for his intellect and more for his interpersonal skills. To be successful, according to the course, the interrogator "requires tact, skill, patience, and a good knowledge and understanding of life."[143] Sometimes that skill meant not just coaxing information from the aircrew but also sifting through their claims.

Intelligence officer training clearly placed the onus for accurate reporting on the intelligence officer versus the aircrew. "It is a good policy to adopt that the S-2 should always stay on the conservative side in reporting the results of bombing," the textbook insisted. "Should he not do this, there is a tendency to jeopardize seriously the reputation of the crew and the S-2 because a report is submitted in which, for example, an aircraft factory is claimed as completely destroyed, and a reconnaissance mission over the area soon after the mission shows the aircraft factory to be standing and absolutely intact."[144] The intelligence officer was to filter out excessive claims by the crew in bombing accuracy as well as air-to-air kills. The service tended to accept exaggeration by aircrew, as if expected, but made no concessions for potential bias by its intelligence officers. Instead, these intelligence officers were caught between aircrew who needed to feel their sacrifices were validated, commanders who preferred positive feedback (to reinforce promotion), and an imperative to find the truth with inadequate analytical tools and training. This put them in a position to make the strongest claims they could reasonably defend with the information they teased out of the aircrew. General Arnold noted that this predicament drove behavior reminiscent of an entirely different profession: "Intelligence Officers . . . seemed to me . . . to use psychologists' methods in getting accurate answers from the crewmen."[145] Without any means of independent verification at the group level, unless photos were available and of adequate quality, aircrew claims prevailed.

Furthermore, since the squadron and group commanders for whom the intelligence officer worked were pilots, this arrangement put the intelligence officer in a position to not only speak truth to power, but also extract truth from power. Even the most mature and professional of intelligence officers could be caught between pragmatism and cynicism, either leaving threads of aircrew exaggeration uninvestigated or potentially irritating the boss by doubting a mission's success. A training text concluded with a macabre threat to the intelligence officer's conscience: poor interrogation or reporting "may lead to the loss of aircraft and bomber crews. . . . this loss is directly attributable to the S-2 who carried out the interrogation."[146] Positive motivation was not a strong suit of the Harrisburg school.

The school's photographic interpretation training during this era had its own challenges: an awkward mix of caveats, unreasonable expectations, and an idea—borrowed unfiltered from the RAF—that interpreters should limit subjectivity in their assessments. One course text set the apologetic tone up front: "Photo intelligence is comparatively a newcomer in the field of military science and tactics," cautioned the 190-page textbook, declaring itself to be "preliminary in nature . . . [until] a more thorough knowledge of what the problems are and what type of photo-intelligence organization and procedures are necessary to cope with them."[147] Despite the course's limitations, this observation was spot on. The Harrisburg school showed a prescient self-awareness that technical demands levied on air intelligence were reaching beyond the experience of the organization charged to meet them. Much of the rest of the volume bore either a speculative tone or a notably narrow viewpoint, reflecting the limited operational experience possessed by Harrisburg's instructors. The fledgling school, beginning to sense its inadequacy, could not yet determine the nature of its shortcomings, much less how it might address them.

When the photo interpretation instructors did feign confidence, they placed unreasonable expectations upon their students. In stark contrast to the S-2 course, the photo interpretation instructors prized different traits of their student-analysts than those sought of unit intelligence officers. "Patience, a flair for detail, and a retentive photographic memory" were required for this type of work, so "the research-minded type of individual will probably make the most success of this job," a course text stated.[148] The pool of patient researchers willing to sign up for AAF intelligence was shallow indeed. Further, a brilliant mind for research was not enough; the school demanded of its students the same passion for flight exhibited by the AAF pilots. This type of work also required a "keen interest . . .

in all activities regarding flying, airdromes, air forces, and the aircraft industry," declared a course book.[149] These were lofty selection criteria for a new school with a large enrollment.

In addition, the gifted mind and interest in aviation had to be augmented by a foundation in target information. The photo interpretation course attempted to incorporate the AAF's budding relationship between air intelligence and industrial knowledge. This linkage derived directly from the AAF's strategic bombing doctrine, but the school lacked the resources to teach to the depth it desired. Knowledge of industrial target systems had to be acquired by the interpreter because the quality of his or her assessments depended upon it. Here, the photo interpretation course was aspirational beyond reason: "A good interpreter must have first of all a knowledge of what he is looking for, what it looks like, and where possible, how it works. He must become thoroughly acquainted with the enemy country, that is, the geography, the economic structure, the industries and transportation system, and the military organization. He must know their life as it is today and keep himself currently informed of everything of significance happening in their country as well as his own, gleaning the information from all possible sources."[150]

Even had the school's preferences for student selection held true, the depth of knowledge necessary across various industrial systems could not be obtained in a six-week course or have been reasonably possessed by incoming students. Just as it had with the S-2 training, the school levelled the apparent contradictions of photo interpreter duty squarely onto the shoulders of the student intelligence officer. As it stood, unless the interpreter was gifted with a mind for detail and highly motivated to acquire an understanding of enemy intelligence, then his analysis could be incomplete, inadequate, or inaccurate.

Conscious that their students could not meet expectations after graduation, the school's leadership taught students to hold back on subjective assessments. Both aircraft interpretation as well as damage assessment training captured this sentiment. In aircraft interpretation, for example, the course argued there were "no substitutes for knowledge and practice," so the intelligence officer should "work conservatively in his early 'learning stage' . . . [because] a good aircraft interpreter never guesses."[151] The point at which intelligence officers possessed enough experience to offer subjective assessments was unclear, but as they had learned to offer only objective assessment from the start, they would be unlikely to buck this routine.

Damage assessment training, given only a cursory two pages in the primary course text, was also clearly lifted from the RAF and included examples from before the U.S. entry into the war. The final paragraph concluded: "It is stressed that the work of damage assessment is highly scientific and absolute accuracy must prevail. Often damage assessment reports given by interpreters will clash with pilots' reports and the ground sources available to intelligence officers. The interpreter must be accurate enough so that intelligence and operations will have confidence in his findings. Raid assessment is a most complex and responsible task and is ultimately bound up with operational problems and general bombing policy."[152]

The burden of proof would be on the intelligence officer to resolve contradictory evidence and to convince skeptical aircrew of intelligence findings. Further, the text's tone skirts the issue of intelligence subordination to operations as it captures the political nature of bomb damage assessment. As intelligence professionals, the appeal was to seek the truth. At the unit level, however, where intelligence was subordinated to operations personnel, this task could be exhausting. In situations where intelligence officers worked for each other, such as at Medmenham, they possessed greater flexibility in their assessments along with having autonomy. Effective BDA had to address two audiences: the intelligence staffs at higher headquarters, and the operational commanders. Given the limits of bombing accuracy and the political pressures on the generals to show results, BDA analysts were left to fend for their own credibility.

A FALL OF SHORTAGES: BOMBERS, ESCORTS, AND ANALYSTS

While the AAF's newest analysts trained in Harrisburg, Spaatz's Eighth Air Force settled its headquarters and subordinate units down in the United Kingdom and began operations. Major General Ira Eaker, after establishing VIII Bomber Command headquarters at High Wycombe (near the RAF Bomber Command headquarters) on 15 April, had relayed back to Washington that "Intelligence represents the section of activity in which we are weakest."[153] But the task load grew over several months to include sixteen functions, beginning with "providing the Commanding General and his staff with intelligence required. This includes: the strength, composition and location of the enemy air force; performance of enemy aircraft; airdrome details; state of the enemy defenses, especially flak defenses; information concerning targets under consideration;

raid assessment; in fact, all information concerning the enemy."[154] Other duties varied widely and required the creation of subordinate units within the intelligence section for security, operational intelligence, analysis, duty room, training, photo intelligence, reports and reporting, RAF liaison, as well as public relations and the command historian.[155]

Many heavy bomber groups, committed by the combined chiefs to Operation Torch (the invasion of North Africa) and thus redirected to the Mediterranean, were beyond Spaatz's control in the near term.[156] With the paltry numbers at his disposal, Spaatz's Eighth Air Force busily practiced and experimented with each raid as the tail count and combat range of his bomber forces all too slowly increased. Weather frustrated bombing efforts, which he limited to coastal targets. By the end of October, Eisenhower constrained the highest priority to attacks on U-boat bases in order to protect forces flowing to the Mediterranean.[157] Further complicating Spaatz's progress were the evolving variants of Focke-Wulf 190s menacing his bombers and causing losses that drained morale.[158] As David Mets noted, a stalwart Spaatz "cautioned Arnold not to leap to conclusions on the evidence of the early missions because they would contain too few planes to saturate the defenses."[159] Between September and November, more heavy bombers finally trickled into England, increasing Spaatz's precarious tally of B-17s from 144 to 180 and of B-24s from 34 to 41.[160]

Even as the numbers grew, only a little over half the planes were expected to be flyable in combat at any given time. As a planning factor, Eighth Air Force statisticians estimated that 75 percent of aircraft in theater would be allocated to combat units (others were either in transit or temporarily possessed by service command), of which only 75 percent would be serviceable for bombing raids at any given time.[161] Holding for reserves, this meant that fewer than one hundred heavy bombers could be made available per raid—well below Eaker's then-preferred threshold of three hundred, which he felt "could attack any target in Germany by day with less than 4 percent loss."[162] Armed with a doctrine that depended upon massed formations, Eaker felt he had too few bombers to accomplish much at reasonable cost.

The bomber shortage was not the only aircraft issue affecting operations, however, as escort aircraft during this period were not much help either. They were too few in number and lacking in performance and range to compensate for bomber self-protection challenges. P-39s, introduced in October but phased out after just a few months, were outclassed by the German fighters. P-38s, despite struggling in the cold and humidity of the European climate, boasted improved performance and range.[163] Unfortunately, P-38 numbers peaked at just 184 in October, even before Arnold siphoned them off to North Africa.[164] Only the short-legged British Hurricanes and Spitfires remained available for the escort role. "This limited the range of our operations to a narrow area over Northern France and the Bay of Biscay," Hughes grumbled. "With the possible exception of the German submarine bases, there were virtually no targets of any military or economic importance."[165] Even as small numbers of German fighters spiraled to earth defending the coast, attacks on German submarine bases contributed little value to the emerging air superiority battle. Eighth Air Force was off to a slow start with its bombing operations, and its shortages in aircraft were also matched by shortages in intelligence personnel.

Colonel George MacDonald, then Spaatz's assistant chief of staff for intelligence, had left target planning throughout the fall of 1942 to Hughes' office while he focused on personnel issues. Expressly prioritizing arrival of fresh intelligence officers in theater over the time it took to train them at Harrisburg, MacDonald pressed the air staff to fill his rosters fast. Sizing the Eighth Air Force Headquarters staff wasn't the immediate problem. Its subordinate VIII Bomber Command intelligence staff, however, was overwhelmed at just two-thirds strength as its newly trained officers were splintered into four new units. In a frustrated dispatch fired uphill, Lt. Col. Harris Hull, the VIII Bomber Command intelligence chief, declared, "It is not believed that any officers in the Intelligence Staff at VIII Air Force are familiar with the organizational problems and the *combat* intelligence load now being carried by the Intelligence Staffs of VIII Bomber Command" (emphasis in original).[166] By taking his anger straight to Arnold's staff, Hull bit the hand that was trying to feed him.

There was much work to be done setting up subordinate units in England, and many of those trained for intelligence work found themselves engaged in whatever unrelated duties local leaders deemed expedient. Colonel Ed Sorensen, a reluctant pilot-turned-intelligencer with a particularly forceful personality serving as Arnold's A-2 in Washington, followed up on MacDonald's request and sent officers "without training, but earmarked for intelligence work," adding a not-so-subtle threat "to take every precaution to fasten on to those fifty-one men and not lose them from intelligence."[167] Arnold had already expressed concern to Spaatz about "the diversion of intelligence officers," as word even made it back to Harrisburg about its early graduates "being employed . . . as mess officers, counter-intelligence officers, or simple clerks in the headquarters to which they are assigned."[168] Many of Eighth Air Force's carefully selected and trained intelligence officers took on other tasks while they were backfilled by untrained recruits yet to be acculturated to the combat theater. The lack of aircraft arriving in theater left Eighth Air Force at inadequate strength to meet its operational goals, as the paucity of trained intelligence and analysis personnel left it unable to effectively evaluate its results.

NEW TACTICS AT ST. NAZAIRE

Not every commander was discouraged by the lack of expected resources. In fact, there may not have been an air commander during the entire war more in tune with validating assumptions, selecting metrics, or driving for efficiency than Curtis LeMay. His appreciation for BDA and operations research began during his own brief tenure as a group commander. LeMay was tired of returning his 305th Bombardment Group to the submarine pens at St. Nazaire because they were unable to put enough bombs on target, much less do much damage with the bombs that did hit. In fact, the British Air Ministry's intelligence section began to push for antisubmarine patrols versus bombing the land-based targets: "The most rapid, effective and permanent means of reducing the submarine menace is considered to be direct sinkings by surface and air attack. . . . Certainly the effort required to attain a similar result by bombing of bases and building yards alone will be quite disproportionate to the results."[169] This advice did not sit well with the AAF and had not yet gained traction with the combined chiefs. The AAF had flaunted the argument that its long-legged heavy bombers could perform coastal defense, but a wartime backfire appeared imminent.

The AAF was already operating its antisubmarine command with assets siphoned from its bombing campaign. In good faith, the AAF stood up the 1st Antisubmarine Squadron in England in November 1942. By the end of December, the squadron possessed six B-24Ds but could only claim one U-boat "probably sunk" of two total sightings for that entire month.[170] The Allies lost seventy-five vessels worldwide in December, fifteen of which were participating in Atlantic convoys.[171] There was much yet to be done to stop the U-boats, but the bomber airmen preferred attacking shore-based facilities because they would maintain flexible control of their own forces.

Meanwhile, LeMay was bull-headed about improving his results, so he tried to calculate everything he could imagine. He worked out the numbers using a Reserve Officers Training Corps artillery manual and concluded that enemy fighters were a more significant threat than was flak, so he held his crews to a tight defensive formation to mass their machine-gun firepower against the pouncing Luftwaffe.[172] He also believed maintaining formation integrity would improve bombing accuracy; this would shrink the bombing pattern as well as compensate for variations in experience and ability. In other words, a tighter

Photo 1-3. BDA photograph of 3 January 1943 raid on St. Nazaire. Smoke from bomb damage appears mixed with defensive smoke screens.
Reprinted from Central Interpretation Unit, "Preliminary Interpretation Report No. S.A.188," annotated print No.1, 3 January 1943, AFHRA

bomb pattern meant the bombs would fall in a more precise cluster, while if the whole formation bombed using the skills of the best navigator and bombardier in the group, then the whole load of bombs would be more accurate as well.[173]

On 23 November 1942 LeMay led his group through Eighth Air Force's fifth attack on St. Nazaire in just two weeks, and he insisted the entire group maintain his new "multi-level box" formation straight and level from the initial point through the target.[174] "We were going to put some bombs on the target," LeMay contended. "Anyone in his right mind knew you couldn't shoot a qualifying score by zigzagging around every ten seconds."[175] No aircraft were lost to flak and only two to enemy aircraft. Tallying all efforts through this raid, photo interpreters noted "considerable damage has been caused to facilities and property surrounding the main basin," but there was nothing catastrophic, and earlier reports of a port closure due to damage to lock gates were refuted by reconnaissance.[176] The most that could be attributed to the damage on the submarine pen roof at St. Nazaire was a "diversion to Lorient [another submarine base] of the craft normally based at the former."[177] The Germans quickly repaired the damage, so the bombers returned again on 3 January.

This time, the Mighty Eighth sent an entire division. All 85 bombers led by LeMay's group employed his bombing-on-leader tactic, putting nearly 25 percent of the 107 bombs that hit the port area within 1,000 feet of the target—far better than previous attempts.[178] In addition to a number of destroyed buildings, bomb damage assessments showed "sixteen or more bombs have fallen on the railway lines causing severe damage over an area of approximately 14 acres," a floating dock and sea wall were damaged, and "the U-boat pens have been hit at least one, possibly 3 times. . . . There is a 16-foot crater in the roof."[179] If this was the best Eighth Air Force could muster, it was not going to be enough, even if the analysts' accuracy numbers and BDA seemed to be enough to celebrate.

TWO
PICKING UP THE SLACK

I want a group of civilians to be as able as my best officers. . . . I want them free of all operational and administrative duties so that they can go out and investigate a problem and sit down and study it for three days or longer, until they come up with the answer.

—LT. GEN. IRA C. EAKER, COMMANDING GENERAL, VIII BOMBER COMMAND[1]

The Americans at this time were buying their intelligence from the British readymade, and we had to prove ourselves by showing that the British made mistakes.

—CHARLES P. KINDLEBERGER, OSS ECONOMIST[2]

A Committee of Lawyers and Industrialists

By the fall of 1942 Arnold's steps to build and train an air intelligence cadre and to adopt lessons learned from the RAF could not adequately address near-term requirements. The forthcoming meeting of the combined chiefs at Casablanca intensified his sense of urgency, because he knew this event would set policy for the next phase of Allied bombing in Europe. Without a detailed, feasible, and executable plan, or at least a credible estimate of potential targets in Germany—one that could garner support outside of his own staff—U.S. air involvement could get caught playing second fiddle to the RAF's night area bombing. Even more objectionable, there could be pressure from RAF senior leaders or Churchill himself to give up altogether on daylight precision targeting of specific industries. This would undermine both the AAF's bombing doctrine before it proved valid and its precarious bid for resources vis-à-vis the other services.

Although Arnold received regular updates from Spaatz and others on developments in Europe, he wanted the targeting plan developed in Washington. Arnold knew—or so he thought—his generals in the United Kingdom were too busy dealing with operational challenges to help win the Washington battles, much less arguments with the combined chiefs. Arnold also knew that his own planners lacked the intelligence resources, expertise, and time to propose a more thorough and acceptable analysis than what had led to the troubled roll-out of AWPD-42.[3] This predicament left Arnold with few options, and none were ideal.

To address the expertise problem, he could assign additional training or pursue academic credentials for his staff, but either option would take time he did not have. Besides, many of them had already graduated from the Army's Command and General Staff School in succession with the Air Corps Tactical School. Those schools, in addition to the Army's War College and Industrial College, should have met that purpose insofar as the war department was concerned.[4] Alternatively, he could hire credentialed civilians to augment his staff, but assigning them to his existing intelligence or planning organizations might not help with their credibility problem. Arnold went for a third option, which was to hire a team of premiere civilian analysts who could operate independently of his staff—at least in appearances. This team of reputable civilians, he conjectured, would fill his intelligence gaps with industrial expertise.

An Air Force history posits that Arnold and Fairchild "may have believed that the establishment of a group outside the normal intelligence and plans organizations, especially one including prominent civilians, would carry greater weight with the other services and with political leaders such as the Secretary of War and the President."[5] This logic is plausible, but it also suggests that Arnold may have been more interested in employing civilians for the purpose of adding credibility and rigor to his intent for bombing over Germany than having any real hopes for original thought on their part. Arnold's idea was that his special committee might add meat to the bones of ACTS doctrine without jostling any skeletons in view of the other services. In either case, Arnold needed them to track down and assemble vast sources of information that his existing intelligence staff could not obtain (or that was otherwise blocked by war department G-2). He needed their study to convey impartiality, and he needed it quickly.

As for the more tangible problem of near-term intelligence deficits regarding Germany, Arnold had turned to Robert Lovett, special assistant for air affairs to the secretary of war, for advice. "The easiest way to secure the information would be to get it from engineers, bankers, or construction people who had actually done the construction in foreign countries; men who had loaned money, and in loaning money, had secured descriptions of the various plants," suggested Lovett.[6] Arnold latched onto Lovett's idea. He could directly hire some of the brightest civilians available, who could use their connections and influence to reach out to others.

Arnold then bypassed his planning and intelligence chiefs and directed Col. Byron Gates, his assistant chief of staff for management control—a position "normally concerned with staff procedures, correspondence channels, and management techniques"—to begin hiring a new team of civilians for this purpose.[7] Gates, who had instructed at ACTS with Fairchild just a few years prior, was the only regular Air Corps officer originally associated with the committee, and, along with juggling the demands of his other duties, he was unable to commit to full-time participation.[8] Gates was soon promoted to brigadier general and could provide just enough oversight as the military chairman of committee meetings when he was available. This arrangement helped to keep the civilians from straying too far from ACTS doctrine, while he maintained a duty title innocuous enough not to undercut Arnold's intent to portray his outside group as unbiased.[9]

Arnold's intelligence staff, already exasperated by its own shortcomings, was demoralized to lose a responsibility that seemed so clearly in its lane. Arnold had anticipated that disgruntled staff members might undercut the new committee with security and classification barriers, so he expressly ordered "all personnel having knowledge or custody of relevant material, including such as may be classified, to place the same at [Gates'] disposal."[10] This arrangement permitted Gates to then distribute information to the committee as he saw fit. From the start, Arnold's civilian committee operated in an environment hostile to its existence, so its survival remained a central concern.

Arnold's Committee of Operations Analysts (COA) formed as a core group of prominent economists and lawyers who orchestrated a legion of subcommittees, each representing a different potential target industry and comprising its own set of expert advisors.[11] This arrangement—much like a tree trunk with branches and vines—gave the COA its identity and shaped its behavior among other intelligence organizations. Committee leaders could attract highly educated participants and foreign industry experts with relative ease to the nation's capital, particularly while the war still seemed an existential threat to Western democracy. This arrangement also meant the committee's individual members did not need to acquire massive amounts of personal knowledge about German industrial systems because the organization could collectively invest less energy by finding additional experts (or at least someone who presented as such).[12] Thus, the COA's challenges centered less on creating new experts and more on validating the expertise they had found. It also needed to tie disparate expertise into reports that linked industrial conclusions with strategic bombing doctrine and elusive operational factors—an even knottier problem for the COA's cadre of nonflying civilian experts.

Aside from Gates, other notable members included Col. Guido Perera, a Harvard-educated lawyer previously activated to duty as a reservist judge advocate; Lt. Col. Malcolm Moss as the A-2 (Targets Section) representative; Lt. Col. W. Barton Leach, a Harvard law professor; Dr. Edward Mason, an Office of Strategic Services (OSS) representative and Harvard economics professor; Fowler Hamilton, a Board of Economic Warfare and former Department of Justice antitrust lawyer; Dr. Edward Earle, a Princeton economist and historian; Dr. Elihu Root Jr., a New York lawyer and director of the Carnegie Foundation; and Noel Hall of the British Ministry of Economic Warfare (MEW).[13] From their résumés alone, they were as credible and eminently qualified for intellectual endeavors as the war department might muster. How such a team would approach its problem remained to be seen.

Elihu Root Jr., son of the former secretary of war, proved extraordinarily valuable to the COA's formational period. Despite his lack of experience with industrial economics or strategic bombing, he brought "good judgment and all-around wisdom," as purported in the COA's official history, along with "many years' acquaintance with corporate problems . . . and had maintained close personal contact with leaders in the field of business."[14] In other words, he could navigate bureaucracy and knew who to call to find the industrial expertise that the air staff lacked. The COA clearly placed a higher premium in its core members for their persuasiveness and connections than their ability to verify subcommittee reports or to tackle the operational challenges of strategic bombing. In a sense, the committee operated like a business within the air staff; it relied upon corporate-style leadership and ensured its survival by peddling ideas to the generals who mattered.

Some of the committee's members had other allegiances. Participation by representatives from intelligence organizations outside the war department (notably Hamilton and Hall) and from the OSS injected a dual-edged phenomenon: On one side, they shared information, though sometimes selectively, and they facilitated common perspectives among the various intelligence organizations. Open discussions would help reduce friction where compromise was possible. On the less obvious side, external participants also conveyed information to their home organizations and prepared counterarguments as disagreements arose.

The COA subcommittees also included a handful of notable foreign experts. Their general contributions regarding target system analysis could be valuable, but their specific insights regarding German industrial practices were on occasion priceless. These were insights, according to Col. Ed Sorensen, that the British did not have, and they helped to arm the theater commander "with the thorough analyses which should have been made during the past twenty years of peace."[15] Preeminent among these foreign experts were Dr. Max von der Porten, former president of the German aluminum industry; Dr. Ludwig Homberger, former vice president of German railroads; Henry Behrens, German citizen and former director of Diesel Elektron, a Dutch locomotive company and close collaborator with German locomotive works; Otto Stern, who oversaw Shell Oil interests in Romania; Mauritz Straus, German citizen and former owner/general manager of Argus Motoren Gesellschaft, a leader among German aircraft engine manufacturers; and Lippmann Bloch, a Polish citizen with university experience in Berlin and Munich and owner of Ore Trading Corporation.[16]

Employ of foreign experts brought risks as well. At least four of the initial consultants were actively seeking U.S. citizenship while providing their insights on German industry to the war department.[17] These personal motives could undermine the consultants' objectivity, since the experts would not have felt comfortable offering contrarian opinions for fear of possible deportation. Further, they may have been more likely to offer contrived information than to acknowledge information gaps since they wanted to appear as helpful as possible. Finally, as Hughes had complained of some of the American economists, the situation with foreigners was much worse: since they did not have security clearances, they could not provide comparative analyses to other industries, detect omissions, or even offer suggestions to final reports.[18] It all added up to a potential for less objectivity and less expert review as the committee generated reports for Arnold.

The preponderance of the committee's Ivy League–educated participants internalized a superiority complex toward military leaders, at least insofar as scholarly prowess. Even as a uniformed member initially junior to most of the air staff (including Sorensen), Perera admitted witnessing from his Harvard days that "the military were treated by the intellectuals as second-class citizens inhabiting a limited world of their own."[19] The COA's core members saw themselves as an organization that could tackle any problems they might find in the military's limited world—especially those of their boss, "Hap" Arnold. To Perera, Arnold "was in no sense a thoughtful, precise thinker, but a doer."[20] They aimed to earn and maintain their favor with Arnold, which would give them greater autonomy and influence over AAF actions. Arnold's favor could at least ensure the committee would survive the remainder of the war, as it would also grant them due regard from Arnold's subordinate generals, especially Eaker, who knew better than to swipe at Arnold's pet projects.[21]

The COA members sprung with zeal into their impossible implied task of thoroughly dissecting German industry in a little over a month. A side effect of the time crunch they faced was that the committee members had to prioritize their focus areas quickly in order to manage their time and the scope of their task, which spilled over into target priorities. When committing their positions in writing, however, the COA members carefully maneuvered to downplay this necessary evil. The analysts' approach came across in the form of subtle contradictions, as if offering Arnold a choice of passages in hopes that he might find something he liked. For example, with a nod toward their own impartiality and thoroughness, the COA analysts purported to be "well advanced in a general Survey of Western Axis industry . . . as a safeguard against omission," then revealed in the same memorandum that they had honed in on "industries which have seemed to it the most promising . . . aircraft, oil, transportation, electric power, coke, and rubber."[22] Without yet completing its broad survey, evaluating the bombers' potential to locate or even to reach their targets, or projecting Eighth Air Force capacity, the analysts had set de facto priorities by virtue of which industries they selected first and about which they acquired the most information.

Pressure on the committee's experts to generate reports quickly meant that good ideas could come from anywhere. One remarkable episode occurred on the evening of 20 December 1942. COA's Guido Perera met Sexton Wolmar, who was then vice president of an American branch of SKF Industries (a subsidiary of a Swedish ball-bearing manufacturer with a similar subsidiary in Schweinfurt, Germany). Wolmar offered, "Why doesn't the Air Corps knock out the ball-bearing plants at Schweinfurt? Germany could not get along without them."[23] Interestingly, Wolmar's boss, William Batt, was both president of SKF and vice chairman of Roosevelt's war production board with duties including "responsibility for international supply."[24] After SKF's Swedish owners placed their American interests into a five-year "voting trust" held by Batt, his incentive to knock out the competition for ball-bearing production in Germany is not hard to fathom.[25] Ball-bearing production quickly found its way into committee deliberations.

A tacit contradiction soon arose over bombing policy recommendations. COA leadership planted a seed in an early update to Arnold that served to undercut a mindset of continuous air campaign assessment: "It is clear that results are cumulative and that a master plan, once adopted, should be adhered to with relentless determination."[26] They wanted their recommendations to have a chance to succeed. It was also clear from the start that most industries would require many targets to be destroyed, in most cases including repeat attacks on the same areas. This language survived in their final report four months later. In that report, however, the COA analysts added a recommendation for "continuing evaluation of the effectiveness of air attack on enemy industrial and economic objectives in all theaters," with an express purpose: "for the information of the appropriate authority charged with the allocation of air strength."[27] This last piece, following their trip to England, echoed Eaker's wishes to limit General Arnold's impetuous control of all AAF aircraft.

The idea behind the evaluation add-on was to have enough patience to stick with the plan until evidence could prove or dispute its effectiveness. Such evaluations (or air campaign assessments) might also inform whether each theater was appropriately resourced. Although it is unlikely the COA analysts had considered it at the time, assessments might also show whether the theater commander was following the plan. Unfortunately, no entity picked up the ball for ongoing assessment for several more months.

The Calculating "Quiz Kids"

A team of six operational researchers led by John Harlan arrived in England in late October 1942.[28] Eaker declared their mission as "[to analyze] bombing operations with a view to finding weak points in our method of attack in bombing and also any weaknesses in the employment of the enemy defense system; to ascertain the cause of casualties with a view to their reduction; to assess and evaluate the effectiveness of bombing attacks and also to investigate various communications problems relating to this command."[29]

Too much of this strategic bombing trial had been untested in combat conditions, and the early results did not seem to match stateside expectations. Informal trial and error was better than nothing, but the stakes were too high not to learn as quickly and as smartly as possible. If these operations research quiz kids got it right, they could "dig out the lessons of this war for application in this war rather than to await postwar analysis for use in future wars."[30] In many cases, however, data were not readily available, and any recommendations the researchers might have would necessarily await direction from above to implement. Eaker extended to his operations researchers unprecedented autonomy and access, including "contact with air crews, authority to visit operations rooms, situation rooms, attend briefings of crews, and in short, all activities that would aid them in their work."[31] Eaker's Operational Research Section (ORS) researchers had open access to talk to whomever they wanted, as long they were focused on improving the mission.

The Eighth Air Force ORS was a different sort of team with an entirely different dynamic. The inaugural six members were swamped from day one with producing fourteen distinct studies covering VIII Bomber Command's "most pressing" operational challenges.[32] As for their internal leadership, Harlan and Leslie Arps were both attorneys at the same New York law firm. Having lawyers in such leadership positions, either in Arnold's COA or in Eaker's ORS, was not a coincidence. COA's own Barton Leach played a role in establishing the framework for operations analysis sections within the war department, and he had stipulated that they "should be led by a non-scientist, preferably a lawyer."[33] Scientists would produce the research, and the lawyers would argue its value.

Operations researchers typically resisted pressure to take officer commissions, though all of them in any combat theater were required physically to wear the uniform; civilians went without insignia.[34] From the service's standpoint, commissioning of analysts was the preferred option because it gave their commanders more control over them in terms of both accountability and authority. Senior commanders thought groups of civilians leading civilians might stray too far from task, so the chief and deputy of the Eighth Air Force ORS eventually received commissions.[35] This option also offered more flexibility to the more senior commanders as to how these scientists could be employed and when they might be released from service.[36] Recruitment required intellectual courtship, but retention required rules.

Most operations analysts preferred to remain outside the rank structure if they were not forced into a commission. This would eliminate the distractions and obligations of military decorum and put them "on an effective working basis with either enlisted men or general officers."[37] Their civilian status also served, in a way, to shield them from criticism and to reinforce their objectivity, especially when they produced critical reports. This helped as they routinely received delegations from bombardment wings—typically skeptical commanders and lead bombardiers—who probed their work.[38] Coupled with their civilian status, the fact that these analysts reported to a higher echelon commander kept their arguments substantive and disarmed protesting officers from any attempts at pulling rank.

These operations analysts were math people—serious researchers and scientists—but they knew that their work could have value only insofar as it had operational applicability. An independent charter did them no good if their work was sequestered or stovepiped. In their minds, "The nearer [we] were to the actual operating units and, at the same time, have available sufficient data for study, the more effective the section could be."[39] They spent considerable time interacting with and learning from the bomb groups, especially those of the 1st Bombardment Wing, made available by their then-commander, Gen. Newton Longfellow. As the operations analysts saw it, their contributions should be judged not upon scientific merit or individual recognition, but by whether "results were used effectively by the command being served."[40] To this end, their relationship with the command mattered, and their incentive was to reinforce the command's preferences.

While the researchers lived, ate, and worked together, sharing camaraderie underscored by "none too dignified poker games," they did not all share the longer term sense of commitment or sacrifice exhibited by members of Donovan's OSS serving in the EOU or of the WAAFs at Medmenham.[41] In fact, just three months into the job, Harlan sought to leave Eighth Air Force and return to Washington in a recruitment role, an act of self-interest that Eaker personally blocked.[42] Brigadier General H. M. McClelland, an ACTS classmate of both Eaker and Sorensen serving as AAF's director of technical services, shared his insights in a response to Eaker's concerns: "These Operational Research people are, in a sense, prima donnas, or perhaps I should say strong individualists. . . . that is why they are able to do the work that they do."[43] The egocentric personality traits that made them tough to keep on the team were the same traits that gave them the personal confidence and self-driven focus to accomplish research others could not.

ACCURATELY ASSESSING ACCURACY

The ORS bombing accuracy subsection members furthered the practice of examining poststrike photographs as overall hit-or-miss snapshots into effective learning tools for Eighth Air Force. ORS analysts found data reported by crews and recorded by unit interrogators to be unreliable and inaccurate, so they needed to develop more objective measures.[44] Prior to their formal approach to the study of bombing accuracy, each bomb plot produced by a USAAF liaison to the CIU had included a composite view of all strikes in the target area. While these images could reasonably answer the question, "Where did our raid's bombs land?" they could not be used to determine why some formations or individual aircraft had bombed with greater success than others.

This process was relatively straightforward, as long as the cameras worked and the photographs were of suitable quality. The contentious limitation was that the bomb plots accounted only for bombs that appeared in photos as craters, collapsed roofs, damaged infrastructure, or other visible rubble. A bomb that might not appear in a strike photo for any number of reasons, such as a double hit, delayed fuze, dud weapon, or obscured impact, could not be counted, thereby falling into the same category as bombs that had fallen too far off target to appear in the image anyway. This was a limitation of their source data, which was beyond their control, not their math, so the researchers adamantly defended their process.

They also developed a standard for measuring bombing accuracy. One method was to determine, using all identifiable craters, a mean point of impact assessed by "the length (along track) and width (across track) of the pattern" from the intended target.[45] Another method involved depicting arbitrary, but standardized, five hundred-, one thousand-, and two thousand-foot circles around each target, then determining the percentage of bomb craters found within each for the total bombs released. After evaluating a multitude of other possible metrics, they selected the one thousand-foot circle, despite its limitations, as the measurement against which bomb scores were graded.[46]

The researchers had their customers clearly in mind—not only General Eaker, but all levels of their assigned Air Force—as they approached their work. They had to select methods and draft arguments that could be grasped easily by both the scientific community and the airmen fighting the war. Hugh Miser, an ORS mathematician, reflected, "In practice the tool adopted should be the simplest one that will be effective."[47] As Leach argued, "These officers are so inevitably absorbed with carrying out today's mission and planning tomorrow's they simply don't have the time and uninterrupted attention which most of these matters required."[48] Whatever method ORS mathematicians selected for assessing bombing accuracy had to be both within their capacity (in terms of manpower and available data) and useable by their customers. As a result, they gravitated toward leaders like Curtis LeMay, who appreciated their work, and used their reports "to keep his commanders on their toes."[49]

A TALE OF BOMBS AND FUZES

Connections between members of Arnold's committee in Washington and Eaker's ORS in England seemed to propagate on their own. For example, on 14 December 1942, Sorensen's COA subcommittee, then comprised of pilots, intelligence officers, a lawyer, a businessman, a mathematician, and a physicist, gained a much-needed "expert on explosives" in Dr. John Burchard, director of the National Defense Research Committee's structural offense and defense/effects of impact and explosion division.[50] Burchard had been teaching architects and engineers a two-month course in ballistics and bomb damage at Princeton University.[51] Based on his own operations analysis experience with the AAF, Burchard dispatched two of his students to work with Eaker's ORS under John Harlan; one, Bissell Alderman, was a graduate and assistant professor of architecture at the Massachusetts Institute of Technology; the other, Charles U. Kring, was a structural engineer.[52] They arrived the following month in England, where they founded the ORS bombs and fuzes subsection.[53]

Architects and structural engineers who consulted Eighth Air Force offered strategic bombing advice antithetical to their own training. While Burchard attempted to "reverse their peacetime practices and use their knowledge to destroy buildings rather than build them," their instincts persisted.[54] Alderman was notably part of a legacy more deeply rooted than his own career, as he was also the son of a prominent Massachusetts architect. His father designed or improved more than fourteen churches and chapels in the Holyoke area alone in addition to a multitude of schools and other buildings.[55] Professional architects like Alderman were trained to respect buildings built by others, especially those intended for religious services or envisioned for posterity. John Ruskin's *Seven Lamps of Architecture*, written in Alderman's father's era, captures well this sentiment toward buildings: "The dead still have their right in them; that which they labored for, the praise of achievement or the expression of religious feeling, or whatsoever else it might be which in those buildings they intended to be permanent, we have no right to obliterate. . . . It may hereafter be a subject of sorrow, or a cause of injury, to millions, that we have consulted our present convenience by casting down such buildings as we choose to dispense with."[56]

Although Alderman never alludes to this cognitive dissonance in his own wartime history, it is nevertheless evident in his philosophy toward bomb selection and his attitude toward senior commanders. For example, Alderman speaks disparagingly about General Longfellow, whom he declares was among the "big bomb enthusiasts," while he praises Gen. O. A. Anderson for his discretion: "He wanted to use the smallest weapon . . . providing it would be the most effective."[57] Alderman had undoubtedly picked up his assumptions of bomb effects where ACTS had left off: smaller bombs were better if you could carry more of them. While U.S. bombers in the European theater may have dropped a lot of bombs on unintended locations and on targets of opportunity, they tended not to over-kill their targets (if they killed their targets at all).

New members of the bomb and fuzes branch preferred not to prioritize a liaison mission with the British, because they decided it was "more important to follow very closely the developments at our headquarters."[58] This was unfortunate, because Eighth Air Force relied on raid assessment reports by analysts from the British Ministry of Home Security (MHS), which suffered from lack of coordination with and expertise from ORS experts.[59] For example, MHS produced reports oriented toward estimating production losses and expected repair timelines, but as the ORS researchers critiqued, the MHS analysts seemed to struggle with bomb damage analysis, and their reports "were never published until long after the raids had lost all interest," if they were completed at all.[60] ORS researchers fixed on Eighth Air Force leadership as their customer, not the MHS, and the small team of three preferred to work together with no one within their subsection in charge. The ORS bombs and fuzes branch continued to exert its unusual autonomy in determining its own priorities throughout its early period. "We were more interested in the behavior of the individual weapons on certain targets," Alderman offered, "than we were in summarizing the results of all the attacks on all targets."[61] Eaker's grant of autonomy may have backfired.

Poststrike images gave the researchers more reliable feedback on structural attacks, so they could prove what they had learned. In this sense, both their past experiences and desire to demonstrate outcomes led them astray and cuffed their analyses. For example, in their reports, they classified damage as: "STRUCTURAL damage, including the destruction of trusses, beams, columns and so forth; and SUPERFICIAL damage including the stripping of roof cover and skylights and damage to secondary structural members such as roof purlins" (capitalization original).[62] Anticipated bomb damage to contents—which is what really mattered for industrial production—was omitted. In this sense, the mathematicians and scientists chose metrics and analytical methods that served only to exacerbate the tendency already shown by photo interpreters to overestimate damage to building contents.

As the bombs and fuzes section gained confidence, they offered recommendations expressly refuting War Department Training Circular 50—the only existing publication governing bomb selection. They met with little resistance from the chain of command to radical recommendations. "This I think was probably because we had been built up as 'experts' by Mr. Harlan, Col. Sims, and a few others," Alderman confessed, "and, possibly, to some extent by ourselves."[63] However, the typical aircrew members were not so easy to convince.

When the operations analysts attempted to adapt the British preference for incendiary bombs, which were ideal for RAF area attacks, more prominently into U.S. plans, they met considerable opposition. "A large part of our efforts were [sic] spent in convincing them [the aircrew] of the effectiveness of IBs [incendiary bombs] and in searching for data to prove our beliefs," revealed one operations analyst.[64] U.S. aircrew resisted dropping incendiary bombs because incendiaries were notoriously inaccurate, which did not sit well with the idea of being graded on their raid results. The aircrew also believed they were taking precise aim to destroy factories, not to burn large urban areas. Operations researchers eventually proposed the idea of mixing the two bomb types on each bomber, which added even more bomb-loading time and aiming complexity to a job that was difficult enough already.[65] Perhaps most importantly, in the words of an exasperated researcher, the aircrew "could not see that the dropping of incendiaries produced any results."[66] Fires that burned long after the bombers escaped the flack and fighters near their targets did not leave the crews with the same sense of satisfaction they received when they saw the explosions themselves.

The bombs and fuzes subsection found challenges not only with the aircrew, but with the military intelligence officers as well. ORS researchers recommended weapon selections during the planning process based upon timely and accurate target folders from Eighth Air Force's A-2 division, which the ORS researchers found to be incompetent. In some cases, "target folder material was pathetically inadequate" or required corrections, while in other tasks they found the A-2 was unbearably slow: "We were . . . constantly being blamed for delays which were not due so much to the time that we required for our selections but more to the time required of the Intelligence Officers in getting out the folders."[67] There may have been a shortage of synthesized intelligence, but there was certainly no shortage in spirited competition.

THE OSS ARRIVES IN LONDON

For Richard Hughes and the Eighth Air Force planners, a dearth of quality information about potential German targets quickly became a mind-boggling mass of incomprehensible reports. No one at the air staff or Eighth Air Force had developed a systematic approach to prioritize and analyze the data, much less sort it, until the OSS showed up in London. The OSS analysts also brought another benefit: they could establish relationships in the Allied intelligence community the military officers could not, which would help not only to obtain preferred reports from the British, but also to shape how they were written. Civilians in British intelligence preferred to work with U.S. counterparts rather than directly with military officers. If a functionally equivalent office or entire agency did not exist, the OSS nimbly restructured or added a branch and hired more academics.

This behavior suited both the British and U.S. air intelligence organizations. The British shored up their status quo amid shifting military strategy and political priorities, while the OSS validated its expansionist aims. According to an OSS internal history, "Every British office of importance made an effort to distinguish the one American agency which most closely corresponded to its own function, and to establish more or less exclusive relations with that agency."[68] Relationships formed that were both competitive and symbiotic as both sides vied for influence over the combined chiefs while they both helped to justify each other's existence. For Hughes' team at Eighth Air Force, the OSS delivered intelligence products with expanded access and sharpened analysis, although time would show the finer edges tended to resemble the analyst.

How exactly the OSS came into the role of Eighth Air Force targeting is historically equivocal. By one account, the OSS would have had no such opportunity but for Hughes' request directly to Ambassador John Winant, the former World War I pilot then running the state department mission in London, and Winant's eagerness to help.[69] Alternatively, an OSS version suggests that Hughes extended the request to Chandler Morse of the OSS Washington research and analysis branch during the latter's visit to London.[70] Yet a third account credits Dr. Edward Mason, also of the OSS (prior to his joining the COA), for arranging "a unit that would sort of work for the Eighth Air Force and which would do two things: help pick targets and help assess bomb damage."[71] Collective memory may tend to spread the credit for good ideas, as a combination of all three of these events is likely what transpired. The result was the formation of the Enemy Objectives Unit (EOU) by the OSS and a most unusual arrangement with its gargantuan British counterpart, the Ministry of Economic Warfare. A comparison of these two organizations reveals their character and their influence on the air campaign. Offering its economic brainpower along with inroads to other U.S. intelligence organizations, the EOU expanded OSS influence and secured connections to British intelligence.

Targeting by Economists: A Micro- and a Macro-enterprise

Although their sizes and origins were starkly different, the two organizations would become similar in function over time. Throughout its three-year existence, the EOU was a small but industrious outfit, with only fifteen people passing through its employ; of these, all but two were on the OSS payroll.[72] Further, as with similar spin-off agencies and committees in Washington, the EOU roster comprised almost entirely economists. Their way of thinking could contribute to strategic bombing evaluation in ways that other approaches often underemphasized.[73] If they were not tuned in to the enemy mind, they were at least inclined to consider how the enemy might mitigate the effects of bombing. As one EOU member asserted, "I would say the most important idea that as an economist I had, all of us economists had, which wasn't in ordinary military thinking, was the idea of substitution. If you take the whole strategic materials business, we were among the first people to see through this argument about 'strategic materials' and say this is going to be crap, because they'll find ways around it."[74]

The economists' specialization contributed in other ways as well. Through the crucible of war and its swirling ideas of how to win, they valued intellectual rigor over keen intuition in decisionmaking processes. The downside of this intellectual rigor was that they were not prone to appreciate the style of quick decisionmaking prized by military leaders. In their own words, they had "learned that theories, no matter how elegant or attractive, had to be disciplined forcefully against the facts before a policy decision is reached."[75] Of course, not every policy decision had time for all the facts, and facts, like statistics, can be spun to support different theories. The economists tended to project a sense of personal valuation into their arguments, as many of their debates and reports would later show.

Loaded with unremitting and cocksure personalities yet limited in manpower, the EOU leadership selected both its personnel and its outputs carefully. Since the United States did not employ a system such as Britain's Central Register, which allowed civilians to be selected for government service according to their qualifications, the OSS relied upon its senior professors at prestigious academic institutions to recruit the best of the younger generation.[76] The EOU economists were among America's brightest, and they saw themselves as the all-star team. As one EOU economist, Walt Rostow, later reflected, "Britain had the Air Ministry full of people, Lansdowne House [used by the RAF and the MEW] full of people, and we were about five or six fellows who operated like the Globe-Trotters basketball team."[77]

In fact, the EOU members sensed they were compensating for decades of failure by the military to recruit and develop highly capable intelligence officers. "The military services put overriding priority on operational virtuosity and consigned their least competent permanent officers to intelligence," purported

Rostow, "and there was no way that situation could be rapidly changed from the top."[78] This team of ambitious analysts sought to perpetuate their penchant for quantitative methods into air intelligence writ large.[79] The EOU's small but significant team saw the opportunity to influence the air campaign with its own brand of intellectualism and seized it.

SACRED COWS GO MEW

The MEW, by contrast, included a ponderous cast of about a thousand, and "a truck load of paper emerged from their offices every day," or so it seemed to Hughes.[80] The Americans weren't the only ones taxed by the MEW's prolific but unsystematic writing; RAF's Bomber Command became so saturated by the MEW's "vast and rapidly obsolete" reports that the Air Ministry requested a more simplified analysis of industrial targets.[81] Sifting through the MEW's analyses was more complicated than simply sorting the wheat from the chaff.[82] It was best to manage the MEW's outputs with relationships and specific requests.

Despite their difference in size, the MEW and the EOU shared an economic bent. From the Air Ministry's perspective, as both a rival and a customer, the MEW "would appear to have been designed almost exclusively to manage the naval blockade"; it grew into the mission of target selection to the extent that air action could substitute for "other forms of economic warfare."[83] Insofar as airpower might topple the Third Reich, MEW economists sought to crumble the foundation of the German economy—an unsurprising inclination given their organizational title—but the implications for British bombing policy were significant. MEW personnel saw themselves as contributors to an analytical behemoth, and they defended their reputation for the depth and complexity of their reports. An EOU economist complained of the less-focused MEW that "its papers tended to be collections of economic data, rather than intelligence studies."[84] The larger organization hedged against irrelevance by reporting on everything it could.

Whereas the EOU had materialized at the behest of a dire AAF need, the British committee of imperial defence installed the MEW into a position of superiority vis-à-vis the Air Ministry; its charge was to monitor and advise targets related to "distribution of enemy industry, centers of storage and sources of supply, and to the key points of his transport system."[85] The MEW was to be a check against the RAF because military service intelligence tended to reflect and reinforce rather than to regulate service behavior. This was especially pertinent since the RAF's own intelligence apparatus could assess the enemy's "economic situation and the morale of the civil population."[86] Nevertheless, the British consolidated in the MEW an overall advisory role for target selection apart from the Air Ministry and the RAF, while all three would have inclinations of their own.

Despite its relative primacy among the British air intelligence organizations, the MEW was marginalized by RAF Air Marshal Sir Arthur T. "Bomber" Harris' Bomber Command. MEW analysts had lost credibility with Harris because of their dogmatic pursuit of industrial "bottlenecks" ("panacea mongering" to Harris), largely because they had falsely assumed, during blockade planning years prior, that German industry had been operating at "fever pitch."[87] Harris challenged the idea of bottlenecks in the absence of definitive proof that German industries faced shortages, workarounds were limited, or repairs would not be expeditious. Such proof in wartime was not easy to come by, but these assumptions and the arguments behind them were critical because they underwrote the RAF's targeting theory.

In Harris' view, the MEW had misjudged not only Germany's internal production situation, but also its access to external resources. The MEW, he felt, had been "in its glory, planning a campaign against Germany's synthetic oil plants, together with factories making aluminum, and aircraft works," because their myopic study of Germany in 1940 had overlooked German access to foreign resources through its "non-aggression pact" with Russia as well as its conquest of French aluminum and sources of Romanian oil.[88] Disputes about Germany's industrial position were not Harris' only concerns. He also found the MEW's analyses and target recommendations to be a ceaseless source of misdirection, because they had not adapted to Bomber Command's operational realities.

Throughout 1942 Harris' inclination to incinerate German morale city by city chafed the MEW's increasingly bloated but detached sense of purpose. Jockeying to restore its relevance to bombing policy, the MEW economists sought to co-opt Bomber Command's morale-bombing practices into a scientific approach to targeting for economic effect. A narrow strip of common ground finally emerged for the various competing interests after two key events. First, Bomber Command had finally received formal approval for area bombing on 14 February 1942. This gave Harris authority to commit his forces full time to night attacks, and it forced the intelligence organizations to find ways to support those attacks. Second, the order was reinforced the following month by a memorandum from

Frederick Lindemann (Lord Cherwell), Churchill's top scientific advisor, to the prime minister himself, professing the merits of "de-housing" the German population.[89] The memorandum read, in part: "Investigation seems to show that having one's house demolished is most damaging to morale. People seem to mind it more than having their friends or even relatives killed. At Hull signs of strain were evident, though only one-tenth of the houses were demolished."[90]

Lord Cherwell added a modicum of scientific credibility to morale bombing at a precipitous moment. His approach, the RAF's intelligence history contended, "provided an opportunity to estimate the effect of the destruction of housing and amenities on the capacity or determination of the working people," though the report also admitted that "in this period judgment on this question tended to be based on more speculative reasoning which had a strong appeal to certain minds."[91] Lord Cherwell had data to demonstrate that the bombers could demolish houses, but any assurances that "this would break the spirit of the people," as he contended, were spurious at best.[92]

In January 1943 the MEW analysts followed suit with a scientific report of their own, the first of several volumes entitled *The Bomber's Baedeker*. In appearances, it was a prioritized hit list of towns with a population greater than 15,000 inhabitants with special preference to those of greater than 250,000—certain to rouse an interest from "Bomber" Harris. What the report provided was actually an internally consistent logic that connected "the economic importance of each town" to "Direct effects: a) Destruction and damage to dwellings and de-housing of population; b) Destruction and damage to factories and commercial property and the interruption of public utility services and communications; [and] Indirect effects: c) Loss of working time due to general dislocation of economic life; d) Expenditure of manpower and materials in rehabitation measures."[93]

The economists' logic was a best seller as long as the report's audience was willing to accept some sleight of hand on its assumptions. Bomber Command certainly was. The following passages from the report's introduction, laced with the MEW's seductive logic, are worthy of review to this express this point:

> At this stage of the war and with the tactical methods at present employed, the heaviest effect on the enemy's war effort is probably produced by the combination of a) and d). The proportion of the nation's manpower and economic resources which the enemy can devote to the manning of the Armed Forces and the production of equipment and munitions

> for them is only the surplus left over after the minimum allocations essential for the maintenance of the civilian population and the national economic machine generally have been met. These needs will always demand the attentions of the major fraction of the working population. The devastation of the cities produced by night bombing serves to raise the proportion of the national resources which must be devoted to meeting these needs. . . . This result can be obtained in theory by the devastation of any built-up area in Germany regardless of the economic activities of its inhabitants. It is, however, likely in practice that the German Government will be induced to spend its resources more freely for rehabilitation purposes in cities which play a vital part in the national war effort. . . . Concentration of night bombing effort on such targets would not only produce at least as great a drain on the enemy's economy as elsewhere through the destruction of houses and the diversion of resources to rehabilitation measures, but it would also ensure the maximum direct and indirect damage to economic activities which are of primary importance to the enemy's war effort.[94]

To this end, the report would later classify highest priority targets as those "reserved for factories with pronounced 'bottleneck' characteristics which would merit specific attack if this were practical. This distinction is applied only to factories possessing the following qualifications: a) that the activity involved is of primary importance to the enemy war effort; b) that this activity is concentrated in a large degree in a small number of places; c) that the supply and demand position is sufficiently tight to ensure that effects of loss of productive capacity would be serious and immediate."[95]

The cleverness of the MEW report lay not in the expanse of its supporting data or its industrial analysis, although both were immense. The MEW economists had engineered a logic, notably ex post facto, to suit Harris' brutish intentions given his Bomber Command's operational realities: industrial dislocation would lead to victory. In other words, the MEW analysts reestablished their preeminence, justifying their staggering energies into economic and industrial reports, if only to determine which cities should be de-housed first. Harris would unleash hell as city after city went "up in flames."[96] He was content as long as his hands were not tied; but if the MEW had regained any credibility with Harris, it would not last long.

EOU: ECONOMISTS ON A MISSION

Unlike the MEW, the EOU economists had no recognized charter, no formal authority, and limited resources. They compensated for these shortfalls by deliberately cultivating the skills and reputation of their small team and farming out their expertise. The EOU grew slowly along with the scope of its opportunistic mission after the first five members arrived in the fall of 1942, and they became, as they saw it, "the only organization in theater devoted solely to the development of target intelligence and target thinking."[97] The EOU's position outside of the AAF's chain of command gave it credibility for objective assessment in ways that the AAF's internal air intelligence could not enjoy. The EOU team was close-knit with consistent membership, and its economists were able to form personal relationships with their Eighth Air Force customers as well as their British counterparts.

Consistency among its core membership was essential. Because they were outside of Washington, working close to the war effort and to each other, the EOU members could sense the impact of their contributions. This made them less apt to leave for other employment opportunities—at least until the war was over. Had Hughes marginalized their access, rejected their ideas, or simply shelved their reports, the ambitious EOU economists may have risked irrelevance or disbanded entirely. For the high-achieving competitors that they were, with long-term designs on government service, an early and unceremonious return home would have been perceived as failure.[98]

The relationship between the EOU and Hughes indeed proved reciprocal. In a pragmatic sense, EOU members appreciated Hughes and ingratiated themselves with him because their success depended upon it. But he was also the type of character to whom they could relate. Carl Kaysen, an EOU economist, later reflected of Hughes, "He really was a terrific guy, very focused, very smart, he understood what we were doing, he was a good politician, he had *enormous* courage. . . . He was our marketing agent, our contact with the Air Force and he was quite adept at it."[99] Hughes had expressed frustration with the economists and lawyers who supported the war department in Washington, but he had nothing but praise for EOU members: "They backed me up, supplemented me, and supported me, in every way possible through the next two hectic years."[100] Mutual reliance formed an extraordinary bond and tendency for cooperation between Hughes and the EOU.

The command environment added another reason for this cooperative arrangement. According to Hughes, "General Eaker kept even the most minute administrative details in his own hands, and seemed to have very little time, or inclination, for discussing operational plans. . . . With no sympathetic intellectual support, or understanding from my Commanding General it was a difficult and heavy burden."[101] Hughes needed support with both the intellectual weightlifting and the slog of day-to-day planning. The EOU was eager to offer its services.

The EOU mission steadily evolved into four functions, which kept its members busy "almost every night and most Saturdays."[102] In EOU economist Walt Rostow's words: "First came the Aiming Point reports, the detailed analyses of the layouts of the targets, and the objectives within them whose destruction would cause the maximum loss of production; Second, were the analyses of the industries as target systems, furnishing the basic data for the comparative calculations of cost of systematic attack and of probable returns; Third, were the occasional but important ventures in drafting air plans; Fourth, were the jobs carried out by various individuals within EOU in helping to guide particular branches of the Air and Ground Staffs."[103]

When there was breathing room, they would seek out other opportunities. The EOU economists tended to channel their efforts toward those most likely to expand their influence and prestige, while steering clear of those likely to draw ire from the AAF.[104] For example, aiming point reports were tedious but comprised the bulk of day-to-day duties. Rostow admitted that these reports tested the economists' "energy and inventiveness" but failed to satisfy their intellectual affinities.[105] So the group took on something more interesting, initially bypassing the AAF's urgent need for a robust damage assessment methodology, to propose a targeting theory instead.

TARGETING ECONOMICS 101

The ACTS graduates filling the most senior positions of the AAF and Eighth Air Force command and operations staffs, given their confidence in doctrine they had published at Maxwell Field, were not likely to accept new ideas from anyone who had never flown an aircraft much less attended their hallowed school. Undeterred by this, the EOU economists applied their deeply ingrained habits of mind to target thinking. Whether or not they adopted the approach espoused by ACTS graduates, the economists sought to be efficient in their support of Hughes and Eighth Air Force. Likewise, their training as economists oriented them toward guiding Eighth Air Force to be efficient in the air campaign. To these ends, the economists needed a methodical approach to help prioritize target selection. In the absence of command-level guidance, they attempted to develop their own targeting theory.

The economists began their task with an analytical model, published internally on 17 December 1942, which they divided into two parts. The first was to develop criteria for the selection of target industries, and the second was to prioritize individual targets for attack. As to industry selection, they identified eleven potential criteria, including "importance of product to war production," "tightness of supply situation," "ease of repair," and "possibility of substitution."[106] However, they decided that mathematically prioritizing targets by these criteria was too complex to "bear a simple additive relation to each other."[107]

They encountered another problem as well. Although the economists were confident their approach had incorporated all criteria relevant to target selection, they also regarded "the judgment factor," which "may be required to fill gaps in factual data or to re-evaluate appraisals previously made."[108] Recognizing that economic theory might not explain enemy behavior, Rostow opined that "the balance may be turned by judgment concerning the intentions of the enemy, the relative degrees of disorganization likely to be created, or the manner in which the enemy is likely to react to the destruction of alternative targets."[109] In short, they lacked the experience to make the judgment calls.

It would seem there were too many factors to consider, too much information unavailable, and too much judgment at play to impart such a robust model.[110] In order to limit their assumptions, the economists simplified their model. Instead of attempting to weigh all of the potential criteria, they narrowed their focus to three questions: "1) How great is the impairment of the enemy's efforts of per unit of physical destruction? 2) How many units of physical destruction will be achieved per ton of bombs dropped on the target? 3) How many tons of bombs can be dropped per unit of air effort, or per unit of cost? (Including losses and wastage of planes and crew, expenditure of bombs and gasoline, etc.)."[111] These questions were reduced and represented mathematically as:

$$\frac{\text{Impairment to enemy}}{\cancel{\text{Physical damage}}} \times \frac{\cancel{\text{Physical damage}}}{\cancel{\text{Tons of bombs}}} \times \frac{\cancel{\text{Tons of bombs}}}{\text{Cost to us}} = \frac{\text{Impairment to enemy}}{\text{Cost to us}}$$

Since physical damage and tons of bombs cancel out, the solution was simply "the ratio of impairment to enemy's effort to cost to us."[112] With their elegant formula, the EOU had developed a model for efficient target nomination—one that injected an assumption of risk aversion that was otherwise absent from ACTS doctrine and Arnold's expectations in Washington.

ACTS OF AIR INTOLERANCE

Colonel Ed Sorensen also maneuvered into COA meetings from his duties as Arnold's chief of air intelligence.[113] His advocacy of emerging bombing theory was as aggressive, confident, and informed as any from the school, though he took views that deviated from the norm, and his tact (or lack thereof) engaging with senior leaders left him sideways with Eaker and cast out from the inner circle of ACTS graduates.[114]

In early January 1943 as the COA was preparing its first round of subcommittee reports, Sorensen sent a letter to Brig. Gen. Laurence Kuter—then departing his tour as a bombardment wing commander in England—offering "some advance information on what we [the COA] are attempting to do . . . for quicker action in case we ask you for certain pictures or other data by cable or by mail."[115] Sorensen acknowledged that Eighth Air Force was likely developing plans of its own but that the COA would eventually send a team forward "to compare notes," adding "that the better plan would be recognized by our people."[116] If there was a diplomatic way to suggest that a committee in Washington would be intruding on a theater commander's targeting plans, Sorensen had not found it.

Moreover, Sorensen expressed views that were unusually pragmatic regarding the joint environment for a former ACTS instructor. He insisted upon several controversial observations in his letter, including that "any plan must have the concurrence of Ground and Naval forces"; that the "initial or air phase proper" was preliminary rather than in lieu of an eventual ground invasion, during which it would be necessary to destroy "transportation structure . . . in the protection of a bridgehead for an invasion force"; and that arguments he had heard from group commanders returning from theater that gross bombing inaccuracies had been due to unexpected enemy antiair resistance (both fighters and flak) were "not well founded," because "none of the units which have operated in the U.K. thus far had reached a satisfactory degree of peacetime bombing training."[117] In other words, Sorensen decided from a continent away that enemy resistance was not the primary issue with their bombing performance; training was.

Not only was Sorensen's approach inflammatory, but his ideas may also have ignited a firestorm with Eaker, who shared his group commander's frustrations "to see their little force dwindling," as he expressed to his friend, Maj. Gen. George Stratemeyer, a few weeks later.[118] Eaker was trying to win the war, and while he claimed to be open to advice from Washington, particularly if it came from a peer that he respected like George Stratemeyer, what Eaker really wanted was replacement crews and the bomb groups he had been promised.

Kuter, who was apparently underwhelmed by Sorensen's prose, did little with the correspondence until handing off wing command to Haywood Hansell with a brief note: "This baby [Sorensen's letter] is now in your hands. . . . It is my personal belief that you should not simply give this paper to Ira Eaker, but must discuss it with him and build some foundation upon which he may accept it. Ira is not impressed by Ed Sorensen's views."[119] If Kuter had begun to socialize Sorensen's contrarian viewpoints with Eaker, he clearly had not made much headway.

Hansell then reassured Sorensen that he need not feel apprehension about "unwanted meddling with [Eaker's] affairs . . . so long as the approach is tactful and through the highest channels." Additionally, Hansell recommended that Sorensen steer his committee toward rather than against AWPD-42 (Hansell had evidently already convinced Eaker of its merits), but "do not harp too much upon small precision targets. . . . We find they are hard to hit, particularly in the face of heavy [antiaircraft] fire and determined fighter opposition."[120] Hansell recognized that hitting targets in combat was proving far more difficult than expected, especially as the missions were planned—"so much like the old days of the Air Corps Tactical School," as Hansell reminisced with Fairchild in another letter the same day.[121]

George Stratemeyer (then Arnold's two-star chief of the air staff), finally weighed in directly with Eaker in an attempt to settle the dust-up. "He is just so intent on precision bombing like all of us are that when, in his mind, the bombing isn't good, or heavy bombers aren't used properly," Stratemeyer explained of Sorensen, "I guess he can't help but sound off."[122] The ACTS graduates maintained their strong opinions and their open dialogue, but they still had a pecking order that seemed to have as much to do with tactical credibility and old relationships as rank. By any measure, Sorensen had emerged from under Arnold's wing to represent the air staff's increasing role in air intelligence, and the forceful impression he gave to his senior officers in England had cost him their respect. Sorensen and Eaker did not see eye to eye, and relationships were not going well for Sorensen in Washington, either.

Ostensibly responsible as Arnold's A-2 for steering all of the AAF's intelligence functions and special reports, Sorensen was the one most proximally snubbed by Arnold's decision to place the COA under a division other than the A-2. This arrangement also led to unresolved bad blood between Sorensen and Perera, who noted that Sorensen "bitterly resented" the COA's role as "a sort of super reviewing authority."[123] As Sorensen struggled to defend A-2 influence, he stumbled into a difficult task with the COA as well.

As the only of the committee's core participants with a background in bombing principles, Sorensen led the subcommittee on bombing probabilities. This was the one area of military specialization in which no amount of previous experience could compensate for practical knowledge of bombing. Among this subcommittee's considerations were: "Estimated probable error, the state of training, the effect of combat conditions, the height from which bombing was carried out, the percentage of assurance of securing a hit on a given spot postulated, the number of abortive sorties . . . the method of dropping bombs whether in train or otherwise, the ballistics of the bombs used, the selection of aiming points and the blast effects of the bombs themselves."[124]

Outputs from Sorensen's subcommittee were vital to the COA's ultimate task of determining a timeline for the dislocation of German industry, although these outputs informed the work of all other subcommittees as well.[125] According to historian Stephen McFarland, during Sorensen's time instructing at ACTS, he'd "analyzed 40,000 bomb drops and concluded that 'any categorical answer to the question [of] how many airplanes must be dispatched to obtain a reasonable chance of destroying an objective is of no practical value because of the many factors that must be considered in each case.'"[126] This was precisely the task he now broached along with COA analysts. Sorensen's conundrum was that any uncertainties or errors factoring into his equations could drastically influence the force-sizing requirements and expected operational outcomes when applied across entire industries. Put another way, none of the industrial intelligence had any meaning to an air campaign plan unless it was mated with realistic assumptions about bombing. Meanwhile, the mounting tension between commanders and pilots serving in senior intelligence positions reflected a similar budding resentment at lower levels.

OVERCOMING AIRCREW ANIMOSITY

Intelligence officers were not the only ones receiving intelligence training. The AAF also attempted to educate aircrew about photo interpretation and BDA via both publications and film. Because of a secondary purpose to inspire and reinforce credibility of intelligence officers, they tended to mix hyperbole with reality. For example, the February 1943 edition of *Air Force*, the official service journal of the USAAF, featured an article loaded with exaggerated claims about stereoscopic photography—the act of using an optical device with two images in order to perceive depth. "Advances in aerial photography and photo interpretation make the camera a super-human military observer who seldom, if ever, is fooled," claimed the article's author. "It would not be out of the question to plan an entire campaign from a stereoscopic study of terrain as revealed in modern aerial photographs."[127] Intentional or otherwise, this romanticism for an emerging field embodied the general lack of awareness throughout the service of its limits. Since the article's author was assigned to AAF headquarters, it was nothing short of propaganda to foster confidence. The downside was that it reinforced a tendency to overrely on visual intelligence. Aircrew tended to remain skeptical.

An official AAF training film produced around the same time was intended to curb the animosity typical of bomber aircrew. Harrisburg's AAFAIS sent a photo interpretation instructor, Capt. Frederick M. Brown, to serve as technical advisor. The school's first commandant supported the effort, but he also contributed to the tensions between intelligence personnel and aircrew by inculcating his attitude into his students. "Neither pilots nor combat crews have the faintest appreciation of the value of intelligence and the assistance which it renders them in accomplishing their mission and returning alive," noted the commandant.[128] The video's narrator opens with deprecating sarcasm toward the B-17 aircrew, capturing service culture of the 1940s AAF: "This is the story of Bill Wayne, a bombardier, with a two day leave in London. He's just been out on his first bombing mission and he's sure he's blown up his target single handed. Boy is he cocky. . . . He's a real hero all set for a binge."[129]

The video portrays a U.S. photo interpreter as a mature, almost paternal figure (though both officers were lieutenants) who explained the detailed process of BDA to the bombardier. Strike photos, taken by the bombers themselves in six-second intervals after release, had several purposes: "It gives you a quick summary of the results of the mission without waiting for reconnaissance pictures. In case the high command wants an immediate report, it'll tell you pretty closely what percentage of the bombs landed in the target area. The strike plot comes in very handy for the damage assessment interpreter because it's a sure way of ruling out old hits when he's examining reconnaissance pictures. Finally, it can be referred to at any time for the bombing record of the lead bombardier."[130]

The AAF wanted its aircrew to understand that all of the perceived hassle associated with uploading, operating, and downloading cameras was part of a scientific record for assessment, not a contrived scorecard or a meaningless waste of time. After viewing his own results, as annotated by the interpreter, the bombardier concludes, "Next time I'm going to keep my big mouth shut until I see those snapshots of yours."[131]

The idea was to get aircrew to stop speculating and spreading word of raid results and to trust in the intelligence assessment. The training video also depicted a bias by the U.S. photo interpreter favoring the RAF's one-thousand-bomber "saturation bombing" raid as the acme of destruction to the enemy's cities, as he concluded: "We didn't decide the means by which this war is being fought. . . . They brought that type of war to us and we have to use the same white gloves."[132] This idea of white-glove weapons delivery might have supplanted any ethical reluctance either by crew members or those charged with assessment with an emphasis on the dedication, teamwork, and attention to detail necessary to achieve the most from every raid. This film and another supported by the Harrisburg school became part of the curriculum. Both were also widely disseminated to both air and ground forces.[133]

Although the air staff met its production goals for air intelligence personnel, the harried effort was not without consequence. Rather than view the Harrisburg school as the deliberate development of a new air-minded profession, AAF leadership saw it as a factory for stamping a minimum of intelligence training onto recruits to get them overseas quickly. In essence, they tried to make up for "too little, too late" with "too much, too fast," and the result was to send to Medmenham unit intelligence officers who lacked confidence and photo interpreters whom the British found to be "pretty useless" or otherwise "completely lacking in any interpretation of operational photographs."[134] This led to a misguided AAF effort to educate the rest of the service about air intelligence, and a search for other agencies to support growing requirements for intelligence assessment.

Early school administration drew the ire of a series of unsatisfactory inspection ratings covering just about every facet required of a military post: housing, mess facilities, appearance and discipline of personnel, management of post funds, medical attention, post regulations, and handling of orders and regulations.[135] Well-intentioned but overzealous efforts by the third commandant to correct all of the school's administrative shortcomings met with subversive resistance from a pocket of disgruntled instructors led by a frustrated previous commandant, who had been relieved after less than two months but remained at the school.[136] They convinced a visiting intelligence officer from VIII Bomber Command, Lt. Col. Carl Norcross, to report observations of the school's "serious decline" to the assistant chief of staff, A-2: "Resentment against the present Commanding Officer boils down to the following: He is not an intelligence officer," Norcross suspected. "In over 10 weeks he has done nothing to convince the faculty that he is even mildly interested in the instruction given to students."[137] The nascent community of air intelligence officers, who did not respect a leader whom they viewed as an outsider, would rather have been led by one of their own. Although much of Norcross' report was proven unsubstantiated, it nevertheless precipitated an intrusive investigation by Technical Training Command that hung a cloud over the school until its dissolution.[138] The school saw five commandants in its short tenure—hardly a recipe for continuity, even in the best of circumstances. On the positive side, six weeks after the investigation completed, General Arnold transferred oversight responsibility from Technical Training Command to his A-2, a move that immediately boosted the school's access to "intelligence data, training aids, and equipment."[139]

The school chose as its motto the word *apprehension*, an apparent reference later noted by an Air Force historian to "signify the prowess basic to the learning of intelligence procedures."[140] However, a dictionary available to the faculty at the time shows prophetic irony. The school may have intended the word in the sense of "the act of conceiving [or] perception" necessary for intelligence officers, but another meaning, "fear or distrust of the future," more closely aligned to the faculty attitudes.[141] New air intelligence officers streamed into the European theater despite having ineffective training and a lack of a collective identity as intelligence officers. Since they also lacked the experience and credibility in Europe to engage in immediate target intelligence challenges, those duties would fall to other organizations.

Photo 2-1. AAFAIS students listening to a news broadcast, 1943.
Reprinted from Army Air Forces Air Intelligence School, "History of AAFAIS," USAF, 1945, AFHRA

EAKER SAVES CASABLANCA

While Eighth Air Force continued to batter unsuccessfully at U-boat targets, Arnold's COA forged ahead, adding more subcommittees and increasing its research scope as it ran out of time to prepare Arnold for the Casablanca conference. Although a dozen or more subcommittee reports were in progress, Arnold would have only two for his trip: a two-page interim update offering little save a few preliminary observations, and a tentative memorandum that unsurprisingly suggested that "the Axis oil position, especially as regards its aviation gasoline, is closely balanced and may become critical."[142]

What mattered most to U.S. airmen leading into the first phase of the combined bomber offensive was not the details discussed at the Casablanca conference or those of the directive released thereafter, but rather the ambiguity and lack of coordination in both. As to grand strategy, in January 1943, little had been resolved since Arcadia. The series of battles in the Atlantic and in Africa were not yet culminated, Italy was still hanging on, and Russian resilience was far from certain.[143] The airmen wanted the flexibility to pursue their bombing doctrine as they continued to build up force.

Discussions at Casablanca neither reopened the Germany First debate nor altered the Allied subtext for an eventual cross-Channel invasion, though no date was set. The question at hand was what to do with strategic bombers and who would control them.[144] Roosevelt did his part by deflecting pressure from Churchill to consolidate the AAF's bombers under RAF control, but he offered little resistance to giving up on daylight bombing.[145] He left the counterarguments to the airmen.

As a subordinate general to Arnold, Eaker would not have been present, except that Arnold had sent for him after it became apparent that U.S. air strategy was at risk and the entire entourage—Arnold included—had been handily outclassed in preparation.[146] "They swarmed upon us like locusts with a plentiful supply of planners and various other assistants with prepared plans to ensure that they not only accomplished their purpose but did so in stride," groaned Gen. Albert Wedemeyer, in attendance from Marshall's operations planning division. He added, "From a worm's eye viewpoint it was apparent that we were confronted by generations and generations of experience in committee work and in rationalizing points of view."[147]

If anyone could gin up facts in short order to support arguments for daylight strategic bombing, it was Eaker. In a private meeting with Churchill, Eaker regaled the prime minister with four concise arguments: (1) a switch to night bombing could increase losses because U.S. crews were not equipped or trained for it; (2) day bombing could destroy targets undiscernible by night area bombing; (3) the twenty-four-hour pressure of day-and-night bombing would guide the RAF "by fires set by day," and ensure "the devils will get no rest"; and (4) day bombing would force the Luftwaffe to fight.[148] Eaker's argument prevailed, and the AAF would stick to its doctrine, its training, its equipment as designed, and its own chain of command. Target priorities, however, were yet another issue.

The Casablanca directive was conveniently vague. Rather than resolving most points of conflict between the Allies, the directive simply lumped the various perspectives together. With a tip to the targeting proclivities of both countries' air forces, the combined chiefs defined their objective for Allied bombing in theater as "the progressive destruction and dislocation of the German military, industrial and economic system, and the undermining of the morale of the German people to a point where their capacity for armed resistance is fatally weakened."[149] The Americans could hone their focus on the German economy, while the British would emphasize morale. The distinction was not clear-cut, but the two approaches could be complementary and served by the same order.

Target priorities were the sticking point. Until a date could be determined for a ground invasion, airpower was free from pressure for direct support of it. However, the British Admiralty maintained extraordinary pressure on both air forces to step up their efforts in the antisubmarine campaign. The Eighth Air Force had already launched twelve raids on U-boat bases on the Bay of Biscay between October and the January conference, in addition to five more by the RAF against Lorient in the northwest of France.[150]

However, if perceptions of their success could keep them tied to the submarine targets, then the early attacks backfired. The AAF's own A-2 maintained sanguine expectations on most types of attack, while the British Admiralty slanted the bomb damage estimates with as much positive impact as possible. As to the former, for example, an A-2 report suggested that attacks on the pens themselves did not seem profitable, but "there are certain European targets which if heavily and consistently bombed would so seriously interrupt and demoralize the

U-boat organization that the number of submarines operating in the North and South Atlantic would be considerably reduced"; this included continued attacks on the Bay of Biscay bases.[151]

The Admiralty supported the A-2 position with a tenuous evaluation that begged for increased bombing intensity. Royal Navy Captain E. C. B. Mobray argued that changes in port activities, dry dock operations, and movement of subs between the Biscay bases showed signs of cumulative effects.[152] He was backed by a 20 November 1942 Admiralty intelligence report: "The U-boat bases are showing signs of disorganization which must be attributed to these raids. . . . If the series of attacks on these U-boats is sustained . . . the cumulative effort will considerably effect the whole U-boat campaign."[153]

Pressure did not come from only the Admiralty. Based on his frustrations the previous summer, Eisenhower was also sensitive to losses at sea. "Each week brought us records of additional ships sunk or damaged by enemy U-boats, ships that were included in our programs for the transport of troops, equipment, and supplies," he lamented, adding, "Each sinking causes revisions in operational and tactical plans."[154] Even VIII Bomber Command's analysts appeared swept up by the sentiment of the cooperative Allied and joint effort. In the A-2 report, the analysts argued that "British and American naval and air opinions are in agreement that these operations, although they have been few and light, have done material damage to the submarine war effort in this theater, have enhanced Allied morale, and done corresponding damage to the Axis morale."[155] If any real evidence of progress existed beyond the anecdotal boost in morale, no one seemed to be looking for it or considering it necessary.

Transportation and oil fell even lower in the initial target list. The directive did offer some latitude to deviate from the proposed priorities, but only temporarily: "The above priority may be varied from time to time according to the developments in the strategical [sic] situation."[156] Arnold encouraged Eaker to press toward the targets of his choice, whenever the directive's nominal target choices were "interfered with by weather."[157] Weather was a problem for visual bombing on more days than not during the winter. During this early part of the campaign, however, attempts to strike deeper into Germany meant tangling in the air with the Luftwaffe's day fighter force. Eaker found the fight he was looking for, but Haywood Hansell, as one of Eaker's wing commanders, would argue just a few weeks later that "the single most important factor facing us today is that of combat crew replacements. . . . The loss rate from fighters has been pretty severe. . . . They literally fly right through our formations."[158] The Eighth Air Force command echelon already seemed more concerned with losses than with their bombing effectiveness.

TRAVELING SALESMEN WITH ARNOLD'S BAGGAGE

While the Allied leaders sparred at Casablanca, a few COA analysts ventured to England on their own. They had recognized that their assumptions regarding operational bombing capabilities, especially as they pertained to Sorensen's committee, might create friction with Eighth Air Force. This type of friction that arises from competition between similarly charged organizations might lead Eighth Air Force to retaliate and undermine the COA's credibility or even to threaten its survival by rejecting its inputs outright. From the committee's perspective, it would be best to resolve potential disputes before publishing the final reports, and it would best to do it in person.

Despite Sorensen's leadership role on the committee, as well as his close relationship with Brigadier General Kuter, a fellow ACTS instructor then commanding Eaker's First Bombardment Wing (immediately prior to Hansell), he did not participate in the trip. Sorensen was aware his personality seemed to cause more harm than good. "I would, of course, be glad to come over," Sorensen wrote to Kuter, "but since I am obviously not in good standing here and probably not with General Spaatz [who had turned Eighth Air Force command over to Eaker in the ensuing weeks], I doubt the advisability of it."[159] Fairchild also refused the trip, which left the COA's temporary colonels, Perera and Leach, along with two civilians to fend for themselves without a regular officer insider to help them establish trust.

In London, the COA traveling team discovered the EOU was already actively picking targets for Eighth Air Force. The official COA history notes that Eaker's senior staff "believed it advisable for target information matters to be handled in England rather than by A-2 in Washington."[160] This was probably an understatement. The COA analysts trod lightly, seeking common ground and rationale for coexistence. After a two-and-a-half-hour meeting with Hughes and EOU members, they discovered their approaches were nearly identical except that Eighth Air Force had emphasized that "integration of RAF and USAAF activities must be a constant major consideration" as it pertained to intelligence, target selection, and synchronization of the missions themselves. They then agreed on a common framework for industrial analysis:

1. The indispensability of the product to the enemy war economy
2. The enemy position as to current production, capacity for production, and stocks on hand
3. The enemy requirements for the product for various degrees of activity
4. The possibility of substitution for the product
5. The number, distribution, and vulnerability of vital installations
6. The practicability of destruction of such installations with forces expectable
7. The recuperative possibilities of the industry
8. The lag time between the destruction of installations and the desired effect upon the enemy effort.[161]

Of course, this list created more questions than could be answered in detail about every industry.

COA members would have an uphill battle to prove their worth to General Eaker (by then back in London from Casablanca) and Lieutenant Colonel Hughes, though they disarmed immediate apprehensions by openly sharing and explaining their preliminary recommendations, working with the EOU rather than bypassing it (especially as pertained to engaging with the British MEW), and calming Eaker's concerns by committing their intended process to paper before they departed for Washington.[162] They had seemed surprised by Eaker's cordial demeanor despite a tipoff to expect a "decidedly cool" reception.[163] Leach knew of Eaker and had anticipated resistance, particularly if Eaker detected that their plan had not been clearly thought out. "He is not an 'oh, hell, I can do whatever it is' officer," Leach said of Eaker during a COA meeting before the team's departure. "He is a thoughtful, analytical mind."[164] Of course, Eaker would not have overtly treated this team sent by his superior disrespectfully, as he was duly reverent with correspondence or actions he thought might get back to Washington.

Besides, Eaker was choosing his battles carefully with Arnold and was already trying to make him feel guilty for "stealing" Eaker's P-38s for Africa. In a message to Arnold that same week, Eaker wrote, "That decision . . . is going to mean the loss of many bombers and their fine crews."[165] Eaker, along with Newton Longfellow (commanding general of VIII Bomber Command), clarified his take on the Eighth's operational assumptions to the COA team. These included a near-term range limitation of four hundred miles (which he attributed to current B-17 range with a "full load"), requirement for a month of training for new crews, expectations for 70 percent of theater aircraft operational (which proved too high), and the necessity to "saturate the defense by dispatching forces of not less than 300 aircraft."[166] This was useful data for the COA team members to bring back to Washington, though it was clear they would not be able to keep in tune with such dynamic operational considerations from thousands of miles away. Despite the overall positive tone of the visit, Eaker followed up with several concerns he addressed directly to Perera: "That the analysis of prospective targets be done by agencies best equipped to do it and closest to the sources of information; that we do not set up another agency to do work already being done by existing agencies; that we do not harass over-worked British organizations with additional requests for information, duplicating work already being done, or calling in slightly different form, for Intelligence work already being prepared."[167] In short, Eaker told them to do whatever Arnold had asked them to do, as long as they stayed out of his hair and avoided muddling up any of his existing intelligence routines or relationships.

A number of meetings with other intelligence organizations in London helped the COA members socialize their preliminary findings and feel out their own relationships with the established players. For example, Mr. Lawrence, director of the Ministry of Economic Warfare's objective department, leapt at the COA members' recommendation to target ball-bearing factories, and he also seemed supportive of attacking grinding wheels. Ball bearings would "form extremely vulnerable targets to incendiary attack," he thought, adding that "effective attack on all ball bearing plants would be felt almost immediately."[168] The MEW had less information on grinding wheels, as Lawrence admitted that they had only conducted preliminary studies on the abrasives industry (if at all).[169] This type of target "lay lower in the industrial process," Lawrence felt, but "its effectiveness would be felt within a reasonably short period," although investigations had yet to show favorable evidence as to "concentration of the industry or as to its recuperative powers."[170] Grinding wheels had to be heated in the production process; Lawrence "was suspicious, however, of any statement that kilns were difficult to replace."[171] All of these factors mattered to industrial target selection, and much of a target's value toward dislocating the enemy economy depended upon how the enemy might respond—the most difficult factor to determine.

In the MEW, the COA members had clearly found another intelligence organization set on pursuing quick victory through airpower. However, MEW's economists placed a higher premium on targets that were highly vulnerable and hard to repair. Unfortunately, these variables were often difficult to prove with available intelligence. As such, they formed the central arguments on many future debates. In some cases, opinions would dominate the facts.

THREE

EAKER'S IMPERFECT PITCH

I am enthusiastic about the possibilities of using this report of an impartial group of analysts as a means of presenting to the Combined as well as to the Joint Chiefs of Staff the concept that Airmen have known for years to be sound.

—GEN. H. H. ARNOLD, COMMANDING GENERAL, AAF, 24 MARCH 1943[1]

We know that the selection of the most vital targets must come as a result of thorough analysis. We know that the strength of our fighting force will always be relatively limited. We must, therefore, apply it to those specially selected and vital targets which give the greatest return. We cannot afford to apply it where, or in such a manner that, the return is not eminently worth the cost. We know that there is room for doubt as to whether friend or enemy is worn down faster by bombing unless it is applied with precision against vital objectives.

—GEN. H. H. ARNOLD, 10 APRIL 1943[2]

By the third week of March, the COA's core members completed and cosigned their final report on the Western Axis, then submitted it to Major General Fairchild, who was bounding his way up the Air Staff as Arnold's Potomac-based protégé after skipping the rank of colonel on his way from major to two-star general in a span of five years.[3] In his final review,

Fairchild insisted on deleting the single paragraph that had actually estimated German industrial dislocation for Arnold. A force of five hundred heavy bombers, they projected, "free for the bombing of industrial targets for a period of eight months, the effect would be to impair very gravely the capacity of the Western Axis to resist; and if a force of 1,000 such planes could be maintained, equally free for a similar period, the result might be to cripple the Western Axis war effort."[4]

With this statement, the COA members' months of research culminated in an assertion that the AAF could not risk committing to paper. Perhaps there was no need to suggest that strategic bombing could enable a cake walk of an invasion by January 1944 because the Army would not be ready by that time anyway. Why risk an unnecessary claim? Moreover, even if the AAF leaders hoped to end the war before a ground invasion was possible, to propose such a feat would undermine the combined chiefs' plans and their build-up program, thereby drawing criticism the research could not support. Perhaps Fairchild sensed there was no chance of consistently generating raids with one thousand bombers in 1943, or he doubted the accuracy of the assumptions. If the timeline assertion did not pan out with the committee's credibility on the line, then the rest of their report would lose its clout. In any case, the AAF's generals wanted victory through airpower as soon as they could get it, but they knew they were best off not yet committing to a date.

In addition to its list of targets and rationale, the remainder of the report offered insight into the team members' desire to establish their own enduring purpose. The COA members attempted to cement their credibility with Arnold by emphasizing collaboration with diverse entities in Washington. "The Committee has had the assistance and hearty cooperation of A-2, G-2, the Board of Economic Warfare, the Office of Strategic Services, the War Production Board, other government agencies, and the best qualified experts in private industry," they touted.[5] In reality, this list was a reflection of the COA's own composition from the start, though the individual members had reached back to their parent organizations.

Further, the report also highlighted collaboration with the influential actors they had met in England, including "Eighth Air Force staff, the Royal Air Force, the Air Ministry, the Economic Warfare Division of the American Embassy and the British Ministry of Economic Warfare," although many of their meetings were more diplomatic than substantial.[6] Perhaps even more important to the COA members than learning which intelligence organizations in England had which preferences, they could now show they had quickly established peer relationships with the many intelligence organizations sharing a stake in air campaign targeting. The COA proved its opinions mattered and succeeded, at least outwardly, in establishing partners rather than foes.

Finally, the COA showed regard for Eaker's Eighth Air Force. On paper, Eighth Air Force was the subordinate air command to European Theater of Operations, United States Army (ETOUSA), at that time led by Lt. Gen. Frank Andrews, not AAF headquarters, although Arnold's extraordinary influence was no secret. COA analysts had been reticent to declare target priorities on their final report, ostensibly for security reasons, although they later awkwardly recommended "that the current selection of particular targets be left to the responsible authorities in England, subject only to such directions as may be called for by broad strategic considerations."[7] They had left their target selections in priority order but removed the labels, making their final recommendations less contentious. The COA analysts tiptoed in the space between the limits—both official and unofficial—of General Arnold's authority and the wishes of the command responsible for carrying out its recommendations. While Arnold devoured the report's appetizing front matter, competing intelligence organizations criticized its shortcomings.

A look at the internal responses by these other organizations, particularly the British MEW and the American EOU, reflects their respective organizations' behavior and helps to dissect the reasons behind the targeting preferences of all three groups before assessing their impact on the air campaign. The MEW deputy director general, Geoffrey Vickers—a former British infantry colonel and "an almost dangerously brilliant lawyer"—penned a critique of the COA analysts' reports to Air Chief Marshal Sir Charles Portal.[8] Vickers vehemently defended the MEW's army of intelligence bureaucrats, who collectively sought a reputation for amassing all relevant details for Germany's economic collapse. To MEW economists, the idea that a handful of American Johnny-come-lately analysts would outdo them from Washington was unthinkable.

Moreover, Vickers' defensive posture also reflected his own insecurities about leading an enormous intelligence organization with no previous experience of his own.[9] He had to save face that the plan for the combined bomber offensive

(CBO) would be based largely on COA rather than MEW inputs, or he would risk being discredited from within his own organization. Despite these factors, British senior military and civilian leadership enticed all forms of U.S. support, so any excessively disparaging comments might have met with a fierce rebuke from above. In fact, according to the COA history, Portal later submitted only glowing praise to Arnold on behalf of the British air ministry despite the content of Vickers' report.[10]

In his collegial-yet-supercilious review, Vickers took the opportunity to reinforce the MEW's preferred reputation for more critical analysis by gently besmirching the COA analysts' lack of depth and factual credibility. He argued that much of the COA work constituted a "somewhat superficial examination of the enemy's position" and that there were problems related to "a certain divergence of opinion between us on questions of fact."[11] Vickers cast doubt on COA sources. Nevertheless, he voiced no substantial concerns over the COA analysts' five highest priority targets—aircraft, ball bearings, petroleum, nonferrous metals, and synthetic rubber—while he rejected outright the COA analysts' final two recommended categories, transportation and submarine yards, as "subject to a very substantial time-lag."[12] Although the MEW economists maintained a greater focus on inducing economic collapse (as opposed to imposing military matériel shortages) than any other intelligence organization, they also sought to attack industrial bottlenecks.

Apart from ball bearings, however, the MEW economists pushed for different bottlenecks in a variety of industries, as if preferring to place independent bets. For example, MEW economists proclaimed a "less optimistic" stance on grinding wheels, pushed to target "internal combustion engine components and accessories" rather than assembly plants for motor transport and aircraft, and argued that aircraft production might be impacted best by attacking propeller factories.[13] The MEW economists followed up Vickers' assertions with detailed commentary in a separate report of their own. After all, the MEW organizational prestige depended not particularly on nominating targets, but on producing superior economic reports.

It is worth noting that MEW economists were enthusiastic about targeting petroleum and sought to increase the number of synthetic oil plants on the COA target list; there was "no question that the destruction of either the 13 Bergius plants or the leading Romanian refineries at any time in the next twelve months would have a critical, and perhaps decisive, effect on the enemy's war effort," Vickers claimed.[14] By comparison, the COA analysts' draft oil-targeting conclusions had been considerably muted, noting only that "loss of production would make almost inescapable some curtailment in direct military consumption of oil."[15] Oil was a worthy target to the COA members, as its depletion would help dry up the roaring engines of both the Luftwaffe and the Wehrmacht, but results would take some time. In their final report, the COA members noted it might take only four months for Germany to feel the "full impact of their destruction," even though they were heavily constructed.[16] The COA members also gravitated to the idea that so much Axis oil seemed to originate in so few locations, giving to it the quality of a bottleneck, albeit not one as attractive as ball bearings.

The EOU Bites Back

Economist Charles Kindleberger took a different tack as he drafted the EOU response to COA for Colonel Hughes. Kindleberger's approach, adopting the pugnacious character typical of the EOU economists, attacked the style and consistency of the COA reports in addition to their substance: "The reports have been written by a variety of people of differing talents," he argued, "and from various points of view."[17] Despite the detailed background provided in some COA industrial studies, Kindleberger ridiculed them as "focused mainly on the industry in the abstract without relating potential destruction to military operations."[18] He genuflected to the few reports he commended with veiled self-praise, noting they were "written from a viewpoint practically identical with that developed here . . . with persistent attention to 'depth,' and to the actual possibilities of affecting the enemy military capabilities within a reasonable period of time."[19] Kindleberger did not share Vickers' penchant for dampening the extremes of his assessment, which also broadly reflected the EOU economists' attitude toward their competitors as the air campaign later reached a crescendo.

Matters of tact aside, Kindleberger pointed out his opponent's fatal flaw. The COA experts-for-hire consistently struggled to connect their knowledge to bombing outcomes. The committee's ad hoc meeting format had put each industrial expert in a position to convince the uninitiated of the merits of his particular industry as a potential target. In that environment, persuasiveness could be more important than data since the other members lacked the expertise to critically evaluate the supporting evidence.

Further, this approach meant a target system could be rejected if its advocate failed to represent it well or had latched on to either a flawed assumption or an erroneous conclusion. However, an industry with the appearance of a more complete puzzle and a stronger advocate would come out on top regardless of whether it was truly vulnerable to airpower. Kindleberger added, "The reports prepared by industrial experts tend to suffer from a lack of perspective and objectivity—each industrial expert naturally thinks of his own field as a prime objective. On the other hand, the papers prepared by economists are apt to have less detailed technical information."[20] Some COA experts may not have had enough research experience or sufficient time to ensure consistency across all of their subcommittee reports, but the result was to give the impression that they had stacked the deck to favor the industries they had identified from the very start.

In sum, the COA analysts had framed their initial understanding of the problem months earlier—to create a "pattern of destruction" to the German war machine based on "analysis of industrial, utility, and military bottlenecks."[21] They never deviated from this approach, and they focused on trying to achieve victory through airpower as quickly as possible. For this reason, the analysts tended to bet heavily on obscure shortcuts such as ball bearings, grinding wheels, nonferrous metals, and optical glass rather than the "progressive deterioration" of systemic industries such as coal, electricity, and rail traffic.[22] None of these three systems made the COA top eight despite the fact that rail and electricity had been the highest priorities in AWPD-1 (behind only the German air force).[23] If systemic effects against these larger target types could not be assured by a small force of bombers, the COA analysts dropped them in priority or discarded them altogether. For example, their transportation report maintained that "limited and scattered attacks upon transport targets are of little consequence because the recuperative powers and flexibility of the transport system permits rapid and successful readjustments in transport operations."[24] The COA gave Arnold what they thought he wanted: a list of short-cut targets destructible as quickly as possible by the least number of bombers. Ball bearings were an incomparable choice, surpassed on their list only by German fighters (to enable air superiority). With their top choices made, the COA offered plenty of pessimistic speculation to rule out larger target systems.

A similar rationale clouded their judgment on coal and the coking industry, in terms of both attacking the sources and the transportation thereof. The COA analysts felt that German civilian coal requirements could be reduced to a miniscule fraction of prewar usage, leaving the industry with excess capacity, especially if Germany curtailed its exports.[25] COA subcommittee experts struggled to sync coal as a target area with realistic bombing capability and industrial vulnerability. As one COA expert reported in a pivotal committee meeting, "If we could deprive them of [coal], we could accomplish a great deal, but no one knew how we could do that, except indirectly."[26] They also balked at coal because of a perceived lack of enough bombers: "Coke and coal tar products are very attractive in that they bring a single aspect on many industries," an industrial expert reported, "but you have hundreds of installations. About 25, however, do supply about half of the output, but to get further proportions, you have to get a very large number of coke ovens. They don't give too much hope."[27] Experts without hope do not make very good advocates.

Before Arnold could even pitch the COA report to the joint chiefs, Colonel Cabell—newly promoted and reassigned to Arnold's advisory council—energized the COA members to plan a motion picture film to accompany their report.[28] The analysts jumped into the propaganda project and produced a full script in just a couple of days. The film would sell the top three COA-recommended targets with their indisputable footage and facts. To a scene of bombers, bombs, and a burning aircraft factory, the narrator would pitch that the venerable Focke-Wulf 190 and Messerschmidt 109 "form two-thirds of German fighter strength. Cut down their numbers and Allied effectiveness in the air would sharply increase with fewer losses of planes and personnel, fewer planes grounded for repairs, [and] greater bomb loads in place of ammunition, all resulting in heavier blows at German industry . . . paving the way for less costly invasion."[29] The implication of this argument was that the battle for air superiority—not the battle against submarines—was the key to efficient victory. Ironically, albeit unintentionally, a Navy film crew, ignorant of the argument behind their efforts, would shoot the footage.[30]

The pitch for oil was no less embellished. Against a backdrop portraying the German war machine, a narrator read: "Her planes grounded . . . Her panzers immobilized . . . Germany could not endure such a famine of fuel."[31] Finally, the pitch for ball bearings would be the film's visual coup de grace. A diagram would show that the bombers' range could reach all recommended factories from England and would depict a destroyed factory along with "a great fleet of bombers coming out of the clouds" as the narrator boasted: "Destruction means wide industrial stoppage—no bearings for aircraft engines—no bearings for locomotives—or auto-engines—ordnance—machine tools. Special precision tools take months to build—Recovery would take as long. Anti-friction bearing factories are essential to the German industrial strength—and they are all vulnerable."[32] Regardless of whether the Committee of Operations Analysts were impartial to the preferences of AAF doctrine, they were certainly partial to their own analysis and eager to market their conclusions.

Without waiting for the film, Arnold approved the report and dispatched Colonel Cabell to carry it to England along with a personal letter to Gen. Frank Andrews—his friend, rival, and subordinate—ordering him to study its contents: "I am enthusiastic about the possibilities of using this report of an impartial group of analysts as a means of presenting to the Combined as well as the Joint Chiefs of staff the concept that Airmen have known for years to be sound," Arnold confessed.[33] He then begged Andrews for "particular attention to the ball-bearing industries, because its [sic] destruction would virtually paralyze all German industry, and secondly because it may well be within our capacity to destroy this industry with the size Air Force that we happen to have in the United Kingdom in 1943."[34] If the COA analysts were selling air intelligence, then Arnold was buying it wholesale. Ball bearings seemed like the perfect efficiency in a target system, because attacks on their production would serve as a short cut to securing objectives on other industries. Arnold added, "If we could destroy the ball-bearing industry, it would be unnecessary to destroy airplane or airplane engine manufacturing establishments, or, for that matter, the submarine manufacturing installations, for in a very short time their operations would be vitally affected."[35] He had injected the COA report directly into the European theater with his cordial influence on Andrews, and he used it to keep his micromanagerial thumb pressed firmly on Eaker.[36]

The Sheen of Success at Vegesack

While Arnold's COA analysts developed their target plans in Washington, Eaker's commanders and researchers experimented to improve bombing results in Europe. A few weeks of data at the end of 1942 offered ORS researchers a chance to leverage LeMay's assertions about formation bombing accuracy; if the entire command would switch to Lemay's bomb-on-leader technique, then the researchers might share in the credit. The opportunity was delayed because Haywood Hansell, then acting commander of VIII Bomber Command, refused to act until Gen. Newton Longfellow returned. Longfellow finally directed LeMay's bomb-on-leader technique for every group in their 18 March mission on the Bremer Vulcan submarine yard at Vegesack, near Bremen. Though it may have been the aircrew whose lives were in jeopardy, the ORS members felt enormous pressure with this mission. They had weighed in supporting LeMay's bombing procedure, and their "entire reputation and future were at stake," according one ORS member.[37]

Preliminary raid results suggested extraordinary accuracy relative to previous raids. The average bomb score across all groups, 97 aircraft dropping 270 tons of bombs, was 26.1 percent inside the 1,000-foot circle, making it the Mighty Eighth's best accuracy performance of the first half of 1943.[38] LeMay's 305th dropped an astonishing 76 percent of its bombs within the 1,000-foot circle.[39] Just two days later, the ORS produced a report recommending "(1) that all groups be instructed to drop their bombs on the lead ship; (2) that the aiming points for the lead ship be selected with a view to placing the formation pattern most effectively over the target area; and (3) that every effort commensurate with defensive needs be made to reduce the length of the bomb pattern of existing formations."[40] They were going to take the credit for tightening up bombing accuracy, and they doubled down on their success by winning a policy change.

Interestingly, an ORS history makes no mention of aircrew use of the B-17's C-1 automatic flight control equipment on the Vegesack mission. The C-1 was essentially a mechanical autopilot that coupled the aircraft's flight controls to the bombardier's target-aiming solution on his Norden bombsight. The idea was to get the aircraft as stable as possible so that, as one former Eighth Air Force group commander wrote, "When the bombardier takes over the ship for the run on the target he is in command," both in terms of his direction to the crew as well as his literal control of the aircraft.[41] However, it was a complicated and finicky arrangement of servos, gyros, and extra cables that were clamped onto the normal flight control linkages; it took nineteen manual steps, including a ten-minute warm-up period, just to engage the system.[42] That was if the system worked properly. It depended upon a time-consuming preflight, tricky troubleshooting, and sensitive airborne fine-tuning—especially under combat conditions. The system proved unreliable on early combat sorties from England, so crews lost confidence in it while engineers from Honeywell worked out the kinks.[43]

Eaker was well aware of the C-1's difficulties and efforts to fix them. The Army's director of bombardment wrote him to praise its performance at Vegesack: "Because of the bad reputation that the old automatic flight control equipment has developed, it is most necessary at this time that all possible action be taken to indoctrinate personnel, by lectures and demonstrations, in the present effectiveness of this equipment. . . . We have known for some time that large bombing errors of units in combat have been caused to a large extent by poor piloting technique" (emphasis in original).[44]

Engineering teams corrected autopilot glitches just prior to the Vegesack mission, and the 305th's lead ship employed the C-1, which coupled well with LeMay's guidance not to maneuver on the bomb run.[45] In the final analysis, it was not clear how much of the bombing accuracy attained at Vegesack was due to LeMay's techniques, the ORS recommendations, improvements to the C-1 autopilot system, or even the 305th's crews' increasing familiarity with the target area after returning on multiple occasions. Perhaps it was all of the above.

While various teams shared in the Vegesack mission's apparent success, one team's performance decidedly did not. For bomb damage assessment, Vegesack proved among the more pronounced failures for photo interpreters. Reports categorized the raid damage as "extremely heavy," emphasizing complete destruction of the power house and several other important structures, in addition to a capsized U-boat and others potentially damaged.[46] The interpreters assumed that the apparent increase in accuracy, since so many bombs fell inside the target area, correlated to a commensurate increase in effective damage, and there was a lot of damage for them to see, but the challenge for the interpreters was to help convey what the apparent damage meant.

Conservative judgment was overruled by optimistic views. They wanted to see destruction, so they were easily fooled by damaged camouflage. They also assumed that visible damage to buildings would equate to long-term loss of production. As a result, CIU interpreters' inputs to Eighth Air Force's mission reports were exaggerated, and German recuperative capacity was equally underestimated. Neither the interpreters nor Eaker yet knew that Arnold's A-2 would report that the total impact for all raids on Vegesack would be to delay the U-boats completed by 1 July by "an estimated average of 2 weeks."[47] The increase in accuracy did not correlate to any meaningful effect on U-boat production.

Because other sources of intelligence were either highly compartmentalized or not yet adequately incorporated, the CIU interpreters failed to receive adequate and timely feedback. ULTRA decrypts of German communications traffic, for example, had been funneled to a single individual at Medmenham and kept from the eyes of photo interpreters. "In some cases, intelligence was withheld from the interpretation unit, on the grounds that it was too dangerous to share certain information," reflected one photo interpreter, "thus depriving the interpreters of material vital to the success of their work."[48] There was no meaningful way for Eaker's leadership team, Harlan's ORS, or Hughes' target planners with the EOU to confirm the accuracy of the CIU's assessments; the latter were in position to trust what they received. In the meantime, the most important intelligence customer in Washington seemed to be Hap Arnold, who needed to see little more than the "pictures of your strike at Vegesack" to conclude, "The results of that magnificent show are certainly encouraging to those of us who are convinced of the soundness of high-altitude daylight precision bombing. Keep it up and we will yet convince the skeptics."[49] It seemed everyone was selling their own take on the ideas represented in the photos, including Arnold.

Eaker's Audible and Muffled Feedback

What Arnold sought from Andrews, even though the request had been carefully worded to appear flexible, was for theater air commanders to validate the COA report and his own understanding of the required bomber force. Arnold's intent for Andrews was more political than it was scientific, because Arnold would not permit his generals in Europe to request more bombers than he could give them. Assumptions about the necessary size of the operational bomber force would be critical. Cabell, who'd drafted Arnold's letter for him, had written: "It must be within our capabilities to provide the force recommended," and the minimum size of that "operationally efficient" force would be twelve hundred bombers.[50] The planners assumed a dispatched force of three hundred bombers could make "deep penetrations" into Germany, while a minimum of two hundred could "provide self-protection and at the same time carry out worthwhile destruction" into Germany, as long as fifty bombers with a fighter escort were available to provide a diversion attack to draw off the German air force.[51] Cabell was now in position, after having drafted Arnold's letter to Eaker and delivered the message himself, to remain in England and participate on Eaker's planning team.

The other key assumption, as eventually briefed by Eaker himself, was that "experience in the Theater to date indicates that at least 800 airplanes must be in Theater to dispatch 300 bombers on operations."[52] This meant just over 37 percent of all bombers Arnold could put on English soil would fly in any given raid. The difference, then, between eight hundred and twelve hundred as the size of the bomber force in theater was more about the rate of operations—Arnold's preferred metric—than the size of the bomber force per raid. Sustaining those operations with good results was Eaker's problem, but first he needed to develop the plan.

The COA report, including the size of the force required to destroy the targets, had relied upon several other fundamental assumptions. For example, Sorensen's committee presumed that 50 percent of all bombs—"sighted and released"—from 25,000 feet would land within 1,000 feet of the target, and that 60 percent of all dispatched bombers would successfully attack their targets in combat conditions, yet they acknowledged that only 40 percent had done so through December 1942.[53] They had also calculated that 153 hits from 500-pound bombs across the 5 ball-bearing plants at Schweinfurt would knock them out of service, based upon the idea that a single bomb per 20,000 square feet would do the trick.[54] Put otherwise, 1 in 10 bombs from a force of 200 bombers (each carrying up to 8,500-pound bombs) would each strike a vital impact point or otherwise destroy the contents of 141 square feet of single-story, light machine shop space. Time would tell if the assumptions behind this "conservative estimate"—as Sorensen saw it—would prove true, but Eaker would first develop and brief his own plan for the CBO.[55]

Upon receiving direction from Andrews, Eaker assembled his team, including two of his subordinate wing commanders (Hansell and Anderson) and his senior air planners (including Hughes), along with Cabell. They would study the COA report and craft its findings into a theater-level air plan.[56] Eaker's plan was not to be a major departure from previous guidance, but data included in the COA report gave him plausible rationale to make the change he most wanted, which was to get his bombers focused back on the Luftwaffe. His plan now included German air force targets as an "Intermediate Objective," which he contrived to mean even higher priority than the "Principal Objectives." Eaker argued, "If the growth of the German fighter strength is not arrested quickly, it may become literally impossible to carry out the destruction planned and thus to create the conditions necessary for ultimate decisive action by our combined forces on the Continent."[57] Eaker knew that battling through the German single-engine fighters, incidental to raids on the U-boat industry, was an ineffective way to deplete their numbers.

The COA report refrained from choosing between targeting airframe assembly or aircraft engine plants, simply listing all of them, although neither target set had been enough to satisfy Eaker. Advocating another slice at the Luftwaffe's front-line strength, Eaker wanted to add airfields as well as repair depots and aircraft storage facilities to the target lists, especially since weather was no longer written into the directive as a viable excuse for manipulating target priorities.[58] Hughes, as the intelligence officer and a junior member of the team, remained uncharacteristically mum until he attempted to steer Eaker from adding aircraft repair depots into the plan based on his own inaccurate assumption that Air Chief Marshal Portal would not approve. Hughes may have preferred to avoid taking on the hassle of convincing the British Air Ministry and RAF leadership of the add-on targets in addition to the extra work for his shop in planning them, but more likely he was echoing the EOU members' sentiments from a memorandum he had just received from Kindleberger, which purported to cover "the various lines of investigation" into attacking the German aircraft industry.[59] They had concluded that "the airframe industry suffered from the disadvantage of containing few vulnerable or even highly specialized installations," and that aircraft engines were more likely to be the "limiting factor."[60] They had not considered the import of airfields or repair facilities at all, though their logic would have ruled them out. In any case, Eaker overrode the recommendation, and Hughes redeemed himself by rattling off the repair depot locations at Antwerp, Paris, and Romilly-sur-Seine as possible targets.[61]

The intelligence organizations most oriented toward inflicting economic collapse saw little value in airfields and repair facilities, even if these targets were essential enablers to keeping the Luftwaffe out of the fight. Targeting the aircraft industry proved a contentious challenge, not only because there were differing opinions about how to attrit the Luftwaffe, but also because the reich creatively modified its production locations and practices throughout the war.[62] Eaker doggedly pursued these targets while disinterested intelligence organizations struggled to provide the feedback he really needed on the attacks. Despite the absence of aircraft repair facilities in the COA report, Eaker's Mighty Eighth raided all the locations Hughes had mentioned by the first week of September.

Eaker also sought to leverage a recent boost in bombing accuracy to lend credibility to his plan. "General Arnold wants to know what percent we can destroy of the targets we must hit, based on experience, with examples to prove our statements," Eaker had said to his team. "[I] do not think we should use theoretical statements such as mil error in stating bombing accuracy. We should use photographs of Vegesack, Renault, etc., as examples and accentuate our increase in bombing accuracy."[63] Eaker did not need the photographs to predict the industrial impact of the raids as much as he needed them to project a psychological impact on his audience—in this case, Arnold and then the rest of the combined chiefs.

With his references to Vegesack and Renault, Eaker was cherry-picking two of the better accuracy performances and using the photographs to tell a convincing story of bombing accuracy and likely future success. Bomb plot reports for the 4 April raid on Renault (a factory in Paris attacked the day prior to his planning meeting) showed 15.3 percent of bombs within 1,000 feet of the target, which outstripped the 14.9 percent average for all raids from January through March.[64] Moreover, the ORS bombing accuracy reports showed Eaker that 4 consecutive raids between 8 March and 22 March (including Vegesack) had attained an average of 21 percent in the 1,000-foot circle, while the previous 4 had averaged just over 10 percent. Eaker wanted to impress his boss, and the ORS data apparently suggested an exceptional learning curve for his organization, doubling its earlier accuracy performance.

Unfortunately, the ORS research later showed that for the rest of April through June, Eighth Air Force could not sustain a new accuracy standard. Of the 19 assessable raids after Vegesack and Renault, only 9.9 percent of the total bombs dropped fell within 1,000 feet; only a single raid outperformed the 20 percent mark for bombs inside 1,000 feet; and 8 raids had yielded all bombs outside of 2,000 feet.[65] Visual bombing accuracy, at least by the 1,000-foot-circle metric, had found its plateau at 10 percent.

Given what he knew at the time and since Eaker's plan had to receive the combined chiefs' approval, Hansell and his planning team dared not move submarine bases below second place on their final plan. At third priority, Eaker's team swapped ball bearings in for transportation targets—as they had been listed in the Casablanca directive, acknowledging Arnold's request. Petroleum remained at fourth. Finally, Eaker's team dropped grinding wheels and nonferrous metals—the other two obvious panacea targets on COA's list—from their new plan altogether.[66] Perhaps Hansell only felt comfortable with marginal deviations from AWPD-42, so ball bearings as one high-priority outside bet was his limit. Hansell was prone to avoiding operational risk, just as Eaker was apt to accept a plan that briefed well. As such, the plan went out for review.

Air Chief Marshal Arthur Harris' feedback on Eaker's plan showed a depth to his strategic and political thought not often credited to his character. To the major aims of Eaker's plan, Harris extended his full support. After all, Harris held command over roughly half of the bombing forces necessary to enact its purported devastation, even though Eaker would shoulder the burden of convincing the military and political leadership—on both sides of the Atlantic—to give both air forces a chance to consolidate their aims under a more formal construct.

Harris' two areas of concern, however mild they may have seemed, were prophetic. Harris detested the arguably absurd sense of precision with which Eaker had prescribed a year's worth of highly specific targets, as if to suggest the plan obtained a perfect grasp of the enemy. "The plan as it stands may prove somewhat inelastic," Harris reasoned, adding, "In practice, it could and would be modified as necessary to meet developments in the general situation and to accord with new information as to the effect of past attacks on different types of objectives."[67] Harris knew Eaker's plan was based largely on speculation, and the Germans would undoubtedly respond. Harris seemed to value the importance of ongoing assessments, regardless of whether he would choose to accept them. The plan would have to be flexible as the campaign developed, and this was a point he felt worth highlighting.

Harris also mocked the primacy Eaker's plan afforded to attacks on submarine bases. Harris would not object if Eaker wanted his day-bombing force to continue whaling away fruitlessly at concrete submarine pens, but he had no intention of trying to crack into them with his night-bombing force. Finally, Harris revealed his sense of airpower and the magnitude of the political situation in which both he and Eaker found themselves: "There is no difficulty in achieving our object at minimum cost in life, material, and effort," Harris avowed. "There is difficulty only in convincing those in whose hands lies the power to grasp this opportunity."[68] For Harris, the assured success of the combined bomber offensive had less to do with the Germans or their industries and everything to do with receiving the permission and the equipment to unleash hell—first on the Luftwaffe, then on the moral backbone of the German *Vaterland*. The air intelligence organizations were not the only ones selling their agendas.

Eaker's amended plan was completed and approved by both Andrews and Air Chief Marshal Sir Charles Portal by mid-April 1943. Eaker's adept briefing skills "without notes and with compelling command of his subject" certainly mattered, but there was also work behind the scenes that helped it flow back uphill smoothly.[69] The EOU economists, ever struggling to get out from behind Hughes' curtain and onto the main stage, would not be shut out of the credits. As Eaker's plan was recorded in their history, they had played "a hand in shaping the basic analysis and to some extent its final form," though they conceded it was Hughes who bore the "brunt of the laborious salesmanship at higher levels."[70]

Andrews had been a fan from the start. He sought to temper Arnold's relentless drive for dispersed raids and constant pressure with operational flexibility. "An intensive, continuous search should be maintained for a critical system," he suggested to Eaker, "so that at any time a part of the German economic structure becomes critical we can strike it with increased effort."[71] As Harris had also recognized, there was a balance to be struck between presenting a plan that was detailed in its analysis, but not so much so that it appeared overcommitted to its predictions. Andrews wanted to ensure that more lucrative target systems were not overlooked once the plan was set in motion. It was up to the analysts to keep searching.

Eaker kicked off his final brief for the CBO to the joint chiefs leveraging the COA analysts' trumped-up credibility more than their actual expertise. For example, despite the fact that much COA research had been accomplished by officers with wartime commissions (i.e., Colonel Perera and Colonel Leach) as well as by the A-2 and G-2 officers who had joined the team, Eaker curiously credited only the COA's "eminent civilian authorities" in his opening remarks.[72] Eaker shamelessly plugged the COA analysts' business, academic, and interagency credentials as well as their external coordination with the Board of Economic

Warfare, OSS, Air Ministry, war department G-2, war production board, Ministry of Economic Warfare, and others. Eaker's opening gambit reflected an awareness that the air staff had been branded as biased in senior defense circles, so he established the plan's credibility by emphasizing only the role fulfilled by civilian consultants. No intimations of the air staff or his Eighth Air Force planners, no matter how valuable or necessary their contributions might have been, would help to wheedle a thumbs-up from leaders outside of the air arm.

Despite the ease with which Eaker painted his plan's attractive veneer, the closed-door question-and-answer period following his brief to the joint chiefs foreshadowed several elements that would require future adjustments. General Marshall had the foresight to press Eaker on his fighter escort requirements. Eaker's talking points included excruciating detail of the German fighter force and his plans to curb its production. Not even once, however, did his script include a mention of Allied pursuit aircraft with respect to his plan's requirements. Eaker maintained utmost confidence in the venerable Flying Fortress, despite the crippling losses he had already taken.[73] In fact, the only range Eaker had described in his entire brief, including all four three-month phases, was a four-hundred-mile limit on penetration during the second phase. This was peculiar, because he had declared that the "German fighter force must be kept depleted" for subsequent phases and targets that would require deeper penetration.[74] Eaker believed he could eliminate the German air force without an escort that could reach Berlin, as he retorted to Marshall that the only escort he needed was the P-47 with its four-hundred-mile range.

Eaker also put extraordinary faith in blind-bombing techniques enabled by the advent of onboard radar, which afforded the ability to map the ground and aim at targets through the weather. With adequate forces, Eaker felt he could squeeze up to ten missions per month out of his bombardment wings, even during the worst months of the often-overcast North Atlantic winters. "The weather would actually be an aid rather than a hindrance," he argued, "in view of new devices which have been developed for bomber aircraft which act as leaders."[75] Bad weather was no problem for bombing accuracy, he thought, but it could help reduce the attrition numbers on his bombers, as they would be obscured from the Luftwaffe and from flak.

Finally, Chief of Naval Operations Adm. Ernest King pushed to expose any possibilities that Eaker might try to wriggle his bombers away from the battle against submarines. King's exchange with Eaker continued the trend of passive-aggressive manipulation between the Navy and the AAF. Just a few months earlier, General Fairchild had easily dredged up the expertise of eager Navy officers willing to contribute to COA's subcommittee on submarine targets, but the sailors could not obtain permission to participate from the top of their sea service.[76] Despite the best intentions of midlevel officers, Navy brass could not risk being coopted into a joint report that might condemn the feasibility of air attacks on submarine bases. However truthful such studies might have been, it was safer for the Navy's interests not to play. They wanted the air component supporting their mission.

King, who had the "sparkling eye and animated countenance" suggested by the equine meaning of his father's middle name—Clydesdale—trained his gaze on Eaker.[77] "U.S. officers think they can strike at Submarine bases," Eaker crowed, but "the British are not in full agreement."[78] Eaker had avoided addressing some of the thorniest challenges ahead, but he was going to need informed intelligence, robust assessment, imaginative operations analysis, and a healthy openness to feedback in order to succeed. As it stood, the joint chiefs opted to defer final decision until the Allied combined chiefs met at the Trident conference in mid-May.[79]

SHARPENING FOR TRIDENT

While Eaker and his staff had been busy drafting and selling his proposed version of the CBO plan, Arnold was busy losing patience with the lack of quantifiable detail on Eaker's bombing progress. Damage assessments flowing back to Washington were delayed, lacked depth, and seldom included correlation with other intelligence sources. Arnold was not able to answer questions he was getting from above, and he was beginning to sense that Eaker could not answer them either. Arnold wanted reports with increasing regularity and accuracy; the time for haphazard experimentation was over. Arnold expressed this sentiment to Eaker in a 10 April 1943 letter:

> It is very natural for many people in high places to note that so many bombs were dropped on a given occasion by units of your striking force. The very natural question is, what was destroyed? Did you hurt the

> enemy's ability to wage war? Did you destroy any facility or part of a factory which is directly supporting the war effort? How much damage was done and to what?
>
> We are in a difficult position here when it comes to answering questions of the above character. We get your reports and pictures ultimately, but they are rather long delayed. We also are handicapped here in making an assessment of damage which will satisfy your people because as you have told us, pictures alone do not give all of the evidence. Additional information comes from espionage or other sources. We appreciate the fact that information from espionage or other such sources is not immediately available.
>
> It will help us a great deal in defending your operations and in building up a correct picture of the results being accomplished if you make a special effort to have a summary on the subject gotten back here about every two weeks. . . . This report should cover your bombing operations, including target pictures before and after bombing, and should particularly include your most thorough assessment of damage done to the enemy that can be made in the time allowed.[80]

Another reason for Arnold's request was that time was running out as preparations for the Trident conference of the combined chiefs of staff, a meeting scheduled for the following month in Washington, reached fever pitch. The Washington locale for this follow-on to Casablanca offered the U.S. joint chiefs an enhanced opportunity to commit their assistants and planning staffs to preparation, which was a lesson learned from their relative lack of preparation (compared to the British) at Casablanca.[81]

From President Roosevelt's perspective, two considerations were at stake for the European theater at Trident. First, if Allied forces were to emphasize the Mediterranean and take Sicily by August, then U.S. troops would sit idle in Italy until an invasion of Germany became possible in 1944. This was unacceptable to Roosevelt, because "it would have a serious effect on relations with Russia, who was bearing such a disproportionate weight."[82] These troops would need to either move to England or take on another operation in the Mediterranean. This was a key strategic decision, because further Mediterranean operations could consume resources necessary for Roosevelt's second consideration: the timing and scope of the potential cross-Channel invasion. Now was the time, he thought, that the limited and opportunistic plan known as Sledgehammer or the large-scale operation known as Roundup (later Overlord) "should be decided upon definitely as an operation for the spring of 1944."[83] This strategic fork in the road depended upon the success of the forthcoming CBO to negate the Luftwaffe and to forestall any unanticipated or unnecessary increases in the size of Allied invasion forces.

During conference preparation, General Marshall's planners, led by Brig. Gen. Thomas Handy, gave him an earful that victory through airpower alone could not be assured, so it was necessary to push the president to help shift priorities toward invasion preparation.[84] The Army staff preferred the larger-scale plan with a definite invasion date. Marshall agreed, and he emphasized his confidence in airpower to help with invasion preparation along with the need for greater precision in planning for troop movements. "Great faith was being pinned to the results of the bomber offensive," Marshall said to the combined chiefs. "We must be ready to take advantage of these results," he added, conceding that "the exact results of the air attacks might be problematical, but the availability of tonnage to move troops could be calculated."[85]

Both Roosevelt and Marshall were aware of the delicate balance of keeping the Russians in the war by taking just enough pressure off the eastern front. However, pulling the Luftwaffe toward the western front meant that invasion timing was critical, since the Allies needed to muster an adequately sized force and more time to establish air superiority. The figures projected in Eaker's plan seemed optimistic, but there was not much reason to question them, provided Eighth Air Force did not compete with ground component priorities, and Eaker might show progress toward controlling the skies over the eventual invasion lodgment on coastal France.

As the combined chiefs got around to considering Eaker's plan, Air Chief Marshal Portal, ostensibly the senior Allied air commander for the CBO, seized the opportunity to drive this point home to the ground commanders. "One of the main features of the air plan outlined by General Eaker was not only its tremendous effect both on production and morale, but also, and perhaps most important, the elimination of the German fighter force," he argued, adding, "This would have an immense effect on any operations against Germany, whether across the Channel, in the Mediterranean, or on the Russian Front. . . . The longer the destruction of the German fighter force was delayed, the longer would the ultimate defeat of Germany be delayed."[86] In other words, air superiority was to be a joint problem and a necessary precondition for success.

In sum, Trident was a conference of compromise, and General Marshall's argument for the large-scale invasion ultimately held sway. The enormous Anglo-American cross-Channel invasion was planned for 1 May 1944, which set into motion the need for an even tighter coupling between the strategy and the resources required for the remainder of the war.[87] Despite its approval "as presented" at the conference, the Pointblank directive, which officially initiated the "Plan for the Combined Bomber Offensive from the United Kingdom," was not published until 10 June 1943.[88] With its delayed signature and an air commander (Eaker) who had seemed deaf to feedback, dumbfounded by possible escort requirements, and hopeful about blind bombing, the combined bomber offensive began.

The Devil and the Deep Blue Sea

Between 1 April and 1 July 1943, as Allied generals updated their grand strategy and future bombing priorities, Eaker's Eighth Air Force was busy shifting its weight of effort—at least on paper—to the first phase of the CBO. Eaker's bombers conducted raids on just twenty days of the three-month period—a tempo that had actually exceeded the plan's expectations, as the bombers managed thirty-four attacks on thirty different locations (many were repeats).[89] Of the raids Eaker reported had been projected for this first period, nineteen attacks featured submarine bases and yards, eight were aircraft storage and repair facilities in occupied countries outside of Germany, and one fell on the Focke-Wulf factory (collocated with a submarine yard) at Bremen.[90] Additionally, Eaker marshalled six attacks on targets outside the scope of the Pointblank directive's plan for the first phase, including three on airfields, one on the Renault vehicle production facility in Paris (collocated with an aircraft factory), a naval depot, and the synthetic rubber plant at Hüls.[91] Rounding out the top seven target priorities, German oil refineries received no attention at all because, as Eaker put it, "these targets were not to be attacked unless Ploesti were successfully attacked."[92]

The apparent reason for Eaker's hesitance to focus on oil early was, first, that the Ruhr refineries were deeper than the "relatively shallow penetration" he'd planned for the first phase of the CBO.[93] He would be ready, based upon the plan, to strike either the oil targets in the Ruhr or the more distant ball-bearing factories at Schweinfurt, but he preferred to wait on both target areas. As Eaker understood it, the more bombers he could send per raid, the proportionally lower the losses he would take because of the improved defenses of larger formations, which would also exact greater damage on the targets per raid.

Eaker also knew that once he initiated an attack on a new target system deeper into Germany, he would need to sustain the attack in order to increase pressure on that industry. If he had to follow up too often or too soon on heavily defended targets with too small of a bomber force, he might not achieve his desire to build up the larger force required for later phases. In his brief on Pointblank to the combined chiefs, Eaker suggested that in a possible attack by the Mediterranean Allied Air Forces (MAAF) on Ploesti, "We will be forced to operate against the Ruhr refineries in order to exploit the advantage achieved in Romania."[94] That Ploesti had not yet been attacked by MAAF by July was a boon as far as Eaker was concerned, because he could focus on holding to his plan and building up his forces.

As for the Schweinfurt ball-bearing factories, Eaker claimed in his June report, "Adequate force for this still lacking"; then in July, the mission was "postponed until longer nights make it possible for RAF to supplement our day attack with a heavy night attack."[95] Eaker had reiterated the COA's (and Arnold's) fanaticism about ball bearings in the Pointblank plan, noting in it that the "critical condition of the ball bearing industry in Germany is startling" and "outstandingly vulnerable to attack," but his concerns about attacking too early were even more pronounced for this target system.[96] He had briefed the combined chiefs that "it would be most unwise to attempt it until we are perfectly sure we have enough force to destroy the objective in a single operation," adding prophetically, "Any attempt to repeat such an attack will meet with very bitter opposition."[97] Eaker sought ideal circumstances before he would undertake the risk to his force of an attack on Schweinfurt; not only did he insist upon sending a formation larger than he could muster by July, but he also wanted the RAF to attack the same night in hopes of hitting this ideal target with a perfect one-and-done raid. The COA offered a victory shortcut endorsed by Arnold, but Eaker was holding off for just the right moment.

KEELHAULED AT KIEL AND HÜLS

Regarding day-to-day target selection, Eaker followed the EOU's recommendations to Hughes, as he seemed content to attack submarine yards for much of the spring, if only for training and respite from the more costly raids into Germany.[98] In June, however, Eaker would venture back into Germany; his 4th Wing was devastated when twenty-two of the sixty bombers that fought their way to the target failed to return from the submarine yards at Kiel, and another sixteen were lost the following week in a raid Eaker's assessors had otherwise declared successful against the rubber factories at Hüls.[99] Eaker's bombers let loose 243 1,000-pound and 1,202 500-pound general purpose bombs in this first large-scale daylight raid against Germany's Ruhr valley.[100]

The Kiel raid was a disaster for both operations and intelligence. The VIII Bomber Command operations officer reported that the 4th Bombardment Wing "was subjected to the heaviest enemy fighter attack any of our forces have ever been subjected to on any raid," which was probably not hyperbole. This outcome might have been anticipated, however, because Eighth Air Force had planned the mission without fighter escort.[101] Concerns over intense engagements with enemy fighters dominated the postmission reports. In fact, the 94th Bombardment Group intelligence officer became so bogged down in paperwork supporting the gunners' forty-one kill claims that he was still submitting forms for the wing commander's reconsideration "from the standpoint of morale" over a month later.[102] If the intelligence officer thought he could defend a war-weary staff sergeant's combat record with a photograph discovered later and an interview with another tail gunner, he was going to take the time to make the argument. Morale may not have been among Eaker's calculations, but it certainly counted down in the squadrons.

As for BDA, not a single bomber managed to return with a usable photograph, and most crews had not observed their own bombs due to a combination of navigation issues, overcast weather, enemy opposition, and formation disarray.[103] The lack of debrief data did not leave much for the group S-2s to piece together. For example, the best the 94th Bombardment Group intelligence officer could determine from crew interrogations was "approximately 10 bombs were observed bursting just south of the Kiel canal—observation somewhat limited due to enemy activity."[104] Since no photographic evidence could support a favorable assessment, the wing's report instead relied on alternative intelligence methods such as bomb plots "based purely on verbal reports" and an unsourced claim that "German broadcasts after the mission indicated that the damage done by our bombs was very extensive."[105] If there was evidence of positive mission impact hiding somewhere, the intelligence officers found it, and the wing commander put it in his report.

A postmission photoreconnaissance assessment for Kiel was disappointing but reasonable given the circumstances. Photo interpreters detected only slight damage compared to images taken the following week. Bombs had demolished a few small sheds and a couple of commercial buildings, but there was no damage of note to the Kiel shipyard or any submarines.[106] Sapping any remnants of positivity from the previous reports, Eighth Air Force operations analysts determined several weeks later that two consecutive raids on Kiel, including this one in June that resulted in 236 aircrew casualties, had failed to produce a single bomb within 2,000 feet of the aiming point.[107]

The "battle of Kiel," as Brig. Gen. Fred Anderson saw it, was noteworthy because it left an ACTS graduate and combat wing commander scraping for intelligence that could justify his wing's desperate effort as he clung—along with Eaker—to the positive.[108] After suggesting his crews had probably shot down more than double the figure they had actually claimed and citing the high end of intelligence estimates of enemy fighters encountered, Anderson argued: "Almost all bombs dropped were dropped on the target area with what is believed to be considerable damage to enemy installations . . . the reckless and futile attacks by German fighters indicates a desperate but vain attempt to stop the Daylight Bombing of their war installations. This suicidal defense by the German fighter force will quickly attrite the one opposing factor of any consequence to our heavy bombardment force."[109]

By the time reality set in and more detailed analysis was available, missions such as this one could be weeks or even months in the past, well after commanders had already internalized their observations from immediate reports and moved on. In this case, not even two weeks later, Fred Anderson was promoted to major general and succeeded his boss, General Longfellow, at VIII Bomber Command.[110] Kiel was a disastrous raid that, if analyzed patiently along with accurate and timely postraid intelligence, might have shocked the generals out of their mindset of bomber supremacy or at least opened discussions to loosen their control of escort fighters. Instead, it was just another airborne duel for Eighth Air Force and the Luftwaffe. But Eaker appreciated and rewarded Anderson's optimism.

Follow-up attacks—the penalty for failed raids—were not much better. The 305th Bomb Group S-2 portrayed the positive side despite his aircrew's challenges in another Kiel raid in July: "Bombing results were extremely difficult to observe due to heavy smoke screen, smoke from previous bombings, and dense haze. The main concentration of our bombs landed to the right of the covered basin. . . . Scattered hits were seen on slips around the covered basin. Sighting was extremely difficult and lead bombardiers did a very good job of finding the target."[111] The group S-2's use of the words "our bombs" certainly conveyed unit-level teamwork in Curtis LeMay's former outfit. Unfortunately, there was a big difference between finding the target and actually damaging it. This S-2 may have overstepped the guidance in the First Bombardment Wing's S-2 training manual that "there is much combat intelligence which S-2s are expected to collect, assemble, and report on. But it is never their function to evaluate such items as tactics."[112] While S-2s might have contributed valuable insights into the mission's tactical employment, in this case, another form of intelligence contradicted his impression of the bombardier's Norden bombsight work. ULTRA intercepts indicated "negligible damage" as far as the German naval situation was concerned, and the Kiel U-boat yard persisted as an elusive target.[113]

SMOKESCREENS AND BURNING RUBBER

The mission to Hüls was an altogether different episode. A combination of 1st and 4th Wing bombers would pound the Buna rubber plant at Hüls in two waves, aided by a smaller diversionary force to lure enemy fighters over the North Sea.[114] While the rubber industry ostensibly fell below oil and ball bearings in priority, the plant's location west of the Rhine offered a target of reasonable penetration into Germany, dependent upon fighter escort support on the ingress and egress routes.

A new target area and a new type of target added impetus to preraid intelligence reports. The target intelligence portion of the mission briefing kicked off with a motivational statement to the crews: "Your target today is vitally essential to the successful prosecution of the war by the enemy. In order to keep its mobile units on the move it must have rubber. . . . This plant has never been bombed before, there are no craters, and it is responsible for 17½ percent of the German annual output of chemical products."[115] Crews undoubtedly felt some trepidation, but the intelligence marketing of the mission's value to the war effort would give them confidence in their day's purpose. In addition to forecasts of spotty cloud decks, reports also suggested that the plant's important facilities were meticulously camouflaged, so sighting the target for accurate visual bombing could pose difficulties.[116]

During the mission, typical operational challenges ensued. Ineffective communications by VIII Bomber Command ended up delaying the diversionary force by an hour, rendering it irrelevant. Further, an unusual number of aborted aircraft, including those of both the leader and deputy leader of the 94th Bomb Group, led to confusion since the briefing had not covered that contingency. General Armstrong reported that the bombing otherwise went as briefed.[117] However, postmission damage reports for the Hüls raid would give a hazier impression.

After the lead group botched its aiming, the successive seven bomb groups serviced the target in a compressed five-minute period. Crews of the trailing groups within each wing tended to express confidence that some group—if not their own—had hit the target, as the plant became increasingly obscured by smoke. For example, the 305th Bomb Group S-2, whose group flew in the middle of the pack, reported that "bombing results were particularly good. Large fires were seen in the area."[118] However, the S-2 for the 306th Bomb Group, which had tagged along just behind the 305th, emphasized his own group's questionable success by accentuating that of the previous groups: "From all reports it would appear that the bombing of this group was only fair with hits in the extreme north end of the target area. Preceding group scored direct hits in the center of target."[119]

The trend only continued from there. The S-2 for the group bringing up the rear did not specify his group's results at all, as if it no longer mattered: "Large fire and heavy smoke observed over target. Fighter support spelled out letters 'U.S.' with vapor trails. Morale of our crews high after raid."[120] This tendency was not missed by the scrupulous and forthright Col. Curtis LeMay, then commanding the 4th Bombardment Wing. Of his crews' performance, whose spirited efforts comprised the final three groups across the target, LeMay reported the following up the chain:

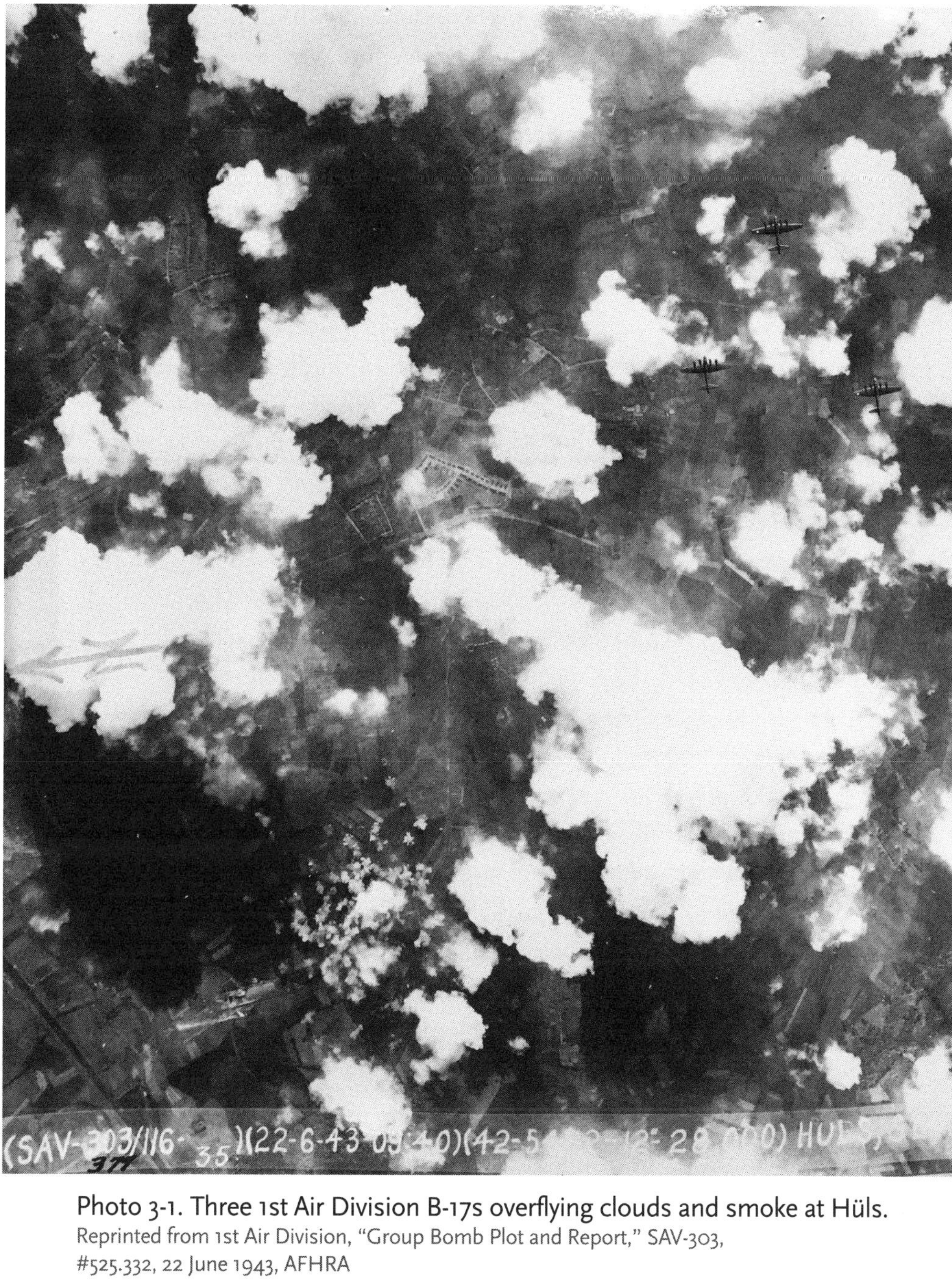

Photo 3-1. Three 1st Air Division B-17s overflying clouds and smoke at Hüls.
Reprinted from 1st Air Division, "Group Bomb Plot and Report," SAV-303, #525.332, 22 June 1943, AFHRA

> All bombardiers on this mission were convinced they had made a good run on the target. This is doubtful, however, in view of the cloud conditions shown in the photographs and of the elaborate camouflaging known to exist in the target area. The cloud conditions were further aggravated by the smoke developing from the previous Wing's hits, which shows again that if one Wing or Group has been successful in bombing the target, the groups immediately following may be seriously handicapped.[121]

For LeMay, every bomb mattered, and so did the intelligence. He expected perfection of every crew and every intelligence officer, showing little patience for ignorant performance or blustery reports. He made a habit of reviewing the pre- and postmission intelligence carefully.

As it turned out, the 305th Bomb Group's photo interpretation officer's report and bombardier's plot showed 104 of the group's 180 500-pound bombs as hitting the target, although fewer than 20 appeared within 1,000 feet of the aiming point, 15 fell in a field short of the target, and 10 could not be located at all.[122] The entire pattern appeared offset about 1,000 feet to the left of the planned track, but the far-right edge of the bomb pattern had hit dead on the aiming point (see photo 3-3). This was all that mattered to the group's lead bombardier, who claimed that "observers reported bombs hitting directly on the aiming point, the pattern being exceptionally good. This was later confirmed by photographs."[123] Crews participating in each raid were motivated not to return to that target, so they were inclined to share others' credit or exaggerate their feats if it helped to prove overall mission success. Their group intelligence officer's reports reflected sympathetic optimism. Insofar as crews cared about their accuracy, it only took a few good bombs to validate a mission and boost morale, so the rest of the bombs did not matter. For group-level intelligence officers, if bomb bursts could be located in the target area and appeared to hit at least something of perceived value (typically based on sketchy preraid target intelligence), then there was no reason to question the group's accuracy or the bombardier's claims.

Interpretation reports by Medmenham's CIU streamed in two days later bearing a similarly optimistic sense. The CIU's seasoned experts verified the 305th Bombardment Group's claims as they added confidence with their review of the entire mission. Preliminary photo interpretation from the bombers' on-board

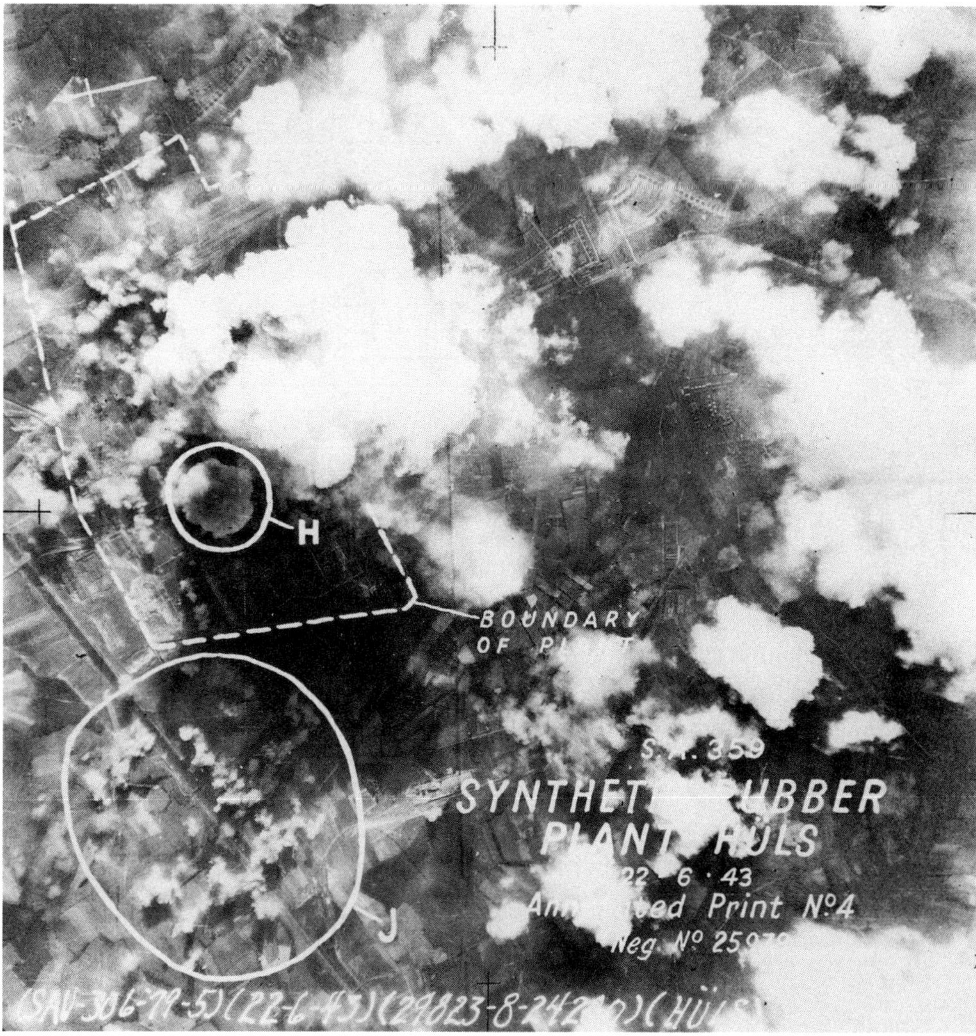

Photo 3-2. BDA photograph of raid on Hüls. Smoke and steam from the plant frustrated the BDA process. Reprinted from 1st Air Division, "Group Bomb Plot and Report," SAV-303, #525.332, 22 June 1943, AFHRA

cameras showed a significant concentration of bombs in the target area from both waves of bombers, including hits on "the main power plant, chemical plants, acetylene plants, and other vital installations."[124] A Spitfire from RAF 542 Squadron tore overhead a month later, capturing outstanding reconnaissance photos at high noon on a clear day. The CIU interpreted the high-quality photos and remarked, "A high proportion of the bombs dropped fell within the target,"

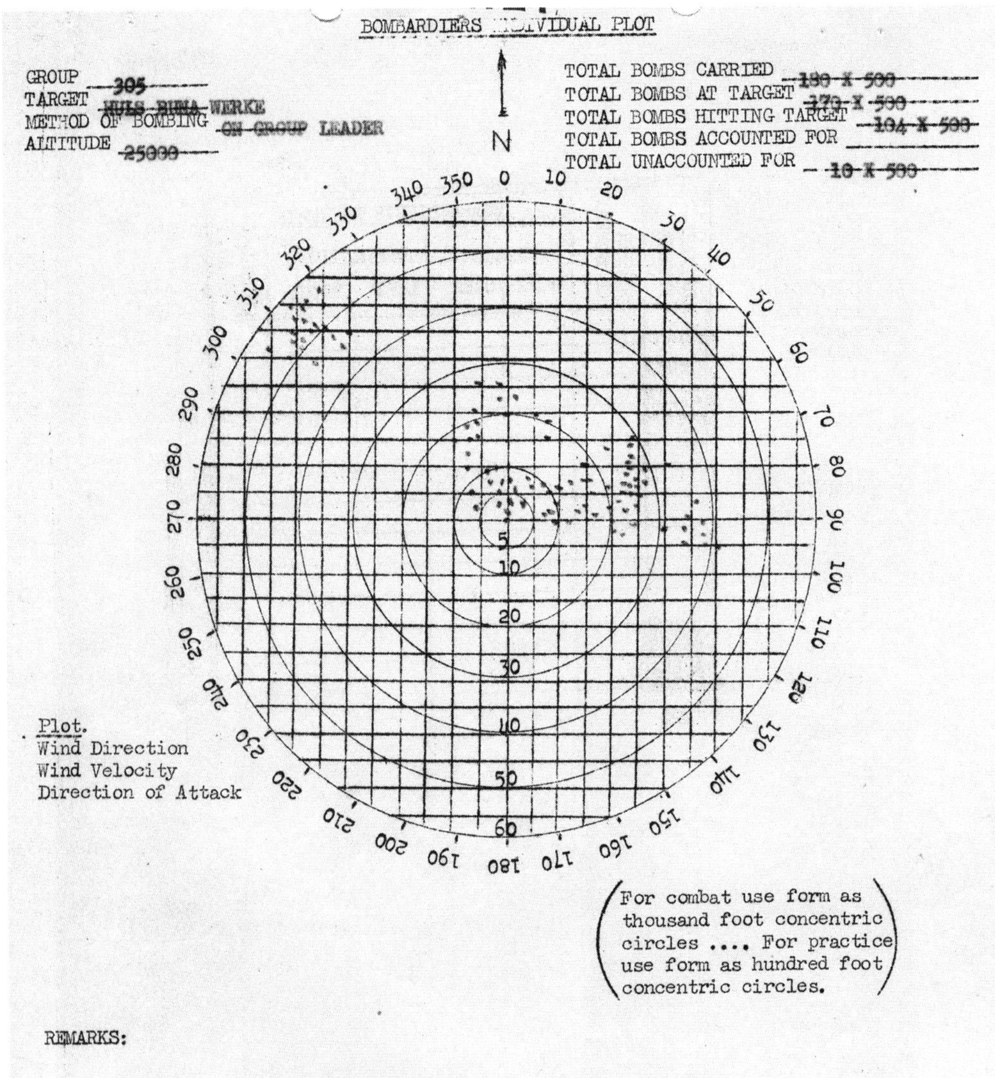

Photo 3-3. 305th Bomb Group Bombardier's individual plot. Reprinted from Headquarters 305th Bombardment Group, enclosure "J," Group Bombing Plot and Report, in Narrative Report of Operations, Field Order No. 153-A, AFHRA

adding to show consequence, "Considerable damage is seen throughout the plant."[125] The presence of such value judgments in the interpretation reports is intriguing: High compared to what? Considerable relative to what? What expectations did the photo interpreters have in mind, and with whom were they coordinated?

If judged on accuracy standards alone, the Hüls raid might have been considered a failure. Only 50 bombs—less than 4 percent of the total expended—fell within 1,000 feet of the aiming point, and less than 12 percent fell within 2,000 feet.[126] By these measures, the raid had failed to meet expectations by an order of magnitude short of those previously set by Brigadier General Sorensen's probabilities committee report. However, accuracy issues were inconsequential for this target. Misses over 2,000 feet still had a fair chance of striking essential elements of a target as large as a 541-acre rubber plant.[127] The one-thousand-foot standard developed by the ORS mathematicians simply did not account for the size and shape of the target.[128] As it turned out, the bombs dotted a broad swath over "an area 4.2 miles long and 2.8 miles wide, including a strip about 80 yards wide diagonally through the plant."[129] In this case, quantity compensated for accuracy, and the results appeared to be devastating.

The Germans accounted for nearly every bomb dropped on the previously undisturbed manufacturing community of Hüls. Although they had found that "386 bombs landed within the plant confines," approximately 10 percent of them had failed to explode, adding insult to the task of safely clearing debris.[130] The bombs inflicted human injuries as well. According to plant records, 186 workers perished and another 1,000 were wounded, primarily due to delays in air raid sirens, inadequate shelter space, and the fact that 2 bombs unpredictably managed to hit the air raid shelters.[131] The Germans were determined not to let this happen again.

The plant did not remain damaged for long. Unknown to the target analysts and photo interpreters, the reich considered the Hüls plant vital to its war economy and prioritized its repair; the plant resumed partial operation after about forty days, and surveyors later noted that "full production of rubber was reached in six months."[132] The Germans also responded by limiting "all traffic behind the front (military and civilian) to a maximum speed of 17 miles per hour in order to save tires."[133] If intelligence analysts were aware that the speed restriction was a useful indicator that the reich was desperate to control its rubber expenditure, the insight did not appear to inform decisionmaking for follow-on attacks. But Berlin's willingness to take such drastic measures also showed it had administrative tools available to ration stocks and limit the impact of the bombs.

Intelligence reports from Arnold's A-2 staff varied their tune as the summer of 1943 progressed. Captain James Lowe (also a COA participant) submitted an update on the rubber industry ten days after the Hüls raid. Interestingly, he was undeterred by not yet possessing even preliminary photo intelligence from this first major attack on the industry. Adding no further explanation, he assumed "total destruction" and touted "the loss of this plant for 12 months, which is the time estimated to get it back into production, means that Germany will be deprived of 25,000 to 50,000 tons of synthetic rubber in 1943–1944."[134] This was another overly optimistic assertion, especially given the Eighth's track record until that point. The air staff, thousands of miles from the nose-searing stench of burning rubber at Hüls, had not considered how the Germans might react.

While Lowe overestimated the bombers' capability to destroy the plant, he compounded the error by underestimating the Germans' recuperative ability. He concluded the Germans would not meet their rubber production requirements by 25 percent into 1944—even without further attack on the Hüls plant as available rubber stocks depleted.[135] In the case of Lowe's report, his series of flawed assumptions seemed to result in the right conclusion from the standpoint of air campaign strategy, which was not to bother with further attacks on the rubber industry. Lowe added a takeaway to the report, based more on instinct than any evidence he provided, that rubber shortages would not lead to any reduction in German fighting strength, merely "a marked deterioration in both the quantity and quality of rubber tires and other rubberized equipment."[136] How could Eaker justify the cost to his own forces if the result might be merely a nuisance to the enemy? As it were, Lowe did not have enough information to assess that the Hüls plant recovered at break-neck speed, as Germany's excess rubber stocks were already down to only about a month's supply.[137] Despite Lowe's argument, if the rubber industry was an important target and not just a costly sideshow to attacks on the aircraft industry, then further attacks were necessary and urgent—not only on other rubber plants but on the Hüls plant as well.

Arnold's A-2, Brigadier General Sorensen, attempted to make this point in September as he fought to reenergize rubber industry attacks. At the time, Sorensen was also serving as the senior military member in COA meetings regarding Japanese industries, including rubber, which was undoubtedly on his mind.[138] Sorensen argued that "further attacks on other rubber plants may be expected to yield dividends in the form of actual curtailment of essential uses, but only if made before the effects of the Hüls raid have worn off."[139] He, along with Lowe, had been part of the committee that pushed the rubber industry as a priority target since 1942. Sorensen's argument proved too late to influence Eaker. The 22 June raid by Eighth Air Force was the last planned attack on Hüls for eighteen months, and the rubber industry—vulnerable as it may have been—was never seriously threatened for the remainder of the war.[140]

Despite the raid's positive results and some inconsistent encouragement to exploit its success, Eighth Air Force leadership did not emphasize the rubber industry for good reason. Indeed, additional attacks may have kept the plant out of operation or forced the Germans to commit further resources to the rubber industry that were more useful elsewhere. But as Lowe aptly noted, such attacks were unlikely to have any appreciable impact on the German armed forces. Attacks on rubber may have increased in utility later in the war as the Eighth's bombing capacity increased. However, in the fall of 1943, as the combined chiefs shuddered over the thought of conducting a cross-Channel invasion without a guarantee of air superiority, other targets had to come first.

Gunships and Negative Aims

If Eaker was going to sustain his planned six missions per month, he knew he needed to decrease the cost of each raid (as well as maintaining hopes for increased reinforcements from Arnold).[141] Long-range fighters were not yet available, and he still believed in the defensive primacy of the bomber, so he had anxiously awaited testing in the European theater for the YB-40, a B-17 modified exclusively as a gunship to protect bomber formations. Eaker had dispatched eleven YB-40s along with his 1st Division on their raid on Hüls. The gunship bombers contributed to claims of twenty-six kills and another eighteen probable kills by bombers against German fighters, and they all reportedly overflew the target area, although not necessarily in tight formation.[142] Eaker expected better. On 29 June, he wrote to Maj. Gen. Barney Giles, who'd taken over as Arnold's chief of air staff, to express his disappointment. "I had great hopes for that airplane," Eaker groaned, "and I was most loath to render a derogatory report."[143] The plane was too heavy and dirty with the additional drag of machine gun modifications to hang in formation with the bombers.

Making matters worse, Eaker discovered that his bomber crews did not want to fly the YB-40 because the bombardier position had been removed and the bomb bay filled with bullets. Bomber crews derived their identity from placing steel on target, not solely in spraying their .50-calibers at enemy fighters, so the conversion disrupted their morale. Group intelligence officers seemed to adopt their aircrews' sarcasm. An S-2 included in a formal mission report after a raid on the nitrate works at Heroya, Norway, the fact that a YB-40 had failed to bomb the target "as it carries no bombs."[144] The YB-40 might have gleamed with brilliance on an Air Corps Tactical School drawing board, but it struggled in the operational and organizational reality of the air campaign.[145]

Eaker's force was meager, so the fact that the preponderance of his effort was still oriented toward targeting submarine installations warranted investigation. Were these attacks successful? If so, what did they accomplish, and at what cost? Assessments emanating from Eaker's headquarters were hopeful. Summarizing the attacks on submarine bases, his official report stated, "Much physical damage has been done to all of these bases and it is increasingly difficult for the enemy to turn around their submarines on scheduled time," adding without further evidence that "there is no doubt whatsoever that they have contributed materially to the marked diminution of the U-boat effort and the resultant reduction in our shipping losses."[146] The report may have seemed like hyperbole in Washington, because any direct linkage between visible facility damage and lost U-boat production had yet to be proven (and never was).[147] If Eaker truly desired to shift his focus from the U-boats, the spin on these reports did not show it.

Raid after raid, the Luftwaffe took its toll. Eaker started April on pace to build his projected CBO bomber force, but he closed out June with just 806 of an expected 944 bombers for the second phase.[148] This shortage consumed Eaker's attention. In a sense, he was caught between the devil of the Luftwaffe and the deep blue sea of U-boats. He believed that he needed to build up a larger force before he could get at Germany's vital industrial centers, much less sustain raids that would help to attrit the Luftwaffe and disrupt the German aircraft industry. However, the unproductive attacks on U-boat targets continued to bleed down his bombers and crews faster than he could build them up. Furthermore, Eaker's personal desire to sense his air campaign's success crossed with pressure from above to engage in these submarine industry attacks, which were still second only to aircraft in the Allies' targeting priority. The resulting conflict left him clinging to the positive bits of feedback he received from his intelligence sources.

By June 1943, however, the EOU economists noted that "it was clear that the attacks on production and bases were making no significant contribution to anti-submarine warfare," so they sought "to remove them [submarine targets] from top priority and to clear the way for attack on the main target systems."[149] Meanwhile, the economists had gained confidence and information resources, so they added a "systematic comparison of the attractiveness of various target systems,"[150] which they would use to push alternative target choices.

At about the same time, they drafted a *Handbook of Target Information* and socialized it with analysts back in Washington.[151] The idea was to consider both "the importance to the enemy of each potential target" as well as "our ability effectively to destroy it."[152] The upshot was that targets too vast or too difficult to attack would be purged from the economists' analytic grind, even if a target's connection to the German war effort could be immediate and significant (such as the electric power grid). The downside was that assumptions about the size, accuracy, and destructive capability of the available bomber force would have to be captured thoughtfully and revisited continuously.

The handbook also included a new target selection model that could be summarized as "high wastage plus high production equals high value." They argued: "Equipment like airplanes which are wasted rapidly and in which monthly production is large in relation to strength in combat units, is a more desirable objective of attack than items like range-finders, in which annual production forms only a small increment to total stocks in use."[153] For example, the Luftwaffe's high demand for a fresh supply of airplanes increased that industry's sensitivity to supply interruptions. This was not true of submarines. Since relatively few submarines were in production at any time and submarine wastage rates were much lower than those of aircraft, submarine bases were less lucrative objectives in terms of near-term benefit for the effort expended. Even if the attacks on submarine yards and bases had been more successful, "the effects will be long delayed."[154] The economists' rationale had side-stepped the ongoing debates over submarine yard vulnerabilities and equipped them to push harder for attacks on German aircraft assembly plants.[155]

Eaker's thinking the following month seemed to reflect the economists' viewpoint. He had become particularly interested in attacking aircraft factories while he was concerned about his losses. Eaker expressed to Arnold that he was increasingly concerned about German innovation in air-to-air attacks that could "increase greatly the cost of our bombing," and he sought to intensify attacks on fighter factories before "the enemy has discovered a way of making our bombing uneconomical."[156] Hughes may have been the conduit, but the EOU's economists appeared to have had Eaker's ear as they worked out the cost-benefit analysis of his raids.[157]

Unfortunately, the economists had assumed away any possibility that Germany might disperse its aircraft production industry—until Charles Kindleberger, pushing his argument like a lawyer rather than an economist, presented in his own words "evidence for the jury, together with a suggested verdict," that the reich had surreptitiously moved Focke-Wulf 190 production from Bremen by June.[158] To make his case, he assembled his evidence into fifteen separate lines of reasoning and backed them with forty-five significant intelligence reports and twenty-nine ground intelligence reports, all involving the same factory over a span of thirty-one months.[159] While the quest for research perfection was commendable for its accuracy, an earlier call based on intuition might have conserved considerable resources—at least the twenty-six AAF bombers and the crewmembers lost when they attacked the Focke-Wulf factory at Bremen two months earlier.[160]

The economists were likewise not content to commit foremost to the air superiority fight. Without specifically referencing Clausewitz, Rostow admitted, "Since the attack on aircraft was essentially a defensive action, designed to achieve a condition favorable to later air and ground exploitation, it was conceived proper to devote some part of our effort to more positive attack affecting other finished armaments."[161] The economists could analyze the kill ratios and cost-benefit of bombers lost to targets struck, but they did not understand air superiority as either a necessary precondition or a positive aim for the air campaign—not just a potential ground campaign, a target that drives enemy behavior and imposes further costs as it allows further offensive action. As a result, the EOU set Eaker's Eighth up to smash his bombers against the Luftwaffe in attacks against ball-bearing, aircraft assembly, and vehicle plants, not because these were particularly effective at dislocating the German economy or even winning air superiority (due to plant dispersion), but because a mathematical formula seemed to indicate such attacks might have short-term results on German matériel production (that is, if the enemy behaved as expected). In any case, the economists' underlying logic was straying from that of ACTS doctrine, but it was not yet influential enough to prevent U-boat attacks altogether.

A Firestorm of Postmission Assessments

The 25–26 July attack on Hamburg's shipyards served as another case in point of these deceptively futile U-boat attacks. Blohm and Voss was the largest submarine shipyard in Germany (comparable in size to that of Newport News, Virginia) and reportedly produced almost 18 percent of German U-boats.[162] The RAF had launched six small, ineffectual attacks on the dockyards and the city area of Hamburg during 1940–41, but this was to be the first large-scale, coordinated day-night *Katastrophe* raid by the RAF and AAF on the city.[163] Harris' Bomber Command ignited "the Hamburg firestorm" with four attacks on the city between 24 July and 2 August, though the concentrated portion on Blohm and Voss shipyards fell on the night of 24–25 July by the RAF and the day after by the AAF.[164] The first night, Harris' force of 739 bombers dropped more than 349,000 incendiary bombs (a mix of 4- and 30-pounders) on the city, then Eighth Air Force complemented the onslaught with attacks on the port and industrial areas over the next two days.[165] On 25 July 68 U.S. bombers dropped 144 tons of bombs on Blohm and Voss, and 54 bombers dropped another 97 tons (using almost entirely 500-pound bombs) on neighboring Howaldswerke shipyards the next day.[166]

Despite the effort against Blohm and Voss' expansive 145 acres with its 112 structures, raid reports could claim visible damage to only 10 buildings, 2 dry docks, and a few vessels.[167] A photo intelligence officer assigned to the 1st Bombardment Wing acknowledged only four buildings struck, though he noted each of them as "direct hits."[168] Despite the anemic photographic evidence, Arnold's intelligence staff later concluded the combined attacks, along with the other attacks by the RAF against the city itself, had cut production during the period from July to November by about half (only fifteen of twenty-nine possible U-boats were produced by the yard).[169]

The British Ministry of Economic Warfare released a report on 12 August 1943 that attributed success at Hamburg to the RAF's style of attack. The report conceded that "the amount of active shipping in the port at the time of the first raid is not known," but that "complete evacuation of active shipping" was surely of "the most important" results.[170] Turning the focus of success toward the RAF, the MEW economists argued, "Although the direct damage sustained by the shipping in port and by port handling facilities is severe, the primary cause of the evacuation probably lies in the complete disorganization of the life of the city, the disruption of local and through communications, the destruction of public utilities, dwelling houses and food stocks necessary for the maintenance of the port community."[171] From the point of view of the MEW economists, the key implication of this successful onslaught on Hamburg had nothing to do with U-boats but would place even "further strain" on the other German ports of Emden and Bremen.[172] The MEW sought to reinforce blockade-style victory through economic dislocation, so choking off German sea lines was a worthwhile endeavor.

Arnold's Committee of Operations Analysts was repulsed at wasting effort against such unprofitable targets and had pushed the submarine yards down their list to seventh priority. The committee released a report concluding that even if all Axis U-boat production could be reduced 80 percent by 1 October 1943, there would still be 443 of a possible 455 U-boats operating in April 1944.[173] This was because postproduction U-boats took seven months for "testing and training" after they left the construction yards, and the pipeline at that time was healthy.[174] Thus, attacks on construction yards, even if successful, could not impact near-term numbers of operating U-boats. In short, challenges presented by assessors were threefold: postraid assessments of submarine shipyards and bases often revealed deceptively enticing damage to irrelevant structures; the effects of bombing upon U-boat production and their associated towns were speculative or due to other factors; and the time frame necessary even for best-case results to mature had rendered the entire endeavor moot.[175]

In summary, the various organizations had offered assessments limited to their own point of view, none of which were particularly focused on air superiority first. For Eighth Air Force, the cost of training crews, generating aircraft, and fighting to reach a target only to drop mostly ineffective bombs was too high to justify sustaining the offensive, even given some of the overly optimistic assessments. By VIII Bomber Command's report of the 25 July raid, of 182 aircraft of the 1st Air Division that took off intended for the Hamburg area, only 68 bombers managed to strike their primary target (including the Blohm and Voss shipyard), 32 bombers attacked a marshalling yard as a target of opportunity instead, and 82 bombers failed to bomb anything at all.[176] The Luftwaffe and German flak claimed fifteen.[177]

If Eaker's dilemma between the Luftwaffe and U-boat attacks, along with an increasing proportion of losses with deeper attacks into Germany, had not yet maximized his frustration, another demand from Washington seemed likely to. Grinding wheels were decidedly not among the targets necessary to achieve air superiority. Nevertheless, Arnold continued to meddle with target selection from Washington, due in part to his impetuous personality and the relentless influence of his advisory council, but also to the COA's swelling stature as his analytical brain trust. Newly emboldened after the combined chiefs had signed the final CBO plan, COA analysts weighed in because Hughes (and the EOU) had eliminated attacks on precision grinding-wheel plants from Eaker's plan. As a target system, the grinding-wheel plants had been the COA analysts' fourth priority.[178] To COA members, whose organization's survival was by then all but assured for the remainder of the war, securing support for their research was a matter of pride.[179] An opportunity to force Eaker's hand to attack grinding-wheel plants would also reinforce the agenda they shared with Arnold to seek out the catastrophic raids; if successful, quick victory could be attributed to the COA's collective genius along with Arnold's omniscient view from Washington—or so they thought.[180] Unfortunately, as with ball bearings, the analysts' push to attack grinding wheels would perpetuate the tendency in Washington to overestimate the bomber's ability to attack such targets and to underestimate the Germans' ability to cope.

The committee's lawyers-turned-intelligencers cornered Isaiah Frank, the single Washington-based OSS abrasives industry expert who had weighed in with evidence against recommending attacks on grinding wheels in the first place. Months prior, Frank had provided a statement based on "conversations with technical men. . . . It appears that grinding wheel plants do not constitute profitable targets, because, with the exception of the hydraulic presses, the major apparatus can be constructed in about a month."[181] This view had undercut the committee's argument to bomb this industry, because it meant Germany could bounce back too quickly. The committee offered him a chance to change his testimony.

As one of the COA's lawyers tells the story, Frank admitted—under the pressure of interrogation—that he "had never personally contacted the individuals referred to in [his] memorandum," and that his statement was based on single phone call involving "narrow hypothetical questions" with one expert.[182] Embarrassed, he recanted his opposition to the target. The subtle inaccuracy in Frank's internal office memorandum may have been inconsequential to the

COA's grinding-wheel report itself, but Frank's earlier slip-up provided the committee's lawyers with probable cause to reattack Eaker with a modified report.

The COA team then reinterviewed other abrasives industry experts, who unsurprisingly verified the importance of their own industry as "a target of the highest economic priority"; then the committee added for clarity: "Mr. Frank's question referred to one kiln. If you knock out the dozen or fifteen kilns at a plant like Precision Grinding Wheel Company or the Abrasive Company, it would take three to four months to get them back under the best conditions."[183] When it came to expert witnesses, how questions were asked and to whom they were asked could result in completely different conclusions. In this case, the committee found the expert they sought, and he provided the opinion they expected.

Ignoring written protests from the EOU's Kindleberger, who contended differences over both vulnerability and recoverability of grinding wheels as targets, COA analysts ultimately pitched a supplemental report directly to Arnold, which even the analysts admitted "did not materially differ from that of the original."[184] General Arnold gladly sent Colonel Perera and Colonel Leach forward to meet with Eaker on 1 July, bearing a memorandum he had personally signed. Arnold directed Eaker to acknowledge the committee's "further study . . . that there should be a reconsideration of grinding wheel plants as a target."[185] This was Arnold's subtle way of increasing the weight of his thumb on Eaker's plans.

Eaker fumed. Just two weeks earlier, Arnold had sent a scathing missive accusing Eaker of mismanaging his force in three areas, specifically that he was "leaning over backwards trying to get 100 percent perfect planes when 90 percent would do the trick," that he spent time and manpower modifying aircraft with changes that Arnold did not feel were "absolutely necessary," and that he arbitrarily held partial crews together such that "when a plane is shot up the whole crew is knocked out."[186] Eaker fired back that German fighter tactics "could increase greatly the cost of our bombing," as he pled with Arnold to stop diverting his bombers from attacking German fighter production.[187] In short, Arnold blamed Eaker for shortfalls in operational readiness as Eaker's frustrations mounted with the Germans as well as with Arnold.

When Arnold's analysts, Perera and Leach, showed up in Eaker's office and slapped their familiar grinding-wheel intelligence onto his desk, Eaker snapped. To Eaker, these gentlemen represented and facilitated Arnold's impulsive micromanagement. First, he held them accountable for diverting his desperately needed bomb groups to support the upcoming Ploesti mission, although the committee members conceded only to helping plan the targets. They were stunned by Eaker's outburst: "Damn it Perera, you are stealing my air force. I don't like it!"[188] The COA's modus operandi had been to press its agenda up to the point of receiving pushback but never to cross the line with commanders. In a draft letter to their champion back on the air staff, Brigadier General Gates, they reacted defensively: "He seemed to feel that we were responsible for that project!!!!"[189] Eaker was not particularly interested in listening to them or in targeting grinding wheels, for that matter. The general retorted that any additional objectives would require resources he did not have.

The fact is, these types of machines were difficult to destroy, Eighth Air Force lacked quality intelligence products about the industry, and substitutions were possible.[190] More importantly, however, it was too late to push what seemed like another distraction from the more pressing imperative to engage the Luftwaffe, and its planes were killing Eaker's crews by the dozen. Meanwhile, Perera and Leach had destroyed any previous credibility they had established with Eaker with their demanding approach. They were behaving more like the lawyers they were than targeting experts.

Eaker resolved the argument by suggesting the RAF might attack the plants with their Mosquito bombers instead. Then he left the COA emissaries, in their own words, "standing by awaiting word to appear and present our case" to the British.[191] While the various analytical organizations each marketed their own brand of information toward nominating targets, assessing bombing performance, and solving Eaker's (or Arnold's) problems, none had yet offered to look at the progress of his air campaign as a whole. Eaker had not asked for it.

FOUR

"THE APPEARANCE OF THE BOTTOM OF THE BARREL"

The appearance of the bottom of the barrel under present conception of requirements of military and civil man-power is beginning to force serious consideration on the strength of the War and Navy Departments and directly on the strength of the Army Air Forces. . . . Here in Washington, we have many agencies receiving data on the results of your operations but there is no single office which can answer the general question, "What is the overall effectiveness of the combined bomber offensive?"

—BRIG. GEN. L. S. KUTER, 6 JULY 1943[1]

Any Air Force Commander operating against the enemy is primarily concerned with the effect his bombing has on the target he sends a force to destroy. If they destroy that target he will never willingly report the bombing as other than superior.

—MAJ. GEN. IRA C. EAKER, 15 SEPTEMBER 1943[2]

As Eaker concluded his first phase of the CBO in June (as he reported, not based on the combined chiefs of staff's signatures on the Pointblank directive), the war department finally was confronted by the reality of severe manpower concerns. What seemed like the separate challenges of raising, equipping, and transporting forces were, in fact, all tied to the limits of available American manpower. The original victory plan, as directed by

President Roosevelt in 1941, had called for an Army of 8.8 million troops, assembled into a bewildering 213 divisions; of these, 61 were to be armored and another 61 of mechanized infantry.[3] Equipping a force of that magnitude was a colossal undertaking. Assumptions underlying these original requirements were the possible collapse of the Soviet counteroffensive, a 273-group Air Force potentially still locked in an ongoing battle for air superiority, a massive and continued Lend-Lease program for U.S. allies, and the additional manpower necessary "to service its lines of communications extending around the world."[4] As overstretch became apparent with waxing congressional interest, Marshall chartered a series of committees to reevaluate the scale of the military program. The American "arsenal of democracy" was proving finite.[5]

Colonel William W. Bessell had led a committee in April to report a "Survey of Current Military Program," which adjusted troop requirements down to match the presidentially approved level set in 1942 for 8.2 million; of equal importance, it reduced the number of divisions to 155.[6] But this was not enough. Another committee, chaired by Col. Ray Maddocks of the Army's operations planning division (OPD), followed up in June with another cut. This time, the Joint Strategic Survey Committee, a team of three including Major General Fairchild as the air member, engaged with OPD for a more assertive view of airpower's role: not only would the CBO achieve air superiority by 1944, but it would also relieve pressure on the Soviet Union in the meantime.[7] This shift in assumptions, accepted by Marshall, conceded that "the Joint Planners had gone astray in trying to match Allied forces, division for division, with the enemy."[8] The Allied airpower advantage, if proven, would reduce the need for parity in ground forces. The Maddocks committee returned to Marshall in June with three recommendations: "First, it proposed the reduction of the strength of the Army authorized for 1943 from 8,248,000 to 7,657,000. Second, it called for modification of the current troop basis to provide a balanced force built around eighty-eight divisions, the number already activated. . . . Third, it recommended that the ultimate size of the Army and of the major units in it (air and ground) should be decided at the end of the summer."[9]

Adjustment of the military program and its underlying assumptions placed new pressure on the CBO as well as the air staff. Eaker had to not only accomplish the Pointblank directive's intermediate objective of rendering the Luftwaffe impotent, but also prove his progress before the end of the summer or risk losing the resources to finish the job. The size of Eaker's bomber force was already contentious, even within the air arm. Eaker's statistical control office reported that Eighth Air Force closed out 30 June with only 806 heavy bombers, just 85 percent of the plan's required 944.[10] Just three months into Pointblank, Eighth Air Force was already playing catch-up, especially if there was to be any chance of achieving Eaker's desired 1,192 bombers by the end of September.[11] Of course, responsibility for pushing bombers into theater was ostensibly Arnold's problem.

The task to report on the CBO's progress, dated 1 July 1943, fell initially to the AAF in the form of a memorandum to General Arnold from Marshall's staff, including the following:

> Determination of the ultimate size of the Army and the major units required (divisions and Air Force groups) . . . will depend, to a large extent, on the outcome of the Russo-German operations this summer and the effectiveness of the Combined Bomber Offensive, the trends of which should be sufficiently apparent by early September to warrant a decision [including by the Commanding General, AAF] . . . An analysis of the overall effect of the Combined Bomber Offensive on Germany's war potential, and an estimate of its future capabilities.[12]

The order stirred frenzy on the air staff as tasks rained like poorly aimed incendiaries on Arnold's unsuspecting subordinates. The memo had exposed with startling clarity that no one, much less any standing committee or air staff office, had undertaken a broad air campaign assessment. Despite Arnold's plea months earlier for recurring data from Eaker, processes inside the staff remained fragmented and myopic as information from Europe seemed to fly into various offices and die where it landed. An organized review of Eaker's reports might have been helpful, but these were deep questions, requiring analysis that could connect the dots from bombs on target to future capabilities of German fielded forces. Eaker had enough challenges with bombing accuracy and aircraft losses.

Brigadier General Kuter (Arnold's assistant chief of staff for plans and combat operations) assumed the lead role on a special committee established by the air boss. Kuter, who had instructed at ACTS as a lieutenant when Eaker attended the course as a major, engaged directly with Eaker a few days later. In an attempt to pull the right information from England and to push the analytical effort onto Arnold's COA, especially since Col. Guido Perera happened to be in London at the time, Kuter wrote:

> On first glance, it appears to us that the necessary data is available in England in probably greater detail and surely at earlier dates, than it could be available in Washington. We believe that Colonel Perera and Lt Col Barton Leach from this Headquarters who are now with you are well qualified, and with your introduction may have the best contacts to obtain an answer to the question our committee has to solve.
>
> Our broad problem is this: What change, if any, should be made in the troop basis for the United States Army because of the success or failure of the combined bomber offensive against Germany? It is realized that there are a great number of variables in this problem. It is immediately apparent that solutions might vary all the way from giving an open and first priority call on man-power to all essential elements of your offensive against Germany (and conducting a ground invasion with a very small force at a quite distant date) to halting the expansion of the Air Forces (and forming a large and powerful ground Army to force an invasion at an early date). At this point, our committee has no formula to suggest whereby this question might be answered.[13]

As target planning challenges had emerged for the CBO nearly a year earlier, questions about assessment again plagued the generals responsible for conducting war with a staff ill prepared to gather and analyze appropriate information, much less inform their strategic decision-making. They did not even appear to understand how to approach the problem. In their haste to sort out the targeting plan, AAF leadership had not given serious consideration to assessment once the campaign started. While they had clearly approached the targeting problem as an iterative sequence of steps, they had overlooked the interactive nature of their air campaign and their commensurate need to evaluate it on a broad scale in order to monitor its progress and resources and the response from the enemy.

More than just information-gathering or assessments, Kuter needed help conceptualizing the problem. He was a brilliant and highly respected airman, but he was also very busy, and he was not planning to meet with his team again for nearly six weeks.[14] The same day Kuter had reached out to Eaker, a memorandum internal to the air staff intelligence division captured the mood of the Washington-based air staff:

> At present, no organization in this Headquarters or abroad keeps complete bomb damage records on which to make the following assessments—
>
> a) The extent to which the industrial installations of the enemy have been structurally damaged;
> b) The production the enemy has lost as the results of such plant destruction;
> c) The effect such lost production has had, is having, or may have on enemy front line strength
>
> There are a half-dozen or more organizations in this Headquarters doing different parts of this work. At present, their activities are uncoordinated. A similar state of confusion exists abroad.[15]

The work simply was not being done. The air staff was characteristically in over its head and underequipped, while its leaders shot reactively from the hip.

While temporarily in London, COA members Perera and Leach received the task from Eaker (presumably before he dismissed them to talk to the RAF about grinding wheels) and attempted to dissect the problem while they began procuring the necessary data from the various forward agencies with relevant reports. Their approach would be straightforward and tied to basic mission statistics, extent of physical damage, and potential economic impact, relying primarily upon raid reports from the British Ministry of Home Security.[16] But they also picked up on the nuance demanding a strategic-level view of air superiority embedded in the war department task, so they decided to include more detail under an "additional accomplishments" subheading: attrition to the German air force and "aid to Russian and Mediterranean fronts by diverting fighters from those fronts."[17] With the phrasing of a single question, Marshall's staff had caused a peculiar non sequitur for CBO assessment: the war department was now principally concerned with air superiority for its invasion, not with the economic objectives of the CBO as officially agreed by the combined chiefs of staff. In other words, insofar as the Army was concerned, the Pointblank directive's intermediate objective was now its sole objective.

The Army and its air arm depended upon each other for planning assumptions based on tangible and reasonable expectations. In this case, a ground force with friendly aircraft overhead could be much smaller and less armored than one facing an air onslaught while attempting to seize ground from another army. The industrial impacts of the CBO on the German military, while desirable, would be much more difficult to quantify and harder to prove, would take longer to develop, and would be less useful as a planning factor for the Allied military program. In any case, both sides sought to guard their resources, and the airmen were not truly giving up on victory through airpower.

Noting the missing ingredients and adding a layer of irony, Perera informed Kuter of an inconvenience with the economic damage reports produced by the British MHS. "Due to lack of personnel, these reports unfortunately do not, at this time, cover every raid by the VIII Air Force under the Combined Bomber Offensive plan," wrote Perera.[18] These were the same reports from the same office that Bissell Alderman and Charles Kring of Eighth Air Force's bombs and fuzes subsection had been hired to support, but they had subsequently rejected it as routine work. In Alderman's words, "Kring and I were of course in no position to estimate production loss and were not immediately concerned with dates of re-attack," even though they were the ones most proximally connected to the information necessary.[19] Harlan had hired the wrong people for that job, and while they went on to exert tremendous analytical effort for bombing accuracy, Harlan never revisited the need to ensure the economic reports were completed. The AAF paid the price for affording its hired analysts too much flexibility in their duties.

Eaker did not see the problem as a lack of information or analysis in the European theater or even of insufficient reporting, but rather as the absence of a coherent spokesman in Washington. He signaled to Kuter: "The reporting, as we have established it between the RAF and ourselves, covers the field. . . . What is required by you and Barney [Giles] is not a new reporting agency in this theater, but a good mind, a qualified statistician to digest, compile, and brief the data which reaches Washington and may otherwise be separated and go to various staff agencies unless there is someone there to compile and make it available so that it can readily be digested by your committee."[20] Eaker envisioned an opportunity to build advocacy in Washington, where he knew his biggest problem was getting on the same page with Arnold—a place from which they seem to have strayed since they had cowritten *This Flying Game* seven years earlier.[21] Rather than levying yet another reporting requirement onto his own staff, Eaker pinned the rose for building advocacy on Leach, who was more than happy to gain the responsibility and the excuse to remain comfortably in Washington—perhaps with the occasional visit forward to England.

That Eaker would have selected a member of a committee with whom he had significant differences of opinion over target selection preferences was odd. Perhaps Eaker assumed Leach would simply compile and regurgitate reports he received from Eighth Air Force. Eaker had little rapport, much less a strong foundation of trust, with either Perera or Leach. While Eaker's rationale for nominating Leach is not clear, he may have underestimated the importance of the position—that of owning the responsibility for overall assessment, because the statistics and words that described them would matter in such an opinion-charged environment. Although it is unlikely Leach played much of a role other than to support the COA's assessment, Eaker certainly missed the opportunity to find an advocate he could trust. What really happened here was that the generals in Washington and the generals in England were pushing the responsibility for air campaign assessment onto each other. The result was to set the stage for a showdown of air intelligence organizations to control the CBO narrative.

The Campaign for Air Assessment

The same U.S. air intelligence organizations that had battled for influence in air campaign targeting again locked horns to influence assessment as well. Their incentive was clear from the start: any thorough assessment would also imply an evaluation of planning and targeting in addition to the bomber's operational performance. Put simply, the analysts recognized the opportunity to grade not only the bombers' efforts and adherence to the plan but their own target selection homework as well. Thus, each organization had a vested interest in controlling the assessments and the CBO narrative they portended.

The emergent "jurisdictional difficulties" to control the assessments were not missed by the Committee of Operations Analysts; they aligned with Arnold's plans division to "prepare an appreciation of the effectiveness of the CBO for use at the Quebec conference," while Arnold's A-2 (still led by General Sorensen) teamed with OSS personnel to produce an "evaluation of the results of the CBO."[22] The tasks were indistinct, and the result was a passive-aggressive competition to produce the dominant document. Each organization produced an assessment that reflected its own interests.

AIR CAMPAIGN ASSESSMENT BY ECONOMISTS

Both the air staff intelligence division and Leach reached out to the EOU economists at the U.S. Embassy over the perplexing issue of CBO assessment. Loath to forego an opportunity to play intellectual one-upmanship or to exploit an AAF expertise shortcoming, the EOU (with support from the OSS research and analysis branch) proposed an initial framework for air campaign assessment.[23] Though references to the original war department task were scrubbed from the final draft of the EOU study on strategic air bombardment evaluation, the members had included it in their drafts, which indicated their awareness of General Kuter's concerns over his staff having no formula from which to approach the problem.[24]

The economists understood that an analyst, no matter how brilliant, cannot solve a problem without first understanding it. "There is neither precedent nor established methodology for making an evaluation of the effects of bomb damage on a complex economic structure," the economists acknowledged.[25] Proposing such methodologies was well within their professional wheelhouse. They had recognized the need for such work in 1942, but they had preferred to stick with targeting instead. Had they delved into assessment methodology earlier, they would have risked being consumed by work even more routine than the grind of building target folders.

The joint EOU/OSS study on bombardment evaluation showed clearly the economists' orientation in their work, which was both helpful and detrimental in its analysis. By mid-1943 the EOU economists had matured in their understanding of both targeting and planning through their months spent with Hughes' team. They drew from this experience and contributed an assessment methodology as part of a comprehensive air campaign cycle beginning with estimates of essential enemy warmaking resources, noting "their relative vulnerability to air attack" and linking them via "the progress being made toward the objectives" back to changes in original estimates.[26] This was a novel concept for assessment, but it had eluded the minds of the airmen.

Interestingly, the OSS study acknowledged not only tangible effects, but also the importance of assessing "highly imponderable" effects such as enemy morale (though they may have conflated political will of the elites with public support by the general populace). These imponderables tended to stray from concrete methodology, so interest in them trailed off as the economists recognized that "to state the problem of evaluation . . . is not, however, to solve it."[27] They then offered a methodology based entirely upon tangible decreases to enemy resources available, and they tied the outcome to friendly resources required. The economists captured in their typical pedantic prose that objective measures of assessment for an air campaign were inextricably linked to ground force requirements: "This reduction in enemy resistance to our final occupation of his vital territory is reflected in a reduction in the resources which we must make available to our ground task forces for this victorious termination of hostilities. The amount of that reduction, properly related to the time factors involved, is the only fundamental and realistic measure of the effectiveness of the bomber offensive."[28] Economists working for the Office of Strategic Services—not Air Corps Tactical School graduates or the AAF's organic air intelligence officers—had devised and recommended an enduring framework for air campaign assessment. The answer this solution provided, of course, was a measurement of German war matériel—the EOU economists' preferred targeting scheme.

While EOU members cautioned against eliminating targets that were difficult to assess, they were nevertheless partial to targets with calculable impacts on the enemy military. As economists, they relied upon their backgrounds in maximizing quantitative factors and efficiency, while attempting to validate their preferred targeting recommendations: "That system or pattern of targets should be selected for attack in which a given expenditure of effort produces the greatest reduction in enemy military capability within desired time limits."[29] The implications of this assertion, while subtle, were significant. A target's post-attack calculability, if considered in depth during (not after) the planning process, might inform target selection—or at least identify intelligence gaps early enough to act upon them. Whether an attack could be assessed was not one of the EOU's original eleven criteria for target selection.[30]

ASSESSMENT BY A COMMITTEE OF LAWYERS AND INDUSTRIALISTS

The Committee of Operations Analysts, however, preferred to tell Arnold what they thought he wanted to hear, as they sought to reinforce their own targeting plan. The committee's approach to assessment was threefold: to focus on the Eighth's greatest successes, to overlook the obvious struggles, and to blame the lack of progress in German industrial dislocation on the fact that Eighth Air Force had committed an alarming 55 percent of its effort to the submarine facilities, which "are not profitable bombardment targets."[31] In other words, if bombing progress should be criticized, it was because the air campaign as executed did not match the COA's recommendations.

Most remarkably, the reality in theater did not support its assertions, which made the entire assessment read as embellished propaganda rather than objective evaluation. For example, COA members submitted in the leadoff section of their report: "The heavy bombardment force has indicated its ability (a) to fight its way to a target and back (b) to bomb with such precision from high altitude that industrial targets can be put out of action," which seemed a reasonable proposition, until they added, "This applies to all types of targets in all geographic areas within range against all degrees of opposition."[32] Maybe the AAF's top generals wanted to accept this, whether they believed it or not.

However, this assertion from Washington that the bombers were effective against all degrees of opposition might have seemed preposterous to a closer observer of the human costs paid by the thousands of dead, missing, and injured Allied airmen battling the Luftwaffe in Europe. As a single case in point, Staff Sgt. J. J. Dalinsky, who bailed out from the waist gunner position of his B-17 named "Dear Mom" over Regensburg contemporaneous to the committee's report, might have offered a more reasonable perspective about enemy opposition; instead, Dalinsky simply made a request to "put mike buttons on gun handles" after he had spent the next six months evading capture while returning to friendly territory.[33] Perhaps the COA analysts had not taken the time to discern a more human and realistic sense of how the air campaign was actually fought from the airmen who were fighting it.

A few examples from the BDA the analysts cited in their reports reflect their salesmanship. For the Vegesack mission, they plugged photo interpretation claims that "damage to buildings was such as to 'reduce efficiency to a minimum if not dislocate the yards entirely.'"[34] These findings had not materialized, and the COA analysts understood this well enough to contradict their own argument in the same report: "The current successes against the submarines at sea and the growing realization that bases and construction yards are unfruitful targets releases up to 55 percent of the net effort for attacks on the GAF [German air force] and basic industry."[35] A tendency for contradictions, seemingly offering a range of viewpoints from which the AAF's commanding general might select his preferred brand, undercut their credibility.

The COA also touted the Hüls raid, referencing both CIU interpretation and joint intelligence sub-committee reports to make its case: "This mission shows the Eighth Air Force fighting its way into the heart of Germany, locating an isolated industrial plant of considerable dispersion and great structural resistance, laying a bomb pattern all over it, and putting it 'out of action for several months.'"[36] There was no doubt the raid had shown great promise, especially if they had accepted the language at face value in the bimonthly report by Eaker's A-2, which argued that the Hüls attack "looks like the most effective bombing ever done by the Eighth Air Force. . . . bombs clearly hit many, many vital installations."[37]

But Hüls was part of the Ruhr valley, located on Germany's western fringes, and even if the COA could not yet have known that the plant was out of action for less than six weeks, available damage reports were conflicting.[38] The bomb plot (see photo 4-1) showed significant bomb damage in the north and west of the plant, but there were hardly any bomb impacts on the south and east portions of the plant, while much of the concentration fell harmlessly in nearby fields.

Even more peculiar, the COA made no attempt to connect an estimate in projected rubber production losses to an impact upon German forces or the Allied army necessary to overcome them, perhaps because that impact would have been minimal.[39] An MEW report, which may have been available to the COA several weeks prior, noted that tightening of the rubber position by mid-July would have been due to "non-arrival of blockade runners during the winter," not from immediate impacts of rubber production. Although there were some delays in Berlin, the report added, "Old tyres are usually delivered."[40] Even if full results of the Hüls attack were not yet known, this was the type of information Marshall had asked of Arnold, only the source was British—not American.

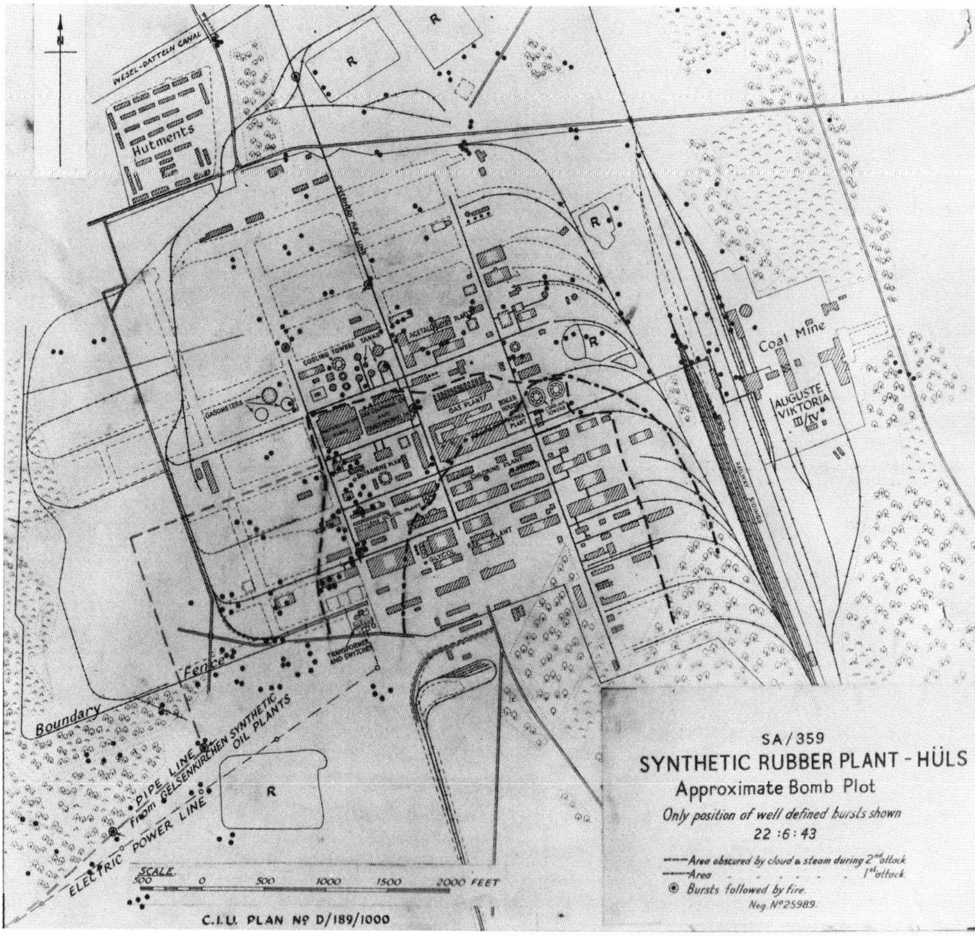

Photo 4-1. Bomb plot of damage at Hüls. Reprinted from Central Interpretation Unit, "Approximate Bomb Plot No. SA 359," in Synthetic Rubber Plant—Hüls, 22 June 1943, AFHRA

COA analysts also touted the raid on the Renault vehicle factory in Paris, claiming that "Eighth Air Force produced at least as great destruction by an attack from 22,000 to 26,000 feet as the RAF produced from 1,200 to 4,000 feet."[41] In spite of the impressive accuracy with which the bombs fell and the British Ministry of Home Security's prediction of the loss of three thousand trucks over three months, the report lacked any evidence to support the AAF's superior damage claim. Further, even before the committee submitted its assessment, MEW economists released one of their weekly reports recognizing "substantial progress was being made in the clearance, repair and reconstruction of the Renault Billancourt factories. More than 30 workshops were under repair, one or two were apparently completely repaired and even the most seriously damaged had been cleared of wreckage and prepared for further reconstruction," all within six weeks of the Eighth Air Force attack.[42] If COA analysts saw this report, it did not seem to deter their confidence in their claims or cause them to question other reports as to the German industrial position.[43]

A consistent and considerable flaw in the committee's assessment was its assumption that photo interpreters tended to underestimate rather than overestimate damage. The COA lawyers and industrialists acknowledged that material damage within bombed buildings could be difficult to determine, especially since "precise function of those buildings is frequently inexact or outdated," but they argued, "The photographic interpreter cannot make guesses without objective evidence and hence states only that minimum which affirmatively appears."[44]

The logic was sound, but the reality was opposite. Both photo interpreters and operations researchers tended to simplify their problems by assuming that damage to structures correlated to damaged contents. From this flawed assumption, COA analysts asserted "a virtual certainty of strikingly accelerated destruction of the industrial resources of the German war machine" in the months to come.[45] As later assessments and postwar surveys would show, most estimates incorporated into their analysis had been needlessly exaggerated.

Next, the COA boasted of the Ploesti mission's success with its special reverence to Arnold, who'd later claim, "No mission in the war was more carefully planned, with full knowledge of the odds against it, nor carried out despite mishaps in identifying the target, with more amazing courage."[46] In spite of the earlier A-2 meeting intended to cap intelligence estimates at a much lower figure, the committee pulled from a "well-authenticated" source, including the refinery's managers, that "the damage to the production facilities of all the refineries as a whole was estimated at 70 percent subject to upward revision."[47] Plant managers themselves had incentive to exaggerate production losses in their pleas for recuperative resources. There was an increased risk of fallacy when pulling the estimates from the high end of intelligence sources.

COA analysts also attempted to reframe the losses taken at Ploesti to seem less distressing. Since Ploesti contained nine separate refineries, they figured that "losses were 4 aircraft destroyed and 1 interned for each objective attacked," which made the numbers seem smaller by comparison.[48] Of course, the percentages were the same no matter how the statistics were carved up. Hap Arnold was proud of Ploesti, but for him it was about the crews' bravery, not downplaying the losses; while writing his memoir, he still grieved that 54 of 177 aircraft—over 30 percent—had failed to return from that single brutal mission.[49] Ploesti hardly proved a sterling example that the bombers could fight their way to any target and back against any opposition—at least not without taking unsustainable losses.

Finally, the analysts winced at the challenge of quantifying results of the RAF's area raids and even of differentiating which of those raids had linked directly to Pointblank industrial targets. According to Perera, the rare cases when the RAF had attacked "specific segments of enemy industrial capacity," results might be measured along with the AAF attacks, "but so far as the RAF strikes at industrial areas or at manpower generally or at morale its relation to the plan was indirect."[50] Measuring indirect effects was not the analysts' bailiwick. In short, they made no effort to correlate the impacts of the two complementary air forces except to identify that assessment of the RAF attacks might be forthcoming in separate reports from the British. The problem with discounting indirect effects was that no area-bombing contributions could then be factored into the U.S. military program.

The British responded posthaste. However, the report released two days later on 22 July by their Joint Intelligence Committee (JIC) openly struggled to connect dehousing metrics to industrial production losses, so they simply accounted for direct damage. The JIC showed, for example, in the RAF's bombing of the industrial city of Essen, that "60 percent of the total loss, and almost all of the short-term loss, is attributable to direct damage to factories," which had been incidental to the area attack on the city itself.[51] They determined that dehoused Germans merely lived with others until a very high "saturation point" could be reached through bombing, and "there is no reason to believe that saturation point has been achieved in the larger cities," with the exception of the densely populated and highly industrialized Ruhr area.[52] Furthermore, manpower for industrial repairs came from the workers themselves as soon as plants shut down, meaning there were no recognizable shortfalls in repair crew capacity.

As for morale, intelligence showed German troops regularly received letters from home detailing "the terrors of air bombing," but the JIC found that "there is nothing to show that their fighting spirit has yet been reduced."[53] While there were notable successes, the tone of the report conveyed a sobering message that lacked confidence in the less quantifiable area bombing results. Among British intelligence organizations, the JIC notably operated independently of the Air Ministry and the RAF, so it lacked incentive to support Harris' preferred strategy.

In summary, the COA likely realized, from its position in Washington, that the total size of the Army depended on the success of the CBO, so any indications of CBO shortcomings could lead to a decision to curtail the AAF in order to build up more ground strength. Its members anticipated what Arnold wanted to hear, and that is how they oriented their report. In truth, the COA's report did little to help Arnold, Eaker, or the AAF by accentuating positive claims and downplaying loss figures. Their selection of exemplar raids (or so they thought) for each of the Pointblank directive's industrial categories seemed a premature argument to redistribute, in their words, a "weight of attack sufficient to produce significant economic damage to the German war machine."[54] They appeared to be building a case to force Eaker's hand toward attacking their preference in industrial targets before he could secure air superiority, and they gave the impression that Eaker had placed too much effort on submarine attacks, whether he'd wanted to or not. The committee had Arnold's ear, and that was not good for Eaker.

While his staff and the various air intelligence organizations scrambled to extinguish CBO assessment fires, Arnold set about invigorating a public relations campaign on the home front. If the Army would not appreciate an independent role for airpower, maybe the American public would. Maybe they would believe in his air arm's capability to win the war, not just to perform the preparatory actions for an invasion. With more time and its full share of resources, the Army's air force could do more than just negate an enemy's bid to control the air. That was the message he hoped to convey in a personal letter to Eaker:

> It is important for the people to understand that our prime purpose is destruction of the enemy's ability to wage war, by our planned persistent bombing and sapping of his vital industries, his transportation, and his whole supply system. . . . It is important for them to realize that this takes time, as well as money and planes and planning and work—but that it will win the war and save perhaps millions of lives which otherwise would be sacrificed in bloody ground combat. . . . In short, we

> want the people to understand and have faith in our way of making war. That faith can grow in strength only as we show them what we are doing, and how well we are doing it. . . . We must put before the public information as to actual results of our bombing; preferably clear photographic evidence showing the before, during, and after phases of the operation. With this—in easily understandable form—should be included the vital statistics and a reasonable assessment of damage inflicted.[55]

The idea buzzing around the Army's planning division that air superiority could reduce the size of the Allied invasion force had merit; but to Arnold, the idea of the air campaign extended much further. He privately articulated his faith that strategic bombing *saved* lives. More Americans would return home and—better still—fewer mobilized troops meant fewer disrupted families, a stronger economy, and less disturbance to the American way of life. This was the promise of victory through airpower, and he was not about to give up on it as the war department focused on invasion planning. His message was to just keep the damage assessments reasonable and let the photos portray the airpower story. Whether intentional or not, Arnold had placed extraordinary pressure on Eaker to help him tell the story that he wanted to tell, and he was going to hold Eaker accountable if demonstrable results were not forthcoming.

Retapping Ploesti and Synthetic Oil Assessments

Adding to Eaker's predicament, earlier that month Arnold had redirected the inbound 389th Bomb Group and transferred Eaker's 376th and 98th Bomb Groups to join Maj. Gen. Lewis Brereton's 9th Air Force on another raid against the heavily defended Ploesti oil fields; 54 of Eaker's B-24s were shot down, and 532 crewmen were lost when they finally executed what turned out to be—both temporally and figuratively—an August mission to remember.[56] Most raids, if successful at all, seemed only half-steps forward, and they left Eaker's bomber force licking its wounds and short on replacements. Ploesti was no exception.

While the raid, code named operation Tidal Wave, was technically a Ninth Air Force mission, everyone with an interest in the European theater had an eye on the results. The idea was to deal a crushing blow to Romanian natural petroleum refineries (as opposed to the synthetic plants in Germany), which offered the Axis ample quantities of the highest grades of fuel and lubricants—the lifeblood of the Luftwaffe.[57] The importance of Ploesti stemmed not just from the one-third of all Axis petroleum it provided, but also from the geographic location of its "panorama of high-chimneyed refineries, tanks farms, and rail network" in Eastern Europe.[58] Ploesti fed Hitler's eastern front from its advantageous proximity, so the loss of this source of refined oil would, as the assistant chief of air staff for intelligence eventually concluded, "necessitate the transportation of crude oil hundreds of miles for refining to Italy, southern France, or southern Germany, thence to the Eastern Front, thus placing an additional burden upon the already strained transportation facilities of the Axis."[59] A weakened petroleum industry would further stress other industries.

Ploesti's location also had a downside for the Allies. From its position nine hundred miles northeast of Tripoli, it was a trek for the bombers and an even greater challenge for reconnaissance flights, as the range pushed the RAF's specially equipped Mosquitoes to their limit.[60] The first of two flights intended for poststrike reconnaissance stole a glance of Ploesti while fires still filled the sky with black smoke. The reconnaissance mission failed to capture the whole target area, and it returned to base with mostly low-angle, oblique images. The second flight, accomplished from medium altitude two weeks later, became "the principal source of Allied intelligence on the effectiveness of the attack, despite all of the known limitations of photographic intelligence."[61] In general, the oil industry was one for which photo intelligence was well suited, since capacity could be measured and operating status confirmed via photo reconnaissance.

Bomb damage assessments deemed the raid worthy of its "Ploesti Smashed" headlines, and the theater photo interpretation chief was ecstatic.[62] The marketing value alone of destroying Ploesti was as great as the impact on the Axis because the BDA images could be used to rally public support behind the air campaign. For this purpose, the low-angle shots were helpful, even if they failed to capture the scope of the attack. The commander of the Middle East interpretation unit also realized from the poststrike photos that preraid threat information had been out of date. "In addition to the excellent photographs of the Ploesti raid itself, which, quite apart from their propaganda value, were most useful for assessment of damage in conjunction with later vertical photographs," wrote the chief of intelligence for Ninth Air Force, "a number of obliques were taken disclosing many points of interest which we might not otherwise have discovered."[63]

Plans for preraid reconnaissance flights were scrapped for fear of tipping off the Germans, so planners and operations analysts in theater were left to work from dated assumptions.[64]

Surprise was paramount, but the U.S. bombers were surprised as well.[65] It turned out the Germans had surreptitiously employed an aggressive defensive countermeasure program since the first raid on Ploesti (the Halverson project) a year earlier. ULTRA intercepts compensated somewhat by indicating as early as December 1942 that the Germans anticipated additional attacks, and messages the month prior to the raid, signed by a new fighter group at Ploesti, had sought "re-arrangement of the existing forces there."[66] Though the intercepts were cryptic and tightly controlled within Allied intelligence circles, the Germans clearly had emphasized Ploesti's defense since the Halverson project mission had exposed Allied interest in Ploesti as a target. Other new measures, albeit not ones addressed in ULTRA, included camouflage, smoke-screen generators, barrage balloons, antiaircraft guns, and dispersed dummy sites; intelligence and operations analysts considered all of these as possibilities but downplayed them to crews, who were told, for example, that "it would be advantageous for a plane encountering a balloon cable to attack it downwind and at as low an angle as possible."[67] Intelligence analysts would later claim that the countermeasures had little impact on the crews or the mission overall.[68] The crews of the unfortunate Liberators lost to barrage balloons probably felt otherwise.

Analysts from the British Ministry of Economic Warfare published in their *Intelligence Weekly*, which they released prior to the second postraid reconnaissance mission, their aspirations for the raid's potential impact. Confident in the "great precision and much damage wrought" by the bombers, they felt the raid's ultimate success depended not as much on the bombs' immediate explosions as on the fires that burned long after the bombers departed.[69] "The firing of oil tankage will cause a dead loss of oil which may well be on a considerable scale and is sufficiently serious in itself," argued the MEW analysts, "but fires among the operating units, if not put out very rapidly, will have caused damage that will take a considerable time to repair."[70] From their economic perspective, losses in existing oil supply were inconsequential compared to lost future production if the refining equipment had burnt up in the intense heat that followed the attack. For the analysts to reach their hopeful conclusions, Ploesti would require considerable additional reconnaissance or ground intelligence.

Not all of their assessments strove for concrete details, however, as the economists also delved into less tangible factors. "It is evident from reports that the accuracy of the bombing has impressed upon the Roumanians their vulnerability to further attacks," the MEW claimed, "and there is no doubt that this event has added to the growing disillusionment that is being felt toward the [prime minister Ion] Antonescu régime."[71] Without divulging evidence to support their claim, the economists insinuated that the daring bomber raid began to drain the loyalty of the Romanian people in addition to their oil. Implications that bombing-inspired uprisings in the minds of an occupied populace actually allied to Germany were significant and likely to gain favor with the bomber generals. Even if unsubstantiated, that King Michael I successfully overthrew Antonescu by coup a year later could be testament to the MEW economists' claim, even if the Soviets were, by then, across the Romanian border.[72]

Finally, in an effort to corral the opinions of "all interested agencies" on the raid's petroleum production impact, the air staff's target information branch called a meeting to force a consensus that the raid destroyed "42.5 percent of total Romanian capacity."[73] Given the political implications of such an important raid, it was best for the credibility of all intelligence organizations if their conclusions were not so widely varied. In the weeks and months following the raid, hasty repairs and idle capacity compensated for some of the deficit, so the best that could be stated of the raid's long-term results was that the Axis was left "with no margin of spare refinery capacity which is efficiently located."[74] In other words, the Germans lost their convenient cushion, but the raid was not enough to stop any engines. This allowed the intelligence organizations most interested in the Axis oil position to insist there must be more attacks on oil.

The following week, an enthusiastic charge circulated among the 4th Bombardment Wing's groups as they prepared for a raid against the synthetic oil plants at Wesseling, near Bonn. The message proclaimed, "The importance of the oil industry cannot be over-emphasized, and with the destruction of the Ploesti fields, the synthetic oil plants take on an added importance."[75] Now that Ploesti had received its due, other petroleum targets—especially those producing gasoline—were central to Pointblank. Eaker's rationale for delaying attacks on them six weeks earlier had expired.

New to striking oil plants, crews received excruciating detail of the target's likely appearance from their intelligence briefer, and they were instructed to aim

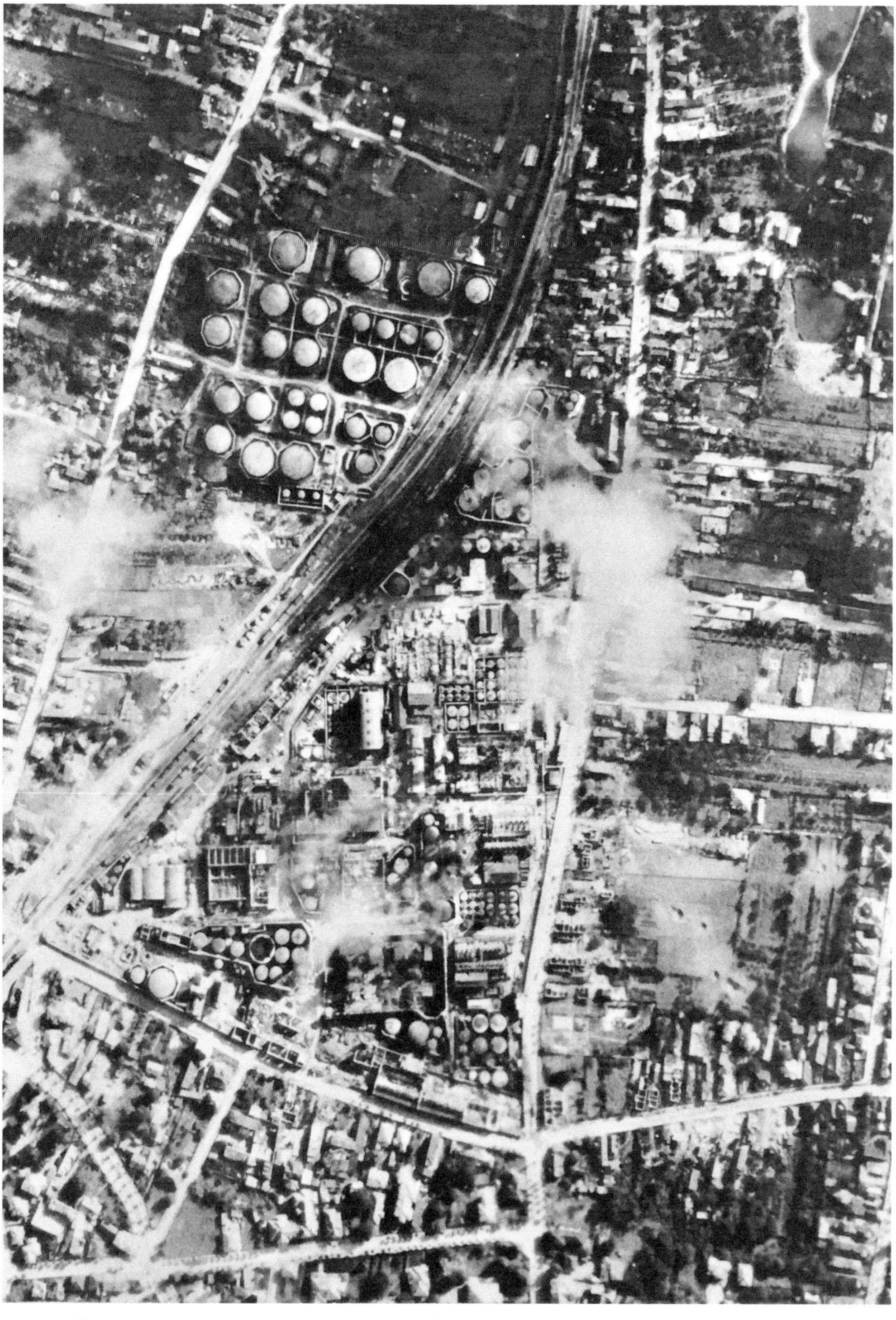

Photo 4-2. Reconnaissance photo of the Steaua Romana Refinery (Target Red) where destruction of refinery capacity was estimated at 100 percent. Reprinted from Assistant Chief of Air Staff, A-2, "The Ploesti Mission of 1 August 1943," in USAF Historical Study No. 103, Historical Division, June 1944, AFHRA.

their bombs for the gas plant (as opposed to high-pressure vessels), because it "is the most vital point as it is relatively easy to damage and its complete destruction would cause production to cease throughout the works."[76] They focused on the target but underestimated the threat.

What neither the crews nor the intelligence briefers anticipated was smoke, possibly from a defensive screen, and flak that was "much more intense than briefed."[77] One 94th Bomb Group crew reported that the whole target area was full of smoke and three bombs hung up inside their bomb bay because the "bomb release cable was severed by flak bursts!"[78] Their group S-2 followed up despairingly in his own report, "Very few accurate observations of bombing reported, however several reports indicated [that the] primary target was covered with smoke."[79] As the postmission intelligence reports moved up the chain, the wing-level S-2 was unable to make heads or tails of any of his groups' reports. He summarized, "Making accurate survey of damage impossible. Claims of bombing of [the] primary target are not substantiated by any photos taken."[80] Everyone seemed to want to distance themselves from the apparent failure.

The other portion of the day's raid, flown by the 1st Bombardment Wing to attack synthetic oil plants at Gelsenkirchen, fared even worse. Crews from the 1st Wing's 305th Bombardment Group were irate and quick to pass fault through their own S-2: "The target was identified by the navigator and bombardier of our lead [aircraft] and after the bomb run was begun the lead group turned right in front and under our group indicating that the lead group was not going to bomb the primary. Rather than break away from [the] combat wing our leader followed the lead group. A similar situation occurred at the secondary target after the target had been identified. Bombing the target was sacrificed for combat wing discipline."[81] Crews reported an ineffective smoke screen and broken cloud layers in the target area, but nothing that would preclude bombing.[82] The despondent assistant wing photo officer reported, "None of our bombers were successful in their attempt to bomb" either of their assigned synthetic oil targets.[83]

If the Ploesti oil raid had been memorable, the synthetic oil raid of 12 August had been one to forget. On that day, 243 Eighth Air Force bombers dropped 560 tons of bombs with no significant damage to their primary targets. Another twenty-five bombers—just over 10 percent—were lost.[84] For reasons perhaps only General Eaker might have fully explained, the only reference to petroleum targets in a monthly operations summary stated that "attacks on two synthetic oil plants in the Ruhr were abortive on account of weather and smoke screens."[85] Further, Eaker's monthly A-2 report to Arnold blamed the lack of bombs dropped on Gelsenkirchen on the enemy's smoke screen and the "unlikely" chance of effectiveness at Wesseling solely on "6–8/10 cloud [cover]" but noted that "flexibility of attack turned what might have been failure into major successes" since one formation managed to damage a steel mill that was assigned as a secondary target.[86] In fact, flexibility of attack was precisely what had kept the raid from achieving success, but this was not what Eaker chose to report.

Eaker had little motivation to press further on oil attacks. Oil targets fell lower in priority than the urgent challenges posed by the Luftwaffe, the pressure to engage in U-boat attacks, and the COA's insistence that ball-bearing attacks would yield quick victory. Further, the COA analysts had considered from their early discussions that the Ruhr synthetic plants were of questionable vulnerability with their "small, rugged structures" that would necessitate "almost direct hits."[87] Available intelligence thus implied that even if the bombers had managed effective attacks, these targets would require continual follow-up against heavy resistance. Even still, Eaker struggled to sustain his force with a reasonable rate of operations against the higher priority targets, including the ineffective U-boat attacks, and he had not yet waged an attack against ball-bearing factories at all. Targeting plans did not return to oil with any consistency for eight more months.

Schweinfurt-Regensburg and the Risk-Reward Calculus

The mid-August sun signaled the approaching end of summer along with the waning opportunity for Eaker and his wing commanders to prove the value of their air campaign. As Col. Richard Hughes put it from the pressure-cooker atmosphere in the Eighth Air Force planners' map room, it was time to "go for broke."[88] After all, no amount of meticulous or informed BDA could compensate for missed opportunities if they failed to put enough bombs on the right targets. It was time to increase their intensity on aircraft factories and to test the theory of Germany's ball-bearing bottleneck.

Advancing technology helped. The arrival into the European theater of modified F-model B-17s, which toted an additional eight hundred gallons of wing-tank capacity, added more than just a few hundred miles of range per aircraft.[89] They added new mission possibilities as well, although the extended range brought with it a temptation to press farther beyond their escorts. The modified B-17Fs now had the range to reach North Africa by way of a deep mission into Germany.

After weeks of soupy weather frustrated the Mighty Eighth's bombing accuracy as well as its plans to synchronize an attack with the three bomb groups on loan to Spaatz in Africa, the skies finally cleared.[90] The plan then in place and ready to execute would include a shuttle mission: 147 B-17s of Curtis LeMay's Third Bomb Division, with their long-range tanks and the preponderance of escort, would wreak havoc on the ME-109 plant at Regensburg and continue on to bases in North Africa; 10 minutes in trail, 230 unmodified B-17s of the First Bomb Division, led by Brig. Gen. Robert Williams, would deal a crushing blow to the ball-bearing factories at Schweinfurt, then reverse their routing back to England due to their lesser range.[91] The brilliance of the plan, had it been executed as designed, was to surprise the German fighters when LeMay's lead division turned south, leaving diminished opposition for the Schweinfurt attack as the enemy fighters refueled and rearmed.[92] The grandiose mission would mark the anniversary of the first full year of U.S. heavy bombing in Europe.[93]

As with all great plans, reality intervened—in this case, in the form of ground fog and an overwhelming sense of urgency. Eaker's force, better trained for instrument takeoffs, launched their Fortresses close to schedule as bad weather blanketed England to ensure they could arrive in Africa before dark. Williams' larger force of twelve groups delayed another ninety minutes before they received the green light from Gen. Fred Anderson.[94] The benefit of the coordinated attack had thus been negated by the delay. The result, as a dismayed Colonel Hughes later reflected, meant that "Curt LeMay's force was exposed to the full fury of all the German fighters all the way to Regensburg. . . . The German fighters then had ample time to fly back to their bases, refuel, and rearm, and to throw their entire strength against the delayed attack" by Williams' lesser escorted forces.[95] Despite the shattered plan, the bombers fought valiantly to place their bombs on target.

Bomb damage assessments and bomber losses were equally stunning. No sooner had the surviving crews limped in to their separate destinations, group S-2s began to tally up the numbers and review photographic evidence. To avoid any shortcuts with the nonstandard shuttle mission recovery, senior intelligence officers were reminded via cable message that "a regular group interrogation will be held for the returning crews of the Regensburg missions" and that "all reports [are] expected within scheduled time."[96] This was a very high-interest mission; the recoveries at North African bases drove additional command and control issues, and there would be a lot of missing crew reports.

The S-2 from the 94th Bombardment Group, one of LeMay's units, wasted no time in transmitting his account. Twenty of their twenty-one aircraft managed to arrive in North Africa, though they had ended up scattered at three different airfields, and one aircraft had landed on a salt flat instead of an air base.[97] Crews grumbled of "constant and eager" German fighter attacks from the time their escort departed (near Antwerp) until close to the target area, although the enemy pilots "seemed green in attacking a formation, riding along parallel, nosing in for a few bursts, and then pulling away."[98] The timid behavior might have indicated that attrition of experienced pilots and hurried training for replacements were taking a toll on the Luftwaffe.

Except for one B-17 that "blew up" before Regensburg, the S-2 reported all crews dropped their ten five-hundred-pound bombs on target with favorable details: "Bombing appeared excellent. All bomb releases observed were immediately in the target area. Smoke and flames enveloped the M.P.I. [mean point of impact]."[99] Interestingly, his interrogation notes and handwritten worksheets included data from only fourteen of the twenty aircraft he incorporated into his report, so the source of the other six remains in question.[100] What was not in question, however, was the crews' sense of accomplishment. Following the report's instructions for the S-2 to "use crew language if you like," he recorded the last two crews' bombing results were "damned good" and "target destroyed."[101] Morale was high in the 94th, and they were confident they had done well.

A successful raid was about more than just the bombs. A reconnaissance flight captured aerial photographs four hours after the raid, and the CIU followed with an urgent intelligence report the next day. Photo interpreters confirmed the crews' confidence: "Damage within the target area is of a high order of concentration, nearly all the craters being within the bounds of the factory," the intelligence report boasted, adding that many of the buildings had still been ablaze when the photographs were taken.[102] Unfortunately, what appeared to be outstanding damage was offset by losses. Of the 146 B-17s dispatched, 127 attacked the target and (optimistically) claimed 140 enemy fighters destroyed, but the cost was devastating: 24 aircraft were lost, including more than 200 aircrew killed or missing.[103] Over 15 percent of the attacking force was lost in just one raid on one of twenty-two targets that comprised key elements of industry supporting single-engine fighter production.[104]

As higher headquarters staffers added their impressions of postraid results, their gusto grew more pronounced: "Heavy damage was inflicted on the factory and nearly all the buildings were affected in some degree," claimed the bomber command report, loosely referencing photoreconnaissance intelligence.[105] When Arnold's A-2 staff in Washington incorporated the attack into their own assessments, they extended the enthusiasm: "Our attack of 17 August 1943, made in conjunction with the attack on Schweinfurt, was probably the most successful attack ever made by aircraft on an industrial target. Nearly every building of this large plant suffered severe damage. . . . It is estimated by competent authorities that this attack caused the loss in production of five hundred Me-109s."[106] There was no doubt that the bombers had accomplished their mission after struggling to get airborne that dreary August morning, and the words marketing their success picked up steam as the reports moved uphill. Larger questions on the path ahead were whether the cost to the Germans was worth the price paid by Eighth Air Force, and how the Germans would respond.

The OSS research and analysis branch waited only a month before delving into a tentative appreciation of the raid's near-term and long-term impacts. OSS analysts, along with their economists serving in the EOU, strongly favored continued attacks against the German fighter industry, as they had from the start. Their intelligence assessment reflected this viewpoint. They felt the raid was just a small part of an opening salvo, albeit an effective one. Probable results of the Regensburg raid, they felt, would cost the Germans at least three months of production. Along with an attack three days earlier on the Me-109 factory at Wiener-Neustadt, the raid imposed "a prompt and considerable impact on [German air force] front line fighter strength."[107] Near-term impacts were undoubtedly positive.

However, OSS analysts sought to keep pressure on both the Luftwaffe and Eaker's future plans. They argued the bombers had merely chiseled the tip of an iceberg: "While the results of the recent [Eighth Air Force] attacks on German fighter aircraft plants represent only a portion of the minimum effects required to achieve a decisive weakening of Germany's fighter defenses, they may nevertheless be regarded as an encouraging beginning."[108] The EOU economists, operating in closer consultation with Eaker's planners than the analysts in Washington, fancied Eaker's focus on the air superiority battle per their targeting methodology. While they would let Eaker's crews enjoy their pat on the back, it was far too soon to celebrate victory over the Luftwaffe.

The assessments and reality grew increasingly muddled as the months ticked by without the Eighth revisiting Regensburg. The CIU's photo interpreters expressed alarm as they noted extraordinary efforts to repair the plant by the middle of October. "Activity is seen at many points in the factory area," they noted from follow-up reconnaissance, "though little of it is likely to be directly concerned with aircraft production."[109] Whatever was going on at the Messerschmitt plant involved an unusual number of workers and a stockpile of resources—well beyond the efforts of a slapdash repair job.

The COA analysts, when identifying Regensburg as a target, understood it to be vulnerable in the same way they understood "all [aircraft] plants are vulnerable to HE [high explosive] and incendiary attack," provided the attack incurred sufficient damage to "component erecting shops and final assembly sheds."[110] It turned out the Regensburg plant was uniquely vulnerable due to the plant's lack of preparedness, although such indicators had not been available to Allied air intelligence organizations.[111] Reconstruction efforts at the plant were therefore more robust than the original plant design, and this took time. Maybe the plant did not need another attack yet after all.

The British Ministry of Home Security's research and experiments department (RE8) also weighed in with a reattack recommendation but with a more open-ended approach, including a range of possible options for the Germans. RE8 analysts concluded that the target would be optimal for reattack after four months, regardless of whether the Germans chose to disperse some of the plant's production functions.[112] No reattack occurred until further reconnaissance showed unambiguous production activity and attempts to camouflage buildings more than five-and-a-half months after the original attack.[113] If the Germans had not been serious about preemptively dispersing, protecting, and hiding their industries before the raid on Regensburg, they became so afterward. As for Eaker's target planners, if they were relying exclusively on the EOU or the MEW to update their original assumptions, they were getting conflicting information, and they were not following the recommendations anyway.

With a scathing postmission report, Col. Curtis LeMay singlehandedly dismantled any further plans for shuttle missions to North Africa. He had personally conducted an advance trip to Africa, where he found that the bare-base facilities were underequipped and personnel there were ill-trained to service his fleet of B-17s, much less repair battle damage and prepare them for combat on the return leg.[114] The unpredictability of combat left many aircraft too short on fuel to reach their intended destinations, and the entire situation placed inordinate strain on his crews. As to preparing for combat on the return leg from such an austere location, LeMay was partial to his own intelligence officers. He was grateful for the support his wing received in Africa, but he felt "our own S-2 officers, well acquainted with our crews and knowing their background, could have given better service."[115] LeMay placed a premium on trust with his staff and crews, including the veracity of their reports. Nearly two weeks after the raid on Regensburg, Eighth Air Force operations staff acknowledged his concerns, as well as his two airplanes and crews still stuck in Africa.[116]

The Schweinfurt raid was a different story than Regensburg (both raids were accomplished the same day—known historically as the Schweinfurt-Regensburg mission), though it would reveal a similar pattern of conflicting viewpoints. That ongoing debate over the target had been controversial added intrigue to its eventual prosecution and attention to expectations of its success. Air intelligence organizations maintained varying degrees of emphasis on the ball-bearing bottleneck, but their consensus—following the ACTS logic for industrial dislocation—consistently placed the system among top priority targets. The controversy arose with "Bomber" Harris, who did not share this thinking.

As advocated in the Pointblank directive, Schweinfurt made an ideal venue for a combined day-night raid by the Allied air forces, and MEW had pressed Harris since the 1942 publication of its *Bomber's Baedeker*. As MEW saw it, Schweinfurt had been one of only two considerable anomalies in its attractiveness as an area target of economic importance. Along with Bitterfeld (and its chemical factory), MEW economists nominated Schweinfurt as the only other city of a population under 100,000 to grace its list of 33 priority-one cities.[117] However, Harris maintained his ardent rejection of "panacea targets" in the summer of 1943, though according to the AAF's VIII Bomber Command, the only reason the RAF did not participate in the 17 August raid was the unfortunate timing of a full moon—a defensive advantage too risky for an RAF night attack.[118] Harris later clarified his opinion in no uncertain terms: "The target experts went completely mad" when they selected ball bearings.[119] Other histories contend MEW's Sidney Bufton bypassed Harris and appealed directly to Hughes and Eaker.[120] Eighth Air Force would go alone after this single town that allegedly produced 50 percent of Axis ball bearings despite its position as the number-three target industry for the CBO.[121]

VIII Bomber Command compiled its narrative as soon as the interrogation reports and immediate interpretation reports came in. Opposition had been brutal. Of the dispatched force of 230 bombers, 36 went missing, and only 183 had bombed their primary targets at Schweinfurt, dropping more than 1,000 250-pound British incendiaries, 719 500-pound bombs, and another 235 1,000-pounders.[122] Despite the losses, "bombing results were very good," the VIII Bomber Command report claimed, as a number of machine shops and other important buildings had received "direct hits."[123]

Interrogation reports indicated a subtle but important nuance. The assessments of group S-2s tended to align with those of their crews, but this raid was different. Two of the group S-2s, as if conferring or sensing the level of scrutiny of their results, held their crews accountable and made their contradictions evident. For example, the 306th Bombardment Group crews were adamant of their success, but their S-2 was unable to match their excitement: "Crews think bombing better than seems to be borne out by the first photos."[124] Another group S-2 reflected similar skepticism: "Crews report excellent bombing results on the target. . . . Bursts were claimed on the aiming point area and on the marshalling yards to the south. However, photographs taken by our lead [aircraft] do not show hits on our target, but rather on a buildup of factory district about 3/4 mile to the north of our target. There was much smoke near the target, evidently from another formation's bombing."[125] Finally, the 305th Bombardment Group seemed to have earned the credit, though the S-2 still distanced himself from the crews' elation and long-term recommendation: "Bombing of all three targets was described as very good. Huge fires were seen and dense clouds of heavy smoke covered all three targets. The actual aiming point was sighted and good results from our bombs are claimed. Crews were convinced that there would be no use of returning to this particular target and they felt equally strong that no more ball bearings would be produced there for some time."[126] This was one raid where the crews would have preferred to complete the postraid assessments themselves, especially whether the target warranted a reattack. Nevertheless, the tenor of the reports showed the group-level S-2s beginning to show confidence in their responsibility for objective reporting.

Reconnaissance squadrons eagerly produced BDA for the high-priority mission, capturing their first overhead photography just forty minutes after the bombers passed over the target. In an unusually expedient step, the Central Interpretation Unit released its first BDA report from poststrike reconnaissance before the CIU's interpreters had even reported on the images taken from the bombers themselves. They had anticipated the unusually high demand for BDA. Smoke and cloud cover was too dense for a thorough assessment, but the interpreters noted of this first pass, "It appears likely that the greater part of the smoke originates from fires burning within the target area."[127] This was fantastic news. Schweinfurt appeared to be engulfed in flame, just as the crews reported.

Their next report, based upon photos taken by bombers' cameras, noted that "although a number of bombs are seen bursting in the target areas, the heaviest concentrations are slightly north, west, and southwest of the targets."[128] There was undoubtedly considerable damage to the target area. However, the gist was that the bombs had not quite centered on the optimal aiming point, and it was too early to determine the extent of damage. Photo interpretation from a "good quality" reconnaissance pass two days later disseminated better news: "All three factories at Schweinfurt and together producing more than half of the roller and ball bearings of Germany have suffered damage as a result of the raid," they wrote, adding as much detail as possible about damaged buildings and facilities.[129] As the dust settled and smoke cleared, allowing for closer investigation, much of the damage appeared only incidental to the ball-bearing factories themselves.

For the many intelligence organizations that advocated attacks on ball-bearing factories, their assessments largely reflected their proximity to the final decision to conduct the raid. The OSS research and analysis branch, given its self-described position as "more distinctly oriented towards the need of the Armed Services than any other research agency," showed its stake in the results and its close partnership (via EOU) with Eighth Air Force.[130] OSS economists projected a positive outlook. With a cautionary caveat due to uncertainty in their "preliminary reports," the OSS economists claimed:

> If these estimates are valid, the Schweinfurt raid will cause both a sharp curtailment of industrial uses of bearings during the next three to five months and at least a temporary and limited reduction of the supply of bearings used in finished munitions. . . . Since it is estimated that the major plant hit in this raid will lose three months output, it appears production will again be close to normal in the early months of 1944. . . . If the estimates of output loss presented above are approximately valid, the margin protecting military use of bearings has now been eliminated.[131]

What was remarkable about their assessment was not that the OSS dealt with considerable ambiguity, though it was to their credit that they recognized it in their preliminary assessments; rather, it was that they cast the ambiguity in such a positive light given the lack of data to support their findings. Implicit in their assessment was that any further successful attacks on ball bearings would yield a direct impact on German matériel, and that reattack would not be essential until the following year. The data behind their assessments may have been ambiguous, but their support to Eaker's and his crews' morale was not.

Arnold's A-2, supporting his own fascination with the ball-bearing idea, gravitated to the OSS information, arguing that "the previously tight German anti-friction bearing situation has been reduced to a serious deficit position by the USAAF attack on Schweinfurt which is believed to have eliminated one-fourth of the normal production of bearings for a three-month period," later adding, "The Schweinfurt achievement will result in the reduction of deliveries to the armed forces of military equipment which would have been in use within six months."[132] These were magic words in the debate for resources with the Army. The bombing success against ball bearings could justify a smaller invasion force and more resources allocated for the AAF's heavy bomber program. The A-2 assessment was aimed directly at helping their boss.

Such optimism was not universal. Just two days later, with the ink of Sorensen's signature still wet on the air staff A-2 report, a separate stack of raid reports circulated among the air staff. These reports, stunning in their sobriety, were attributed by internal correspondence to Col. Harris B. Hull, the plank holder leading VIII Bomber Command's intelligence division since 1942 and an Eaker confidant.[133] Indicating a complete reversal to A-2's perspective, Hull

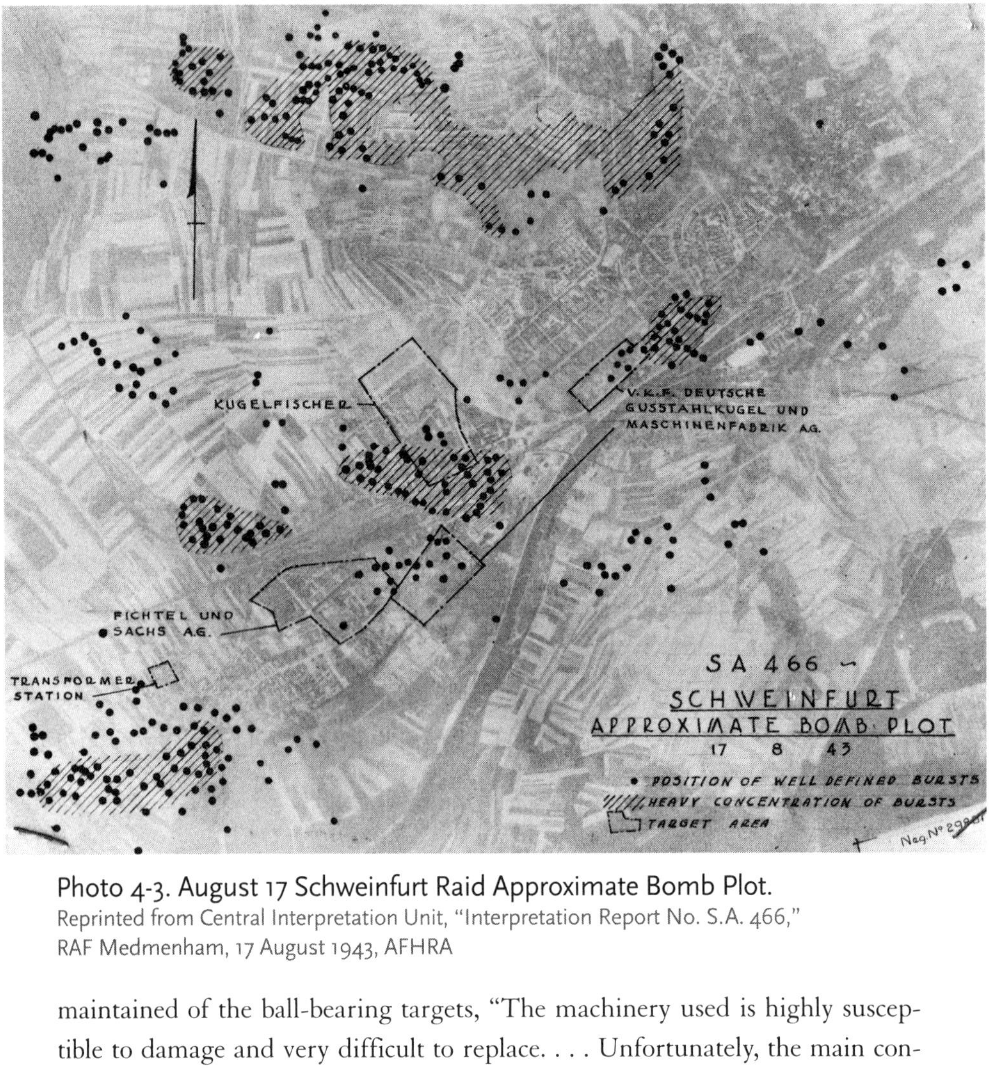

Photo 4-3. August 17 Schweinfurt Raid Approximate Bomb Plot.
Reprinted from Central Interpretation Unit, "Interpretation Report No. S.A. 466," RAF Medmenham, 17 August 1943, AFHRA

maintained of the ball-bearing targets, "The machinery used is highly susceptible to damage and very difficult to replace. . . . Unfortunately, the main concentration of bombs fell between the plants and on the railway track sidings and stations," adding that "great damage was done to the communication and transportation system of the city."[134] That the machinery was highly susceptible to damage was not yet evident (and never would be), and neither was the impact of incidental damage to Schweinfurt's transportation system. It was, however, evident that the target needed another visit if it was to receive the type of damage the target analysts demanded.

Elsewhere in Washington that week, two air staff plans officers attended a peculiar meeting. Rather than rendezvous in their typical war department spaces, however, they convened privately at the office of Mr. Batt, who was continuing his leadership duties with both the War Production Board and SKF Industries. Batt argued that the ball-bearing industry in the United States grew limited in "certain important articles . . . due to the labor difficulties in the industry," but that these articles could be purchased from Sweden, which "would deny them to the enemy."[135] Further, Batt sought an arrangement for additional military aircraft able to transport the ball bearings out of Sweden. When the planners brought this information to their boss, Brigadier General Kuter, he replied skeptically, "If there is a real requirement for these ball bearings or if it is proved that damage could be done to the enemy by our purchase rather than letting them become available to the enemy. [O]ne, two, or three C-47's can and naturally will be made available for this purpose."[136] Batt's motives were anything but transparent, but Kuter was not going to take any chances that the Swedes were taking pressure off of Schweinfurt.

Economists from British RE8 continued their own trend of conservative estimates, and they pulled no punches as they countered the OSS and A-2 assessments with an even more pessimistic outlook: "The attacks on the ball-bearing plants at Schweinfurt caused relatively light damage. . . . This amounts altogether to a loss of about 1 week's supply of total anti-friction bearing output available to Germany. . . . Both plants will have been ready for re-attack immediately after the raid, since the reduction in the rate of output at each was very small."[137] They confidently concluded from the same source material that the raid accomplished negligible results. As they saw it, the raid had not been worth the lives of the many airmen who had perished or even the more fortunate fate of those who had parachuted into harvest wheat fields—probably the only ones who were grateful the RAF had not followed up with a night raid.[138]

Hitler's Vengeance and the Blue Hour

"Bomber" Harris had not simply opted out of the AAF's first attack on ball-bearing plants. In fact, his Bomber Command launched its own massive raid under the lunar glow of 17–18 August 1943, and it did so en masse. However, Harris received a competing priority from an unusual targeting source—Winston Churchill himself—and the highly secretive target had nothing to do with the Pointblank directive. The target was too challenging to attack even with the help of the RAF's radio navigation (OBOE) and the bombers' onboard radar (H2S). Each of these technological inventions warrants brief discussion.

OBOE used ground stations to transmit a signal that a single bomber could process and echo back to the ground; the system could achieve impressive accuracy of just a few hundred yards, but the range was limited to about three hundred miles, which would aid the bombers only about as far as the Ruhr.[139] The British feared that the signal frequency or even an entire avionics unit could wind up with the Germans; this kept them from offering the system for routine AAF bombing.[140]

Creatively nicknamed "Home Sweet Home" by British scientists, H2S employed a "downwards-pointing, rotating antenna" that reflected its "9-cm wave pulses" off of the terrain, which then presented a rudimentary monochromatic picture in the bomber's cockpit.[141] This meant navigators and bombardiers had some ability to see terrain through the weather, although the British had used the system since 1942 to navigate their bombers to the target area, not to aim bombs.[142] The system had inherent errors and limitations, many of which were electronic, but there were other sources of error as well. Operators required considerable training and interpretation proficiency with H2S to decipher the radar returns. For example, variations in terrain reflectivity could make some targets appear differently than reconnaissance photographs of the ground, and highly built-up areas, such as Berlin, could appear as "solid white returns."[143]

As for this special target, Harris knew his crews would need more than their existing technology; they needed ideal environmental conditions and a new tactic. Harris declared, "I knew that I should have to use the main force to ensure destruction of a target of such strategic importance; and that the attack would have to be made in moonlight; there could be no question in trusting only to H2S for the identification and marking of a target of this nature and Peenemünde was far beyond OBOE range."[144] Reacting to unprecedented pressure to produce results, Harris also had his crews practice a "master bomber" tactic, whereby a specially trained crew of his elite Pathfinder force would make a real-time call for trailing bombers to trust the Pathfinder's target markers or to switch bomb releases to "time and distance" from Rügen Island—the initial point prior to the target.[145] It was an innovative scheme, the type that arises from extraordinary circumstances—or at least from extraordinary pressure to succeed.

But the mission's true purpose, to destroy Hitler's dastardly experimental rocket facility at Peenemünde, was too secretive even for the aircrew to know. Instead, crews were fed a contrived but plausible cover story that they were hitting a "radio-location laboratory and aircraft testing site"—a threat against the bombers themselves.[146] The crews were also told they had better get it right on the first attempt or, as Harris put it, the raid "would have to be repeated on the next night, and on all suitable nights thereafter, regardless of casualties."[147] Harris motivated his crews in his own way, dispatched his force of 597 bombers on a one-time operation (dubbed Hydra), and lost 40 bombers and 215 crewmen in the effort—a toll that might have been far worse had Eighth Air Force not absorbed the best of the Luftwaffe's brutal parry earlier that day.[148]

As a target, Peenemünde had been hyped by mystique and controversy.[149] It had indeed emerged as a symbol of British fears for the worst-case scenario—Germans had advanced their long-range rocket program, and the skies over London might soon bellow in clouds of "powerful explosives, poison gas, or perhaps even biological or nuclear weapons."[150] Fear is a powerful human motivator and an extraordinary marketing tool.[151]

As touted by British intelligence, the threat aroused such alarm in Churchill that he had hired his own son-in-law, Duncan Sandys, to lead a hasty investigation into the V-weapons program.[152] Codenamed Bodyline—the act of intentionally aiming at a cricket batsman—Sandys' investigation intimated German foul play by aiming rockets at civilians. Such play "was not only against the rules but certainly unsportsmanlike," later highlighted a British photo interpreter.[153] Behind the British hysteria and Duncan Sandys' report was a power struggle among competing factions of scientists, photo interpreters, and other intelligence analysts to control the narrative of V-weapons discovery as well as the Allied response.[154]

The factions involved in targeting Hitler's V-weapons, a target set that had been unpredictable to operational planners, shifted influence over Allied targeting away from the generals toward a small circle of upper-level intelligence analysts, many of whom were scientists. Photo interpreter Constance Babington-Smith later recalled of the campaign against Hitler's V-weapons, "There were the intelligence experts who weighed all the varied evidence, and upon whose judgment depended what action was likely to be taken."[155] In other words, the analysts who controlled the intelligence about the V-weapons program also controlled the target priorities. Operational commanders had little choice but to follow suit with an emergent target of such apparent political consequence.

The resulting power struggle induced lasting enmity between three groups: British scientists (Lord Cherwell notably among them), who preferred not to admit that German rocket scientists could accomplish what the British scientists could not; photo interpreters, one of whom would be chastised indefinitely by the other factions for allegedly refusing to label "a vertical column 40 feet high and 4 feet thick" as a rocket; and analysts, who represented the increasing importance of nonphotographic forms of intelligence into the realms of targeting and assessment.[156] After Churchill held a war cabinet meeting on 29 June 1943, during which he addressed viewpoints of the disparate factions and committed all sides to disrupting the threat, the feud became more about saving face and seeking prestige.[157] The one argument the three British intelligence factions could agree upon was that locating and neutralizing German long-range weapons demanded maximum effort from the combined bomber offensive. Nevertheless, their differences in opinion over the origins of V-weapons targeting was illustrative of their organizational biases.

The scientists' perspective, promoted by Dr. Reginald Victor "R. V." Jones of British MI6, insisted that credit for pursuing the V-weapons threat (especially rockets) belonged to elite scientists and top-level intelligence analysts. As historian Allan Williams offered, Jones held to a small circle of trust, partly for security, but also because he felt that "a few clever people, even a single individual, can be more effective and efficient than a large organization."[158] He guarded his sources and his side of the story closely.

Jones claimed he was tipped off to German developments in 1942 by a secretive report by a Danish engineer, which purported prototype V-2 launches from Peenemünde that October, as well as the transcript of a bugged conversation between two captive German generals.[159] He even later argued that high-profile fear-mongering by Sandys' report complicated rather than supported his clandestine work, because such reports "resulted in ill-considered questionnaires being sent out to all parts of our agent network."[160] Those such as Jones, who were charged with particularly clandestine inquiry, preferred that their work remain that way, lest their sources became less reliable and their influence more diffuse.

Much to the photo interpreters' dissatisfaction, Jones claimed to have personally identified the first V-2 rocket several days after the CIU's interpreters unsuccessfully reviewed the same images, which gave him "the kind of pulse of elation that you get when after hours of casting you realize that a salmon has taken your line—especially when someone else has had an exhaustive first chance at the pool."[161] Despite a considerable effort by a historian and former photo interpreter to extricate the truth from the disparate claims and probable timelines of V-weapons discovery, perhaps the most that can be said was that the relationship between the scientists and the photo interpreters was "fraught with friction."[162] It seemed everyone with an investigative role wanted the credit for discovering and locating Hitler's V-weapons, but the only near-term certainty would be more battling over target selection by analysts and the commanders they informed.

Photo interpretation advocates did not accept the scientists' argument. They held that their opinions might have cast meaningful shape to the shadows in their images, had their leadership permitted them leeway from "only reporting known facts."[163] For example, Ursula Powys-Lybbe, a British photo interpreter, later argued of the Bodyline investigation: "It must be stressed once again that interpretation officers were not permitted to make definitive statements about any object they might have seen until it had been established by the authorities for what it was in actual terms, no matter what the [photo interpreters] might have deduced personally."[164] The photo interpreters blamed their leadership for unnecessarily stifling their creativity in solving targeting problems.

The photo interpreters also had advocates outside of their own ranks. Notably, General Arnold had been enamored by the story behind the interpreters' role in V-weapons and ski site discovery and of one photo interpreter in particular: "Incidentally, this intelligence was not gained through the underground but from the air," Arnold later quipped in his memoir. "It came from a detailed study of aerial photos by [photo interpretation] experts at Medmenham, including a young WAAF officer named flight officer Constance Babington-Smith."[165] Known to her friends as "Babs" and recognized for her "delicate features" and "sparkling deep intelligence," Babington-Smith conveyed the tale with admirable humility in her own memoir.[166] However, it would seem the scent of her often-cited "L'Heure Bleue" perfume pervaded the impression others had of her more strongly than did her own words.[167]

Babington-Smith adopted a zeal for her work that she expressed through defiant bureaucratic risks. She not only bucked the establishment of her male-dominated service by outwardly maintaining her femininity, but she also applied her creative and expertly tuned imagination as she deliberately investigated photographic images outside the immediate purview of her "everlasting watch for new German aircraft."[168] She examined wooded areas and fields that were normally privileged only to the Army interpreters, leading to her remarkable photographic discoveries in June and November 1943.[169]

Babington-Smith was also no stranger to marketing her craft, having appeared in the Air Ministry's 1941 propaganda film, *Target for Tonight*.[170] Incidentally, her choice of perfume, still marketed by its manufacturer after a hundred years as "endearing, unsettling, captivating," might better describe the endearing impression Babington-Smith made on those who met her, the unsettling effect Hitler's "buzz bombs" had on panic-stricken Londoners, and the captivating grasp Operation Crossbow eventually maintained on Eighth Air Force Bombers as they shifted from Pointblank targets to V-weapons sites.[171]

A third perspective posited that credit for early intelligence regarding Hitler's V-weapons belonged neither to photo interpreters nor scientists, but to a collection of human intelligence sources: "disaffected German nationals; foreign nationals who worked with the Germans but maintained contact with [various] underground movements; and prisoners of war captured in North Africa."[172] This viewpoint held that photo interpreters only succeeded *after* they were instructed what to look for by those who were cleared for other forms of intelligence. This position rested on the idea that V-weapons had been present in reconnaissance photographs for months but had passed through the hands of photo interpreters without remark.[173]

Matters of the target's origins aside, the U.S. air intelligence organizations, with their characteristic preoccupation with efficiency, perceived of Crossbow as yet another distraction from their own preferences. The EOU economists eventually accepted that "some effort" may be required "of a strategically defensive character," with the following stipulation: "In view of the important alternative offensive tasks of our force, it is essential that the Crossbow bombing program as a whole be the most economical and effective, within the limits of the intelligence."[174]

Of course, relationships mattered, and Babington-Smith had been assisting the EOU with its analysis of German aircraft production. She later recalled, "I had made a close study of test beds, because Walt Rostow and the American target experts had wanted to know numbers at each German factory—as evidence of potential output."[175] The EOU, aided by its position in the U.S. embassy, surely understood it was powerless to interfere with the full weight of Churchill's influence over the combined chiefs. Further, the EOU had more to lose in jeopardizing its precious connections with influential actors at the CIU than it might have gained in prestige with AAF leaders by holding strong to its previous targeting recommendations. Besides, the EOU members lived and worked within the V-weapons' range alongside their British counterparts, so a small concession to endorse Crossbow targets might have seemed rational on their part, regardless of whether the actual risk of being hit was very high.

Apart from the motives of the various air intelligence factions, this emotionally charged start to the Crossbow campaign revealed an interaction of opposing air strategies with consequences for both the Allies and the Germans. Although Hitler's V-weapons development clearly did not conform to Lord Cherwell's claim that activity at Peenemünde was "an elaborate German hoax," as historian Roy Stanley has described, there was evidence of a deliberate ploy by German leadership to keep the heat off of the Luftwaffe's stumbling defenses.[176] Erhard Milch, one of Hitler's top Luftwaffe officers, saw advantage in keeping the Allied bombers focused on bombing the V-weapons sites on the French coast because "the men and machines eliminated there won't then get to Germany."[177]

Hitler's V-weapons did not require much accuracy to facilitate German strategy. Fear of V-weapons felt by Londoners drove a massive shift in resources, including absenteeism among workers, evacuation of women and children, and appropriation of 40,000 men as repair workers for recovery from attacks.[178] In a broad sense, the eventual V-weapons attacks may have spiked the Londoners' fears and their responsive measures, but the shift of Allied air campaign resources to disarm the threat was not without its price.[179]

On par with its cost to Pointblank's offensive bombing scheme, Hitler's V-weapons program commanded a shift in air intelligence priorities as well. The V-weapons search devoured 40 percent of Allied photo reconnaissance efforts from the British Isles after 1 May 1943.[180] Further, the CIU reorganized a new subsection devoted exclusively to the V-weapons search, pulling scarce human resources away from other interpretation duties.[181] The British air intelligence organizations realigned to face their perceived immediate threat.

Imperatives to solve the V-weapons mystery stimulated an increasing demand for all-source analysis. A select few (such as wing commander Douglass Kendall) who were cleared for ULTRA, photo interpretation, and prisoner of war interrogation sources began to increase collaboration within the air intelligence enterprise.[182] "Our exact contribution to the delay in V-weapon attack and the reduction of their scope is not measurable," concluded an official history of ULTRA, adding that "months later a diplomatic message of uncertain reliability says that the German necessity to re-convert secret weapons back to single-engine fighter production after the American attacks in February [of 1944] materially delayed the inauguration of the secret weapon attacks."[183] Such bits and pieces of high-level intelligence, nearly useless on their own, took useful shape when paired with other forms of information. Hitler had begun to respond to heavy attacks on his V-1 sites by reprioritizing resources toward his defensive fighters.

With their frightful vengeance weapons and their small, distributed launch sites that were not particularly well suited to daylight precision bombing or night area raids, the Germans exploited a political seam in the Allied air campaign; a fearful threat had allowed scientists to assert themselves among intelligence entities and to seize control of the Allied air campaign. The combined chiefs lacked the independent information to contain this influence. Reichsminister Albert Speer even argued that Allied media played a role in stoking support for V-weapons on the German side. Within the reich, "there was considerable opposition to V-1, including Göring," Speer reflected, "but the press publicity in the United States and Great Britain encouraged the Germans and converted some skeptics."[184] Whether intentional or not, the external audience of Allied media impacted the air campaign's strategy.

It was, after all, a shortage in German manpower that compelled German use of French construction companies in building the V-1 launch sites, which, as one history adds, "positively invited the French workers to conduct espionage."[185] The Crossbow campaign was a confluence of compelling forces: political objectives, fearful outrage, intelligence prestige, and strategic interaction. In a sense, the Crossbow campaign and the air resources it consumed darkened the Allied airmen's hopes for victory through airpower alone. Thus, the independent air campaign eased into an early twilight—when "the sun has set, but . . . the night has not yet found its star."[186] The photo interpreters found their shining star in flight officer Constance Babington-Smith as they credited her with the V-weapons discovery—an act that symbolized perfection in her craft. As one Allied air intelligence officer rose to prominence, too many Germans had already perished for Hitler's strategy to succeed in secrecy.

FIVE

QUADRANT TO SEXTANT

We are now suffering greatly from our shortsightedness in failing to develop capable intelligence officers over a period of years.

—LT. GEN. IRA C. EAKER, 15 DECEMBER 1943[1]

The "Party Line" was, then, both a theory of bombing policy and a related method of analysis. It insisted that targets be chosen in the light of an explicitly defined military aim, linked to the full context of war strategy, and especially to its timing. . . . The "Party Line" was, in short, a doctrine of warfare, not of economics or politics.

—WALT ROSTOW, ENEMY OBJECTIVES UNIT[2]

Quadrant Shifts to the Ground

The week of 17 August 1943 brought more than the first major raid on ball-bearing factories; it offered the next opportunity for the combined chiefs to assemble along with their lead planners and senior staffers in Quebec for the Quadrant conference. This time, Arnold would attend after having sat out of Trident with heart trouble—although, uncharacteristically, he contributed "very little" to the otherwise fiery conference.[3] He made no recorded comments directly advocating for strategic bombing vis-à-vis a ground campaign as he had prodded Eaker. Comments he did make on the European theater involved mostly concerns about replacement crews, loss rates (particularly for the Ploesti raid), and the value additional airbases as far north as Florence, Italy, might provide to strikes against Germany despite a possible need for additional troops to hold a line further north than originally planned—a logic that drew a retort from his boss, General Marshall, that any additional forces in Italy should not draw away from the "overriding priority" of the cross-Channel invasion.[4]

General Marshall, by contrast to Arnold, had a very specific agenda for the meeting to gain full support for Overlord. He wanted consensus to eliminate additional operations in the Mediterranean and to keep the focus on the buildup of forces in England. He insisted on a firm decision one way or the other, so "that definite plans could be made with reasonable expectation of their being carried out."[5] The challenge, as Marshall saw it, was not in the plans themselves, but in the political waffling that typically caused unnecessary delays to military operations, led to inefficient transport between theaters, and increased force requirements once operations began.[6]

Shipping capacity persisted as a frustrating check on the combined chiefs' desired strategy. Just as transatlantic shipping space had delayed the start of bombing in 1942, it would also pose a limiting factor for both the scope and the composition of cross-Channel invasion forces. Marshall had declared his irritation at Trident as well, noting, "The only limit to Torch [the invasion of North Africa] had been the availability of shipping," and the same problem reared up again.[7] Troop redeployments between theaters only added to the problem by consuming shipping from the same pool of oceanic resources, so any potential troop movement from the Mediterranean to England needed to happen sooner rather than later. As an official Army history later reflected, "There was a definite trend toward increasing infantry and airborne divisions during 1943 since strategic and tactical demands as well as the need to save shipping space favored the use of forces that were not so heavily armed or so completely motorized."[8] This shift toward nimbler but more vulnerable ground forces, whether an intentional doctrine shift or an externally imposed limitation, would place an even greater demand on the air superiority mission.

Shortly thereafter (though while still at the conference), Roosevelt released a joint statement with Churchill, based largely on British naval intelligence, purporting that U-boat attacks on Allied ships were in decline: "In the first six months of 1943, the number of ships sunk per U-boat operating was only half that in the last six months of 1942 and only a quarter that in the first half of 1942."[9] Images of U-boat bases may have provided useful indicators, but no metric was more meaningful to the U-boat battle in the Atlantic than the numbers of Allied vessels getting through to their destinations. Nevertheless, the incorrigible Chief of Naval Operations Adm. Ernest King was "surprised to learn that the bombing of U-boat bases in France had been stopped or slowed down," and even if they were presently under control, he felt they were being "refitted with a view to renewing the offensive."[10] King had no intention of relenting his pressure on the AAF to keep its bombsights trained against the U-boats. Pressure slackened, however, from Admiral Sir Dudley Pound on the British side, as he recognized that bombing of U-boat bases on the French coast "did not justify a great diversion from the essential bombing offensive against German fighter factories."[11] Arnold held his tongue; there was an even more important conversation looming.

Adding to Marshall's concerns about the pull of further Army resources into the Mediterranean was the fact that U.S. and British airborne troops had only just initiated their assault on Sicily (Operation Husky) five weeks earlier. With an intense combination of air-ground integration, Allied forces crushed Axis resistance, sending Germans and Italians retreating north from the island in the days prior to the Quadrant conference.

Over the two-month stretch of Husky (bombing actually began on 15 June), the Allies shot down 533 Axis aircraft and destroyed many more on the ground; as tallied by Lord Arthur Tedder, Eisenhower's Mediterranean air commander, "2,000 tons of bombs had been dropped on ports and bases, nearly 7,500 tons on airfields, and no less than 15,500 tons on lines of communication."[12] By comparison, over a similar period of July and August, Eaker's heavy bombers had managed to drop less than 8,200 tons—about a third of the ordnance expended in Husky.[13] For Eighth Air Force, they were the two most productive months thus far in the air campaign; July alone exceeded the total weight of bombs expended in the first eight months combined—a fact anxiously reported by the EOU in September.[14]

Spaatz's Northwest African air force (a component of Tedder's command) not only swept up air superiority, but it also demonstrated extraordinary close air support. Radio-equipped air officers embedded with ground formations coordinated bombing attacks and prevented inadvertent fratricide of Allied troops.[15]

The operation left a favorable impression of airpower in the minds of ground commanders, especially Eisenhower. He appreciated the "vast bombing operation" prior to the invasion, but it was the air interdiction that left an indelible mark: "Entirely aside from its success in defeating the enemy forces, it so badly battered the enemy communications in Sicily and southern Italy that the mobility of his forces was materially lowered and the supply of his troops was a most difficult process."[16] If there was a downside to Husky, it had been the bombers' inability (along with Allied naval forces) to either block the retreating Axis forces or destroy them before they fled across the Straits of Messina.[17] As an Allied joint operation, Husky failed to thoroughly exploit the victory.

Nevertheless, the experience left Eisenhower with high expectations and an unflappable optimism for bombing support to the battlefield, while the bombing raid on oil fields earlier that month on Ploesti seemed to him a superfluous diversion. "Too often we had found the factories listed by our experts as destroyed were again working at full output within a matter of weeks or even days," he reflected.[18] Without an assessment process credible enough to demonstrate the successes of strategic bombing, its appreciation was falling victim in the minds of senior commanders who could see the benefits of air support and interdiction with their own eyes.

Though no American, including Arnold, attempted to address the progress of the CBO in appreciable terms at Quebec, the British did. Air Chief Marshal Portal, relying solely on the assessment produced by the British joint intelligence committee, advocated for additional resources by attempting to show that their efforts were working even if they were not yet conclusive. His gambit was to admit, up front, that "damage caused by the air offensive was difficult to assess in precise terms" and that the effect of industrial attacks "on forces in the field was not immediate and results on these forces would increase as time went on"; he relied instead on emphasizing the German response to Allied attacks, insisting they were on the defensive in the air battle and forced to use their night fighters to repel daylight raids.[19] He pushed the point home at another meeting, using language he knew would resonate with his Army counterparts: "There is no need for us to speculate about the effect of 'Pointblank' on Germany. The Germans themselves, when they weaken the Russian and Mediterranean fronts in the face of serious reverses there, tell us by their acts what importance to attach to it."[20] Portal understood the interactive nature of the air campaign and its inextricable link to enemy will, even if the JIC assessment stood feebly beneath his argument. He offered, as though speaking on behalf of the AAF (especially of Arnold's role to equip): "German fighter strength was stretched almost to the breaking point, and in spite of their precarious situation on the Russian and Mediterranean fronts, they had found it necessary to reinforce their fighter forces on the Western Front from these sources. On the other hand, the expansion of German fighter strength was continuing and had increased 13 percent this year. . . . The Eighth Air Force, who were achieving a great task with their existing resources, believed they could achieve even greater success if their strength was increased."[21] In the final analysis, Portal secured what he had desired from the conference: broad acknowledgment that the CBO had been underresourced and undercommitted for the planned numbers of forces in theater.

However, negotiations produced unintended consequences from the airmen's perspective, especially those whose unvoiced opinions included a belief that airpower could still win on its own. The combined chiefs again revised the Pointblank directive, subordinating the air campaign's success to that of the ground forces. The directive now wove in the primary employment of heavy bombers for interdiction: "The progressive destruction and dislocation of the German military, industrial and economic system, the disruption of vital elements of lines of communication, and the material reduction of German air combat strength by the successful prosecution of the Combined Bomber Offensive is a prerequisite to Overlord (barring an independent and complete Russian victory before Overlord can be mounted). This operation must therefore continue to have highest strategic priority."[22]

Once air superiority might be assured, whether to forego further independent airpower or to support ground forces was an unnecessary argument. The lingering ambiguity was whether interdiction of German transportation or dislocation of economic resources would be the better use of airpower, not only in the months leading into the invasion, but all the way to victory. Eaker's air campaign had not shown appreciable success with submarine efforts, secured any reasonable degree of continental air superiority, or inflicted industrial impacts beyond reducing the German cushion in oil and rubber. Adding to this list of challenges, Eaker gained the task of closing down ground lines of communication and another new inescapable priority.

The Blind, the Weary, and the Wishful

On 27 August Eaker sent a task force based around his 3rd Air Division to continue Eighth Air Force's foray into delaying Hitler's V-weapons program. This target, described in VIII Bomber Command files as "the Aeronautical Facilities Station at Watten," was raided for the first time by Eaker's 1st and 3rd Divisions just eleven days earlier.[23] The concrete monstrosity located there fell under an even greater shroud of ambiguity than had Peenemünde. A CIU photo interpreter later told of its origin: "In mid-May 1943, a large concrete structure was discovered near Watten in the Pas de Calais. . . . It was a mystery and it could not be connected with any known military objective."[24] Hitler had apparently not intended any sort of grand disclosure, and this made the facility even more attractive as a target to the intelligence analysts. A special inquiry chartered by the prime minister to Duncan Sandys' Crossbow committee (known as the Sanders mission) would clarify its purpose, though not necessarily its importance: "Watten was intended to be a chemical factory associated with Crossbow sites. . . . There are no indications that it was to be used for projection of any type of missile."[25] Watten was a special chemical factory indeed.

As opposed to photo interpreters, British scientists felt no compulsion to base their investigative reports on provable facts. As to Watten's purpose, they reasoned, "The aluminum tanks give some lead, in that they are of a type already associated with German technique for handling hydrogen peroxide. In addition, it can be deduced from the extensive air-conditioning system that the process involved the handling of unpleasant gasses."[26] If the reich planned to produce ample hydrogen peroxide, which could play a role in rockets as well as "the launching gear of the flying bomb," then Watten was a necessary target as far as British intelligence analysts were concerned.[27] As intelligence consumers, the bomber crews needed to know only enough to help them recognize their target and to keep them motivated.[28] The idea that was passed along during the mission brief was to take out this "special construction" while it was still being built.[29] First-time success was paramount.

This 7 September raid was the second consecutive mission to Watten where a mixture of environmental factors and human error trashed the crews' bombing performance far worse than enemy defenses. The previous effort, just two weeks prior, had been stymied by haze and an ill-conceived plan as three of the four formations attacked westbound into the setting sun. Crews of the 1st Bombardment Wing, comprising the third wave across the target, seemed to come unglued as they fought through the blinding orange glare, and their S-2s ensured the postmission reports noted as much. For example, the 306th Bombardment Group's S-2 included little about his crews' bomb damage, but he noted their complaints that "you can't fly formation when you can't see."[30] The 305th Bombardment Group S-2 captured similar irritation: "The crews as a mass were very bitter about having to bomb into the late afternoon sun," he noted, adding with heartbreaking disappointment that the group's lead bombardier somehow managed to locate the target, but "the navigator accidently touched the toggle switch with his arm about 90 seconds before the proper time."[31] Many crews and their group intelligence officers were frustrated, and they called it as they saw it in their reports.

Of the sixteen total bomb groups that dropped more than 360 tons of bombs that afternoon as the crews practically flew blindly across the target, two groups combined to put nineteen weapons close to the aiming point.[32] In spite of the hundreds of stray bombs, the two fortunate clusters of bombs succeeded well enough for the CIU photo interpreter to conclude, "While these [clusters] fell almost an hour apart, together they blanket the target."[33]

Unfortunately, the effort was not successful enough to satisfy Duncan Sandys. The 3rd Air Division S-2 received a message from higher headquarters two weeks later, on 6 September, to brief his crews: "The target was damaged in previous attack by aircraft of this wing, and it is desired to completely destroy the installation before construction has been completed."[34] Perhaps with better equipment, training, and tactics for poor visibility conditions, the crews might have succeeded with the target the first time. In any case, Duncan Sandys had apparently garnered enough influence from Eaker's intelligence and planning staffs to assess the bombing and force the reattack.

On 7 September, Eaker launched his 3rd Air Division, still under the command of Colonel LeMay, on a return visit to Watten. LeMay went heavy. All 147 aircraft that he dispatched carried a pair of 2,000-pound bombs in hopes of irreparably damaging the concrete of the main building as it was still being poured (see photo 5-1).[35] Only fifty-eight bombers managed to attack the target, primarily due to weather over the French coast, so they ended up bringing home

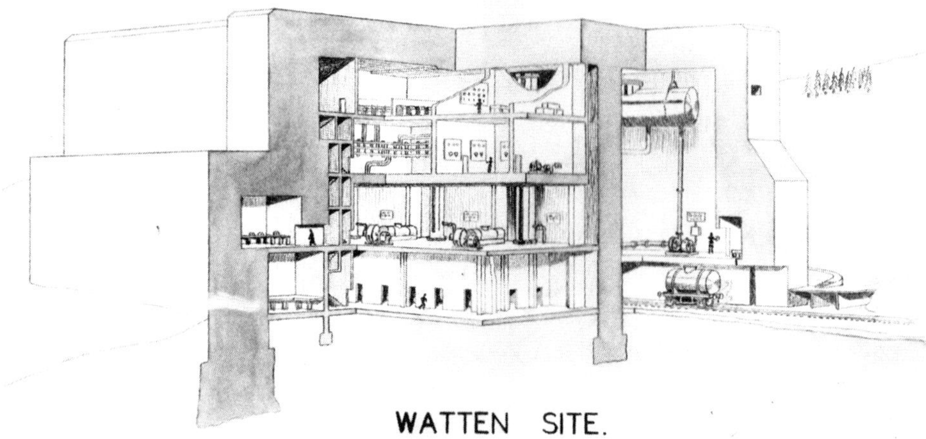

Photo 5-1. Perspective view showing size and strength of main building at Watten. Reprinted from Air Ministry, Investigation of the "Heavy" Crossbow Installations in Northern France, in Report by the Sanders Mission the Chairman of the Crossbow Committee, #505.58–32, 21 February 1944, AFHRA

more bombs than they dropped.[36] Weather at the target was exactly as forecast; about half of the sky was obscured by a mix of swelling cumulus and cirrus clouds—not bad for that time of year, but still too much for the bombers to sort through with their visual bombing techniques, especially given the small target.[37] Most of the bombers simply followed orders—and their leaders—back to England.

The bomber crews were nonplussed. No crew wanted to carry its bombs over enemy territory and back home again, especially after taking flak in the process; not only did they feel robbed of mission performance, but for practical purposes, they would not even gain the boost in aircraft performance from reducing aircraft weight.[38] Having gained visual contact with a secondary target—in this case, "any active airdrome"—and still not bombed anything was enough to inspire the crews to provide remarkably candid feedback up the chain of command.[39] For example, one crew from the 94th Bombardment Group fired back during interrogation that they failed to bomb due to "cloud cover. However,

[we] believe we could have bombed an airdrome in France. Saw St. Omer field and St. Englebert field."[40] The crews had no reservations in blaming the plan or the established procedure of silently following the lead crew. As the crews saw it, their headquarter's leadership was buying into targets that the crews could not hit in bad weather with the equipment they had. As to the name of the secondary target listed on their group's immediate telephone report up to 4th Bomb Wing Headquarters, their S-2 simply listed "none."[41] Maybe the group's lead bombardier and the group S-2 bought so fully into the importance of the primary target that they had not given much thought about listing the day's approved secondary option—one that would have helped gain air superiority for D-day. In any case, the S-2 did not highlight the missed opportunity up the chain of command.

The best that could be said of this second mission to Watten was that no bombers were lost, despite "moderate accurate fire" from flak batteries—some of which appeared to originate from railroad guns in the target area.[42] No enemy fighters even bothered to respond. Nevertheless, bombing performance was abysmal. Of the fifty-seven total bomb bursts that appeared in the BDA images, only five could be confirmed in the target area; a few fell along a roadway, and "the balance are in the woods nearby," noted a CIU photo interpreter.[43] Photos from a reconnaissance mission flown a few hours after the attack showed the same. Though the images were of poor quality, as expected given the cloud cover, the pilot maneuvered to snap the photographs at a favorable angle. A CIU interpreter could see enough to confirm the ineffectual attack: "No significant new damage is seen."[44]

An Eighth Air Force monthly summary produced a few weeks later recorded of this raid: "The attack on the special objective in the Pas de Calais area was again successful, damage inflicted on this installation."[45] While it is unclear who produced the report, whether Eaker acknowledged it, or if Arnold read it, it is clear that the Eighth Air Force report did not include an accurate impression based on the bomb damage assessments or the crews' candid feedback. Eighth Air Force had taken on a character of selling its success and scrubbing negative feedback as reports proceeded up through channels.[46] If the Watten mission should have demonstrated anything to Eighth Air Force, it was that daylight precision bombing, weary crews, and blind visibility did not mix, no matter who promoted the target or how wishful they were about stopping the enemy's cheating intentions or even winning the war with airpower.[47]

COUNTING BOMBS AND FEIGNING INTEREST

In addition to the attack on Watten, Eighth Air Force attacked another target on 7 September. After Schweinfurt's losses, Eaker spent the subsequent weeks focused on German airfields and aircraft repair facilities in occupied territories. Although airfields were not Pointblank targets, aircraft repair depots such as the one at Brussels-Evere fell broadly under the Pointblank directive's guidelines, though neither had been endorsed by the air intelligence organizations.[48] As reported by VIII Bomber Command, this raid on the German-occupied facilities in Belgium featured 104 B-17s dropping more than 1,200 500-pound bombs; the crews achieved direct hits on hangars, factory workshops, and barracks and left a multitude of craters across the airfield while taking zero losses.[49] The raid seemed an easy feather in the cap for Eaker, and certainly one that might aid the aim of achieving air superiority for the eventual cross-Channel invasion, but that still did not make the airfield itself—or any of the seven airfields that Eaker attacked with his B-17s during the second half of September—a Pointblank target.[50]

Nevertheless, the plan for 7 September called for "two forces of three groups each" from Brigadier General Anderson's 1st Bombardment Division; all six groups were to employ the bomb-on-leader technique, meaning all aircraft in each group would drop simultaneously from their position in the formation based upon the navigation and aiming solution of the leader.[51] In a composite formation with the 92nd, the 306th Bombardment Group formed the rear group, which gave them the best view of the devastation from the preceding groups. After the exhilarated aircrews landed in England, the 306th Bombardment Group S-2 completed the postflight interrogation and reported on his crews' apparent success, along the aggressive mindset of the group's lead bombardier: "Bombing excellent, as confirmed by photographs. Aiming point of this group had been hit by previous group when our A/C arrived over the target. Lead bombardier quickly changed aiming point further north and our bombs were seen to hit along northwest edge of field, amongst hangars, workshops, barracks, and administrative buildings."[52]

Using the bomb camera prints the next day, the Central Interpretation Unit's photo interpreters attempted to characterize the damage. Smoke from the bomb impacts partially obscured the airfield images, but the interpreters were able to describe several concentrations of bombs in and around the target area, including direct hits on the airfield and factory area where "the concentration is so heavy that an accurate count is impossible but at least 150 distinct bursts are seen."[53] From the appearance of it, the raid had been a dazzling success, though the group's bomb plot showed only 33 of the 1,243 bombs (2.7 percent) dropped within 1,000 feet of the aiming point, and 979 of the bombs dropped could not be located at all (see photo 5-2).[54] Perhaps there was more to learn than could be gleaned from counting bombs on the strike photos or the bomb plot. None of the methods—the verbal reports, the photo interpretation, or the bomb plotting—seemed particularly reliable, and the accuracy could not account for the fact that an entire bomb group had deliberately shifted its aim point.

A single reconnaissance pass a little more than three hours after the raid failed to capture anything of value, due partly to clouds, although much of the area of interest was not within the area covered by the photographs.[55] The CIU released a follow-up report anyway, but any real sense of what the raid had accomplished would have to wait. Another report two weeks later finally tallied up the damage, including "210 craters on the airfield," but offered no insight into the airfield's operational status, repair activity, or any other indicators of enemy intent.[56] For reasons that could only be described as a lack of priority, probably due to Bodyline and Crossbow requirements, reconnaissance flights did not capture images suitable for further analysis until nearly four months after the raid. The first effort to produce a "clearance and reconstruction report" required an additional two weeks after the eventual reconnaissance flight.[57]

The results in the follow-up BDA report were not worth the wait. Along with a list of buildings under repair, it offered a generic summary: "Reconstruction of the framework of damaged buildings and fresh roof covering is visible, but constructional work and re-equipment may continue after roofing material has been re-laid before a factory is once more in production."[58] Flight officer Babington-Smith's L-section, specializing in aircraft reports, added commentary that several aircraft appeared, including "nine light-colored Me-110s."[59] Their analysis was scientific in its description but safely devoid of creative insight, as their training had taught them "a vertical air photograph is not a picture but a precise mathematical document."[60] Was the repair facility active or not, and why had they referred to it as a factory? These sorts of questions were neither anticipated nor answered.

From the Brussels-Evere bomb damage assessments, a number of observations began to emerge: crews did what they could to get their bombs on the target area; the images neither showed all the bombs nor told the full story of their effects; reconnaissance opportunities might be sparse amid competing priorities; and the assessments—especially if single-source—could be inconclusive, if even complete. The CIU's interpreters were comfortable with their routine work, but reconnaissance efforts were clearly not committed to Eaker's attacks on airfields.

Eaker had added targets and shifted priorities partly because he wanted to show his plan was "a practical job from an active theater" and not something they could produce in Washington, even if he had to "accentuate our increase in bombing accuracy" to justify his inclusions into his plan.[61] That those targets came from him, not the air intelligence organizations, did not provide the latter with much incentive to generate assessments contrary to their own targeting recommendations, in the same way they did for the ball-bearing raids. None of the repair facilities or airfields Eaker added were in Germany—behind the Luftwaffe's defensive curtain—where the air intelligence–recommended targets were.

AN AIR INTELLIGENCE BOMBSHELL

On 10 September 1943 Brig. Gen. Ed Sorensen finally submitted the response concocted by his A-2 division with a heavy dose of OSS assistance to answer Arnold's task from the war department of two months before. It was far too late to have helped Arnold at Quebec, but it was not too late to continue his longstanding disagreement with Eaker—especially that of injecting influence from Washington. With the Quadrant conference, the Schweinfurt-Regensburg mission and the blusterous COA assessment in hindsight, Arnold's most senior intelligence officer completed his sobering and focused appraisal. Sorensen stipulated up front that "much of the basic material presented was provided by the Office of Strategic Services and the Office of Economic Warfare."[62] His opening remarks, while seemingly innocuous, served to not only bolster the report's credibility, but also snub the COA, which was the theme throughout the argument that followed.

For example, Sorensen continued, "This report attempts to go beyond the mere cataloguing of physical damage," as the COA report had done, "by evaluating the significance of such damage to German war production from the point

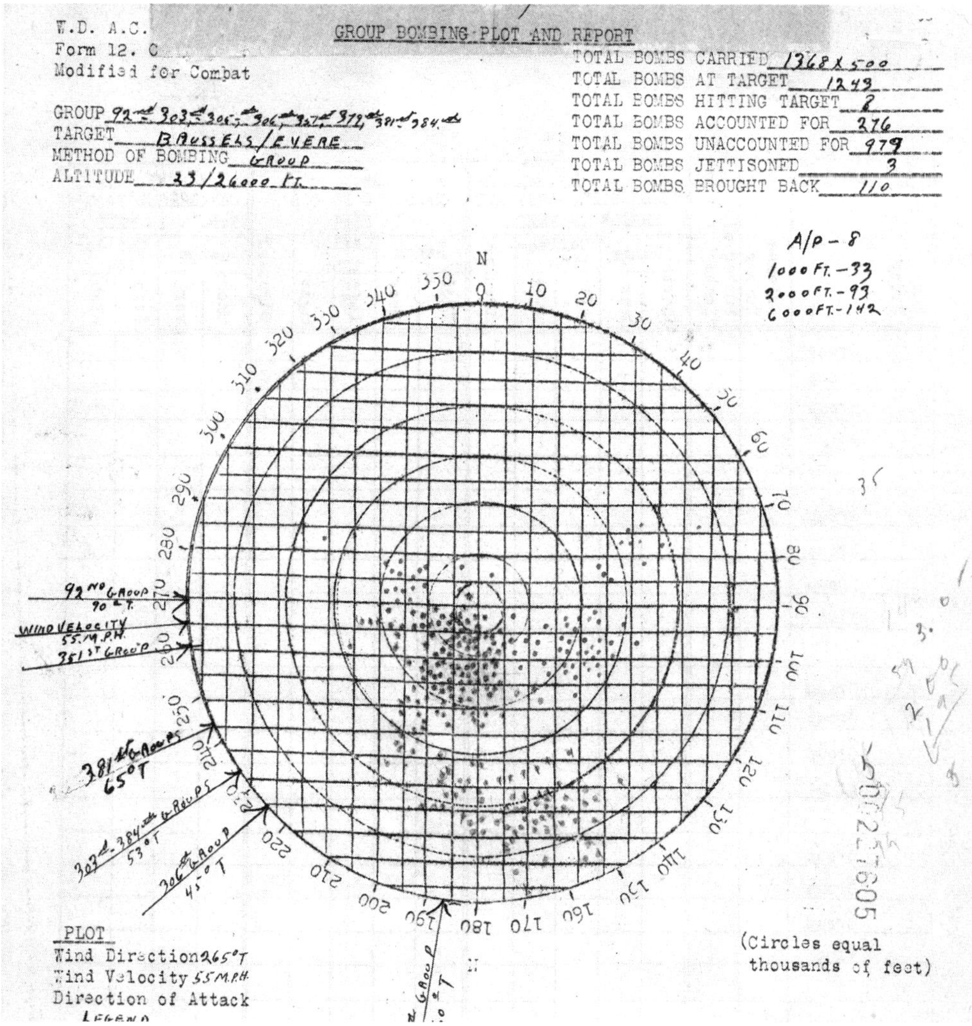

Photo 5-2. Group bombing plot—Brussels/Evere Mission.

Reprinted from Headquarters, 1st Bombardment Division, "Group Bombing Plot and Report," in Brussels/Evere Mission, 7 September 1943, AFHRA

of view of military capabilities."[63] He then added, as if echoing Arnold's private words to Eaker, the report would "fairly review the accomplishments of the bomber offensive," which the COA report had not done.[64] Sorensen sensed he had the bureaucratic advantage, and he exploited the opportunity.

Sorensen steered his report clear of explicit references to BDA, choosing instead to project the trends suggested by the small but rapidly increasing weight

Photo 5-3. Bomb-damage photo of Brussels Airdrome. Reprinted from Headquarters, 1st Bombardment Division, "Bomb-damage photo, Brussels Airdrome," in Brussels/Evere Mission, 7 September 1943, AFHRA

of Eighth Air Force attacks.[65] Of Eaker's Eighth, Sorensen reflected that it had "passed from infancy to promising adolescence," along with the "patterns" formed by its combined raids with the RAF's indirect effects, and its ever-deeper penetrations into Germany.[66] He had even ventured into the space left incomplete by the COA and British JIC reports by attempting to assess indirect effects such as absenteeism (due to "deaths, injuries, damage to communications and utilities, and housing damage"), the cost of repairs, and the political and social consequences of bombing.[67] Sorensen had outmaneuvered the emergent air intelligence bureaucracy and assumed control of air campaign assessment for the U.S. side, and he owned it with a nuanced argument to win over Arnold as well as Marshall.

Two distinctions of the A-2's report exemplified its newfound power to influence the air campaign narrative. First, Sorensen conjured an image that Eaker's Eighth had cast the German air force onto the horns of a dilemma—not the other way around:

> The Eighth Air Force effort to date is justified even if judged solely in the light of its effect in reducing the GAF [German air force] fighter strength. In this connection it has—
>
> 1. Cut German single-engine fighter production for 1943 by 1,200 planes, the equivalent of a complete stoppage of all German fighter aircraft plant for six weeks;
> 2. Destroyed in combat 2,100 GAF fighters, excluding "probable claims";
> 3. Increased GAF combat losses to the point where Eighth Air Force claims alone amount to 75 percent of current production;
> 4. Lowered the percentage of serviceable planes available to the GAF by damaging major repair facilities;
> 5. Compelled the GAF to concentrate over 51 percent of all its single engine fighters (and best pilots) in the west at the expense of urgent needs of the Russian and Mediterranean fronts—itself an eloquent tribute to the threat of the bomber offensive.[68]

Over the coming months, the Luftwaffe's predicament could become increasingly dire as the Allied bombers amassed their strength. Sorensen projected, "Bombing sorties of the Eighth Air Force may increase from 1,960 during August, to approximately 7,685 during March, 1944, a 400 percent increase," along with a commensurate "5 to 1 ratio of bomb tonnage to be dropped."[69] Attacks against the German air force, as the top priority for the Eighth, would pitch the Luftwaffe into an even more precarious position, he argued, "suffering prohibitive single engine fighter wastage or conserving fighter strength through refusal to intercept or to close with the bombers."[70] The reich could use and lose its

Luftwaffe or hold it back as Allied bombers lay waste to its base of industrial support. Now was the time, Sorensen contended, to build unrelenting pressure on the reich and prove the value of independent bombing. The report was not simply a reflective air campaign assessment, but a complete evaluation of the present situation along with specific policy recommendations for Arnold.

Second, Arnold's A-2 finally committed to a clear argument that submarine attacks had not been worth it. Sorensen's argument was a complete reversal from the intelligence estimates from the same office after Casablanca. His report revealed its support from the EOU economists, as it reflected their position that any positive bombing results on U-boat bases were "nullified by the sharp drop in the number of U-boats at sea which followed increased sinkings."[71] In short, the Navy and British Admiralty, not the squandered bombing effort, had turned the tide against the U-boats. The entire bombing effort against the submarine industry proved only to keep a measure of balance in the German position with no reasonable potential to impact the war, and it was no secret that Eaker had elected to attack U-boat bases (for training and reprieve) more than his boss preferred.

Most remarkable of A-2's newly established dominance of CBO assessment was not its evaluation of past performance, or even its eerily accurate forecasts of potentialities—influential as they were. Through his thorough assessment, Sorensen not just reinforced but also extended the argument made against the G-2 by General Arnold (with support from two brigadier general ACTS graduate pilots on his staff, McNarney and Brett) two years earlier: airmen should own air intelligence, and that included assessing the air campaign. Sorensen, undoubtedly keen to point out this achievement, bothered to highlight that his report was prepared by his office "and is concurred in by the ACofS, G-2"—a statement unconscionable during Brigadier General Miles' earlier tenure in the G-2 seat.[72] As A-2, Sorensen gained an independent voice in shaping General Arnold's perspective on future expectations for Eighth Air Force. In fact, on 30 August 1943, Sorensen also literally secured independence for his A-2 division from the Army's G-2. Major General George V. Strong, then the assistant chief of staff of the Army, G-2, disseminated a memorandum officially abolishing the air unit within the Army's military intelligence division.[73] From then on, the Army G-2 would depend upon the Air Force A-2 to provide all matters of air intelligence.

Sorensen celebrated with a word of caution to his own division, reminding them that this recognition came with new responsibility. He emphasized that "the intent of the G-2 to lean more heavily" on the A-2 meant that air analysts had to rise to meet increasing demand; Sorensen insisted his analysts provide the G-2 with "high priority" and "efficient service," such that the air intelligence received by the G-2 be "as good as or better" than that previously provided by its own air unit.[74] Finally, he summarized where the A-2 fit in his service's broader fight for independence: "The closest liaison, cooperation, and understanding between the officers and offices of [the A-2 and the G-2] is an absolute necessity of the just value of and emphasis on the proper use of air power [and] is to be reflected in the overall intelligence studies of the War Department."[75] Sorensen intended to follow through on his victory, and he did so with his report's discussion of ball bearings.

To Sorensen, Schweinfurt symbolized the complexity of air target selection and the depth of industrial, economic, and military intelligence uniquely necessary to the air component's mission. With Schweinfurt, he proved to the G-2 that the epitome of an air target was too different from that of traditional Army intelligence and that air intelligence was truly a different endeavor requiring different specialization. For example, Sorensen explained in his report that the raid on Schweinfurt, along with the indirect effects of several RAF area attacks on other ball-bearing factories, had caused a loss of just 10 percent of annual ball-bearing production for the Axis, but that resulting damage would account for 30 percent over the period from 17 August to 17 November. Moreover, "the impact of this loss will be aggravated by the specialization of production facilities which will make it impossible to concentrate all undamaged capacity on output of highest priority."[76] In other words, bearings were not readily substituted in manufacturing. He wanted his audience—Arnold as well as war department staff—to recognize the industrial complexity inherent in such target analysis, and that his office firmly grasped this complexity. As to "future possibilities," Sorensen redoubled his argument:

> It appears likely that production will again be close to normal by December 1943, unless further raids on the industry are undertaken. The tightness of the Axis bearing situation prior to aerial attack, the apparent major success of the Schweinfurt raid, and the fundamental significance of anti-friction bearings in the production of military equipment, all

> emphasize the conclusion that further attacks on the industry will greatly intensify a deficiency which already seriously endangers the enemy's fighting capabilities. Maximum effects of additional raids will be realized by bringing such pressure to bear during the next three critical months.[77]

As Sorensen would have it, Eighth Air Force should not relent on Schweinfurt under any circumstances, and Sorensen would not relent on controlling the narrative. In all, the A-2's 10 September report became the rubric through which Arnold might evaluate future CBO phases, including Eaker's performance over the next three months. As the various air intelligence organizations jockeyed for influence and produced their campaign-level assessments, the one thing they had in common was that they had all seemed to have turned the spotlight on Eaker. His bombers had not yet produced results commensurate with their targeting recommendations.

Bombing Blind and the Emden Do-Over

Before the month was out, Eaker's Eighth raided Germany for the first time using onboard radar navigation technology for bombing. Eaker had been keenly aware since the year prior that the British were ahead of the Americans in this area and had requested of Washington "that we employ to the fullest extent possible all the late instrument navigational and bombing devices so that we can operate in a wider range of weather than has been possible in the past."[78] That opportunity had finally arrived. The AAF evaluated both the British OBOE and H2S with an aim to improve blind bombing. However, H2S made for the better near-term option for Eighth Air Force while engineers at the Massachusetts Institute of Technology's radiation laboratory worked on producing an enhanced version (later known as H2X) for American use.[79]

Because the H2S radar signal did not reflect off water as it did off terrain, small coastal targets appeared distinctly on the cockpit display. According to Eaker's semimonthly report, he selected Emden as a target for this reason, along with the idea that the bombing of Hamburg had increased German reliance upon the port city, and because it was "indeed a pinpoint objective . . . and therefore required precision bombing of the utmost accuracy"—an add-on Arnold probably read as an excuse in the ex post facto report.[80] Two facts Eaker did not list on the report were that Emden was within escort range of P-47s carrying seventy-five-gallon drop tanks, which was certainly a positive, and that Emden was (as Air Force historians pointed out) "not a CBO target," which it was not.[81]

Lieutenant Colonel Carl Norcross (whose formal complaint had triggered an investigation into the Harrisburg Air Intelligence School in 1943) authorized a message to motivate the bomber crews: "This port has come into greater prominence since the bombing of Hamburg and the increasing difficulty of using Rotterdam. . . . The exact amount of tonnage being handled at the present time is not known but with added traffic it is sure to be far in excess of 500,000 tons. . . . The objective is to knock out the shipping traffic."[82] Crews were to believe that their bombs would shut down an entire port on this first blind bombing mission. Nothing in the message implied that the target might be easy to locate, with or without the new H2S, how difficult the task to shut it down might be, or how long the analysts expected the port to remain out of service—answers to any of which might have added credibility to the embellished mission statement.

On 27 September, VIII Bomber Command dispatched 305 bombers from its 1st and 3rd Bombardment Divisions. They split into two formations, each led by H2S-equipped Pathfinders from the 482nd Bombardment Group, to bomb the port facilities at Emden. According to the 3rd Bombardment Division's tasking order, "if visual bombing is not possible, combat wing mass bombing procedure . . . will be followed."[83] The order specified Pathfinder pyrotechnic signals—large, colored parachute flares—to "skymark the target," and subsequent bombers would aim on the flares.[84] The procedure was relatively straightforward, even given VIII Bomber Command's reliance on "tentative operations instructions."[85]

As expected, weather over the target was poor. Unexpectedly (at least from Eaker's perspective), so too were the bombing results.[86] VIII Bomber Command's roll-up of events reported, "The Pathfinder plane was to drop markers over Emden if the target was obscured by cloud. This plan was followed but the crews did not have sufficient experience in this type of operation to take full advantage of the flares."[87] As their command reported it, the crews needed more training.

Crew reports from the lead formation explained little of what had actually occurred over the target area. It was as if no one had told the crews what they were supposed to do. Many crews reported during postflight interrogation that they had simply withheld their bombs because of the weather, while others seemed to pile up excuses to see if one of them would work. For example, one crew from the 410th Bomb Squadron recorded a hodgepodge of unrelated remarks: "Could not see town . . . 8/10 undercast; not over pathfinder flares. Lead group did not drop."[88] Another from the same squadron did not drop on the target because "clouds covered it," so they jettisoned their bombs "near coast at mouth of river," presumably to shed weight, but it was clear who had given the order.[89] From the crews' perspectives of events, the failed performance sounded more like a leadership problem.

Group S-2 reports from the trailing formation, flown by 1st Bomb Division, reflected a different experience. Crews apparently understood their task, but the mission still went awry. After resigning himself to the fact that only two aircraft in the entire group dropped bombs in the vicinity of Emden, the S-2 from the 305th related his crews' concerns that the entire mission had nearly turned to disaster: "Two groups from another combat wing were crossing directly under our group over the target area and that our bombs would have fallen on these groups if released."[90] The 92nd Bomb Group S-2 accepted his crews' arguments that they had dropped as directed on the Pathfinder flares, though results were, understandably, "unobserved."[91] Finally, the 306th Bomb Group S-2 oriented his feedback toward the elite Pathfinders: "Crews report flares over the IP [initial point] instead of the target," so the confounded crews ended up bombing anywhere "from [the] IP to the target to [the] coast going out, making intense concentrations unlikely."[92] Crews of the 1st Bomb Division reported their results with candor to their intelligence officers, who helped to articulate the mission's challenges up the chain of command.

Unfortunately, the plan had called for a red flare at the IP, a yellow flare for "bombs away" of the lead wing, and three more red flares for bomb release of the trailing wing.[93] The Pathfinders may well have dropped their flares according to plan, but the glow of fire through the low-level clouds and smoke undoubtedly made for a puzzling spectacle—especially to crews performing a mission unlike any they had before. Other than what the crews had told them, the intelligence officers had little independent evidence to review, so it was difficult for them to determine what exactly had gone wrong, much less where the bombs had fallen.

Aside from the crews' verbal feedback, group- and division-level intelligence officers struggled to produce meaningful bomb damage assessments. For example, the S-2 from the 94th Bombardment Group recorded, "Resulting bombing believed poor due to target being entirely covered by clouds."[94] Of course, bombing through the clouds had been the intent of the mission in the first place—why should the bombing be poor only because it was unobserved? The 1st Bomb

Division photo interpreter attempted his assessment but found he had nothing to assess; he returned a memorandum to the division's A-2 merely noting that all mission photography was "completely 10/10's cloud obscured."[95]

In another example, a base photographic officer did not even bother to comment on his wing's bombing performance in his photo and bomb plotting report. He simply remarked that an aerodrome and army camp appeared on a photograph of the target area.[96] This may have been useful poststrike intelligence, but it was not useful BDA. The photographic officer installed eight cameras onboard 94th Bomb Group aircraft, but two were lost, and only one returned with images, from which he noted: "Bomb bursts shown on the one roll obtained. Bursts not believed to be of 94th bombs."[97]

As with visual bombing, the CIU interpreters would attempt to pick up where the unit-level interpreters left off. After reviewing all available images, the CIU interpreters concluded that most of the bombs landed in nearby fields and villages.[98] Nearly all of the bombs dropped had been of the lighter five-hundred-pound general-purpose and one-hundred-pound incendiary variety, which did not help the interpreters spot craters and damage, and there was no dedicated reconnaissance sortie. The BDA from this mission was disappointing, if not from the bombers' inaccuracies, then from the absence of usable information.

After scrubbing a repeat mission just two days later, which allowed a little more time for all involved to think through the postmission assessments, Eaker launched another blind bombing raid on Emden on 2 October.[99] Of 349 bombers dispatched, only 2 were lost, thanks to the "magnificent" fighter support all the way to the target.[100] S-2 reports revealed an extraordinarily different mission than the one launched not even a week prior. Both the intelligence officers and the crews seemed to adapt to the new mission. The 306th Bomb Group S-2 reported that the crew's bombs dropped into the clouds "about where the flares indicated, allowing for drift of flares," but the crew felt blind bombing would improve "as soon as there is a pathfinder with each Wing."[101] Handwritten notes from the 94th Bomb Group S-2 suggested a similar perspective. Though the S-2 noted bombing results could not be observed, he added that the bombs appeared "to be a good pattern" as they dropped into the flares. There was no telling from the on-board cameras where the bombs had landed, but at least the crews had a sense that they had done their part correctly. The S-2 also recorded constructive inputs from his crews that the Pathfinder's flares should be reconfigured to smoke sooner since they had "dropped too far down almost to observe."[102] Interestingly, someone crossed the remark off the S-2's teletype request form before the report was transmitted to the 3rd Bombardment Division on behalf of his group commander.[103] It would seem not all of the crews' feedback made it up the chain.

By the second mission, issues with formation-bombing deconfliction, Pathfinder signals, and mission leadership appeared to have been resolved. This time, the field orders (and late corrections thereto) ensured all bomb groups would take lateral spacing from each other well prior to the target, even if they were not yet sure if the target would be visual; Pathfinders switched their "bomb release" signal to a much clearer indicator of "three large green flares"; and the airborne air division leader would now be empowered to make a verbal radio transmission—"king-pin" for blind bombing or "take interval" for visual bombing.[104] No plan could be perfect from the start, but at least they had developed a crystal-clear game plan for the likely airborne contingencies.

The day after the raid, a reconnaissance sortie finally captured photographs to evaluate damage from both missions, and the CIU wasted no time disseminating its report. The CIU photo interpreter noted little damage to the town of Emden but "heavy damage" to Emden Hafen (the port area), including damage to several buildings, floating docks, quay walls, and barges.[105] While blind bombing raids cannot be said to have shut down the port of Emden, per the original mission order for these raids, one thing can be stated for certain: both the crews and the intelligence officers seemed to convert the 1,597 tons of bombs dropped on these two missions to Emden into a crucial ton of learning.[106] Even if some forms of feedback did not survive to final drafts, data captured in postmission intelligence reports had played an essential role in marketing good ideas up the chain of command and in highlighting what had gone wrong the first time. Although General Anderson had levied the blame for the first mission on aircrew training, everyone—including his headquarters-level planners, intelligence officers, and mission leaders—needed to learn as well.

Spinning Wheels over Ball Bearings

The August Schweinfurt raid had not achieved the level of destruction that the targeting theory demanded or the intelligence organizations expected. The mediocre performance, with its inconclusive results, had neither validated nor invalidated the ball-bearing industry as a viable target. ULTRA intercepts, while unclear in their precise intent, added intrigue by indicating the Germans had

Photo 5-4. BDA image after 2 October raid on Emden showing areas of damage to the port. Reprinted from Central Interpretation Unit, Supplement to Interpretation Report No. K. 1756, 6 October 1943, AFHRA

paid very close attention to the Schweinfurt-Regensburg mission.[107] A follow-up raid—maybe more than one—would be necessary, and the pressure was on from Washington.

Just as the intelligence organizations predicted, Schweinfurt factories had recovered their production, so Eaker mustered his recuperating forces to attack again. September had been an intentional recovery month for Eighth Air Force, though to little avail. Eaker still closed out the month and the CBO's second phase was more than 20 percent shy of the nearly twelve hundred bombers his plan required.[108] Nevertheless, after regaining bombers loaned elsewhere and receiving reinforcements from stateside, Eaker finally achieved a core strength of twenty bomb groups—a boost of 30 percent to his combat-ready force in just two months.[109] He felt the pressure to get back to Pointblank's primary target list, and no target seemed more attractive than ball bearings. In fact, the COA analysts were still so hot on the idea of ball bearings that they were busy on 30 September deciding that ball bearings should be "a primary rather than a supplementary target" in the Pacific as well, because "the basic characteristics of the industry in Japan are similar to those elsewhere."[110] Washington was abuzz with ideas of ball bearings as the shortcut to an industrialized victory.

Unfortunately, the bombers still lacked escorts that could take them all the way to Schweinfurt. When Eaker's bombers launched, their plan again deviated considerably. In addition to weather, a variety of problems, including a botched rendezvous, a slew of mechanical failures, and an ineffective diversionary raid by the 2nd Air Division, together thinned the original force of 377 airborne bombers down to a mere 291 as they pressed eastward across the Channel.[111] Despite anecdotes of extraordinary heroism, including a single bomber that broke formation and placed its load of ten bombs dead-center on the target, losses to the Luftwaffe were brutal, as historian Geoffrey Perret captured: "Sixty planes shot down, another ditched in the channel, six wiped out in crash landings, and seven more written off."[112] The day was indeed a "Black Thursday" for Eaker's Eighth.[113]

Deflated by a cost so horrific to his own bombers, Eaker could only hope that the cost to the German war machine had been even worse. This time, there was no doubt as to where the bombs had fallen, and the group S-2s were confident. The 92nd Bombardment Group S-2, whose group ended up flying as lead for its wing, relayed through channels that "our bombs [were] seen to hit squarely in primary target area," and while a single aircraft had "salvoed just before [the] target," he insisted the pictures otherwise confirmed good hits.[114] Any gratification with the apparent bombing results was offset by bomber crews' frustration that their escort had left them an hour prior to their time over target, just before enemy aircraft showed up. The 306th Bombardment Group S-2 similarly reinforced his crew's claims: "Bombing was good. Photographs show our bombs bursting right on aiming point, while a concentration of earlier bombs is bunched on and to the west of target 'a.'"[115] If the crews had a rough day, at least their S-2s had evidence to show something positive for the effort.

Photo interpreters expedited their review of the bombers' cameras: "The brunt of the attack fell solidly on the target area with at least 100 separate distinguishable hits within the factory confines."[116] It was enough for Eaker to rush a message to Arnold: "Unless the strike photos are very deceiving, we shall find that the three ball-bearing factories at Schweinfurt are out of business for a long, long time."[117] Eaker had no reason to doubt the intelligence. A Spitfire reconnaissance sortie flown two days after the raid, this time waiting for the smoke to clear, verified the apparently phenomenal bombing performance: "Very heavy concentrated damage is visible within the target area, and all five works of the Schweinfurt Ball-bearing Industry have been affected. The damage appears as much to fire as to H.E. [high-explosive], and some buildings which have been partly burnt out have received as many as 5 or 6 direct hits."[118] From the sound of the early photo interpretation reports, the bombing could not possibly have been more successful. Photo interpreters paid little mind to the machine tools they could not see. Buildings received damage, and that seemed to be enough to indicate the bombing had taken a commensurate toll.

Two days later, the *Washington Star* newspaper joined the information fray, relaying the symbolic value of Schweinfurt from a newly invigorated public relations campaign by Arnold and his analysts. The article summarized the remarks from Arnold's "unusual press conference," and he was all too pleased to accentuate the positive sentiment of preliminary intelligence reports:

> Taken by itself, the loss by our air force of sixty bombers in a single raid on the German ball-bearing factories at Schweinfurt last week seems appalling. But what we must learn to remember as the aerial warfare against industrial Germany increases, is not to judge the severity of our losses on the basis of single operations and never to count them without striking some sort of balance between our losses and the damage inflicted on the enemy. . . . The Schweinfurt raid accomplished its mission, which was to knock out the remaining large-scale German source of ball bearings for production of engines—not merely airplane engines, but engines for trucks, tanks, and submarines. Our losses were high; but the cost of this successful mission was relatively small.
>
> The reason it was small is that this raid was merely another step in the execution of a pattern of destruction by air force that is the greatest single threat to Germany's ability to fight. It is not the single blow that counts, but the repetition of single blows, the effect of which accumulates as they are delivered. . . . Our losses will be made up. Germany is unable to make up her own.[119]

Photo 5-5. October 14 Schweinfurt Raid Approximate Bomb Plot.
Reprinted from Central Interpretation Unit, "Interpretation Report S.A. 628," in "Attack on Schweinfurt Ball-Bearing Industry" on 14.10.43, RAF Medmenham, 16 October 1943, AFHRA

Eaker was right about pleasing Arnold—at least with this raid. Empowered by the encouraging results, Arnold wasted no time convincing the American public, and perhaps himself, that the effort more than offset the costs. Airpower, as he saw it, was more capable than the other arms of Allied power, and raids such as Schweinfurt made the job easier by weakening German land and naval forces as well. Arnold needed the public to look past the frightful stories of crashing bombers, to continue to accept attrition of his forces, and to buy into his campaign for victory both through and for airpower. The key to Arnold's campaigns—the one in the air over Germany and the one for public support for his air force—was to maintain two types of continuous pressure. For the first, he sought to press home the COA's target recommendations and exploit earlier gains; for the second, he repeated his message of air campaign success to the American public to exploit the war as an opportunity to prove the value of independent airpower.

ANALYSTS RESPOND AS ADVERTISED

On 25 October, reacting to the Quadrant conference and apparent success of the second raid on Schweinfurt, the COA analysts submitted their "Suggested Bombardment Program in Preparation for Overlord." The amended plan furthered "the principles and basic data" the analysts had pushed to Arnold all year, which they noted was now "supplemented by current intelligence."[120] It was a last-ditch effort to corner Eaker.

The analysts clearly understood that the imperative for strategic bombing seemed to shift to air superiority over the cross-Channel invasion, so they used that foundation to accentuate their preexisting argument. Atop their list, the analysts lumped together "final assembly, major component manufacture, and engine assembly plants for those types of aircraft currently utilized for defense against bomber missions"—notably excluding airfields, Crossbow targets, and expressly arguing against Eaker's long-held desire to hit aircraft repair facilities, because "the requirement of reasonable permanence of damage tends to make these relatively low priority for heavy bombers."[121] The analysts wanted Eaker to commit his bombers deeper into Germany, and their plan was not only about the Luftwaffe.

Other than the aircraft industry targets necessary to secure air superiority, the COA analysts suggested committing the full weight of USAAF strategic bombardment from both Germany and Italy to just two target systems: ball bearings and precision-grinding wheels. Their list of six ball-bearing plants excluded

Schweinfurt, because "the successful attack on Schweinfurt has unquestionably already caused the enemy to take measures of various types to protect the ball bearing supply. . . . the longer additional attack is delayed, the more effective those measures can become."[122] The analysts maneuvered to protect their credibility: either the bombers hit their COA-nominated targets with sufficient weight and follow-up, or the analysts could argue their plan had not been followed.

As for predicting specific results for ball-bearing attacks, the analysts shifted their game plan. Too much detail could be a liability if their assessments could not support their predictions. For example, on 11 October, just three days prior to the last Schweinfurt raid, they claimed that renewed attacks on the full ball-bearing industry "will have pervasive effect on the German war effort which will be felt as early as one month after their destruction."[123] Now that Eaker had actually attempted the raid with apparently positive results, they backed off predicting how exactly such effects might be assessed, especially as pertained to such raids' impact upon the German aircraft industry: "While attack upon ball bearings cannot be relied upon to produce any predictable degree of interruption of aircraft and engine production, it will unquestionably have some effect of that nature to a degree and of a kind not now determinable."[124]

With their renewed emphasis on precision-grinding wheels, the analysts chastised Eaker for not including them in Pointblank. For this target set, they boasted confidently, "The destruction of them would have the most serious disruptive effects throughout enemy war industry within a period of weeks."[125] They listed six targets; two of them, Alt Bendek and Dresden, were more than 580 miles from both London and the Rome-Foggia line, from which 15th Air Force would soon begin operations; these were deep penetrations with likely high casualties for the bombers.[126] However, the analysts in Washington were not particularly concerned with operational realities of raids against their preferred target systems. Those were Eaker's problems.

The COA analysts intentionally omitted the rest of the high-priority Pointblank target systems, in particular "submarine building yards, submarine bases, petroleum, synthetic rubber and tires, military transport vehicles."[127] The analysts sought to consolidate all of the bombers' efforts on only their primary recommendations as a last-ditch effort to consolidate bombing density and to prove they had been right all along. Among these omissions, their decision to remove petroleum was particularly interesting.

COA analysts had also included petroleum in their update on Pointblank targets just two weeks earlier on 11 October, yet they highlighted the fact that Germany no longer needed to supply Italy with up to 1,500,000 tons annually, which would relieve some pressure on that industry. Further, even if destruction of Ploesti and Germany's thirteen Bergius hydrogenation plants were prioritized, "it is impossible to state the precise time when effects of such destruction would become apparent."[128] With the invasion plan in place and the combined chiefs crystal clear on the need for air superiority over the cross-Channel invasion, the timing to show success was everything, so the mere suggestion that effects might not be short-term was another way of condemning that industry in priority. There were not enough bomber sorties to hit everything or even to hedge the bets they placed on ball bearings and grinding wheels.

The British Ministry of Economic Warfare, in its study of the six-month period closing out 1943, walked back both Arnold's and the COA's assertions with respect to ball bearings. In fact, the MEW economists refuted any immediate consequence of the August attack, as they framed their raid assessment for October on the German response instead:

> While there is no reason to believe that prior to the raid the enemy was short of ball-bearings, his consistent purchases in neutral countries, reluctance to export, and the attention paid to production facilities in occupied territories, suggest that there is a somewhat precarious balance between supply and demand. . . . There is as yet no evidence to show where the armaments industry has been affected, and Germany will doubtless attempt to mitigate the loss by seeing that it falls on the categories which are least indispensable to her.[129]

There appeared to be two distinct ways to evaluate the enemy's response to bombing such industries. Creative and aggressive measures by the enemy, on one hand, could be read as desperate indicators warranting immediate follow-up. On the other hand, such actions may have indicated that the enemy mind, malleable in ways that were not easily—if ever—understood, could negate the anticipated effects of bombing. When operational factors such as bomber accuracy, survivability, and bomb damage performed to planned expectations but the results still seemed to fall short, the generals and the analysts tended to point at each other.

Fallout from the chilling October performance against Schweinfurt reflected in more profound ways than the analysts' reports. In fact, the raid may have influenced a friendly mind even more so than Hitler's. Eaker's response to the raid, as captured by Colonel Hughes, was as follows: "Operations beyond fighter cover were sharply curtailed, and every effort was made to have long range P-51s and P-47s sent to us as soon as possible. . . . Almost simultaneously, the usual bad winter weather set in over Germany and, of necessity, operations were almost negligible until early 1944."[130] The Eighth Air Force director of intelligence would support Eaker's deflated ambition during the period immediately after the second Schweinfurt raid with a barefaced argument that "the Eighth temporarily lost air superiority in the major target areas of Germany."[131] Eighth Air Force's heavy bombers did not have air superiority in the first place.

The day after the brutal beating at Schweinfurt, Eaker finally declared to Arnold: "Nothing is more critical to our big battle here than the early arrival of P-38s and P-51s, and particularly the earliest possible delivery of three to five thousand 110- and 150-gallon auxiliary droppable tanks for fighters."[132] It had taken the chief of staff of the ground component identifying the weakest link in Eaker's air plan back in April and then six months of painful losses that culminated with Schweinfurt before Eaker finally accepted that his bombers could not get through without the long-range escort. Nevertheless, Arnold pressed Eaker to consider "possible changes in your formations; dive to minimum altitude coupled with break-up of formations to Squadrons for return home; contact Portal to see if long range fighters can be secured from him."[133] Arnold had little patience for a combat commander who appeared to lack "imagination and aggressiveness," even if that commander had been his long-time friend.[134]

MORE THAN A LITTLE HEARTBURN

Six months earlier, in Arnold's presence, General Marshall and Admiral King had sensed the weak points in Eaker's plan, looked him in the eye, and asked him about his fighter escort, winter weather, and submarine attack assumptions. Still basking in the musk of his "long, delirious" days of flying and debating at Maxwell Field's Air Corps Tactical School, Eaker had confidently sidestepped all three pitches that portended his flawed plan.[135] The problem was not just that Eaker's assumptions proved wrong; it was that he held to his plan long after the panoply of evidence indicated its flaws. The insistent target meddling from

Washington and the mix of excessively positive and contradictory feedback he received from intelligence assessments did not help him to sort out the failures earlier.

He may have seen no choice, but Eaker pulled Eighth Air Force back at precisely the moment when the intelligence assessments by Arnold's analysts in Washington and the EOU economists in England suggested the air campaign needed to thrust forward. Of course, the analysts and economists had not understood the operational limitations or the tactical considerations associated with the air campaign. From their standpoint, they had identified a list of targets, and Eaker's progress did not appear to match their recommendations. As their assessments to Arnold portrayed, the fall and early winter of 1943 was the timeframe of opportunity to capitalize on the few slight yet noteworthy gains and to knock Germany's strained industries further off balance. From the analysts' perspective, either the target recommendations had been ineffective, or Eaker had not followed them.

As Eaker pulled back from deep attacks for his daylight-precision bombers, the Air Ministry locked horns with the EOU over an attempt by Bomber Harris to add pressure on Eighth Air Force to participate in his area attacks. In a 3 November 1943 proclamation to Churchill, Harris argued, "We can wreck Berlin from end to end if the USAAF will come in on it. It will cost between 400–500 aircraft. It will cost Germany the War."[136] Meanwhile, the EOU economists responded by codifying their own target preferences into a "party line," which they saw as "both a theory of bombing policy and a related method of analysis."[137] The EOU economists argued against area bombing on account of its inefficiency as a form of industrial attack and the failure of the Air Ministry to prove that area bombing might otherwise lead to "anarchy or revolution."[138] The ways various analytical constituencies dealt with uncertainty, especially for intangible effects, were easy targets for opposing viewpoints.

The EOU drive for efficiency resonated with its economists' habits of mind and mathematical logic. They'd sought to attack "the minimum number of targets whose destruction would achieve the desired goal."[139] More remarkable was an admission in their history that their party line "opposed attacks designed simply to weaken the German economy or to cause political disruption; and emphasized the possibilities of evading the military consequences of bomb damage in a mature and resourceful economic system like that of wartime Germany."[140] In other words, the EOU economists sought to implement a bombing policy that ran counter to the ACTS graduates. They had apparently become more concerned with rebuilding Germany postwar than with maximizing airpower to win. In any case, it is clear the economists were also interested in proving they were right, even if they had struggled to keep Eaker's bombers focused exclusively on German war matériel, especially single-engine fighter assembly.

While the EOU engaged with the Air Ministry, a bellwether event occurred in Washington. Brigadier General Kuter, then back from England and serving as Arnold's chief of plans, attempted to better prepare his boss for the upcoming Sextant conference by requesting an update from AC/AS intelligence of their September report. The intent of the update, according to Kuter, was "for use in strategic planning" and "for the purpose of comparison with a similar study" by the British.[141] There should have been at least something on paper to represent the American perspective of CBO progress. Three days later, Kuter cut his original three-week suspense on the requested update in half, which grated on Col. William Bentley, a former B-17 test pilot, then serving as the acting deputy chief of intelligence.[142] Bentley shot back at Kuter with a "preliminary" report due to Kuter's shortened suspense and the "sketchy basis for the specific operational plan" provided by Kuter's office. Bentley cautioned that the updated report necessitated "many arbitrary assumptions" and that estimates of future results were "largely speculative."[143] Bentley was forthright that his analysts had done what they could, yet the report was probably not worth much without the time and information they needed to develop it fully.

Nevertheless, Bentley's preliminary report indicated that Eighth Air Force air combat claims against German fighters had exceeded the production losses from bombing German aircraft factories (even when splitting the difference between the Mighty Eighth's inflated claims and the Air Ministry's figures of the same period, since the former nearly doubled the latter.)[144] The bombers were slugging out the battle for air superiority more through attrition than with their bombs. Further, combined results of both attacks on Schweinfurt amounted to losses of only one month's production of ball bearings, suggesting that efforts to exploit the "extremely tight" situation would require seven more attacks on the industry and another projected raid on Schweinfurt in February.[145] Apparently, according to the report, there were "no significant reduction in oil supplies" and no appreciable change in any other industry prioritized for attack under the

Pointblank directive since 1 September.[146] This was bad news. While Arnold's A-2 continued work on a more complete report, Arnold flew to Cairo to meet with the combined chiefs with more than a little heartburn over Eaker's performance.

Sextant: A New Course and a Falling Star

The Sextant conference, held 2–7 December 1943 in Cairo, provided the year's closing meetings for the combined chiefs. Among the critical decisions for the European theater of operations was the long-awaited announcement of the president's preference to command Overlord. After some dithering, Roosevelt selected Eisenhower, but only after realizing that he "could not sleep at night with [Marshall] out of the country."[147] Eisenhower was then free to negotiate the rest of his team, including an American airman who would lead all of his bombers. Given his previous experiences in England and in the Mediterranean, Eisenhower's decision to select Spaatz may have been an easy one.

Eisenhower noted in his memoir that he "desired to take General Spaatz to England," adding that "by agreement made in Cairo the American strategic bombers in the Mediterranean and in England were to be combined under Spaatz's single operational command."[148] It may well be, as other histories agree, that Eisenhower simply insisted on bringing Spaatz as "his airman," who had demonstrated satisfactory understanding of "air support to ground troops," and that this made him the right airman to lead the preparations for Overlord.[149] Personal relationships, previous experience, and imperatives for military unity of command all mattered in Eisenhower's selection of Spaatz. But there were also organizational interests involved on behalf of the AAF and its air intelligence constituency worthy of examination.

Eaker's performance had been a discussion topic at Cairo. Both Eaker and Portal submitted a collaborative progress report to the combined chiefs, but they cited only British intelligence sources and painted a rosy picture from their limited palette of information. They conceded that "a complete and accurate picture of results achieved is not possible" but went on to argue, "The attacks on the ball-bearing industry at Schweinfurt and the synthetic rubber plant at Hüls have undoubtedly produced far-reaching effects throughout the range of German war industry."[150] Further, attacks on aircraft factories at various installations were "likely to have produced effects within that industry far in excess of the sum of the visible damage."[151] Implying that the CBO was halfway complete, the report picked excerpts from a report by the MEW and the Air Ministry, adding that "there is very much greater decline in some individual industries (e.g. ball-bearings and rubber), which may be near the point where they could cause the collapse of the whole war machine."[152] From the sound of it, the bombing had caused the Germans far more problems than dealing with a few squeaky wheels and worn-out tires. If the progress report and its crafty use of language from British air intelligence sources were accepted at face value, then the CBO was proceeding quite well, even if the end of December was supposed to mark the end of the third of four phases per the original plan. Who was Arnold to believe: Eaker's positive spin on his own accomplishments, or the negative perspectives held by Arnold's own intelligence staff?

Portal appeared to back Eaker with sincerity, but his statistics undermined his praise. Portal argued that Eaker had done what he could with "only some 75 percent of his full resources," though he had accomplished "54 percent of the results expected" and was "three months behind" (an entire phase, as the plan had been designed).[153] Portal pointed out that Eaker had predicted nearly this exact outcome in an April memorandum, but the comment served only to deflect culpability toward an already enraged Arnold.[154] Perhaps even more fitting, Portal pointed out that the joint staff of both countries still had much to learn in their endeavors to employ "huge numbers of aircraft," and that "it was not always right nor was it possible to keep rigidly to a plan laid down in advance."[155]

Portal had identified the problems of Eaker's approach and Arnold's impatience, as both American airmen clung to air campaign assessments that suggested their original targeting plan in Pointblank, except for the submarine attacks, was still correct—if only it had been pursued more vigorously. Eaker blamed Arnold for his incessant diversions and the lack of resources, while Arnold blamed Eaker for failing to perform and innovate with what he had. Neither general was particularly receptive to bad news or the other side's perspective, especially when baited into a frenzy by evidence in contradictory intelligence reports or sugar-coated language such as Portal's.

Arnold had spent the last year preaching airpower efficiency in Washington, and COA's convincing plan emboldened his pledge for quick victory. However, for the second conference in a row, the lack of credibility or timeliness in the U.S. air intelligence assessments put Arnold on the defensive. He shuddered as he responded to the British assessments in general and now to Portal's argument in particular. Blame for the air campaign's lack of progress could fall in one or all of three places: Eaker's lack of resources, which would reflect poorly on Arnold in his role as force provider; ACTS doctrine as a failing experiment, which might jeopardize the need for independent airpower; or Eaker's lack of creativity and flexibility as he had underutilized and underperformed the forces he commanded. Arnold chose to articulate the third option.

At the opportune moment, Arnold derided Eaker's performance as he pushed his agenda to the combined chiefs to reorganize U.S. strategic bomber forces in theater. According to meeting minutes, both Arnold and Marshall pressed their proposal to consolidate command of bombers in both England and Italy for a coordinated effort against Germany. Arnold argued this new arrangement would "overcome the lack of flexibility" that led to an inadequate rate of operations out of England, where just 50 percent of Eaker's aircraft were available for combat, whereas "in other theaters 60 or 70 percent of aircraft were used."[156]

Further, Arnold blasted, "the failure to destroy targets was due directly to the failure to employ planes in sufficient numbers."[157] The problem, as Arnold saw it, was not only the size of Eaker's formations, but bombing accuracy and day-to-day target selection as well: "A sufficient weight of bombs was not being dropped on the targets to destroy them, nor was the proper priority of targets being followed."[158] In short, Arnold portrayed a clear case that the plan had been sound and resources adequate, so the blame belonged on Eaker (and Harris).[159]

Air Force historians later concluded, "If Arnold's dissatisfaction over the rate of Eighth Air Force operations entered into the decision [to remove Eaker], the record apparently has left no evidence of it."[160] Perhaps the Air Force historians passed too lightly over the Sextant minutes and the intelligence reports. Arnold concluded his rant with a comment that "training, technique, and operational efficiency must all be improved. Only a new commander divorced from day-to-day routine could achieve this."[161] By *new commander*, Arnold surely referred to a reorganized and consolidated command, and he clearly did not have in mind the man whom he had just disparaged to the rest of the combined chiefs as the one to lead it.

Just three days after Sextant, Arnold's new intelligence chief released an updated version of Sorensen's September assessment, and with it he solidified any remaining doubt in Arnold's impressions of the second half of 1943.[162] Sorensen had been replaced by Maj. Gen. Clayton Bissell, and Bissell's timing could not have been more perfect from the perspective of Washington-based air intelligence interests. Bissell had been a law school graduate at twenty-one years old, a World War I ace, an ACTS graduate, and he participated with Billy Mitchell in sinking the *Ostfriesland*.[163] He clearly had credibility in the air service as a pilot who believed in the primacy of the strategic bomber. Notably, Bissell had also been a war plans division member who was then frozen out of General George's four-member "task force" that produced AWPD-1.[164] To say the least, Bissell had no special affinity for any targeting plan other than the one currently supported by Arnold and his committee of operations analysts.[165]

Bissell's close relationship with Arnold mattered insofar as Bissell maintained credibility with Arnold, who entrusted Bissell as his "detail man."[166] Even Bissell's nemesis, Claire Chennault, called him "a fanatic for meticulous staff work and detailed reports."[167] A detailed air intelligence assessment is exactly what Bissell wrote, and if there was going to be an airman who would expose Eaker for failing to live up to Arnold's expectations or target recommendations as pushed by Arnold's analysts, Bissell would be that airman-turned-intelligence officer.[168]

With damning clarity and a variety of carefully drawn charts and tables, Bissell's report pierced Eaker's integrity and further eroded Arnold's confidence with intimations that Eaker had, at least in some cases, elected to attack targets that "fail to utilize properly the principle of selectivity which is the basis and chief virtue of USAAF daylight precision bombing."[169] Bissell added in a similar vein: "The USAAF, with a *very small proportion of its attack directed against relatively few important targets*, has shown that it can successfully strike at the heart of the German war effort" (emphasis added).[170] The report implied that Eaker had squandered the capable forces under his command pursuing targets other than the ones supported by Arnold's analysts.

Whereas Bissell may have agreed with Arnold on matters of air intelligence, he and Eaker did not. In fact, Bissell's relationship with Eaker deteriorated rapidly while Arnold was away at Sextant. On 3 December Bissell inquired Eaker for his views on installing AAF-level intelligence officers directly into the British Air Ministry. Bissell needed to work through the theater air force component because the only other way he could install AAF officers in Britain would be as attachés, and that meant placing them under the war department G-2.

Bissell's rationale was twofold: first, "so that we may adopt the good ideas therein that are applicable to our problems," and second, "to lay the groundwork for a flow of information of air intelligence direct from the Air Ministry to the AAF Intelligence."[171] Notably, Bissell added his broader concerns about the AAF intelligence. He had visions for the future of his service, and the time was ripe to establish a top headquarters-level partnership with the British. "If we are ever to have a worthwhile AAF intelligence organization," Bissell opined, "we must get assigned to it a certain number of very capable young officers who will make Intelligence work their career. Their hearts must be in it and they must be good." He went on to argue that he needed more regular AAF officers to compensate for the "civilians in uniform" who had "no practical experience with the problems confronting Air Forces in combat."[172] Bissell envisioned the core of future air force intelligence as professional uniformed officers.

Eaker blocked Bissell's request to put AAF intelligence officers in the Air Ministry unless they were to be assigned or attached to Eighth Air Force. "I wish I could agree with you about putting a group of your representatives in the Air Ministry to report directly back to you," Eaker retorted, but he'd been frustrated by "crossed wires" with other war department agencies; he felt himself directly responsible for all activity related to Air Force matters in the theater, and "to have another independent agency in Theater muddies the water, often makes for ill-feeling and results in definite confusion."[173] Eaker's leadership style had been to control information and how it was presented. Eaker wanted his boss to accept analyses from the field, and he was not about to yield influence to Arnold's own staff. "In other words, let us make the command set-up work," he shot back at Bissell, "instead of by-passing it."[174]

But Bissell had already bypassed Eaker with his report to Arnold. As to the ball-bearing attacks, Bissell's carefully worded analysis pinned the lack of success on German response and on Eaker's failure to follow up. Though much of the analysts' rationale for Schweinfurt's high priority had been the relationship between ball bearings and the aircraft industry, Bissell concluded that "this industry will probably not be affected greatly because of the possibility of rerouting the production of undamaged facilities."[175] Though the August raid had little impact on ball-bearing production, the October raid drove November production down by 31 percent; without more attacks, however, full production would resume by March.[176] From Bissell's perspective, ball bearings still seemed the bottleneck target of choice, if only Eaker had figured out some way to sustain the assault on Schweinfurt with lower costs to his own forces.

At a watershed moment for AAF air intelligence, Arnold accepted Bissell's appraisal of Eaker's performance. The AAF's commanding general sided with his top intelligence officer over the semimonthly reports and personal pleas of a commanding general senior to Bissell. In fact, the foreword in Bissell's report, written by Arnold himself, conveyed the latter's sincere frustration. Arnold pointed out that only 20 percent of Eaker's weight of effort (by bomb tonnage) during the preceding four-and-a-half-month period had fallen on industries "vital to Germany's ability to continue the war, vulnerable to aerial bombardment, and within the capacity of our available forces."[177] Arnold was "considerably dissatisfied," noted COA's Col. Guido Perera in an understated tone; the A-2 report, Perera added, was "in some contrast to reports submitted by [Eaker's] Eighth Air Force to General Arnold."[178] While it is unclear which reports Arnold found to be inaccurate, it probably did not help that Eaker's semimonthly reports of bombing results to Arnold, as produced by the Eighth Air Force intelligence section, had taken an extraordinarily positive tone despite the sensible reality of a stalled air campaign.[179] Eaker's October report, for example, had claimed that "Eighth Air Force heavy bombers virtually tore the roof off of Hitler's Fortress Europa," before claiming that "most of the 475 tons dropped found their individual targets" during the "extremely effective attack on Germany's ball and roller bearing industry."[180] Bluster spewing from Eaker's intelligence team overstated the bombing results, and Bissell ensured that Arnold knew it.

"HEARTBREAKING TO LEAVE"

Eaker was, in Arnold's words, "moved down to commanding the Mediterranean Air Force"—in position as well as geography—at least in part because Arnold needed to know that he had a general in place in England who not only could overcome operational challenges as the war intensified, but who also would respond and report openly to Arnold's concerns from Washington.[181] To Arnold, the chance of proving the independent worth of airpower was more important than personal friendship. With Bissell at the top, Arnold's air intelligence gurus had convinced him that Eaker failed in England for the growth and prestige of their own enterprise. Both Arnold and Bissell placed their respective organizational imperatives first.

If Arnold was displeased with Eighth Air Force's progress and with its commander, he had been pleased in equal magnitude by the air intelligence organizations, their targeting recommendations, and their air campaign assessments.

He later noted in his memoir, *Global Mission*, "The information available to us when we considered attacking any target in Germany reflected a combined knowledge about that specific place which included everything known about it at that minute. . . . details ranged from the most abstract evaluations of civilian scientists through the best British-American photo interpretation; the latest reports of our own and the R.A.F.'s combat crews; the reports of General [William] Donovan's OSS operatives behind the German Lines; the careful estimates of British Ministry of Economic Warfare experts, of our own Bureau of Economic Warfare, and what not."[182]

If there was any remaining doubt as to the sources of Arnold's rationale behind his decision to replace Eaker, he summed it up on 5 January 1944 in a way that could only be fully explained by the foregoing narrative: "A study of reports, covering the heavy bomber effort of the Eighth Air Force during the past several months, forces me to conclude that aircraft and crews available in the United Kingdom are not utilized as fully and effectively as possible toward achievement of our aims in the European theater."[183] However, to generate the most damning statistic—that only "20 percent concentration" of USAAF bombs had fallen on "vital target systems" under Eaker's watch between 1 July and 15 November 1943—Bissell's intelligence staff had to twist the facts in their own way.[184] To calculate a percentage that low, Bissell's report included only attacks on aircraft production (omitting Eaker's elective attacks on repair facilities and operating airdromes), ball bearings, oil, and rubber in his calculations. Per the Pointblank directive, these categories were priorities 1, 3, 4, and 5, respectively.[185] Bissell's statistic omitted Eaker's attacks on U-boat installations (priority 2—40 percent of Eaker's bombs) and vehicle factories (priority 6; e.g. the 15 September raid on Renault motor works in Paris), even though these targets fell as legitimate priorities on his governing directive during that period.[186] Bissell's list was an arbitrary reformulation reflecting the COA's original preferences, since neither U-boat installations nor vehicles had been in the COA's top six categories.

In truth, attacks on U-boat installations were not removed as a Pointblank objective by the combined chiefs until 13 January 1944, by the same document that finally added Crossbow objectives as well as "installations supporting the German Air Force" to the list.[187] This meant that Eaker did not receive credit for targets (including the V-weapons site at Watten) he had attacked at the direction of Air Chief Marshal Sir Charles Portal, who technically directed the CBO "as agent of the CCS" during 1943.[188] Eaker also did not receive credit for the attacks he waged on German airfields in occupied territories, even though they were added as an official Pointblank objective within thirty days of his reassignment. Through another lens—one less shaded by organizational imperatives—Eaker's decision to attack airfields might have been considered prescient rather than deficient.

The 20 percent statistic associated with Eaker's Eighth Air Force, however contrived by AAF intelligence, represented Arnold's frustration with the air campaign as a whole: the continual pull toward British and joint objectives (V-weapons, U-boats, and vehicles); operational challenges that seemed to threaten the validity of ACTS doctrine (bombing accuracy, weather, and aircraft loss rates); and most of all, the inability to achieve quick victory in 1943, despite the war department's plan for a ground invasion before the bombing had even started. Arnold wanted a fresh start with Spaatz in England in 1944, and the air campaign assessments gave him the evidence he needed to justify his decision. If Arnold replaced Eaker on the dubious merits of Bissell's report, on account of Eaker's difficulties with weather, manpower, equipment, training, fighter escort, the Luftwaffe, and all of his other challenges taken together, or simply on Eisenhower's preference for Spaatz, then the decision may have been unfair to Eaker.

However, Eaker had proven a wartime commander who valued his analysts' positive spin on his own success over the imperative for organizational learning in the air campaign, and this flaw made him quicker to beg for more resources than to seek creative approaches with the resources he had. His intransigence also hampered the AAF's development of air intelligence. For all of these reasons, it was in the best interest of the Army Air Force, its air intelligence enterprise, and the success of the ground invasion that followed to get Eaker out of the way, even if he would find it (in his own words) "heartbreaking to leave just before climax."[189] There would be no victory in 1943 for the Allies in the air campaign over Germany, for Army Air Corps independence, or for Eaker's Eighth Air Force. Air intelligence interests were, however, victorious over Eaker, and these interests selected a more amiable proponent in "Tooey" Spaatz for the remainder of the war and beyond.

CONCLUSION

> It would appear to me that new yardsticks for measuring ultimate effect of our bombing on the German military effort must be used. Certainly, we are destroying German industries and facilities from one end of the country to the other. Also, certainly this destruction is not having the effect upon the German war effort we had expected and hoped—not the effect we all assumed would result.
>
> —GEN. H. H. ARNOLD, COMMANDING GENERAL, AAF, 8 JANUARY 1945[1]

Spaatz did his best to navigate the space between Eisenhower's demands and Arnold's pressure to stay the course on the COA analysts' recommended targets, which still promised value for strategic bombing beyond immediate support to the invasion. Arnold would not relent. He even sent Guido Perera and Elihu Root Jr. to England to meet with Spaatz "about a matter of target selection," with a heavy-handed order for Spaatz to give both of them access to "all data and personnel involved in the selection of Combined Bomber Objectives."[2] COA analysts had convinced Arnold that victory still had a shortcut, and he had no intention of letting Spaatz off the same hook that Eaker had been on.

While Spaatz was overcoming Eaker's longstanding operational challenges with weather and fighter escort during Big Week of February 1944, Ambassador Winant was busy sending cables from London back to the secretary of state. It turned out that Sweden was, in fact, shipping significant quantities of ball bearings to Germany despite trade agreement limitations; moreover, the Germans were apparently requesting earlier shipments of different types than originally ordered.[3] Army Deputy Chief of Staff Gen. Joseph McNarney became aware of this fact weeks earlier from another state department cable, which noted that a ship with seventy-six tons of ball bearings set out from Sweden for Germany just three weeks after the October Schweinfurt raid.[4] McNarney managed to get a letter sent from War Secretary Henry Stimpson to Secretary of State Cordell Hull expressing "that the effect of the recent bombings by our Air Forces against the ball bearing plants at Schweinfurt is being nullified to some extent by the importation of ball bearings from Sweden. Our missions against these plants have already cost the United States almost 1,000 lives and 100 heavy bombers."[5] Ball bearings might not prove the bottleneck shortcut to victory if a neutral party was refilling the bottle.

Although McNarney's staff in Washington knew that two more shipments totaling 180 tons of ball bearings were already loaded for Germany, Spaatz held a more pragmatic viewpoint as he ameliorated concerns about Sweden: "Present shipments to Germany are critical only if remaining German production continues at [a] level to permit Swedish special types to fill out shortages. Swedish imports will be of limited value if German production [is] knocked out." His intent was clear: "Continue attacks as outlined in plan for completion [of the] CBO," while leaving the problem of pressure on the Swedes to Winant and the state department.[6] The idea, it seemed to both Spaatz and McNarney, was not that Sweden had the capacity to fully resupply German stocks, but that Sweden's plants were "of the highest type" and nimble enough to adjust output quickly; if Sweden could simply compensate for the components lost from Allied bomb damage, then the rest of the German ball-bearing plants could continue to operate without retooling their production lines.[7] This rationale, however accurate, suggested hitting German factories even harder and as soon as possible.[8]

Two more reports by Arnold's intelligence chief over the next six months revealed statistics of an entirely different bombing effort than the previous year. So much had the focus shifted, in fact, that by 15 September 1944 the preponderance of all bombs dropped since July 1943 "were primarily in support of ground operations."[9] According to a September update, the German air force could "no longer offer effective resistance"; oil output had declined "more than 60 percent," which was "well below the enemy's minimum requirements for mobile warfare"; and "lines of interdiction"—especially bridge attacks—seemed to punctuate the transportation campaign by closing off resupply from the east.[10] If the joint purpose of strategic bombing was to aid the ground invasion, then the bombing seemed to be going well.

Moreover, the assessment captured results of oil and transportation bombing in terms of tactical impact on the battlefield, without any regard to German industry. As to the COA favorite, the ball bearings, intelligence sources still did not indicate any conclusive effects on German industry despite the continued high priority. Spaatz's bombers had apparently done their part by reducing ball-bearing production by 50 percent between February and September, but the Germans appeared to have reprioritized "civil-industrial requirements" to mitigate the impact. Nevertheless, the report insisted that the "qualitative effect" on military equipment had been "greater than the figures . . . would indicate."[11] The report stopped short of any clear recommendations on the way forward, but it made no mention of a change in course.

In late July 1944 EOU economists also committed their targeting recommendations to paper in a scheme intended to persist throughout the remainder of the war. Ball bearings remained high on their list, second only to oil production. As the economists saw it, oil continued to be "the most economical and effective contribution the Air Force could make to ending the war."[12] Ball bearings, on the other hand, remained "difficult to trace in the intelligence," but "in view of the limited number of targets which remain, and the vulnerability of the present German position, this attack shoul[d] be pressed hom[e]."[13] The message was apparently that they were already running out of unstruck ball-bearing targets by June 1944. Despite the lack of provable results, they figured that they might as well keep at it anyway.

The final iteration of air campaign assessment by Arnold's A-2, dated 1 December 1944, attempted to wrestle with the emerging reality that the war was almost over, and it did so with a notably defensive posture. For most of Pointblank's original primary target systems, Arnold's A-2 suggested that German ingenuity was as much to blame as diversions in the bombing effort by the responsible Allied authorities.[14] Despite heavy bombing efforts, German aircraft production had actually increased in the latter half of 1944, but this was due to dispersion and an "expansion" program that German Reichsminister Albert Speer had pulled successfully from other resources.[15] Astonishingly, combat losses of German aircraft were double the losses from bombing production factories.

The battle for air superiority had been won in the air, it seemed, more so by the Luftwaffe defending its gasoline supplies than by direct results of the bombing effort.

The twenty-six Allied attacks on ball-bearing factories by the end of 1944 had not turned out as expected.[16] The Washington-based analysts intimated new reasons why expected results had not panned out, including that the Germans had managed to mitigate bombing through "reduction in requirements," "redesign of equipment," "intensified salvage," "dispersal of plants," and "strenuous efforts to restore output."[17] It was as if the COA failed to understand that options available to the air campaign's interactive opponent should be factored into targeting recommendations. Nevertheless, Arnold's intelligence chief hoped that any reader, not only from the air service but also from "other interested agencies," would accept his argument that ball bearings still made for an ideal target, and that bombing caused shortages "*believed* to have resulted in reduced assemblies of tanks, trucks, and other equipment," and "undoubtedly contributed *somewhat* to the decline of German industrial output" (emphasis added), despite the fact that the industry received only 1.2 percent of the total bombing effort by weight.[18]

After reading this report, Arnold grew increasingly suspicious that bomb damage assessments—perhaps the whole system in place for assessing the air campaign—had been flawed from the outset. The air campaign had not met his expectations, but he was not ready to accept that the assumptions behind his bombing doctrine or the concepts behind the targeting plans had been problematic as well. In January 1945 Arnold wrote a letter to Maj. Gen. Clayton Bissell (then the war department G-2) complaining that the bombers had exacted "great damage" as planned; "nevertheless, the German Army and the German Air Force continue under these circumstances to fight with an effectiveness that would have been considered impossible a few years ago."[19] The enemy found ways to negate the effects of bombing, yet Arnold's analysts did not seem to help him anticipate or understand this through the conclusion of the war.

Phillip Meilinger's *Ten Propositions Regarding Air Power* is worthy of revisit: "In essence, Air Power is targeting, targeting is intelligence, and intelligence is analyzing the effects of air operations."[20] Meilinger's syllogism echoes with airpower application and air intelligence in every high-explosive bomb dropped by modern air forces. Further, Meilinger added, "Not only have most air theorists had a single, key target theory, but they have also been surprisingly prescriptive: their target is the key in all types of wars, in all types of situations and against all types of opponents."[21] Refining Meilinger's observation, it may be that air intelligence analysts, not just the theorists, had their own targeting prescriptions as well. Airpower and air intelligence are "integrally intertwined" in ways that did not apply to land (or naval) warfare, and, as Meilinger suggested, the battle for AAF independence was necessarily coincident with the growth and recognition of an independent air intelligence enterprise.[22] As such, the growth of airpower cannot be thoroughly comprehended without an understanding of the maturation of its air intelligence component.

Air campaigns unfold through targeting decisions and assessments that are necessarily shaped by organizational preferences and political imperatives. The targeting practices of Ira Eaker's Eighth Air Force reflected the pressures placed upon him by the AAF's symbolic grip on the heavy bomber and the air intelligence organizations' fixation with idealized targets such as Schweinfurt. Targets driven by political goals (such as V-weapons sites or U-boat pens), inconsistent with the AAF's organizational aims, were attacked ineffectively, begrudgingly, or only as they appealed to other Eighth Air Force purposes, such as for training and respite from brutal losses.

Eaker's plan, as originally submitted and approved, did not fail to achieve its objectives due simply to operational limitations, resource constraints, and German ingenuity, but also because of the rigidity with which Eaker clung to his assumptions and Arnold's analysts pushed their preferences. As to political diversions and the role of the CCS, Brigadier General Hansell, serving briefly as Arnold's acting assistant chief of air staff (plans), argued in Eaker's defense a month after Eaker was fired:

> [T]he criterion for the execution of the combined bomber offensive to date should be to the faithfulness with which operations have conformed to the approved plan and directive, and the degree of destruction achieved compared to that expected in the plan. Whereas, it is realized that the objectives approved by the CCS did not conform to the requirements of many agencies, it is suggested that the Air Forces carrying out the combined bomber offensive were operating under a rigid directive approved by the highest military authorities.[23]

Hansell cautioned against the COA analysts' assessment and attempted to move the burden onto the CCS. Unfortunately, Hansell's perspective was unfair to a system that necessarily and appropriately subordinates military power to political masters. The CCS, in its role advising Roosevelt and Churchill, could only provide the best military advice based upon the assessments available to them. The responsibility to validate assumptions, monitor progress, revise guidance, and adapt the plan to changing conditions lies with the commanders and their staffs. To this aim, the importance of the relationships between the various commanders and between the commanders and their respective staffs cannot be underestimated.

When Marshall asked Arnold to assess the air campaign in July 1943, Arnold permitted (if not guided) the AAF to evaluate itself through its own concept of victory. That Arnold's A-2 sought to control the assessments in a confluence of organizational biases should hardly have been surprising; there were no sources available for truly objective comparison either internal or external to the AAF. In modern reality, air campaigns are joint endeavors, and political goals are messy. Air campaigns are often fought with imperfect information, conflicting guidance, muddled lines of authority, complicated alliances, short-sighted commanders, unpredictable opponents, harsh environmental conditions, and inevitable friction that "makes the apparently easy so difficult."[24] In short, an air campaign fought for purely organizational goals (as in airpower for airpower's sake) is flawed from the start. However, a wise strategist might consider how such goals would influence political aims since organizational goals will inevitably creep into targeting plans and assessments.

Interwar airmen alleged airpower to be the cheapest path to victory by avoiding the bloodshed and depletion of another long ground war. It is clearly possible to launch aircraft and bomb something without solid intelligence, but without a refined sense of what to target or how to measure bombing effectiveness, airpower will be inefficient if not altogether ineffective. Because conservation of human and fiscal resources came to dominate the strategic context in 1943 (at least until Allied leadership shifted their focus toward postwar advantage), economists were credible as intelligence analysts and as surrogates for experienced air planners. The economists and other analysts were concerned about maintaining their credibility, validating their target selections, and maximizing postwar prestige, so they persisted in obligating Eighth Air Force leadership to bomb their respective recommended targets.

Despite the abundance of postwar analyses and interviews with German industrial experts, there is not enough evidence to conclude whether airpower alone might have brought about German economic collapse or whether a true bottleneck even existed. Efforts to draw such conclusions typically founder on trying to prove a negative or counterfactual argument. The problem with the EOU economists was that they did not pursue resolving the challenges associated with their computational approach to targeting, just as the COA analysts never seriously revalidated their assumptions or accounted for operational realities of the air campaign. Both organizations fervently pushed their recommendations on Eaker and Arnold, yet neither organization earnestly acknowledged their own limitations.

Most books on the CBO suggest that the AAF's top leadership espoused ACTS doctrine as their single decisionmaking framework and that Eighth Air Force simply fell in line trying to bring the AAF's interwar doctrine to reality. The dominant argument is that the AAF's bombing zealots were too fixated on proving the value of independent airpower to learn in the cauldron of war. This was partly true. Extraordinary pressure to show results extended directly from General Arnold as he responded to the pressure placed upon him. Taking the AAF as a single entity, it appeared to be applying its interwar doctrine with very little adjustment or acknowledgment of its faulty preconceptions.

This book's deeper vantage also showed competing internal perspectives on the efficacy both of ACTS doctrine and of bombing results. Because the war department had not invested in air intelligence personnel, processes, or products in the interwar years, much less permitted collection or analysis on systemic targets prior to Arnold's successful battle with the G-2, failed bombing results and adjustments to ACTS doctrine are as attributable to interwar war department leadership as to the AAF. Consequences of this lack of foresight manifest well prior to the CBO, and there is little room for doubt that many dedicated, brilliant, and creative people throughout the war department (including the AAF) did what they could to help do something meaningful with the bombers available in 1943. Unfortunately, the various groups they comprised had little incentive to learn or inform in ways that might have justified recommendations contrary to their own organizational survival or prestige, and this instinct showed in their work.

When unchecked, organizations may adopt symbols and exaggerate claims to justify their goals and preferences. Organizations use such symbols to market their ideas in ways that mask their optimistic assumptions as their symbols serve as idealized examples of their organizational interests. In the case of the air campaign against Germany, both the B-17 and Schweinfurt served as powerful marketing tools for the AAF and air intelligence, respectively. Unfortunately, both organizations clung to their symbols in ways that stifled their objectivity and creativity.

Further, mission- and campaign-level assessments are important human aspects of an air campaign, even though there is bias inherent in their production (by analysts and crews) and in their use (by commanders). These assessments feed targeting decisions that are also riddled with organizational biases. We cannot remove the biases from the organizations or the humans who comprise them any more than we can remove the interaction from strategy. These are parts of the whole. We can, however, be conscious that bias is part of organizational behavior and of human judgment, and we can be prepared to guard against it. If wars are fought by militaries and militaries are organizations, then organizational behavior matters to endeavors of military strategy.

A common airpower narrative suggests bombing represents a symbol of superior technology, training, and innovation, even offering a shortcut to victory "over, not through" the enemy.[25] As just one element of military power, airpower offers a means to fight at a lower cost to friendly forces along with potential for less political entanglement.[26] However, airpower may not be efficient, even toward goals for which it is well suited, if decisionmakers do not have the requisite information. Launched with inadequate intelligence or defective decisionmaking processes, an air campaign may squander resources (time, money, human capital, and matériel), increase expenses, and impede overall success as political will falters. Further, uninformed decisionmakers may wield airpower to achieve unintended consequences or even counterproductive outcomes. Thus, the promise of airpower brings with it a robust air intelligence requirement—one that starts well before bombing begins and continues after hostilities cease.

This requirement for processed, exploited, and disseminated air intelligence at all levels of military operations necessitates continual support from a large standing air intelligence enterprise, which can be expensive. Unfortunately, organizational complexities, overlapping responsibilities, and classification sensitivity obfuscate dissection of the modern intelligence community budget, especially since the lines between organic functions of military services and national-level support blur. For example, the combined U.S. budget for both national and military intelligence appropriations ballooned to its highest ever at $81.5 billion in 2018—an amount roughly equivalent to the combined salary of every high school teacher in the United States or the annual cost to operate the nation's entire prison system.[27]

However, only a slice of this massive intelligence budget goes to what the intelligence community calls support to military operations, of which targeting and battle damage assessment are an even smaller part. These tasks comprise cross-cutting responsibilities, competencies, and contributions from five service components, six other Department of Defense entities, and four non-defense combat support agencies, including the Defense Intelligence Agency, National Geospatial-Intelligence Agency, National Reconnaissance Office, and National Security Agency.[28] While their respective budgets remain murky, each of these eleven distinct organizations (and likely many more) has its own role and interests at play in the air intelligence enterprise. A wise air commander would have a sense of the ways these interests influence their respective recommendations and available products.

As for future implications, the challenge of understanding airpower and the air intelligence enterprise continues to be complicated by many dynamic factors, such as the security environment, physical environment, alliance politics, fiscal constraints, potential enemy behaviors, emerging technologies, civil-military relations, interservice rivalry, doctrine, training practices, leadership personalities, and organizational preferences. Whether it will save costs or ultimately increase them, advancing technology calls for intelligence modernization. Perhaps no factor is more prescient or insidious than the organizational implications of air intelligence modernization. It may be, as some authors suggest, that combinations of artificial intelligence, machine learning, big data, and advanced algorithms could "enhance decision-making" or result in "improvements to PED [process, exploit, disseminate] [that] maximize the value of the analysts by minimizing the amount of time they spend on mundane and low value-add activities."[29] However, we must be cautious not to assume that such outcomes are foregone conclusions of improved technology.

The problems are twofold. First, automated analytics may remove some humans from the loop, but they cannot remove the organizational interests entirely. Instead, the inherent organizational biases may burrow deeper into the system. If decisionmaking on the future battlefield is determined by which data is selected, how it is processed, and how it is displayed, then we must guard against biases embedded in contract requirements, computer code, system design, and human-machine interfaces that may be locked in place well prior to conflict. The imperative to keep an operational link to the program managers, engineers, contractors, and analysts behind both intelligence and command and control modernization efforts cannot be understated.

Second, we must be cautious about implicit assumptions that large-scale data processing automatically increases the value of analysts or of their analyses. Both are already invaluable to airpower, but commanders must retain a healthy skepticism about both machine analytics and human analysis. Put otherwise, higher confidence intelligence is not necessarily more correct, in the sense that the commander retains responsibility to ensure the available information informs the best decision for the right reasons at the right time. There is risk that an air intelligence enterprise more empowered by technological modernization could assume a collective mindset of presenting ready-made decisions (without alternatives) or even assuming the role of decisionmaker. Modernization must accompany a careful realignment—or at least a clear revalidation—of roles and responsibilities associated with intelligence support to the chain of command. As there certainly was in 1943, there may always be an inherent tension in these relationships, because commanders' and analysts' (and perhaps contractors') interests do not always align.

Finally, there are many ways to analyze and assess air campaigns. For example, in *Fast Tanks and Heavy Bombers*, David Johnson concluded of the CBO: "The combination of fighter escorts and an almost endless supply of bombers and crews allowed the Army Air Forces to continue what had become a bloody battle of attrition for command of the air war over Europe. Because of this overwhelming quantitative superiority, losses returned to an acceptable range. As Eaker had predicted, the side that could make good its losses won."[30] Johnson is not wrong. In some cases, however, air campaigns might be both understood and prosecuted better as trials of organizational learning rather than as competitions between military-industrial complexes.

Understanding airpower requires an understanding of the organizations nominating targets and performing analysis. This imperative does not appertain solely to historical analyses; it is also incumbent upon those preparing for and fighting wars to assess not only external organizations but also their own. This is no easy task, however, especially for those on the inside. Stephen Rosen aptly offers, "Although it is hard to understand others, it is harder to understand ourselves. . . . Organizational self-assessments have rarely displayed a realistic understanding of the strengths and weaknesses of the organization."[31] The effort is worthwhile, because organizational learning may help reduce the costs of war or avoid campaigns of attrition altogether through a more comprehensive strategy. An air campaign may never be fought with perfect information, but we can endeavor to ask the right questions: What are the organizational interests at play? What ideas and symbols are they selling, and why? And how will these affect the air campaign?

NOTES

INTRODUCTION

1. W. W. Rostow, "OSS War Diary," vol. 5, 13 September 1942–30 April 1945, in "Economic Outpost with Economic Warfare Division R&A Branch," ca. 30 April 1945, 520.056–167, AFHRA, 10.
2. Maj. Gen. Ira C. Eaker, letter, Eaker to Giles, 15 September 1943, AAG 312.1, Operations Letters, RG 18, National Archives (NA).
3. United States Strategic Bombing Survey, *Over-all Report (European War)*, vol. 2 (Washington, DC: U.S. Government Printing Office, 30 September 1945), 1–10.
4. Support to ground forces remained the priority until control of U.S. Strategic Air Forces (USSTAF) reverted from Eisenhower's Supreme Headquarters Allied Expeditionary Force to the Combined Chiefs of Staff on 14 September 1944. Wesley Frank Craven and James Lea Cate, eds., *Europe: Argument to V-E Day, January 1944 to May 1945*, vol. 3 of *The Army Air Forces in World War II* (Washington, DC: Office of Air Force History, 1983), 321.
5. Letter, Arnold to Eaker and Twining, cited in Craven and Cate, 8.
6. A-2 United States Air Forces in Europe, "History of Directorate of Intelligence USSTAF, January 1944–May 1945," 8 September 1945, 519.600, AFHRA, 14; Bill Yenne, *Big Week: Six Days that Changed the Course of World War II* (New York: Berkley Books, 2013), 136–46.

7. Henry Harley Arnold, *American Airpower Comes of Age: General Henry H. "Hap" Arnold's World War II Diaries*, ed. John W. Huston, vol. 2 (Maxwell AFB, AL: Air University Press, 2001), 132–40.
8. Carl A. Spaatz, letter to Arnold, 5 February 1944, 145.81–140, AFHRA.
9. Spaatz to Arnold, enclosure: Summary of Eighth Air Force Heavy Bomber Operations, 1 January 1944 to 31 January 1944.
10. Brig. Gen. F. L. Anderson, "Report of Operations, 24 February 1944, Headquarters Eighth Air Force," 5 March 1944, 520.332, AFHRA, 1–2.
11. Headquarters Eighth Air Force, "Eighth Air Force Narrative of Operations, 233rd Operation," 24 February 1944, 520.332, AFHRA, 2.
12. A-2 1st Bombardment Division and A-2 94th Combat Wing, "Teletype Report," 24 February 1944, 520.332, AFHRA.
13. S-2 379th Bombardment Group, "S-2 Mission Narrative Report, Target—Schweinfurt, N. H. Norgren," 24 February 1944, 520.332, AFHRA.
14. Group Bombardier 92nd Bombardment Group, "Bombing Analysis and Results," 24 February 1944, 520.332, AFHRA; Group Bombardier 305th Bombardment Group, "Bombing Approach and Dropping Procedure for the Mission of 24 February 1944, J. A. Mikkelsen," 24 February 1944, 520.332, AFHRA.
15. Central Interpretation Unit (CIU), "Interpretation Report No. S.A. 1047," in "Eighth Air Force Mission No. 232, RAF Medmenham," 25 February 1944, 520.332, AFHRA, 1.
16. CIU, "Interpretation Report No. S.A. 1047," 3.
17. CIU, "Immediate Interpretation Report No. K.1894," in "Eighth Air Force Mission No. 232, RAF Medmenham," 25 February 1944, 520.332, AFHRA; Allan Williams, *Operation Crossbow: The Untold Story of Photographic Intelligence and the Search for Hitler's V Weapons* (London: Preface, 2011), 183–90.
18. CIU, "Immediate Interpretation Report No. K.1904," in "Eighth Air Force Mission No. 232, RAF Medmenham," 6 March 1944, 520.332, AFHRA.
19. Assistant Chief of Air Staff (A-2), "An Appraisal of Accomplishments and Potentialities," in "The Strategic Aerial Bombardment of Europe, USAAF," 1, 20 April 1944, 142.042–11v5, AFHRA.
20. Assistant Chief of Air Staff (A-2).
21. Assistant Chief of Air Staff (A-2).
22. Phillip S. Meilinger, *Bomber: The Formation and Early Years of Strategic Air Command* (Maxwell Air Force Base, AL: Air University Press, 2012), 62.

23. Meilinger, *Bomber*, 61.
24. Phillip S. Meilinger, "A History of Effects-Based Air Operations," *The Journal of Military History* 71, no. 1 (2007): 141–42.
25. Phillip S. Meilinger, *Ten Propositions Regarding Air Power* (Washington, DC: Air Force History and Museums Program, 1995), 22.
26. James Parton, *Air Force Spoken Here: General Ira Eaker and the Command of the Air* (Bethesda, MD: Adler and Adler, 1986), 155.

CHAPTER 1. THE AAF AT WAR FOR A BOMBER

1. Kuter spoke in this quote of the period around mid-1939, shortly after "Hap" Arnold first assumed the position of chief of the Air Corps. At thirty-six years old, Kuter served as 1st Bombardment Wing Commander in the European theater and later commanded Air University. See Laurence S. Kuter, "Address to Air War College: Organization of Top Echelons in World War II," 28 February 1949, in MS 18, Kuter Papers, Clark Special Collections Branch, 4.
2. Maurer Maurer, *The U.S. Air Service in World War I*, 4 vols. (Maxwell AFB, AL: AFHRA, 1978), IV: 367, 498–501.
3. Robert T. Finney, *History of the Air Corps Tactical School, 1920–1940* (Washington, DC: Center for Air Force History, 1992), 7.
4. Finney, *History of the Air Corps*, 7–8.
5. Finney, *History of the Air Corps*, 19–20.
6. Finney, *History of the Air Corps*, 12.
7. Finney, *History of the Air Corps*, 12, 81.
8. Charles Griffith, *The Quest: Haywood Hansell and American Strategic Bombing in World War II* (Maxwell AFB, AL: Air University Press, 1999), 40.
9. John F. Kreis, *Piercing the Fog: Intelligence and Army Air Forces Operations in World War II* (Washington, DC: Air Force History and Museums Program, 1996), 25.
10. The B-17's range was particularly sensitive to its bomb load. The B-17B boasted a maximum bomb load of 8,800 pounds and a range of 3,000 miles, but it could not accomplish either in combat conditions, in which it could nominally carry only 2,400 pounds up to 1,500 miles. The original armament load of five .30-caliber machine guns on the B model was eventually upgraded to twelve .50-caliber machine guns by 1945. See Wesley Frank

Craven and James Lea Cate, eds., *Men and Planes*, vol. 6 of *The Army Air Forces in World War II* (Washington, DC: Office of Air Force History, 1983), 206–7.

11. Dr. Hal Winton defined doctrine as "the conceptual core around which decisions must be made concerning how the force should be organized, trained, and equipped to win the next war," which must then be incrementally tested and rigorously evaluated. See Harold R. Winton and David R. Mets, *The Challenge of Change: Military Institutions and New Realities, 1918–1941* (Lincoln: University of Nebraska Press, 2000), xii.
12. War Department General Staff, *Field Service Regulations, United States Army, 1923* (Washington, DC: War Department, 1924), 23; David E. Johnson, *Modern U.S. Civil-Military Relations: Wielding the Terrible Swift Sword* (Washington, DC: National Defense University Press, 1997), 6.
13. Air Corps Tactical School, "Rules for Umpires, War Department," May 1936, 248.101–17, AFHRA, 5.
14. For more examples of Air Corps' bombing "at the expense of the Navy," see Stephen Lee McFarland, *America's Pursuit of Precision Bombing, 1910–1945* (Washington, DC: Smithsonian Institution Press, 1995), 99–100.
15. Peter Paret, Gordon Alexander Craig, and Felix Gilbert, *Makers of Modern Strategy: From Machiavelli to the Nuclear Age* (Princeton, NJ: Princeton University Press, 1986), 633.
16. Phillip S. Meilinger, *Airmen and Air Theory: A Review of the Sources* (Maxwell AFB, AL: Air University Press, 2001), 123.
17. John Cotesworth Slessor, *Air Power and Armies* (Tuscaloosa: University of Alabama Press, 2009), 63–64.
18. David R. Mets, *Master of Airpower: General Carl A. Spaatz* (Novato, CA: Presidio Press, 1988), 97–98; John F. Shiner, *Foulois and the U.S. Army Air Corps, 1931–1935* (Washington, DC: AFHSO, 1984), 228–29; Thomas H. Greer, *The Development of Air Doctrine in the Army Air Arm, 1917–1941* (Washington, DC: Office of Air Force History, 1985), 73–74.
19. Mets, *Master of Airpower*, 97–98.
20. Finney, *History of the Air Corps*, 65, 74; Barry D. Watts, *The Foundations of U.S. Air Doctrine: The Problem of Friction in War* (Maxwell AFB, AL: Air University Press, 1985), 18.
21. Haywood S. Hansell, *The Strategic Air War Against Germany and Japan: A Memoir* (Washington, DC: Office of Air Force History, 1986), 7, 10.
22. Hansell, *The Strategic Air War*, 13.

23. Brig. Gen. Haywood S. Hansell, "The Development of the United States Concept of Bombardment Operations," 16 February 1951, in MS 6, series 3, box 4, folder 1, 2, Hansell Papers, Clark Special Collections Branch.
24. Jeffrey C. Benton, *They Served Here: Thirty-Three Maxwell Men* (Maxwell AFB, AL: Air University Press, 1999), 59–60; Griffith, *The Quest*, 43; Vicki J. Rast, *The Air University Pantheon of Air, Space, and Cyberspace Power Thinkers* (Maxwell AFB, AL: Air University Press, 2009), 58–62.
25. Col. Guido R. Perera, "Memoirs: Washington and War Years, 1936–1960," 1973, 168.7042, AFHRA, 77.
26. Kreis, *Piercing the Fog*, 26–27. Kreis also highlights a student exercise led by Maj. Byron Gates and Maj. Robert Webster in 1936 for examining U.S. industry. Kreis concludes that the G-2 would not have had the depth of information required to support ACTS doctrine. This is discussed in a later chapter. Many historians fault ACTS for "mirror-imaging" U.S. industry onto Germany; in truth, they had little choice.
27. Finney, *History of the Air Corps*, 111.
28. Jurgen Brauer and Hubert P. Van Tuyll, *Castles, Battles, and Bombs: How Economics Explains Military History* (Chicago: University of Chicago Press, 2008), 207.
29. Air Corps Tactical School (ACTS), "Maps and Photographs," conference 1–12, 1935–36, 248.101-17A, AFHRA, 1–49.
30. ACTS, "Maps and Photographs, Tactical Employment of Aerial Photography," conference 14, 10 January 1937, 248.101–17A, AFHRA, 80.
31. ACTS, "Maps and Photographs, Tactical Employment of Aerial Photography," 6.
32. ACTS, "Maps and Photographs, Tactical Employment of Aerial Photography," 2.
33. ACTS, "Maps and Photographs, Tactical Employment of Aerial Photography," 7.
34. ACTS, "Maps and Photographs, Tactical Employment of Aerial Photography," 2.
35. Office of Chief of Ordnance, ACTS, "Power of Demolition Bombs," 18 August 1927, 248-6892-14, AFHRA, XXII–XXIII.
36. Laurence S. Kuter, ACTS, "Power and Effect of Demolition Bombs," 1938–39, 248.2208A-3, AFHRA, 4.
37. Kuter, "Power and Effect," 6.
38. Kuter, "Power and Effect," 11.

39. Command and General Staff School, “Conference: Effectiveness of Demolition Bombs Against Specified Objectives,” 14 September 1938, AFHRA, tables 1, 2.
40. Kreis, *Piercing the Fog*, 23.
41. Victor H. Cohen, “Air Intelligence,” in USAF Historical Study 87, ca. 1 January 1954, 106–87, AFHRA, IV-13.
42. Cohen, “Air Intelligence,” IV-38.
43. Michael E. Weaver, “International Cooperation and Bureaucratic In-fighting: American and British Economic Intelligence Sharing and the Strategic Bombing of Germany, 1939–41,” *Intelligence and National Security* 23, no. 2 (April 2008): 159.
44. Weaver, “International Cooperation,” 162.
45. Henry Harley Arnold, *Global Mission* (Blue Ridge Summit, PA: Tab Books, 1989), 188.
46. At the conclusion of his thirty-seven-year military career, Gen. Charles P. Cabell would be viewed as a seasoned senior intelligence officer. His service culminated as the Air Force four-star deputy Central Intelligence Agency director. He was adept at guiding the agency’s clandestine operations and synchronizing military activities, but—as with many military officers turned White House advisors—he was less successful at navigating the political constraints on his plans. Cabell’s career foundered with culpability for the failed Bay of Pigs invasion of Cuba. He unsuccessfully attempted to deflect blame on the presidential decision to cancel preinvasion air strikes and the administration’s subsequent willingness to allow it to fail. Cabell had come to appreciate how airpower could ease the burden on later military operations and seize the information advantage through reconnaissance. Those insights came from his experiences of many years earlier. See: Charles P. Cabell and Charles P. Cabell Jr., *Memoirs of War, Peace, and the CIA* (Colorado Springs: Impavide Publications, 1997), 383–88.
47. Cabell and Cabell, *Memoirs of War*, 14–19.
48. Cabell and Cabell, *Memoirs of War*, 20.
49. Maj. Charles P. Cabell, “Memorandum: Final Report of Military Air Observer to Great Britain to the Assistant Chief of Staff, G-2, War Department,” 7 April 1941, 168.7026–2, AFHRA, 5.
50. Charles P. Cabell, U.S. Air Force oral history interview by Henry L. Bowen and Alfred Goldberg, 15 January 1962.

51. Cabell and Cabell, *Memoirs of War,* 23.
52. Cabell, "Memorandum: Final Report of Military Air Observer," 3.
53. Maj. Charles P. Cabell, "Interpretation of Aerial Photographs," 21 February 1941, 168.7026-2, AFHRA.
54. Maj. Charles P. Cabell, "Aerial Photography: Organization and Operation of Photographic Reconnaisance Unit Number One/Benson, England, War Department," 21 February 1941, 168.7026-2, AFHRA, 4.
55. Maj. Charles P. Cabell, "Organization of the Central Interpretation Unit," 21 March 1941, 168.7026-2, AFHRA, 5.
56. Cabell, "Organization of the Central Interpretation Unit."
57. Ursula Powys-Lybbe, *The Eye of Intelligence* (London: W. Kimber, 1983), 35.
58. Maj. Charles P. Cabell, "Night Aerial Photography," 25 February 1941, 168.7026-2, AFHRA, 1.
59. Cabell, "Night Aerial Photography."
60. Maj. Charles P. Cabell, "Aerial Photography: Organization and Operation of Photographic Reconnaissance Unit No. 3," 21 February 1941, 168.7026-2, AFHRA, 2.
61. Cabell, "Interpretation of Aerial Photographs," 2.
62. Cabell, "Organization of the Central Interpretation Unit," 5.
63. Cabell, "Organization of the Central Interpretation Unit," 4.
64. Cabell, "Organization and Operation of Photographic Reconnaisance Unit Number One/Benson, England," 4.
65. Brig. Gen. Sherman Miles, memorandum from Military Intelligence Division, G-2, to the Chief of Staff, War Department, "Responsibility of the Military Intelligence Division for Air Intelligence," 18 April 1941, 203-6v.5 part 2, AFHRA.
66. A-2 Office Chief of Air Service, "Basis for Air Intelligence for an Air Estimate of the Situation—Europe," 22 March 1941, 203-6v.5 part 2, AFHRA, 1–10.
67. A-2 Office Chief of Air Service, "Basis for Air Intelligence."
68. Miles, "Responsibility of the Military Intelligence Division."
69. Miles, "Responsibility of the Military Intelligence Division."
70. George V. Strong, memorandum by direction of the Secretary of War to the Chief of the Air Corps, "Air Corps Intelligence," 5 October 1939, 203-6v.5, AFRHA, 5; Army Regulation 15-10 of the War Department, 18 August

1936, is published as exhibit No. 42 in U.S. Congress, "Hearings Before the United States Joint Committee on the Investigation of the Pearl Harbor Attack, Seventy-Ninth Congress, Second Session, Part 14, Joint Committee on the Investigation of the Pearl Harbor Attack, 1946," 1416-21. See paragraph 9 for Military Intelligence Division.

71. Brig. Gen. Joseph T. McNarney, memorandum from Acting Assistant Chief of Staff, War Plans Division, to the Assistant Chief of Staff, G-2, "Responsibility of the Military Intelligence Division for Air Intelligence," 24 April 1941, 203-6v.5, AFHRA.
72. Brig. Gen. Sherman Miles, memorandum from Military Intelligence Division, G-2, to the Chief of Staff, War Department, "Delineation of Responsibility for Intelligence Studies between the Air Corps and the Military Intelligence Division," 14 May 1941, 203-6v.5 part 2, AFHRA, 5.
73. A-2 Office of the Chief of Air Corps, memorandum from Intelligence Division, Office of the Chief of Air Corps to Assistant Chief of Staff, G-2, "Digest of Information Received," 13 February 1941, 203-6v.5, AFHRA.
74. Arnold, *Global Mission*, 534–35.
75. Gen. George Brett, memorandum from Chief of Air Corps to Military Intelligence Division, G-2, "Non-Concurrence in G-2/271-A-ST," 16 June 1941, 203-6v.5, AFHRA.
76. H. H. Arnold, memorandum to the Chief of Staff, War Department, "Non-Concurrence in G-2/271-A-57, August 11, 1941," 22 August 1941, 203-6v.5, AFHRA.
77. Arnold, "Non-Concurrence in G-2/271-A-57."
78. Arnold, *Global Mission*, 535.
79. Carl A. Spaatz, "Comments on Air Intelligence Items," 11 July 1941, 203-6v.5, AFHRA, 1.
80. Spaatz, "Comments on Air Intelligence Items," 2.
81. David M. Bensusan-Butt, memorandum, "Bomber Command: Night Photograph Analysis, Offices of the War Cabinet, Air 8—Air Ministry and Ministry of Defence: Department of the Chief of the Air Staff," 18 August 1941, AIR 8/1356, UK National Archives.
82. Tami Davis Biddle, *Rhetoric and Reality in Air Warfare: The Evolution of British and American Ideas about Strategic Bombing, 1914–1945* (Princeton, NJ: Princeton University Press, 2002), 1–3.

83. Denis Richards, *Portal of Hungerford: The Life of Marshal of the Royal Air Force Viscount Portal of Hungerford KG, GCB, OM, DSO, MC* (New York: Holmes and Meier, 1977), 303.
84. For the humorous origin of the word *boffin*, see Norman W. Schur, Eugene Ehrlich, and Richard Ehrlich, *British English A to Zed: A Definitive Guide to the Queen's English* (New York: Skyhorse, 2013), 38. Also, for a concise history of RAF's radio navigation development, along with Bomber Command's resultant experimentation with Pathfinder Force tactics (as further discussed in chapter 4), see Randall T. Wakelam, *The Science of Bombing: Operational Research in RAF Bomber Command* (Toronto: University of Toronto Press, 2009), 60–63, 74–76. Not until H2S (air-to-ground radar mapping) became available at the end of 1942 was long-range blind bombing possible.
85. Maj. D. W. Hutchison, "Central Interpretation Unit Training," 27 October 1941, 168.7026-3, AFHRA, 1.
86. Hutchinson, "Central Interpretation Unit Training."
87. Maj. D. W. Hutchison, "Photographic Training," 27 October 1941, 168.7026-3, AFHRA, 1.
88. Although American women had enlisted in the Army Nurse Corps, Signal Corps, and as Navy yeomen in World War I, the first female officers in U.S. armed forces history did not enter training until July 1942. See Wilma L. Vaught, "In Defense of America: Women Who Serve," *USA Today* 122, no. 2586 (1994).
89. Hutchison, "Photographic Training," 1–2.
90. Charles W. McArthur, *Operations Analysis in the U.S. Army Eighth Air Force in World War II* (Providence, RI: American Mathematical Society, 1990), 34.
91. Maj. D. W. Hutchison, "Morale-Welfare of R.A.F.," 27 October 1941, 168.7026-3, AFHRA, 1.
92. Hutchinson, "Morale-Welfare of R.A.F.," 2.
93. Perera, "Memoirs," 55.
94. Maj. Bartlett Beaman, "Progress Report, Air Intelligence Section," 1 December 1941, 203-6v.5, AFHRA, 1.
95. Beaman, "Progress Report," 2.
96. The attacks would have been simultaneous with the raid on Pearl Harbor had weather not delayed the Japanese. As events transpired, the attack was

only hours later since the Philippines are across the date line. According to the official Air Force account, half of the thirty-five B-17s and fifty-five P-40s were lost. See Wesley Frank Craven and James Lea Cate, eds., *Plans and Early Operations, January 1939 to August 1942*, vol. 1 of *The Army Air Forces in World War II* (Washington, DC: Office of Air Force History, 1983), 201–33.

97. Failures of intelligence and military decisionmaking leading into Pearl Harbor shaped perceptions by the American public and senior government officials that critical national and military intelligence lacked appropriate collection, analysis, dissemination, and especially coordination. Though senior military commanders were held accountable and relieved of duty after the attack, the extensive seventy-day congressional investigation did not begin until after V-J day. Despite a variety of intelligence indicators of faltering diplomatic relations and Japanese interest in the detailed berthing plan for the Navy fleet at Pearl Harbor, the extent to which pieces of decoded messages and other available intelligence amounted to a definitive suggestion of imminent attack remains controversial. Nevertheless, Congress cited detrimental organizational rivalry factors among military intelligence offices and senior officers. For example, "The War Plans Division, particularly, appears to have had an overzealous disposition to preserve and enhance its prerogatives." See U.S. Congress, "Report of the Joint Committee on the Investigation of the Pearl Harbor Attack Including the Minority Report, Joint Committee on the Investigation of the Pearl Harbor Attack" (New York: Da Capo Press, 1972), xiv, 251–66 (quote on 264). Pearl Harbor has been exhaustively studied. For a sense of controversial conclusions, also see David Kahn, "The Intelligence Failure of Pearl Harbor," *Foreign Affairs* 70, no. 5 (1991): 147–49; Roberta Wohlstetter, *Pearl Harbor: Warning and Decision* (Stanford, CA: Stanford University Press, 1962), 382–98.

98. Haywood S. Hansell, *The Air Plan that Defeated Hitler* (Atlanta: Higgins-McArthur/Longino and Porter, 1972), 73.

99. With minor tweaks, AWPD-1 was accepted as the blueprint for buildup of air forces at the Arcadia conference, which concluded on 14 January 1942. See Hansell, *The Air Plan that Defeated Hitler*, 97–99. VIII Bomber Command and its higher echelon Eighth AF activated (with their general

officers in place) on 23 February under Eaker and on 5 May under Spaatz, respectively. Operations in the European theater unfolded in a series of incremental firsts. Notably, the first bombing raid by the AAF in Western Europe occurred on 7 July, conducted with aircraft borrowed back from the United Kingdom. The 97th becomes the AAF's first heavy bomb group ready for combat from the United Kingdom on 27 July. Its first B-17 raid occurred on 17 August, just over seven months since the plan was authorized. For more timeline details, see Kit C. Carter and Robert Mueller, *U.S. Army Air Forces in World War II, Combat Chronology 1941–1945* (Maxwell AFB, AL: AFHRA, 1991).

100. While the Army's organization in 1945 differed significantly from the force envisaged in the Victory plan, the total size of the force was remarkably similar. The actual size of the AAF on 31 May 1945 was 2,310,436. More detail is available in Alan L. Gropman, *Mobilizing U.S. Industry in World War II: Myth and Reality* (Washington, DC: National Defense University Press, 1996), 42.
101. Craven and Cate, *Plans and Early Operations*, 238.
102. Greer, *The Development of Air Doctrine*, 123–24.
103. Ronald E. Powaski, *The Cold War: The United States and the Soviet Union, 1917–1991* (New York: Oxford University Press, 1998), 50.
104. Hansell, *The Air Plan that Defeated Hitler*, 59.
105. Craven and Cate, *Plans and Early Operations*, 237–40.
106. Richard G. Davis, *Carl A. Spaatz and the Air War in Europe* (Washington, DC: Deaprtment of the Air Force, 1993), 69.
107. Mets, *Master of Airpower*, 116.
108. Cabell and Cabell, *Memoirs of War*, 110–11.
109. Col. Richard D'Oyly Hughes, "Memoirs: Chapter VIII—1941–1945, USAF," 1957, 520.056-234, AFRHA, 16, 27.
110. Hughes, "Memoirs," 11.
111. Hughes, "Memoirs," 15–20.
112. Geoffrey Perret, *Winged Victory: The Army Air Forces in World War II* (New York: Random House, 1993), 177.
113. Assistant Chief of Air Staff (A-2), "The Ploesti Mission of 1 August 1943," June 1944, USAF Historical Study 103, 101–103, AFHRA, 14. This report includes an extensive review of context and results for both the 1942 and 1943 Ploesti raids. While it is quick to highlight operational failures of an

inadequate attacking force and navigational errors, it suggests that collection of targeting histories was a positive contribution by AAF intelligence. Alan J. Levine, *The Strategic Bombing of Germany, 1940–1945* (Westport, CT: Praeger, 1992), 94.

114. Assistant Chief of Air Staff (A-2), "The Ploesti Mission," 16–17.
115. Levine, *The Strategic Bombing*, 95.
116. Wesley Frank Craven and James Lea Cate, eds., *Europe: Torch to Pointblank, August 1942 to December 1943*, vol. 2 of *The Army Air Forces in World War II* (Washington, DC: Office of Air Force History, 1983), 10.
117. Col. E. F. Koenig, "Final Report to Commanding General, First District, AAFTTC, Headquarters Air Intelligence School (Harrisburg, PA)," 30 September 1942, 266.1-1, AFHRA, 9:2.
118. Maj. Gen. George Brett, "Budget Estimate for F.Y. (Fiscal Year) 1943, Air Corps—Intelligence Items," in "History of AAFAIS, USAF," 1945, 266.1, AFHRA, 2.
119. Perret discusses Arnold's impulsive management style and "aversion to standard operating procedures [that] extended even to his own Air Staff" through several anecdotes; see Perret, *Winged Victory*, 137–39.
120. Cohen, "Air Intelligence," 9:4–9.
121. Koenig, "Final Report to Commanding General," 6.
122. "History of AAFAIS," 3:2.
123. Cohen, "Air Intelligence," 12.
124. "History of AAFAIS," class roster, 9:14.
125. Koenig, "Final Report to Commanding General," 6.
126. Koenig, "Final Report to Commanding General."
127. "History of AAFAIS," 17.
128. Cohen, "Air Intelligence," 9:18.
129. Carl von Clausewitz, *On War*, ed. and trans. Michael Howard and Peter Paret (Princeton, NJ: Princeton University Press, 1984), 187.
130. United States Army Air Forces, draft memorandum, "Intelligence Officers on Temporary Duty in Washington," ca. October 1942, 266.1, AFHRA.
131. Lt. Col. L. W. Johnson, "Investigation of Conditions at AAF Air Intellgence School, AAF Technical Training Command," 16 February 1943, 266.152-1, AFHRA, 38.
132. AAF Intelligence School, "Information Bulletin," 10 April 1942, 266.1, AFHRA, 5.

133. Col. Harvey Holland, "Progress Report, Headquarters Air Intelligence School," ca. 10 March 1943, 266.1, AFHRA, 4.
134. Cohen, "Air Intelligence," 9:10.
135. "History of AAFAIS," chap. 3.
136. Capt. Arthur A. Houghton Jr., memorandum, "Indoctrination Course, Headquarters Air Intelligence School," 4 February 1943, 266.1, AFHRA, 6.
137. Gen. George C. Marshall, "Military Education: The Air Corps Intelligence School," n.d., 266.1, AFHRA.
138. Army Air Forces Air Intelligence School (AAFAIS), *Group and Squadron S-2*, ed. United States Army Air Forces, rev. ed. (Washington, DC: U.S. Government Printing Office, 1943), 5.
139. AAFAIS, *Group and Squadron S-2*, 7–8.
140. AAFAIS, *The Briefing and Interrogation of Bomber Crews* (Harrisburg, PA: United States Army Air Forces, 1942), 16.
141. AAFAIS, *Group and Squadron S-2*, 31.
142. AAFAIS, *Group and Squadron S-2*, 9.
143. AAFAIS, *The Briefing and Interrogation of Bomber Crews*, 16.
144. AAFAIS, *The Briefing and Interrogation of Bomber Crews*, 20.
145. Arnold, *Global Mission*, 223.
146. AAFAIS, *The Briefing and Interrogation of Bomber Crews*, 24.
147. AAFAIS, *Photo Intelligence for Combat Aviation* (Harrisburg, PA: United States Army Air Forces, 1942), 2–3.
148. AAFAIS, *Photo Intelligence for Combat Aviation*, 177.
149. AAFAIS, *Photo Intelligence for Combat Aviation*, 67.
150. AAFAIS, *Photo Intelligence for Combat Aviation*, 18.
151. AAFAIS, *Photo Intelligence for Combat Aviation*, 67, 73–74.
152. AAFAIS, *Photo Intelligence for Combat Aviation*, 154.
153. Eaker, "Bomber Command Plan," 4, in Craven and Cate, *Plans and Early Operations*, 624.
154. Lt. Col. Harris B. Hull, memorandum to Commanding General, VIII Bomber Command, "Subject: Organization of the Intelligence Section," in "Report of Lt. Col. John T. McCall on Eighth Air Force, Headquarters VIII Bomber Command," ca. December 1942, 520.601C V.1, AFHRA.
155. Lt. Col. Harris B. Hull, "Organization Chart, Asst. Chief of Staff, A-2," in "Report of Lt. Col. John T. McCall on Eighth Air Force, Headquarters VIII Bomber Command."

156. Craven and Cate, *Plans and Early Operations*, 588–90.
157. Craven and Cate, *Torch to Pointblank*, 237.
158. Walter J. Boyne, *W 190 Wurger* 92, no. 4 (2009): 80.
159. Mets, *Master of Airpower,* 133.
160. Davis, *Carl A. Spaatz and the Air War in Europe*, appendix 8, 618.
161. In practice, some months of the war, less than 40 percent of the aircraft in theater were available for combat. See Headquarters Eighth Air Force, "Review of Operational Considerations" and "B-17 Statistics" in "Summary of Eighth Air Force Heavy Bomber Operations as Called For in Combined Bomber Offensive Plan: First Phase," July 1943, 168.61-10, AFHRA.
162. General Frank Andrews, as the theater's top airman, would set a more aggressive estimate the following spring, when he insisted that at least two formations of one hundred bombers each per day would "penetrate enemy defenses" and destroy most targets, but those numbers were well out of reach in 1942. See "Notes on Meeting with General Eaker, Eighth Air Force," 3 April 1943, 168.61-10, AFHRA, and Craven and Cate, *Torch to Pointblank*, 236.
163. Craven and Cate, *Torch to Pointblank*, 74, 322.
164. Craven and Cate, *Torch to Pointblank*, appendix 9.
165. Hughes, "Memoirs," 24.
166. Lt. Col. Harris B. Hull, personal letter to Col. Lucius P. Ordway, Assistant Chief of Staff, A-2, Headquarters VIII Bomber Command, 13 December 1942, 520.6031, AFHRA.
167. Edgar P. Sorensen, letter to MacDonald, HQ AAF War Department, 2 October 1942, 520.603-1, AFHRA.
168. Edgar P. Sorensen, "Memorandum to All Eighth Air Force Subordinate Commanding Generals, HQ AAF War Department," 3 October 1942, 520.603-1, AFHRA; Koenig, 6.
169. Air Intelligence Section, "Analysis of Results of USAAF Bombing Attacks on Submarine Bases in France, during November, 1942," in "An Evaluation of the Air Effort Against Submarines (to January 1, 1943), Air Ministry," 7 January 1943, 142.042-6, AFHRA, 2.
170. Antisubmarine Command, "Monthly Summary, USAAF," January 1943, 142.042-6, AFHRA, 4.
171. Antisubmarine Command, "Monthly Summary," 2.
172. McFarland, *America's Pursuit of Precision Bombing*, 170; Parton, *Air Force Spoken Here*, 237.

173. McArthur, *Operations Analysis*, 32.
174. McArthur, *Operations Analysis*, 31.
175. Warren Kozak, *LeMay: The Life and Wars of General Curtis LeMay* (Washington, DC: Regnery, 2009), 104–7.
176. AC/AS Intelligence, "Attacks of U-Boat Bases in Northern France by the USAAF," in "An Evaluation of the Air Effort Against Submarines (to January 1, 1943)," 8 March 1943, 142.042-6, AFHRA.
177. Air Intelligence Section, "Analysis of Results of USAAF Bombing Attacks on Submarine Bases in France, during November 1942," 7 January 1943.
178. McArthur, *Operations Analysis*, 32; Craven and Cate, *Torch to Pointblank*, 250.
179. Air Intelligence Section, "Analysis of Results of USAAF Bombing Attacks on Submarine Bases in France, during November 1942." Of note, the CIU later correlated the titles of their reports to the raid date rather than the date of the reconnaissance flight. In this case, the report addresses the raid of 3 January.

CHAPTER 2. PICKING UP THE SLACK

1. Among the nicknames for operational analysts in Eighth Air Force were "Quiz Kids," "Op Annies," or simply "Doc." Charlotte Knight, "Ask Them Another," *Air Force* 28, no. 8 (1945): 31.
2. Richard D. McKinzie, "Oral History Interview with Charles P. Kindleberger," 16 July 1973, 18, https://www.trumanlibrary.org/oralhist/kindbrgr.htm#transcript.
3. Various histories offer slightly different perspectives on Arnold's formation of the COA, although appraisals of his motives are relatively consistent: he needed credible air intelligence and could not get it from his staff. The COA's official history gives the credit to Major General Fairchild, who had recognized that "the research and analysis necessary to the formulation of plans and solutions of strategic bombing problems . . . was [an activity] for which a regular army career did not necessarily prepare an officer." There may have been problems of competency as well as credibility. Guido R. Perera, "History of the Organization and Operations of the Committee of Operations Analysts," 1944, 118.01 v.1, AFHRA, 3–4.
4. As official Army historians reference the matter of interwar education for officers, "The Army Industrial College prepared senior officers of demonstrated ability for the most responsible command and staff positions and

assisted in the development of war plans. By establishing the Industrial College, the Army acknowledged the high importance of industrial mobilization and logistical training for the conduct of modern warfare." Of course, the school's attendees were trained on the American military-industrial complex since its inception in 1924, not the destruction of foreign industries. Richard W. Stewart, *American Military History*, vol. 2 (Washington, DC: U.S. Army Center of Military History, 2005), 95.

5. Kreis, *Piercing the Fog*, 152.
6. Arnold, *Global Mission*, 534–35.
7. Hansell, *The Air Plan that Defeated Hitler*, 148.
8. Gates previously held the section chief position for both observation and pursuit at ACTS as well as teaching in the department of air tactics and strategy. Even if he was not directly responsible for instructing bombardment doctrine, he would certainly have been aware of ACTS viewpoints as he steered COA. See Finney, *History of the Air Corps*, 106–12.
9. The presence of direct oversight or involvement by ACTS graduates (both Gates and Sorensen) is an important distinction between the COA and the EOU. By contrast, especially given Eaker's alleged laissez-faire role in his staff's operational matters, EOU did not have continuous or direct involvement by ACTS graduates except the intermittent interactions between Fred Anderson, Haywood Hansell, and Curtis LeMay with Richard Hughes. EOU thus had a wider berth to stray from ACTS doctrine. For examples of the latter interactions, see Hughes, "Memoirs," 18, 30, 33; W. W. Rostow, "OSS War Diary," vol. 5, 13 September 1942–30 April 1945, in *Economic Outpost With Economic Warfare Division*, ca. 30 April 1945, R&A Branch, 520.056-167, AFHRA (hereafter, "Rostow Report").
10. H. H. Arnold, memorandum, "Research and Analysis to Fix Earliest Practicable Date for Invasion of Western Europe," 22 December 1942, 118.161, AFHRA.
11. McArthur, *Operations Analysis*, 9.
12. Haridimos Tsoukas categorizes organizations of this type as "distributed knowledge systems, whose effective action is the result not so much of individuals acquiring more and more knowledge as of finding ways of utilizing widely distributed organizational knowledge." Haridimos Tsoukas, *New Thinking in Organizational Behaviour: From Social Engineering to*

Reflective Action (Oxford: Butterworth-Heinemann, 1994), 16. Also, an organizational challenge of hiring outside experts is one of lacking the internal expertise to hold them accountable. Robert Gilpin and Jean M. Gilpin, *Global Political Economy: Understanding the International Economic Order* (Princeton, NJ: Princeton University Press, 2001), 71.

13. Parton, *Air Force Spoken Here*, 249–51; McArthur, *Operations Analysis*, 9; Byron E. Gates, "Memorandum to Maj. Gen. Fairchild," 15 December 1942, 118.161, AFHRA.
14. Perera, "History of the Organization and Operations of the Committee of Operations Analysts," 1944, 7.
15. Edgar P. Sorensen, letter to Kuter, 3 January 1943, MS 6, series 2, box 2, notebook 1, Hansell Papers, Clark Special Collections Branch.
16. Howard Bruce, "Memorandum for Asst Chief of Air Staff, A-2; Subject: Foreign Experts," 12 December 1942, 118.161, AFHRA, 2–3.
17. Bruce, "Memorandum."
18. Hughes, "Memoirs," 11.
19. Perera, "Memoirs," 41-A.
20. Perera, "Memoirs," 55-D.
21. Arnold's seemingly endless diversions of Eighth Air Force bombers in 1943 was a source of serious concern to Eaker, but they also often disagreed on everything from maintenance practices to personnel moves. COA's efforts probably added one more frustration for Eaker. Though Eaker rarely opposed Arnold directly, when he did so, he tried to choose his words and his battles carefully. Despite his subordinate tone, Eaker probably crossed the line on 12 July 1943 and arguably never quite recovered: "One of my greatest concerns is the fact that I have so frequently of late been placed in the position where it might appear that I was opposing an idea which originated in Washington and which from the information available there, seemed to be sound." Maj. Gen. Ira C. Eaker, letter to Arnold, 12 June 1943, box 16, Eaker Papers, Manuscript Division, Library of Congress (LOC).
22. Byron E. Gates, memorandum, "Analysis of Bombardment Objectives in Axis Europe," 23 December 1942, 118.161, AFHRA, 1.
23. Perera, "History of the Organization and Operations of the Committee of Operations Analysts," 18.
24. Hoover Medal Board of Award, "William Loren Batt: Thirteenth Hoover Medalist," 1951, 10.

25. Martin Fritz and Birgit Karlsson, *SKF—A Global Story: 1907–2007* (Stockholm: Informationsförlaget, 2006), 102–3.
26. Gates, "Analysis of Bombardment Objectives in Axis Europe," 2.
27. Committee of Operations Analysts, "Report of Committee of Operations Analysts with Respect to Economic Targets Within the Western Axis," 8 March 1943, tab 22, 118.02v2, AFHRA, 2.
28. As with many other analysis-related initiatives, Americans emulated the British. The Air Ministry had employed a team of scientists under Henry Tizard to develop radar in the 1930s and later employed civilian teams to conduct "operational researches," which was less about new laboratory work or technology development and more about "doing the best you can with what you have." Joseph F. McCloskey, "The Beginnings of Operations Research: 1934–1941," *Operations Research* 35, no. 1 (1987): 144–46.
29. Col. Charles B. B. Bubb, memorandum, "Operation Research Section, to Commanding Officers, 1st, 2nd, 3rd Bomb Wings, Headquarters VIII Bomber Command," 23 October 1942, 520.303-1, AFHRA.
30. Leslie H. Arps, report, "Operational Analysis Section, Headquarters Eighth Air Force," 1 June 1945, 520.303-3, AFHRA, 2.
31. Bubb, "Operation Research Section, to Commanding Officers, 1st, 2nd, 3rd Bomb Wings."
32. Col. Charles B. B. Bubb, memorandum, "Directive to Section Chief, Operational Research Section, Headquarters VIII Bomber Command," 23 October 1942, 520.303-1, AFHRA.
33. Charles R. Shrader, *History of Operations Research in the United States Army* (Washington, DC: U.S. Army Center of Military History, 2006), 25.
34. Knight, "Ask Them Another," 60.
35. According to the ORS history, both commander and deputy had been commissioned by July 1943. See Arps, 3.
36. Civilians in service in World War II, including operations analysts as well as Women Airforce Service Pilots, had "the nonmilitary rights of optional resignation and rejection of assignments." See Jane A. Barlow and Clinton C. Gardner, *World War II Remembered* (Hanover, NH: Kendal at Hanover Residents Association, 2012), 151.
37. Knight, "Ask Them Another," 60.
38. Leslie H. Arps et al., *Operations Analysis in the Eighth Air Force, 1942–1945: Four Contemporary Accounts* (Linthicum, MD: INFORMS, 1997), 196–98, 204–12; Arps, "Operational Analysis Section," 56–57.

39. Arps, "Operational Analysis Section," 9–18.
40. Arps et al., *Operations Analysis in the Eighth Air Force*, 3. Text from Hugh Miser's introduction.
41. Arps, "Operational Analysis Section," 26.
42. Maj. Gen. Ira C. Eaker, letter to McClelland, 10 January 1943, box 16, Eaker Papers, Manuscript Division, LOC.
43. Brig. Gen. H. M. McClelland, letter to Eaker, 15 February 1943, box 16, Eaker Papers, Manuscript Division, LOC; Finney, *History of the Air Corps*, 126.
44. Leroy A. Brothers, "Operations Analysis in the United States Air Force," *Journal of the Operations Research Society of America* 2, no. 1 (1954): 3.
45. For an evaluation of the ORS researchers' methods, see Statistical Control Division, "AAF Bombing Accuracy, USAAF," 31 March 1945, 134.71-83, AFHRA, 52–54.
46. Brothers, "Operations Analysis," 3.
47. Arps et al., *Operations Analysis in the Eighth Air Force*, 3.
48. Knight, "Ask Them Another," 31.
49. Arps et al., *Operations Analysis in the Eighth Air Force*, 208.
50. Perera, "History of the Organization and Operations of the Committee of Operations Analysts," 10.
51. Bissell Alderman, "Report for Colonel Leach on the History and Development of the Bombs and Fuzes Subsection of the Operational Analysis Section, Headquarters Eighth Air Force," 10 April 1945, 520.3033, AFHRA, 2.
52. McArthur, *Operations Analysis*, 39.
53. As Harlan saw it, the bombs and fuzes subsection's purpose developed over time into four tasks: choice of weapons for particular targets, analysis of photographic reconnaissance unit coverage for weapons effectiveness lessons learned, studies of theoretical and experimental data, and estimates of weapons requirements. See John M. Harlan, "The Operational Research Section at the Eighth Air Force," 18 July 1944, 520.303-1, AFHRA, 7–8.
54. McArthur, *Operations Analysis*, 39.
55. John Hoyt Lockwood, *Western Massachusetts: A History, 1636–1925*, vol. 3 (New York: Lewis Historical Publishing Co., 1926).
56. John Ruskin, *The Seven Lamps of Architecture* (London: Chiswick Press, 1880), 197.
57. Of note, both Anderson and Longfellow were ACTS graduates from the classes of 1937 and 1936, respectively. The ACTS pedigree in no way protected a general from "Hap" Arnold's fury. Arnold insisted Eaker remove

Longfellow from VIII Bomber Command in April 1943. Maj. Gen. Barney M. Giles, letter, Arnold to Eaker, 11 June 1943, RG 18, AAG 312.1-G, NARA; Alderman, "Report for Colonel Leach," 5, 18; Finney, *History of the Air Corps*, 116–27; McArthur, *Operations Analysis*, 101.

58. Alderman, "Report for Colonel Leach," 3.
59. According to a COA memorandum, the Ministry of Home Security R. E. 8 (Research and Experiments Department, section 8) was yet another intelligence-related organization composed of "architects, physicists, photographic interpreters, and some economists." Their functions were: "(a) assessment of the results of German air attacks on Great Britain; (b) pre-raid assessment of probabilities of British and American raids upon German targets; (c) post-raid assessment of damage and economic effects thereof of British and American raids; (d) assessment of relative efficacy of weapons." Their reports allegedly circulated to Colonel Hughes, EOU's Chandler Morse, and General Arnold via his A-2, but COA was not receiving them prior to July 1943. See Col. Guido R. Perera, memorandum for Brig. Gen. Gates, 15 July 1943, 118.111, AFHRA, 4–5. According to an Air Force history, "By August 1943, fifteen Americans were assigned to R. E. 8." See Kreis, *Piercing the Fog*, 138.
60. Alderman, "Report for Colonel Leach," 3.
61. Alderman, "Report for Colonel Leach," 4.
62. Alderman, "Report for Colonel Leach," 10.
63. Alderman, "Report for Colonel Leach," 6.
64. Alderman, "Report for Colonel Leach," 8.
65. Arps, "Operational Analysis Section," 77.
66. The mathematicians finally overcame objections to mixed-loading incendiaries with high-explosive bombs by producing improved bombing tables for bombardiers and optimizing loading tables for ordnance and chemical warfare sections. Arps, "Operational Analysis Section," 77–78.
67. Alderman, "Report for Colonel Leach," 14–15, 17.
68. War Diary, R&A Branch, OSS/London, vol. 1, "Early History," 10, 12, 16, 87, reel 3, entry 91, RG 226, NARA, 10, 12, 16, 87, in Nelson MacPherson, *American Intelligence in War-Time London: The Story of the OSS* (Portland, OR: Frank Cass Publishers, 2003), 59–60, 105. Macpherson's analysis suggests these relationships led to unnecessary demarcation between OSS branches and hindered collaboration within the OSS to produce comprehensive analysis as a result.

69. Rostow, who was part of the original EOU team, claims Hughes reached out directly to the ambassador. See W. W. Rostow, "Waging Economic Warfare from London," *Studies in Intelligence* 7, no. 1 (1992): 73.
70. Tyson, who was not an economist like most EOU members, applied his Harvard education to aircraft industry assessments. He claimed Hughes first contacted Chandler Morse of the OSS R&A branch. See James L. Tyson, "The EOU vs. Hitler's Mini-Missiles," *International Journal of Intelligence and Counterintelligence* 12, no. 1 (1999): 81.
71. Marc Trachtenberg, David Rosenberg, and Stephen Van Evera, "An Interview with Carl Kaysen," MIT Security Studies Program (Working Papers), Massachusetts Institute of Technology, 1988, http://web.mit.edu/ssp/publications/working_papers/Kaysen%20working%20paper.pdf.
72. Rostow, "Waging Economic Warfare from London," 73.
73. The economists, it should be noted, demonstrated a tendency similar to that of Gareth Morgan's notion of an egocentric organization. As Morgan recognized of other professions, this also held true for EOU's economists, whose "understanding of the environment was a product of their identity." Their desire to impart models of rational and efficient targeting decisions also inclined EOU to seek its own goals. See Gareth Morgan, "Organizations as Flux and Transformation," in Tsoukas, *New Thinking in Organizational Behaviour: From Social Engineering to Reflective Action*, 142–43.
74. Trachtenberg, Rosenberg, and Van Evera, "An Interview with Carl Kaysen," 2.
75. Rostow, "Waging Economic Warfare from London," 78.
76. MacPherson, *American Intelligence*, 104.
77. Of note, Walt Rostow was a Rhodes scholar and later national security advisor to President Lyndon Johnson. See W. W. Rostow, "Oral History Interview 364 with Walt W. Rostow," 17 October 1970, no. 0016244, Project Corona Harvest, AFHRA, 98; see also Tyson, "The EOU vs. Hitler's Mini-Missiles," 81.
78. Rostow, "Waging Economic Warfare from London," 78.
79. Carl Kaysen, another EOU economist, recommended notably to the Air Force postwar "the desirability of recruiting, as far as possible, economists, economic statisticians, engineers, and to some extent, lawyers for intelligence service, as opposed to a tendency in World War II to recruit people with experience in the advertising, newspaper, publicity, and selling fields." See Carl Kaysen, "Notes on Strategic Air Intelligence in World War II (ETO)" (Santa Monica, CA: Project RAND, October 1949), 29–30.

80. Hughes, "Memoirs," 90. For a sense of MEW's scope, its Enemy Branch in 1943 "comprised 12 technical sections (armaments, engineering, metals and minerals, power, inland transport, chemicals, textiles, petroleum, labour, finance, trade, and administration); a shipping section (strength and movements of merchant shipping controlled by Germany and Italy); three 'country' sections covering Axis Europe, including the occupied territories; a Far Eastern department; a bomb damage assessment section; a Russian section; and finally an Information and Procurement department concerned with the war activities of individuals and firms and distribution of intelligence material." See Peter Davies, "Geoffrey Vickers and Lessons from the Ministry of Economic Warfare for Cold War Defence Intelligence," *Intelligence and National Security* 31, no. 6 (2016): 812.
81. Hohn adds, "In November 1941, it was calculated that 2,400 targets were included in the German target books at the Bomber Commands' stations and that dossiers and maps existed for 1,500 of them." See Uta Hohn, "The Bomber's Baedeker—Target Book for Strategic Bombing in the Economic Warfare against German Towns 1943–45," *GeoJournal* 34, no. 2 (1994): 214.
82. Many MEW reports included obscure data. They reported, for example, that Germany imported 214 tons of Hungarian wheat via rail from Hegyeshalom in March 1944. See Foreign Office Enemy Branch and Ministry of Economic Warfare, Appendix IX, "Summary of Specific Commercial Consignments Passing to and from Balkan Countries, March, 1944," in "Enemy Inland Transport Notes, No. 4," 17 July 1944, 512.6111D, AFHRA.
83. Air Ministry, "The RAF in the Bombing Offensive Against Germany," n.d., 512.041-26, AFHRA, 331.
84. Rostow, "Rostow Report," 15.
85. Charles K. Webster and Noble Frankland, *The Strategic Air Offensive Against Germany, 1939–1945*, 4 vols. (London: Her Majesty's Stationery Office, 1961), 261.
86. Webster and Frankland, *The Strategic Air Offensive Against Germany*.
87. MacPherson, *American Intelligence*, 127–28; Biddle, *Rhetoric and Reality*, 199.
88. Arthur Travers Harris, *Bomber Offensive* (South Yorkshire, UK: Pen & Sword Military Classics, 2005), 45–46.
89. Hohn, "The Bomber's Baedeker," 220.
90. Memorandum, Cherwell to Churchill, 30 March 1942, in Max Hastings, *Bomber Command* (Minneapolis: Zenith Press, 2013), 90.

91. Webster and Frankland, *Strategic Air Offensive*, 1: 270.
92. Memorandum, Cherwell to Churchill, in Hastings, *Bomber Command*, 90.
93. Ministry of Economic Warfare, "The Bomber's Baedeker," in *Guide to the Economic Importance of German Towns & Industries, Enemy Branch*, January 1943, 512.611-39, AFHRA, Part I, 1.
94. Ministry of Economic Warfare, Part I, 1–2.
95. Ministry of Economic Warfare, Part II, 2.
96. Harris, *Bomber Offensive*, 105.
97. Rostow, "Rostow Report," 6, 11, 16–18. John De Wilde, who had been employed by the Board of Economic Warfare rather than the OSS, became a core member in addition to those who were OSS.
98. Most of the EOU's central figures, notably Rostow, Kaysen, Kindleberger, and Morse, went on to leverage World War II service into prominent careers in the federal government or academia with enduring federal influence. Rostow later reflected, "It was an irreversible experience of public service that shaped the subsequent lives of its members. As nearly as I can relate, virtually all of us subsequently spent some time in government." See Rostow, "Waging Economic Warfare from London," 78.
99. Trachtenberg, Rosenberg, and Van Evera, "An Interview with Carl Kaysen," 5.
100. Hughes, "Memoirs," 22.
101. Hughes, "Memoirs," 28–29.
102. Tyson, "The EOU vs. Hitler's Mini-Missiles," 84.
103. Rostow, "Rostow Report," 3.
104. Meyer and Rowan explain organizational worth in environments such as the complex bureaucracy of intelligence organizations. In their view, organizations "become sensitive to, and employ external criteria of worth," such as "ceremonial awards . . . endorsements by important people, the standard prices of professionals and consultants, or the prestige or programs or personnel in external social circles." In the EOU members' case, several of the above are applicable. Among their top motivators were endorsement of their products by Allied senior generals and prestige of their work and individual intellectual ability by any leaders external to their own organization. See John W. Meyer and Brian Rowan, "Institutionalized Organizations: Formal Structure as Myth and Ceremony," *American Journal of Sociology* 83, no. 2 (1977): 350.

105. Rostow, "Rostow Report," 34.
106. William Salant, "The Selection of Industrial Bombing Targets: Some Analytical Notes," 17 December 1942, in Rostow, "Rostow Report," 36–37.
107. Salant, in Rostow, "Rostow Report."
108. Enemy Objectives Unit, "Handbook of Target Information, Office of Strategic Services," May 1943, 118.042-2, AFHRA, 8.
109. Enemy Objectives Unit, "Handbook of Target Information."
110. Both William Salant, who penned the EOU's original notes on target selection and Charles Kindleberger, who led the EOU during this period, were prominent Keynesians—the dominant school of economic thought at the end of the Great Depression into World War II. See Lawrence H. Officer, "Review of *International Monetary Economics, 1870–1960: Between the Classical and the New Classical*, by M. June Flanders," *The Journal of Economic History* 50, no. 3 (1990): 780–81. Also of note, efficiency (especially the marginal efficiency of capital) is central to Keynes' economic theory. The idea of maximizing bombing efficiency in terms of imposing costs on the enemy while minimizing bomber losses would likely have resonated with EOU economists. For a contemporary example, see Carl Landauer, "A Break in Keynes's Theory of Interest," *The American Economic Review* 27, no. 2 (1937): 260–66.
111. Salant in Rostow, "Rostow Report," 39–40.
112. Salant in Rostow, "Rostow Report," 40.
113. Sorensen had graduated from the tactical school in 1936 and served as its commandant at Maxwell Field until just prior to assuming duties as assistant chief of staff for intelligence in July 1941. See Finney, *History of the Air Corps*, 113.
114. All of the participants (Sorensen, Eaker, Kuter, Hansell, and Stratemeyer) in the trail of correspondence that follows were ACTS graduates or instructors.
115. Sorensen, letter to Kuter, 3 January 1943, 4.
116. Sorensen to Kuter, 3–4.
117. Sorensen to Kuter, 3–5.
118. Maj. Gen. Ira C. Eaker, letter to Arnold, 30 January 1943, 168.491v.1, AFHRA.
119. Laurence S. Kuter, letter to Hansell, 28 January 1943, MS 6, series 2, box 2, notebook 1, Hansell Papers, Clark Special Collections Branch.
120. Brig. Gen. Haywood S. Hansell, letter to Sorensen, 11 February 1943, MS 6, series 2, box 2, notebook 1, Hansell Papers, Clark Special Collections Branch.

121. Brig. Gen. Haywood S. Hansell, letter to Fairchild, 11 February 1943, MS 6, series 2, box 2, notebook 1, Hansell Papers, Clark Special Collections Branch.
122. Maj. Gen. George E. Stratemeyer, personal letter to Ira Eaker, 23 March 1943, AFHSO.
123. Perera, "Memoirs,"119.
124. Perera, "History of the Organization and Operations of the Committee of Operations Analysts," 19.
125. The exact wording of Arnold's initial charge to Gates was noteworthy because COA analysts tended to fixate on the time requirement: "Have the group of operational analysts under your jurisdiction prepare and submit a report to me analyzing the rate of progressive deterioration that should be anticipated in the German war effort as a result of the increasing air operations we are prepared to employ against its sustaining forces. This study should result in as accurate an estimate as can be arrived at as to the date when this dislocation will have progressed to a point as to permit a successful invasion of Western Europe." Arnold, memorandum, "Research and Analysis to Fix Earliest Practicable Date for Invasion of Western Europe," 22 December 1942.
126. McFarland, *America's Pursuit of Precision Bombing*, 98.
127. L. B. Wright, "Three-Dimension View of the Enemy," *Air Force: Official Journal of the U.S. Army Air Forces* 26, no. 2 (February 1943): 32.
128. Col. E. F. Koenig, "Final Report to Commanding General, First District, AAFTTC," 30 September 1942, 266.1–1, AFHRA, 6.
129. First Motion Picture Unit Army Air Forces, "Photographic Intelligence in Damage Assessment," in Training Film: War Department, 1943, I-3340.
130. First Motion Picture Unit.
131. First Motion Picture Unit.
132. First Motion Picture Unit.
133. "History of AAFAIS," ca. 1 January 1945, 266.1, AFHRA, 9: 3.
134. Taylor Downing, *Spies in the Sky: The Secret Battle for Aerial Intelligence During World War II* (London: Little, Brown, 2011), 229; Air Ministry, *Photographic Reconnaissance*, vol. 2, May 1941–August 1945 (London: UK National Archives, 1948), AIR 41/7, 79.
135. Col. Harvey H. Holland, "Progress Report," ca. 10 March 1943, 266.1, AFHRA, 4.

136. "History of AAFAIS," 8: 5–6; Lt. Col. L. W. Johnson, "Investigation—AAF Air Intelligence School, Army Air Forces Technical Training Command (Greensboro Headquarters First District, North Carolina)," 18 March 1943, 266.152-1, AFHRA, 368–69, 693.
137. Lt. Col. Carl H. Norcross, memorandum for the Assistant Chief of Staff, A-2: Army Air Force Intelligence School, 22 January 1943, 266.1-1, AFHRA, 1–2.
138. The investigation marked faculty morale at "the lowest in the history of the school," due partly to a failure by the commanding officer "to inspire or imbue [the faculty] with confidence in his ability as a commander and as an educator." See Johnson, "Investigation," 1–10.
139. Victor H. Cohen, "Air Intelligence," ca. 1 January 1954, 106–87, AFHRA, 9: 31.
140. Cohen, "Air Intelligence," 9: 17–20.
141. Noah Webster, *Webster's New Modern English Dictionary* (Chicago: Consolidated Book Publishers, 1922), 46.
142. Committee of Operations Analysts, "Analysis of Bombardment Objectives in Axis Europe," 23 December 1942, tab 6, 118.02v2, AFHRA, and "Western Axis Oil Industry as Bombardment Target," ca. 23 December 1942, tab 7, 118.02v2, AFHRA .
143. R. J. Overy, *The Air War, 1939–1945* (Washington, DC: Potomac Books, Inc., 2005), 73.
144. Craven and Cate, *Torch to Pointblank*, 300.
145. Herman S. Wolk, "Decision at Casablanca," *Air Force Magazine* 86, no. 1 (2003): 81.
146. Hansell, *Strategic Air War*, 69.
147. Personal letter, Wedemeyer to Handy, 22 January 1943 quoted in Maurice Matloff, *Strategic Planning for Coalition Warfare, 1943–1944* (Washington, DC: Office of the Chief of Military History, Department of the Army, 1959), 107.
148. Wolk, "Decision at Casablanca," 81; Craven and Cate, *Torch to Pointblank*, 302.
149. Ira Eaker, "The Bomber Offensive from the United Kingdom," ca. April 1943, 168.61-10, AFHRA.
150. Assistant Chief of Air Staff (A-2), "Air Estimate, The Submarine Situation in Europe, Part I," 12 February 1943, 142.042-5, AFHRA, 9.
151. Assistant Chief of Air Staff, "Air Estimate," 2.

152. Assistant Chief of Air Staff, "Air Estimate," 9.
153. Assistant Chief of Air Staff, "Air Estimate," 8.
154. Dwight D. Eisenhower, *Crusade in Europe* (Garden City, NY: Doubleday, 1948), 85.
155. Assistant Chief of Air Staff, "Air Estimate," 10.
156. Eaker, "The Bomber Offensive from the United Kingdom."
157. H. H. Arnold, personal letter to Maj. Gen. I. C. Eaker, 24 January 1943, 168.61-10, AFHRA.
158. Hansell, letter to Fairchild, 11 February 1943, 1.
159. Sorensen, letter to Kuter, 3 January 1943.
160. Perera, "History of the Organization and Operations of the Committee of Operations Analysts," 32.
161. Col. Guido R. Perera, memorandum for Maj. Gen. Eaker, 30 January 1943, 118.1511, AFHRA.
162. Perera, "History of the Organization," 33–37.
163. Perera, "History of the Organization," 33.
164. Meeting Minutes, War Department, 18 December 1942, 118.151-1, AFHRA, 2.
165. Maj. Gen. Ira C. Eaker, letter to Arnold, 30 January 1943, box 16, Eaker Papers, LOC.
166. As previously mentioned, Eaker clearly understood fighter escort ranges, but these did not appear to be important factors to his plans since his assumption was that large bomber formations did not depend primarily upon escort. Perera, "Memoirs," 108–9; Perera, "History of the Organization and Operations of the Committee of Operations Analysts," 38; Col. Guido R. Perera, memorandum of conference with Major General I. C. Eaker, in Meeting at Widewings, 4 February 1943, COA History tab 18, 118.02v2, AFHRA, 2.
167. Maj. Gen. Ira C. Eaker to Perera, Subject: Response to Memorandum of 30 January 1943, 3 February 1943, 118.1511, AFHRA.
168. The objectives department, according to Uta Hohn, "had the function of providing advice on bombing targets for the strategic offensive against the enemy and occupied territories." See Hohn, "The Bomber's Baedeker," 214. Also Col. Guido R. Perera, Lt. Col. W. B. Leach, and Fowler Hamilton, memorandum of conference with Mr. O. L. Lawrence, Chief of Objectives Department, Ministry of Economic Warfare, 2 February 1943, COA History tab 14, 118.02v2, AFHRA, 2.

169. Interestingly, Levine's research suggests, "During 1941 the Ministry of Economic Warfare had realized that the enemy was dependent on ball bearings,production of which was overwhelming concentrated at Schweinfurt," but it would seem MEW dropped the idea of striking at Schweinfurt until after COA's experience with Mr. Lawrence. See Levine, *The Strategic Bombing*, 38.
170. Perera, Leach, and Hamilton, memorandum of conference with Lawrence, 3.
171. Perera, Leach, and Hamilton.

CHAPTER 3. EAKER'S IMPERFECT PITCH

1. H. H. Arnold, letter to Frank Andrews, 24 March 1943, 168.61-10, AFHRA.
2. H. H. Arnold, letter to I. C. Eaker, 10 April 1943, RG 18, AAG 312.1-E, Operations Letters, AFHSO, NA.
3. Mark R. Grandstaff, "Muir Fairchild and the Origins of Air University, 1945–46," *Airpower Journal* XI, no. 4 (Winter 1997): 30.
4. Perera, "History of the Organization and Operations of the Committee of Operations Analysts," 43.
5. Committee of Operations Analysts (COA), "Report of Committee of Operations Analysts with Respect to Economic Targets Within the Western Axis," 1.
6. COA "Report of Committee of Operations Analysts."
7. COA, "Report of Committee of Operations Analysts," 2.
8. Margaret Blunden, "Geoffrey Vickers—An Intellectual Journey," in *The Vickers Papers*, ed. Open Systems Group (London: Harper & Row, 1984), 27.
9. Peter Davies argues, "As a serviceman with no background in intelligence or Whitehall, a self-employed lawyer lacking professional qualifications in economics, and without management experience of an organization of several hundred staff, he was hardly the go-to candidate to fill such a senior civilian post." See Davies, "Geoffrey Vickers and Lessons from the Ministry of Economic Warfare for Cold War Defence Intelligence," 811.
10. Portal did praise COA's "very valuable report," which he noted was produced in collaboration with MEW, but the rest of his favorable comments were actually intended as compliments for Eaker's plan, not the COA's report. See Air Chief Marshal Sir Charles Portal, Enclosure 'A,' Plan for the Combined Bomber Offensive from the United Kingdom, Whitehall Air Ministry, 15 April 1943, 118.04W, AFHRA. Also, Perera, "History of the Organization and Operations of the Committee of Operations Analysts," 45–45a.

11. C. G. Vickers, untitled memorandum, MEW views on the document entitled "Report of the Committee of Operations Analysis: March 8th 1943," in personal collection of Gen. Henry H. Arnold, part 3 of 6, Ministry of Economic Warfare, 3 April 1943, MICFILM 28253, AFHRA, 1.
12. Vickers, memorandum, 2.
13. Vickers, memorandum.
14. Ministry of Economic Warfare, memorandum, "Detailed Commentary on 'Report of the Committee of Operations Analysis: March 8th 1943,'" in personal collection of Gen. Henry H. Arnold, 4 April 1943.
15. Dr. Edward S. Mason, memorandum, "Proposed Selection on European Industrial Targets, Committee of Operations Analysts," 19 January 1943, 118.04W, AFHRA.
16. COA, "Report of Committee of Operations Analysts with Respect to Economic Targets Within the Western Axis," leaflet 3.
17. Charles Poor Kindleberger, memorandum for Colonel R. D. Hughes, "Subcommittee Reports to the Committee of Operational Analysts," in personal collection of Gen. Henry H. Arnold, part 3 of 6, American Embassy Office of Strategic Services, Economic Warfare Division, 7 April 1943, MICFILM 28253, AFHRA, 1.
18. Kindleberger memorandum.
19. Kindleberger memorandum.
20. Kindleberger, memorandum, 2.
21. COA, "Outline of Proposed Study," ca. 4 December 1942, 118.201-2, AFHRA, 1.
22. Arnold, "Research and Analysis to Fix Earliest Practicable Date for Invasion of Western Europe." Also of note, optical precision instruments and optical glass were equivocal as bottlenecks. Seventy percent of optical glass for military purposes was produced in the town of Jena, and 80 percent of optical precision instruments was produced in only two plants. Although the analysts noted in their final report that "the effects of the destruction of these two targets will not become apparent in the Axis war effort for a considerable time, probably years," both were nevertheless included in the recommended list. See COA, "Report of Committee of Operations Analysts with Respect to Economic Targets Within the Western Axis," 8 March 1943, tab 15.

23. Hansell, *The Air Plan that Defeated Hitler*, 163.
24. Ralph J. Watkins, "Feasibility of Air Attack on European Axis Transport," in COA History (tab 14), 21 January 1943, 118.04-4 V.1, AFHRA, 1.
25. Watkins, "Feasibility of Air Attack," 20.
26. Meeting Minutes, War Department, 15 December 1942, 118.151-1, AFHRA.
27. Meeting Minutes, Oil and Chemicals, War Department, 23 December 1942, 118.151-1, AFHRA.
28. Byron E. Gates, memorandum for Sorensen, "Motion Pictures to Supplement Committee Report," 26 March 1943, 118.04A-5, AFHRA.
29. COA, script, War Department, 1 April 1943, 118.04A-5, report 3, AFHRA, 3.
30. According to COA's Dr. Mason, the OSS would shoot the film using their camera crew who happened to be Navy. That the crew was not AAF was a convenient coincidence for some of the COA members who were concerned that a uniformed AAF officer overseeing film production in a ball-bearing plant might give away their plans. See Meeting Minutes, War Department.
31. COA, script, report 2, 7.
32. COA, script, report 1, 7.
33. Arnold, letter to Andrews, 24 March 1943.
34. Arnold letter to Andrews.
35. Arnold letter to Andrews.
36. Despite the COA's acquiescence to Eighth Air Force not to expressly establish target priorities, the report nevertheless included the list in unlabeled priority order and bumped ball bearings up to second, behind only the German aircraft industry. As published, the priorities reflected the forcefulness and persuasiveness of the committee chairs. See Perera, "History of the Organization and Operations of the Committee of Operations Analysts," 44.
37. Arps, "Operational Analysis Section," 46.
38. Headquarters Eighth Air Force, "Bombing Accuracy," in "Summary of Eighth Air Force Heavy Bomber Operations as Called for in Combined Bomber Offensive Plan: First Phase," July 1943, 168.61-10, AFHRA.
39. Craven and Cate, *Torch to Pointblank*, 343.
40. Arps, "Operational Analysis Section," 46–47.
41. Brig. Gen. Frank A. Armstrong, "Air Discipline," *Air Force: Official Service Journal of the U.S. Army Air Forces* 28, no. 11 (1943): 6.

42. Minneapolis-Honeywell Regulator Company, "Here's How: Operation of the C-1 Autopilot" (Minneapolis: Minneapolis-Honeywell, 1944), 4–9.
43. Lt. Col. James H. Straubel, "Cross Country," *Air Force: Official Service Journal of the U.S. Army Air Forces* 26, no. 10 (1942): 1.
44. Brig. Gen. Harper Eubank, letter to Eaker, 31 March 1943, box 16, Eaker Papers, Manuscript Division, LOC.
45. Craven and Cate, *Torch to Pointblank*, 343.
46. AC/AS Intelligence, "The Strategic Aerial Bombardment of Germany—Submarines, USAAF," 15 September 1943, 142.042-11, AFHRA, 2.
47. AC/AS Intelligence. Although the information was certainly not available at the time, a postwar review of Vegesack shipyard records by the United States Strategic Bombing Survey (USSBS) team revealed evidence in striking contrast to the photo interpreters' raid estimates: "The damage suffered by boats on ways was slight, because most of the bombs that hit the ways either broke open with resulting low order detonations or penetrated below the concrete and were dissipated underground. The damage apparent to the camouflage over the submarines caused the damage to them to be overestimated from air cover. Actually only a few fragment holes resulted. . . . Records show that productive activity was resumed at the yard after one week, and that in six weeks, normal activity was being carried on." See USSBS, *Bremer Vulcan, Vegesack, Germany*, 2nd ed., no. 100 (Washington, DC: USSBS, 1947), 111–12.
48. Powys-Lybbe, *The Eye of Intelligence*, 35.
49. H. H. Arnold, letter to Eaker, War Department, 19 April 1943, AAG 312.1-F, RG 18, Operations Letters, AFHSO, NA.
50. Arnold, letter to Andrews, 24 March 1943. The letter is marked at the top "prepared by Advisory Council," which indicated Cabell's role.
51. Maj. Gen. Ira C. Eaker, "Presentation of Combined Bomber Operations—United Kingdom, Headquarters Eighth Air Force," ca. April 1943, 168.61-10, AFHRA, 6.
52. Eaker, "Presentation of Combined Bomber Operations," 7.
53. Edgar P. Sorensen, memorandum, "The Method of Computing Sortie Requirements," 20 March 1943, 118.04-9A, AFHRA, 1.
54. Edgar P. Sorensen, "Memorandum for the Advisory Committee on Bombardment, Subject: Calculations of Force Required," 21 January 1943, 118.04A-9A, AFHRA.

55. Sorensen, "The Method of Computing Sortie Requirements," 1.
56. Maj. Gen. Ira C. Eaker, Letter of Instructions, Eighth Air Force, 2 April 1943, 168.61-10, AFHRA.
57. Eaker, "Presentation of Combined Bomber Operations," 4.
58. "Notes on Meeting with General Eaker, Eighth Air Force," 5 April 1943, 168.61-10, AFHRA.
59. Memorandum, Kindleberger to Hughes, 15 March 1943, cited in Rostow, "Rostow Report," 66–70.
60. Rostow, "Rostow Report," 72.
61. "Notes on Meeting with General Eaker."
62. Eaker's goal was in part enabled by none other than Flight Officer Constance Babington-Smith at Medmenham's CIU. With a one-off compliment outside their own organization, the EOU credits her for bringing "craftsmanship, enthusiasm, and a creative imagination to the analysis," which sharpened "photographic interpretation of both aircraft types and the aircraft industry" just as it became most necessary for the CBO. Aircraft targets became increasingly difficult to find as they dispersed and moved underground. See Rostow, "Rostow Report," 62.
63. "Notes on Meeting with General Eaker."
64. Headquarters Eighth Air Force, "Bombing Accuracy."
65. Headquarters Eighth Air Force, "Bombing Accuracy."
66. Maj. Gen. Ira C. Eaker, "Presentation: Plan for Combined Bomber Offensive From the United Kingdom," in personal collection of Gen. Henry H. Arnold, 29 April 1943, part 3 of 6, Joint Chiefs of Staff (277), MICFILM 28253, AFHRA. Also, COA, "Report of Committee of Operations Analysts with Respect to Economic Targets Within the Western Axis," 8 March 1943, foldout 1.
67. Air Chief Marshal Sir Arthur T. Harris, personal letter to Eaker, in personal collection of Gen. Henry H. Arnold, 15 April 1943, part 3 of 6, Headquarters Bomber Command, MICFILM 28253, AFHRA, 1.
68. Harris to Eaker, 2.
69. Parton, *Air Force Spoken Here*, 253.
70. Rostow, "Rostow Report," 60.
71. "Notes on Meeting with General Andrews, Eighth Air Force," 8 April 1943, 168.61-10, AFHRA.

72. Maj. Gen. Ira C. Eaker, "Suggested Commentary . . . for The Combined Bomber Offensive From the United Kingdom," in personal collection of Gen. Henry H. Arnold, ca. 16 April 1943, part 3 of 6, MICFILM 28253, AFHRA, 1.
73. Eaker, "Suggested Commentary," 17 pps.
74. Eaker, "Presentation: Plan for Combined Bomber Offensive."
75. Eaker, "Presentation: Plan for Combined Bomber Offensive."
76. Perera, "History of the Organization and Operations of the Committee of Operations Analysts," 40.
77. One of King's own daughters allegedly quipped of the short-fused admiral, "He is the most even-tempered man in the Navy. He is always in a rage." Perhaps the comparison isn't fair to the horse. See Eric Larrabee, *Commander in Chief: Franklin Delano Roosevelt, His Lieutenants, and Their War* (New York: Simon & Schuster, 1988), 155; "The Clydesdale Horse—Dialogue," *The Farmers' Cabinet and American Herd-Book* V, no. 1 (15 August 1840): 25. For a broader characterization of King's personality, see Walter R. Borneman, *The Admirals: Nimitz, Halsey, Leahy, and King—The Five-Star Admirals Who Won the War at Sea* (New York: Little, Brown and Co., 2012), ch. 2.
78. Eaker, "Presentation: Plan for Combined Bomber Offensive."
79. Parton, *Air Force Spoken Here*, 253.
80. Arnold, letter to Eaker, 10 April 1943.
81. Matloff, *Strategic Planning*, 110–11.
82. "Meeting of the CCS with Roosevelt and Churchill," 12 May 1943, document 29, in William Z. Slany et al., *Foreign Relations of the United States, 1943* (Washington, DC: Office of the Historian, Department of State, 1970).
83. "Meeting of the CCS with Roosevelt and Churchill."
84. Ray S. Cline, *Washington Command Post: The Operations Division* (Washington, DC: Office of the Chief of Military History, Department of the Army, 1951), 192; Maurice Matloff, *The 90-Division Gamble* (Washington, DC: U.S. Army Center of Military History, 1990), 70.
85. "85th meeting of the CCS," 15 May 1943, document 37, in Slany et al., *Foreign Relations of the United States, 1943*.
86. "85th meeting of the CCS."
87. Parton, *Air Force Spoken Here*, 263; Matloff, *Strategic Planning*, 130–31.

88. Yenne, *Big Week*, 85.
89. Headquarters Eighth Air Force, "Effort Against Individual Targets," in "Summary of Eighth Air Force Heavy Bomber Operations as Called for in Combined Bomber Offensive Plan: First Phase," July 1943, 168.61-10, AFHRA.
90. Headquarters Eighth Air Force, "Effort Against Individual Targets."
91. Headquarters Eighth Air Force, "Effort Against Individual Targets."
92. Headquarters Eighth Air Force, "Effort Against Individual Targets."
93. Eaker, "Presentation of Combined Bomber Operations—United Kingdom," 8.
94. Eaker, "Presentation of Combined Bomber Operations."
95. Headquarters Eighth Air Force, "Summary by Target Category," in "Summary of Eighth Air Force Heavy Bomber Operations as Called for in Combined Bomber Offensive Plan: First Phase," 1 August 1943, 168.61-10, AFHRA.
96. Eaker, "The Bomber Offensive From the United Kingdom."
97. Eaker, "Presentation of Combined Bomber Operations—United Kingdom," 8.
98. Parton, *Air Force Spoken Here*, 283–84.
99. Craven and Cate, *Torch to Pointblank*, 670–71.
100. Central Interpretation Unit (CIU), "Preliminary Interpretation Report No. S.A. 359," in "Attack on Synthetic Rubber Plant Hüls on 22.6.43," 24 June 1943, 520.365, AFHRA.
101. S-3 VIII Bomber Command, A-3 Section, "Comments on Report of Raid on Bremen and Kiel—13 June 1943," in "Tactical Mission Report, Field Order No. 174," 25 June 1943, 520.332, AFHRA; Brig. Gen. F. L. Anderson, "Tactical Report of Mission, Kiel, 13 June 1943, 4th Bombardment Wing Headquarters," 19 June 1943, 520.332, AFHRA, 2.
102. 94th Bombardment Group Intelligence Officer, "Memorandum for Commanding General, 4th Bombardment Wing, Subject: Resubmission of Claim for Encounter with E/A, Captain Joseph G. Butterworth," 15 July 1943, 527.332, AFHRA; Headquarters 4th Bombardment Wing, "Summary of Operations, Target: Kiel,"13 June 1943, 520.332, AFHRA.
103. Anderson, "Tactical Report of Mission, Kiel, 13 June 1943," 1–3.
104. S-2 94th Bombardment Group, teletype report, "Mission 13 June 1943, 3rd Air Division," 14 June 1943, 527.332, AFHRA, 4.

105. Anderson, "Tactical Report of Mission, Kiel, 13 June 1943," 3.
106. CIU, "Immediate Interpretation Report No. K.1587," in "Damage Assessment," 22 June 1943, 520.365, AFHRA.
107. Headquarters 4th Bombardment Wing, "Summary of Operations, Target: Kiel, 13 June 1943, A-3 Assistant Chief of Staff, Bombing Accuracy," in "Notebooks for Gen. Devers and Gen. Eaker," 30 August 1943, 168.61-2, AFHRA.
108. Finney, *History of the Air Corps*, 127.
109. Anderson, "Tactical Report of Mission, Kiel, 13 June 1943," 8.
110. Stephen Lee McFarland and Wesley Phillips Newton, *To Command the Sky: The Battle for Air Superiority Over Germany, 1942–1944* (Tuscaloosa: University of Alabama Press, 2006), 109.
111. S-2 305th Bombardment Group, teletype report, "Section 'A' to Commanding General 1st Bomb Wing," 30 July 1943, 525.332B, AFHRA.
112. USSBS, "Blohm and Voss Shipyards, Hamburg Germany," in "Plant Report No. 51, Physical Damage Division," 8 October 1945, 137.311-51, sec. 5, AFHRA.
113. National Security Agency and Central Security Service, *ULTRA: History of U.S. Strategic Air Force Europe vs. German Air Force*, vol. SRH-013 (Washington, DC: Held by AFHSO, June 1945), 82.
114. Headquarters VIII Bomber Command, "Bomber Command Narrative of Operations, Day Operation—22 June 1943," 29 June 1943, 520.332, AFHRA, 1.
115. Headquarters 94th Bombardment Group, "Mission Briefing Notes," in "Bombing Annex, Mission 10, Hüls," 22 June 1943, 527.332, AFHRA.
116. Headquarters 94th Bombardment Group, "Mission Briefing Notes."
117. Brig. Gen. Frank A. Armstrong, "Report of Operations, Hüls, 22 June 1943 to Commanding General, VIII Bomber Command, 1st Bombardment Wing Headquarters," 28 June 1943, 520.332, AFHRA; Col. Curtis E. LeMay, "Tactical Reports of Mission, Hüls, Germany, 22 June 1943 to Commanding General, VIII Bomber Command, 4th Bombardment Wing Headquarters," 29 June 1943, 520.332, AFHRA.
118. S-2 305th Bombardment Group, teletype report, "Mission 22 June 1943, War Department," 22 June 1943, 525.332B, AFHRA.
119. S-2 306th Bombardment Group, teletype report, "Mission 22 June 1943, War Department," 22 June 1943, 525.332B, AFHRA, 1.

120. S-2 94th Bombardment Group, teletype report, "Mission 22 June 1943," 22 June 1943, 527.332, AFHRA, 2.
121. LeMay, "Tactical Reports of Mission, Hüls," 6.
122. S-2 305th Bombardment Group, "Photo & Bomb Plotting Report, 1st Lt. Franklin E. Smith," 22 June 1943, 520.332, AFHRA; Headquarters 305th Bombardment Group, "Enclosure 'J,' Group Bombing Plot and Report," in "Narrative Report of Operations, Field Order No. 153-A," 22 June 1943, 520.332, AFHRA.
123. Headquarters 305th Bombardment Group, "Description of Bombing Approach and Dropping Procedure, Mission of 22 June 1943, Capt. Bruce A. Gardner," 22 June 1943, 520.332, AFHRA.
124. CIU, "Preliminary Interpretation Report No. S.A. 359."
125. CIU, "Interpretation Report No. K.1618," in "Damage Assessment," 1 August 1943, 520.365, AFHRA.
126. Headquarters Eighth Air Force, "Bombing Accuracy."
127. Per the USSBS, "The plant is laid out on a very spacious scale, both war time contingencies and normal fire hazards having been taken into consideration in its planning. It covers a roughly rectangular area of 541 acres, of which about 10 percent is built up." It was ideal as an area target for a multiwing attack with a dispersed bomb pattern. See USSBS, "Huels Synthetic Rubber Plant," in No. 128, Oil Division (Washington, DC: USSBS, 1947), 16.
128. Mathematician G. Baley Price described the ORS process for determining pattern-center errors and assessing accuracy from bomb plots. They did not account for target size and shape—only accuracy from the aiming point. While their process suited their purpose, it is important to consider that accuracy and bomb damage may not correlate as closely for area targets as they do for point targets. Only the bombers' cameras could differentiate which aircraft dropped which bombs. This mattered for accuracy evaluations, but poststrike reconnaissance by the PRU proved more important for assessing the overall effectiveness of the raid. See G. Baley Price, "A Mathematician Describes His Work as an Operations Analyst with the Eighth Air Force," Headquarters Eighth Air Force, Winter 1945–1946, 520.310-7, AFHRA, 9–12. Eighth Air Force ORS did acknowledge the importance of optimizing bomb spacing and pattern size for area targets

versus "small precision targets," though this concept was not factored into accuracy assessments. See Operational Research Section, "Memorandum on Salvo and Intervalometer Releases, Headquarters Eighth Air Force," 16 September 1944, 520.310v.7, AFHRA, 3–8.

129. USSBS, "Huels Synthetic Rubber Plant," 33.
130. USSBS, "Huels Synthetic Rubber Plant."
131. USSBS, "Huels Synthetic Rubber Plant," 43.
132. USSBS, "Huels Synthetic Rubber Plant," 1, 74.
133. USSBS, "Huels Synthetic Rubber Plant," 44.
134. Capt. James T. Lowe, memorandum for General Sorensen, "Western Axis Rubber Position 1943, Committee of Operations Analysts," 2 July 1943, 187.2, AFHRA, 2.
135. Lowe, "Western Axis Rubber Position."
136. Lowe, "Western Axis Rubber Position."
137. USSBS, "Huels Synthetic Rubber Plant," 4.
138. Meeting Minutes, War Department, 18 September 1943, 118.151-5B, AFHRA, 1.
139. Assistant Chief of Air Staff (A-2), "An Appraisal of Accomplishments and Potentialities," in "The Strategic Aerial Bombardment of Europe, USAAF," 10 September 1943, 142.042-11v1, AFHRA, 25.
140. This was one instance where the USSBS authors may have violated their imperative to conduct an "impartial and expert study," or they otherwise exposed a degree of ignorance of air campaign strategy through their harsh criticism, as the survey team later cited far more than simply failures to evaluate aspects of the production process at Hüls: "It is apparent that erroneous basic intelligence on the German rubber situation resulted in wrong decisions regarding the importance of the synthetic rubber plants as a vital industry, and also their inter-relationship with other vital industries. They offered an effective target system, easily identified, vulnerable, and slow to repair." See USSBS, "Huels Synthetic Rubber Plant," 33, 75.
141. Headquarters Eighth Air Force, "Summary by Target Categories," in "Summary of Eighth Air Force Heavy Bomber Operations as Called For in Combined Bomber Offensive Plan: First Phase," 1 July 1943, 168.61-10, AFHRA.
142. S-2 1st Bombardment Wing, teletype report, "Mission 22 June 1943, War Department," 22 June 1943, 525.332B, AFHRA.

143. Maj. Gen. Ira C. Eaker, letter to Giles, 29 June 1943, AAG 312.1-H, RG 18, Operations Letters, NARA.
144. 305th Bombardment Group, teletype report, "Section 'A' to Commanding General 1st Bomb Wing." Of note, the S-2 went on to capture his unit's mission success, relaying that a bomb-bay observer saw a single bomb result in a "large sheet of deep red flame 200 feet square and 1,000 feet high," and he corroborated their claims of good hits with photographs. Some reports matched sarcasm with hyperbole.
145. Eaker continued to include YB-40s on missions throughout his tenure at Eighth Air Force in the fall of 1943.
146. Headquarters Eighth Air Force, "Bombing Accuracy," 3.
147. As discussed in further detail below for Blohm and Voss, postwar surveyors at Howaldtswerke found "serious damage was caused by 500-lb and 1,000-lb bombs to principal buildings, but at no time was production stopped or greatly impeded. This can be attributed to the excess amount of structures, stock and equipment possessed by the organization, in relation to the production requirements." See USSBS, "Howaldtswerke Shipyards at Hamburg Germany," in "Plant Report No. 50, Physical Damage Division," August 1945, 137.311-50, AFHRA, 27.
148. Eighth Air Force, "Effort Against Individual Targets."
149. Rostow, "Rostow Report," 58.
150. Rostow, "Rostow Report," 42.
151. Chandler Morse, letter to Perera, Office of Strategic Services, 22 May 1943, 118.042–2, AFHRA.
152. Enemy Objectives Unit, "Handbook of Target Information," 2.
153. Enemy Objectives Unit, "Handbook of Target Information," 3.
154. Enemy Objectives Unit, "Handbook of Target Information."
155. He expressed his growing concern to Arnold about German innovation in air-to-air attacks that could "increase greatly the cost of our bombing," and he sought to increase attacks on fighter factories before "the enemy has discovered a way of making our bombing uneconomical."
156. Maj. Gen. Ira C. Eaker, letter to Arnold, 18 July 1943, box 16, Eaker Papers, Manuscript Division, LOC.
157. Meyer and Rowan note an institutionalized tendency for goals, procedures, and policies to be viewed as "analogous to the vocabularies of motive used to account for the activities of individuals." As an example, they offer: "Some

can say that the engineers will solve a specific problem or that the secretaries will perform certain tasks, without knowing who these engineers or secretaries will be or exactly what they will do." As to the EOU, Eaker received air intelligence marked by standards of efficiency from the economists. See Meyer and Rowan, "Institutionalized Organizations: Formal Structure as Myth and Ceremony," 349.

158. Charles Poor Kindleberger, letter to Chandler Morse and Phil Coombs, Office of Strategic Services, 30 June 1943, 118.04-12, AFHRA.
159. Enemy Objectives Unit, "F.W. 190 Production at Bremen," 30 June 1943, 118.04-12, AFHRA, 1, appendix A, appendix B.
160. Assistant Chief of Air Staff (A-2), "Bremen (Neuenland): Focke Wulf Plant," in "Reports of Attacks on Axis Targets in Europe, USAAF," 12 September 1943, 142.035-7, AFHRA.
161. Rostow, "Rostow Report," 58.
162. USSBS, *Blohm and Voss Shipyards, Hamburg, Germany*, ed. Submarine Branch Munitions Division, 2nd ed., no. 94 (Washington, DC: USSBS, 1947), 1.
163. Assistant Chief of Air Staff (A-2), "Hamburg: Blohm and Voss and Howaldts—U-Boat Yards," in "Reports of Attacks on Axis Targets in Europe, USAAF"; USSBS, *Blohm and Voss Shipyards, Hamburg, Germany*, 19.
164. Richard G. Davis, *Bombing the European Axis Powers: A Historical Digest of the Combined Bomber Offensive, 1939–1945* (Maxwell Air Force Base, AL: Air University Press, 2006), 133.
165. USSBS, "Blohm and Voss Shipyards, Hamburg, Germany," 8 October 1945, table 1, attack data, sheet 2.
166. Assistant Chief of Air Staff (A-2), "Hamburg: Blohm and Voss and Howaldts—U-Boat Yards." According to USSBS records, the RAF's smaller night raid on 2–3 August also had some direct impacts on Blohm and Voss, though certainly the RAF considered all four of their attacks on Hamburg during this period to have affected German workers. USSBS, "Blohm and Voss Shipyards, Hamburg Germany," table 1, attack data, sheet 2, and "Howaldtswerke Shipyards at Hamburg Germany," August 1945, 22.
167. Assistant Chief of Air Staff (A-2), "Hamburg: Blohm and Voss and Howaldts—U-Boat Yards"; USSBS, "Blohm and Voss Shipyards, Hamburg Germany," 4–6.

168. Headquarters 1st Bombardment Wing, "Immediate Interpretation Report, No. 9a," in "26 July 1943, Hannover—Hamburg, 2nd Lt. George Welter," 27 July 1943, 525.332, AFHRA.
169. AC/AS Intelligence, "The Strategic Aerial Bombardment of Germany—Submarines," 15 September 1943, tab A.
170. Ministry of Economic Warfare, "M.E.W. Intelligence Weekly," 12 August 1943, 512.607A, AFHRA, 3.
171. Ministry of Economic Warfare, "M.E.W. Intelligence Weekly."
172. Ministry of Economic Warfare, "M.E.W. Intelligence Weekly."
173. Col. Guido R. Perera and Lt. Col. W. B. Leach, memorandum to General Fairchild, "Timing of Economic Effect of Attacks Contemplated by Eighth Air Force Plan: Submarines," 5 May 1943, Committee of Operations Analysts, tab 64, 118.04–4 V.1, AFHRA, 2.
174. Perera and Leach, "Timing of Economic Effect of Attacks."
175. If production capacity had really dropped so precipitously at Blohm and Voss, it was certainly not a proven result of the AAF's attack on the shipyard, much less the indirect result of Harris' dehousing the Hamburg's workers. Surveyors later found "widespread superficial damage did not cause a stoppage in production" at Blohm and Voss or other similarly robust U-boat production yards. By the spring of 1943 the Germans had already planned to shift U-boat production into bomb-proof facilities elsewhere; unbeknownst to the Allies, the vulnerable but otherwise "excellent facilities" at Blohm and Voss were to be abandoned—hence the curtailment in production. If the raids could be considered successful, it was due to their second-order effect on enemy strategy, which eventually resulted in less efficient, but highly resilient, production methods. See USSBS, "Blohm and Voss Shipyards, Hamburg Germany," 32–33; USSBS, "Valentin Submarine Assembly Plant, Farge Germany," in "Plant Report No. 47, Physical Damage Division," 26 October 1945, 137.311-47, appendix I, AFHRA.
176. Headquarters VIII Bomber Command, "Tactical Mission Report, in Eighth Air Force Mission No. 76," 25 July 1943, 520.332, AFHRA, annex VII.
177. Assistant Chief of Air Staff (A-2), "Hamburg: Blohm and Voss and Howaldts—U-Boat Yards."
178. Perera, "History of the Organization and Operations of the Committee of Operations Analysts," 50–51.

179. Of note, barely two weeks after COA had submitted its final report on the Western Axis to Arnold, he tasked Gates to have them study targets in Italy and Japan, then to "make a continuing study of the Strategic targets located in Germany and occupied Europe." The committee members clearly now had job security. See H. H. Arnold, memorandum to Assistant Chief of Staff, Management Control, "Subject: Analysis of Strategic Targets in Italy," 23 March 1943, 118.02v2, tab 23, AFHRA.
180. Perera states in COA's official history that Colonel Cabell (from his seat on Arnold's advisory council) asked the committee to reexamine grinding wheels after he participated in Eaker's planning discussions. What is remarkable in this episode is the fervor with which the team's civilians acted on the impulse to steer the background research. See Perera, "History of the Organization and Operations of the Committee of Operations Analysts," 51.
181. Isaiah Frank, "Revised Statement on Grinding Wheel Plants and Objectives," 22 January 1943, 118.02v2, tab 19, AFHRA.
182. Perera, "History of the Organization and Operations of the Committee of Operations Analysts," 51; R. F. Robbins, "Memorandum as to Conversation with Mr. Frank of Office of Strategic Services and his Memo with Reference Thereto," 7 June 1943, tab 26, 118.02v2, AFHRA.
183. Perera, "History of the Organization and Operations of the Committee of Operations Analysts," 53.
184. Perera, "History of the Organization and Operations of the Committee of Operations Analysts," 53.
185. H. H. Arnold, memorandum for General Eaker, "Supplementary Data on Abrasives Industry in Axis Europe," 1 July 1943, box 16, Eaker Papers, Manuscript Division, LOC.
186. Arnold, letter to Eaker, 15 June 1943.
187. Eaker, letter to Arnold, 12 July 1943.
188. Perera, "Memoirs," 121.
189. Guido Perera addressed Eaker's frustrations with Colonel Smart and his association of COA with other projects advanced by Arnold's advisory council. All four exclamation points are included in Perera's original. This was an uncharacteristic break from Perera's typically formal writing style of COA's history. Perera, memorandum for Brig. Gen. Gates, 15 July 1943.
190. Hansell, *Strategic Air War*, 130–31; USSBS, *The German Abrasives Industry*, ed. Equipment Division, 2nd ed., no. 51 (Washington, DC: USSBS, 1947), 24–25.

191. Perera, memorandum for Brig. Gen. Gates, 15 July 1943; Perera, "History of the Organization and Operations of the Committee of Operations Analysts," 53.

CHAPTER 4. "THE APPEARANCE OF THE BOTTOM OF THE BARREL"

1. Laurence S. Kuter, personal letter to Eaker, 6 July 1943, 187.1-18, AFHRA.
2. Eaker, letter to Giles, 15 September 1943.
3. Gropman, *Mobilizing U.S. Industry*, 41–43.
4. Matloff, *The 90-Division Gamble*, 366–67.
5. Maurice Matloff, ed., *Strategic Planning for Coalition Warfare* (Washington, DC: U.S. Army Center of Military History, 1994), 5.
6. An official Army history offers that, in addition to Marshall's committee led by Colonel Bessell, the president appointed an additional committee to review shortages in civilian labor. Matloff, *Strategic Planning*, 115–19.
7. Other members of the Joint Strategic Survey Committee were Lt. Gen. Stanley B. Embick and Vice Adm. Russell Wilson, making the brilliant but unimposing Fairchild the junior member. Perera contends the committee's functions were "to study and survey the major basic strategies of the war (past, present and future); to keep the Joint Chiefs of Staff advised on combined basic strategy in the light of devleloping and predictable situations; to advise the Joint Chiefs of Staff on long-range strategy (combined); to study the strategies possible to be adopted when current plans have become impractical and to advise the Joint Chiefs of Staff in regard thereto." Presumably, Fairchild's role in this group, as perceived by Arnold, was important enough to keep him in Washington throughout the war. See Perera, "Memoirs," 75–76; Matloff, *Strategic Planning*, 122.
8. Matloff, *The 90-Division Gamble*, 369–70.
9. Matloff, *Strategic Planning*, 180.
10. Eighth Air Force, "Review of Operational Considerations." Also, Eaker, "Presentation of Combined Bomber Operations—United Kingdom," 10. Interestingly, Arnold sent a memo to the other joint chiefs the same day Eaker briefed them requesting 864 bombers by 30 June, not the 944 Eaker requested. Although it seems implausible Eaker would simply have disregarded Arnold's change to the plan or that Eaker did not get the memo, Eaker was not listed on the distribution list. Commanding General Army

Air Forces, "Plan for Combined Bomber Offensive from the United Kingdom," in personal collection of Gen. Henry H. Arnold, 29 April 1943, part 3 of 6, Joint Chiefs of Staff (277), MICFILM 28253, AFHRA.

11. Eaker, "Presentation: Plan for Combined Bomber Offensive from the United Kingdom," 11.
12. Col. O. L. Nelson, memorandum for Commanding General, AAF, "Revision of the Current Military Program," 1 July 1943, 187.1-18, AFHRA.
13. Kuter, personal letter to Eaker, 6 July 1943.
14. Kuter to Eaker.
15. Capt. James T. Lowe, memo for General Sorensen, "Subject: Bomb Damage Assessments," 6 July 1943, 187.1-18, AFHRA.
16. Col. Guido R. Perera, memo for Major General Eaker, "Subject: General Kuter's letter of 6th July," 20 July 1943, 187.1-18, AFHRA.
17. Perera memo for Eaker.
18. Col. Guido R. Perera, personal letter to Brig. Gen. Lawrence Kuter, 22 July 1943, 187.1-18, AFHRA.
19. Alderman, "Report for Colonel Leach on the History and Development of the Bombs and Fuzes Subsection of the Operational Analysis Section," 3.
20. Maj. Gen. Ira C. Eaker, personal letter to Kuter, 22 July 1943, 187.1-18, AFHRA.
21. Incidentally, the purpose of this coauthored book was openly intended as propaganda "to translate for the youth of today some of the things we have learned in order that they may avoid our errors." The text opened with, "FLYING—What dreams it inspires! What ideas and thoughts it excites in boy and man alike!" Neither Arnold nor Eaker was unfamiliar with the idea of marketing their ideas. See Arnold and Eaker, *This Flying Game*, xvii, 3.
22. Perera, "History of the Organization and Operations of the Committee of Operations Analysts," 99.
23. Office of Strategic Services (OSS), "Bomb Assessment (Draft)," 22 July 1943, 187.1-19, AFHRA.
24. OSS, "Bomb Assessment (Draft)."
25. OSS, "Bomb Assessment (Draft)."
26. OSS, "Strategic Air Bombardment Evaluation (Basic Considerations)," ca. July 1943, 187.2–30, AFHRA, 1.
27. OSS, "Strategic Air Bombardment Evaluation," 4–6.

28. OSS, "Strategic Air Bombardment Evaluation," 5.
29. OSS, "Strategic Air Bombardment Evaluation," 2.
30. Salant, "The Selection of Industrial Bombing Targets," in Rostow, "Rostow Report," 36–37.
31. COA, "Past Effectiveness and Future Prospects of Eighth Air Force Effort Under Pointblank," 11 August 1943, 118.01v2, AFHRA, 6.
32. COA, "Past Effectiveness and Future Prospects," 2.
33. One of the ORS's collateral duties was to take feedback from successful evaders. See Eighth Air Force Operational Research Section, "ORS Interrogation of Evaders," 28 January 1944, 520.362, AFHRA, 1.
34. COA, "Past Effectiveness and Future Prospects," 2.
35. COA, "Past Effectiveness and Future Prospects," 10.
36. COA, "Past Effectiveness and Future Prospects," 5.
37. A-2 Eighth Air Force, "Bi-monthly Report of Bombing Results, for the period of July 16 through July 31," ca. 1 August 1943, 520.307, AFHRA, 1.
38. USSBS, "Huels Synthetic Rubber Plant," 2.
39. The extent of the COA industrial impact statement was: "Between 25% and 35% of synthetic rubber production for some months." COA, "Past Effectiveness and Future Prospects," 8.
40. Ministry of Economic Warfare, "M.E.W. Intelligence Weekly," 22 July 1943, 512.607A, AFHRA, 5.
41. COA, "Past Effectiveness and Future Prospects," 2–3.
42. Ministry of Economic Warfare, "M.E.W. Intelligence Weekly," 8 July 1943, 512.607A, AFHRA, 1.
43. The relationship between MEW's Lawrence and COA members and an offer from MEW to send five of its "engineers, industrialists, and economists" to participate in COA's Far East study the week prior to the COA's report suggest the COA probably had regular access to MEW's weekly reports, though receipt may have been delayed or relayed via Eighth Air Force. Many archival copies on file at AFHRA were Richard Hughes' personal copies. See Laurence S. Kuter, memorandum, Kuter to Arnold, 6 August 1943, 118.201-6, AFHRA.
44. COA, "Past Effectiveness and Future Prospects," 9.
45. COA, "Past Effectiveness and Future Prospects," 10.
46. Arnold, *Global Mission*, 494.

47. COA, "Past Effectiveness and Future Prospects," 12.
48. COA, "Past Effectiveness and Future Prospects," 13.
49. Arnold, *Global Mission*, 494.
50. Perera, memo for Major General Eaker, "Subject: General Kuter's letter of 6th July," 2–3.
51. Joint Intelligence Sub-Committee, "Effects of Bombing Offensive on German War Effort," in J.I.C. (43) 294 (Final), 22 July 1943, 118.04-12, AFHRA, 9.
52. Joint Intelligence Sub-Committee, "Effects of Bombing Offensive," 8.
53. Joint Intelligence Sub-Committee, "Effects of Bombing Offensive," 15.
54. COA, "Past Effectiveness and Future Prospects," 7.
55. H. H. Arnold, letter to Eaker, 29 June 1943, RG18, AAG 312.1-G, Operations Letters, NARA. Emphasis in original.
56. Davis, *Carl A. Spaatz and the Air War in Europe*, 260.
57. Assistant Chief of Air Staff (A-2), "Ploesti Mission of 1 August 1943," 3–4.
58. Assistant Chief of Air Staff (A-2), "Ploesti Mission of 1 August 1943," 6.
59. Assistant Chief of Air Staff (A-2), "Ploesti Mission of 1 August 1943," 4.
60. COA, "Report of Committee of Operations Analysts with Respect to Economic Targets Within the Western Axis," foldout 3.
61. Assistant Chief of Air Staff (A-2), "Ploesti Mission of 1 August 1943,"103.
62. A. Sedgwick, "Ploesti Smashed—300 Tons Rain on Major Gasoline Source of Reich Air Force," *New York Times*, 2 August 1943.
63. Wing Commander Commanding Middle East Interpretation Unit, "Photographs—Ninth Bomber Command," 12 August 1943, 533.923-1, AFHRA.
64. Assistant Chief of Air Staff (A-2), "Ploesti Mission of 1 August 1943," 49–52.
65. Assistant Chief of Air Staff (A-2), 54.
66. National Security Agency and Central Security Service, *ULTRA*, 39.
67. Assistant Chief of Air Staff (A-2), "Ploesti Mission of 1 August 1943," 50–51.
68. Assistant Chief of Air Staff (A-2), "Ploesti Mission of 1 August 1943," 110–12.
69. Ministry of Economic Warfare, "M.E.W. Intelligence Weekly," 12 August 1943, 1.
70. Ministry of Economic Warfare, "M.E.W. Intelligence Weekly."
71. Ministry of Economic Warfare, "M.E.W. Intelligence Weekly," 3.
72. Nick Thorpe and King Michael I of Romania, "Nobody Lifted a Finger," *Hungarian Review* 6 (2011).
73. OSS, "Bomb Damage Report," 18 September 1943, 187.2-16, AFHRA, 9; Assistant Chief of Air Staff (A-2), "Ploesti Mission of 1 August 1943," 106–7.

74. OSS, "Bomb Damage Report," 18 September 1943, 10–11.
75. Form 103A Narrative, Eighth Air Force, 12 August 1943, 527.332, AFHRA.
76. Headquarters 4th Bombardment Wing, "Briefing Notes, Primary Target, Wesseling Mission 36," 12 August 1943, 527.332, AFHRA.
77. Headquarters 4th Bombardment Wing, "Mission 36 (Wesseling)," 12 August 1943, 527.332, AFHRA, 103A Narrative, 94th Bomb Group.
78. Headquarters 4th Bombardment Wing, interrogation form crew 17.
79. 4th Bombardment Wing, "Form 103A Narrative."
80. 4th Bombardment Wing, "Mission 36 (Wesseling)," 12 August 1943, Intelligence Narrative, Mission of Wesseling.
81. S-2, 305th Bombardment Group, "Teletype Report, Mission 12 August 1943," 12 August 1943, 525.332B, AFHRA, 2.
82. S-2, 305th Bombardment Group, "Teletype Report."
83. Headquarters 1st Bombardment Wing, "Immediate Interpretation Report, No. 12, 2nd Lt. George Welter," 12 August 1943, 525.332, AFHRA.
84. Headquarters Eighth Air Force, "Summary of Eighth Air Force Heavy Bomber Operations as Called For in Combined Bomber Offensive Plan: August, 2nd Month of Second Phase, in Heavy Bomber Operations," 1 October 1943, 168.61-10, AFHRA.
85. Headquarters Eighth Air Force, "Summary of Eighth Air Force Heavy Bomber Operations as Called For in Combined Bomber Offensive Plan: August, 2nd Month of Second Phase, in Summary by Target Categories," 1 October 1943, 168.61-10, AFHRA.
86. A-2 Eighth Air Force, "Semi-monthly Report of Bombing Results, 1 August through 15 August 1943," 28 August 1943, 520.307, AFHRA, 3.
87. COA, "Western Axis Oil Industry as Bombardment Target," 8 March 1943, 118.02v2, AFHRA, 4, tab 7.
88. Hughes, "Memoirs," 30.
89. Perret, *Winged Victory*, 264.
90. Thomas M. Coffey, *Decision over Schweinfurt: The U.S. 8th Air Force Battle for Daylight Bombing* (New York: Mckay, 1977), 257–58.
91. Headquarters VIII Bomber Command, "Tactical Mission Report, in Eighth Air Force Mission No. 84," 17 August 1943, 520.331, AFHRA, 1; Parton, *Air Force Spoken Here*, 299.
92. Perret, *Winged Victory*, 264; VIII Bomber Command, "Tactical Mission Report, 17 August 1943," 1.

93. Perret, *Winged Victory*, 265.
94. Perret, *Winged Victory*, 265; Parton, *Air Force Spoken Here*, 299.
95. Hughes, "Memoirs," 35.
96. Commander 4th Bombardment Wing, "Routine Confidential Message, Attn: Senior Intelligence Officer," 19 August 1943, 527.332, AFHRA.
97. S-2 94th Bombardment Group, "Teletype Report, Form 103A Narrative," 17 August 1943, 527.332, AFHRA, 1.
98. S-2 94th Bombardment Group, "Teletype Report, Form 103A Narrative."
99. S-2 94th Bombardment Group, "Teletype Report, Form 103A Narrative," 2.
100. S-2 94th Bombardment Group, "Teletype Report Worksheets," ca. 17 August 1943, 527.332, AFHRA, Report Tabulation Sheet.
101. S-2 94th Bombardment Group, "Teletype Report Worksheets," paragraph 7.
102. CIU, "Immediate Interpretation Report No. K.1671," in "Eighth Air Force Mission No. 84, RAF Medmenham," 18 August 1943, 520.331, AFHRA.
103. Headquarters VIII Bomber Command, "Bomber Command Narrative of Operations, Mission No. 84," 17 August 1943, 519.332, AFHRA.
104. The COA argued that 93 percent of single engine fighters were produced in just seven aircraft final assembly plants, of which the Regensburg Messerschmitt plant accounted for 10 percent. However, the analysts felt that five component-erecting plants were also "deemed essential to achieve effective results," in addition to ten engine assembly plants, which added up to twenty-two total. See COA, "Report of Committee of Operations Analysts with Respect to Economic Targets Within the Western Axis," foldout 1.
105. VIII Bomber Command, "Bomber Command Narrative of Operations, Mission No. 84."
106. Assistant Chief of Air Staff (A-2), "Regensburg: ME-109 Assembly Plant," in "Reports of Attacks on Axis Targets in Europe, USAAF," 12 September 1943, 142.035-7, AFHRA.
107. OSS, "Bomb Damage Report," 18 September 1943, 8.
108. OSS, "Bomb Damage Report," 24.
109. CIU, "Immediate Interpretation Report No. K.S.124, Clearance and Reconstruction," in "Eighth Air Force Mission No. 84, RAF Medmenham," 10 October 1943, 520.331, AFHRA, 2.
110. COA, "Report of Committee of Operations Analysts with Respect to Economic Targets Within the Western Axis," foldout 1; COA, "Summary

of Position of France, Belgium, and Netherlands in Axis Aircraft Production," 2 August 1943, 118.04B-3, AFHRA.

111. Surveyors later determined the plant had been wholly unprepared to withstand attack from the standpoint of "a proper alarm system, air raid bunkers to safeguard personnel, or satisfactory facilities for raw materials and finished products," so the casualty toll exceeded 1,100 workers, along with unrecoverable damage to 70 percent of stored materials and 30 percent of machine tools. See USSBS, *Messerschmitt AG Augsburg, Germany, Part B*, 7.
112. Ministry of Home Security, "Reconstruction Report, Messerschmitt A G Regensburg—Prufening, Germany, Research and Experiments Department," 12 October 1943, 519.332, AFHRA, 1.
113. CIU, "Interpretation Report No. K.S. 407, Regensburg, RAF Medmenham," 3 February 1944, 519.332, AFHRA, 1–2.
114. Col. Curtis E. LeMay, memorandum, "Subject: Difficulties Encountered on Shuttle Raid, Landing at North Africa Bases," 29 August 1943, 168.61-10, AFHRA, 1–3.
115. LeMay, "Subject: Difficulties Encountered on Shuttle Raid," 2.
116. A-3 Assistant Chief of Staff, "Regensburg Shuttle Mission, Headquarters Eighth Air Force," 30 August 1943, 168.61-10, AFHRA.
117. Ministry of Economic Warfare, *The Bomber's Baedeker*, 8.
118. VIII Bomber Command, "Bomber Command Narrative of Operations, Mission No. 84," 5.
119. Harris, *Bomber Offensive*, 221.
120. Coffey, *Decision over Schweinfurt*, 237–39.
121. Hansell, lecture to Air War College, "The Development of the United States Concept of Bombardment Operations," 16 February 1951, 9; Hansell, *The Air Plan that Defeated Hitler*, 163.
122. VIII Bomber Command, "Bomber Command Narrative of Operations, Mission No. 84," 1.
123. VIII Bomber Command, "Bomber Command Narrative of Operations."
124. S-2 306th Bombardment Group, "Teletype Report, Mission 17 August 1943," 17 August 1943, 525.332B, AFHRA, 3.
125. S-2 92nd Bombardment Group, "Teletype Report, Mission 17 August 1943," 18 August 1943, 525.332B, AFHRA, 8.
126. S-2 305th Bombardment Group, "Teletype Report, Mission 17 August 1943," 18 August 1943, 525.332B, AFHRA, 4.

127. CIU, "Immediate Interpretation Report No. K.1672," in "Eighth Air Force Mission No. 84, RAF Medmenham," 18 August 1943, 520.331, AFHRA, 1.
128. CIU, "Interpretation Report No. S.A. 466, RAF Medmenham," 17 August 1943, 519.332, AFHRA, 1.
129. CIU, "Interpretation Report No. K.1677," in "Eighth Air Force Mission No. 84, RAF Medmenham," 23 August 1943, 520.331, AFHRA, 1.
130. United States War Department, *Washington Organization*, ed. Strategic Services Unit History Project, vol. 1 (Washington, DC: U.S. Government Printing Office, July 1949), 344.
131. OSS, "Bomb Damage Report," 18 September 1943, 14–16.
132. Assistant Chief of Air Staff (A-2), "An Appraisal of Accomplishments and Potentialities," 10 September 1943, iv.
133. Arnold, *American Airpower Comes of Age*, vol. 2, 64, n136.
134. Assistant Chief of Air Staff (A-2), "Schweinfurt: Ball Bearing Factories," in "Reports of Attacks on Axis Targets in Europe, USAAF," 12 September 1943, 142.035-7, AFHRA.
135. C. V. Whitney, memorandum for General Kuter, "Ball Bearings from Sweden," 11 September 1943, 145.81-144v2, AFHRA.
136. Kuter, memorandum for Colonel Whitney, "Ball Bearings from Sweden," 11 September 1943, 145.81-144v2, AFHRA.
137. Ministry of Home Security, "Raid Assessment Report, Ball Bearing Plants, Schweinfurt, Germany," 1.
138. Martin Middlebrook, *The Schweinfurt-Regensburg Mission* (New York: Scribner, 1983), 294–99.
139. McFarland, *America's Pursuit of Precision Bombing*, 180; Arnold, *American Airpower Comes of Age*, vol. 2, 51; Arthur Travers Harris, *Despatch on War Operations, 23rd February 1942 to 8th May 1945* (Portland, OR: F. Cass, 1995), 15.
140. Craven and Cate, *Argument to V-E Day*, 691.
141. Horst Boog, Gerhard Krebs, and Detlef Vogel, *The Strategic Air War in Europe and the War in the West and East Asia 1943–1944/5* (Oxford: Clarendon Press, 2006), 18.
142. Operational Analysis Section, "Report on Bombing Accuracy, Eighth Air Force, 1 September 1944 to 31 December 1944," 20 April 1945, 520.310v9, AFHRA, 16.
143. Wakelam, *The Science of Bombing*, 141; Craven and Cate, *Argument to V-E Day*, 14.

144. Harris, *Bomber Offensive*, 182.
145. Harris, *Bomber Offensive*.
146. Hastings, *Bomber Command*, 169.
147. Harris, *Bomber Offensive*, 183.
148. Williams, *Operation Crossbow*, 137; Hastings, *Bomber Command*, 169; Boog, Krebs, and Vogel, *The Strategic Air War,* 42.
149. Even the postwar bombing surveyors could not resist a rare editorial comment that the Crossbow campaign, of which this raid became the ex post facto unofficial beginning, had been "clouded by secrecy and distorted by propaganda." USSBS, *V-Weapons (Crossbow) Campaign*, ed. Military Analysis Division, 2nd ed., no. 60 (Washington, DC: USSBS, 1947), 1.
150. Adam L. Gruen, *Preemptive Defense: Allied Air Power Versus Hitler's V-Weapons, 1943–1945* (Washington, DC: U.S. Government Printing Office, 1998), 1.
151. David Benady has argued, "Politicians and corporations often promise to protect us from perceived threats by playing to our fears." He suggests that deliberate efforts by a handwash brand to inflate public fears of swine flu in order to sell their product serves as an example of this tendency. See David Benady, "Marketing Fear," *Marketing*, August 19, 2009. Fear is a motivator for statesman and militaries alike. Barry Posen offers that military organizations are prone to capitalizing on uncertainty to pursue their own ends—usually budget size and offensive doctrines. See Barry Posen, *The Sources of Military Doctrine: France, Britain, and Germany Between the World Wars* (Ithaca: Cornell University Press, 1984), 47–50, 75–77.
152. Gruen, *Preemptive Defense*, 9.
153. Powys-Lybbe, *The Eye of Intelligence*, 192.
154. V-weapons or *Vergeltunswaffe* ("get even" weapons) included several variations, although only the V-1 "flying bomb" or "buzz bomb" and the V-2 rocket saw operational use against England. Both were remarkably simple in terms of materials and suitability for mass production, though they marked a revolutionary development in unmanned flight. According to the USSBS, both also carried a 2,200-pound warhead. For a more detailed description, see USSBS, *Aircraft Division Industry Report*, 2nd ed., no. 4 (Washington, DC: USSBS, January 1947), 112–19.
155. Constance Babington-Smith, *Air Spy: The Story of Photo Intelligence in World War II* (New York: Harper, 1957), 204.
156. Williams, *Operation Crossbow*, 119; Powys-Lybbe, *The Eye of Intelligence*, 191.

157. Williams, *Operation Crossbow,* 120–23.
158. Williams, *Operation Crossbow*, 107.
159. R. V. Jones, *The Wizard War: British Scientific Intelligence, 1939–1945* (New York: Coward, McCann & Geoghegan, 1978), 332–33.
160. Jones, *The Wizard War*, 339.
161. Jones, *The Wizard War*, 340.
162. Roy M. Stanley, *V-Weapons Hunt: Defeating German Secret Weapons* (Barnsley, UK: Pen & Sword Military, 2010), 46–70, quote on 54.
163. Williams, *Operation Crossbow*, 141.
164. Powys-Lybbe, *The Eye of Intelligence*, 191.
165. Arnold, *Global Mission*, 497.
166. Williams, *Operation Crossbow*, 9.
167. Per flight officer Babington-Smith herself, "The perfume in question was Guerlain's 'L'Heure Bleue,' which I used rather a little too lavishly in those days, on the theory that the masculinity of WAAF uniform needed a little counteracting." Babington-Smith, *Air Spy*, 247; Williams, *Operation Crossbow,* 9; Jeremy Harwood, *World War Two From Above: An Aerial View of the Global Conflict* (Wollombi, AUS: Exisle Publishing, 2014), 71.
168. Babington-Smith, *Air Spy*, 226; Williams, *Operation Crossbow*, 123.
169. Of note, Air Force historians (referencing a *New York Times* article) credited flight officer Constance Babington-Smith with identifying the V-1 flying bomb in May 1943. She corrected the record over a decade later when she first published her memoir. According to Babington-Smith, the object she had originally identified turned out to be a "liquid-rocket" Me-163, not a V-1, and the date was later—23 June 1943; she identified an unknown twenty-foot-wingspan aircraft along with the ski-shaped launcher in November. Babington-Smith, *Air Spy*, 210; Craven and Cate, *Argument to V-E Day*, 84, 89. Further, the source of Craven and Cate's error appears to be the *New York Times*, which had actually published two conflicting articles (not just the one to which the historians refer), and both were incorrect. In the first article, the Air Ministry attributes the find to her in March 1943; the second article, published after the war, claims May. In any case, both the Air Ministry and the media were eager to praise the apparent heroine and sell the story. See "Robot Nemesis a Woman: WAAF Photo Interpreter First Spotted Bomb 18 Months Ago," *New York Times*, 10 September 1944;

"WAAF Tells of Aid in Saving New York," *New York Times*, 6 October 1945. Allan Williams also highlights the discrepancy in the Air Force history, but not the source of the error. Williams, *Operation Crossbow*, 87.

170. Williams, *Operation Crossbow*, 70–74.
171. According to the manufacturer's website, Babington-Smith's choice of fragrance has been in production since 1912, across nearly the entire history of airpower. "L'Heure Bleue," https://www.guerlain.com/us/en-us/fragrance/womens-fragrances/lheure-bleue.
172. Gruen, *Preemptive Defense*, 8.
173. Williams, *Operation Crossbow*, 113; Babington-Smith, *Air Spy*, 210–11.
174. Rostow, "Rostow Report," 123.
175. Babington-Smith, *Air Spy*, 226.
176. Stanley, *V-Weapons Hunt*, 58.
177. GLM meeting, 10 September 1943, BA-MA RL 3/38, 4523-4; cited in Boog, Krebs, and Vogel, *The Strategic Air War*, 422; Brian Mark Rigg, "Half-Jewish Field Marshal Erhard Milch," *World War II* (January 2004), 72.
178. Boog, Krebs, and Vogel, *The Strategic Air War*, 451–53.
179. USSBS surveyors later argued, "The attacks on England caused widespread damage, many casualties, and a considerable reduction of industrial efficiency. . . . They had, however, little or no military effect." See USSBS, *V-Weapons (Crossbow) Campaign*, 16.
180. USSBS, *V-Weapons (Crossbow) Campaign*, 29.
181. Powys-Lybbe, *The Eye of Intelligence*, 197.
182. Williams, *Operation Crossbow,* 142.
183. National Security Agency and Central Security Service, *ULTRA*, 093.
184. G-2 Division Combined Intelligence Objectives Sub-Committee, "Reich Ministry of Armaments and War Production," May-June 1945, 506.620v.102, AFHRA, 28.
185. Boog, Krebs, and Vogel, *The Strategic Air War*, 426.
186. Guerlain SA Département Internet, "L'Heure Bleue," https://www.guerlain.com/us/en-us/fragrance/womens-fragrances/lheure-bleue.

CHAPTER 5. QUADRANT TO SEXTANT

1. Ira Eaker, message, Arnold to Eaker, 15 December 1943, box 324, Spaatz Papers, Manuscript Division, LOC.
2. Rostow, "Rostow Report," 54–55.

3. Arnold noted of Quadrant, "There were some very rough, tough sessions. Angry words were sometimes thrown back and forth." Arnold, *Global Mission*, 444; Parton, *Air Force Spoken Here,* 302.
4. 15th Air Force would bed down farther south, in Foggia, Italy, in November, after Allied forces pushed the Germans north. See Boog, Krebs, and Vogel, *The Strategic Air War*, 102; 108th meeting of the Combined Chiefs of Staff (CCS), 15 August 1943, document 376, and 109th meeting of the CCS, 16 August 1943, document 378, both in Slany et al., *Foreign Relations of the United States, 1943.*
5. Minutes, 104th meeting of the Joint Chiefs of Staff, 15 August 1943, in Matloff, *Strategic Planning*, 220.
6. Matloff, *Strategic Planning*, 112, 221.
7. 83rd meeting of the CCS, 13 May 1943, document 31, in Slany et al., *Foreign Relations of the United States, 1943.*
8. Matloff, *The 90-Division Gamble*, 374.
9. White House press release, 14 August 1943, document 370, in Slany et al., *Foreign Relations of the United States, 1943.* Although other intelligence sources may have been incorporated, the Office of the State Department Historian contends: "The text of this joint statement followed very closely a draft which Churchill had sent to Roosevelt in telegram No. 408, August 11, 1943." This was in opposition to the perspective held by the U.S. Navy.
10. Combined Chiefs of Staff minutes, 14 August 1943, document 373, in Slany et al., *Foreign Relations of the United States, 1943.*
11. Combined Chiefs of Staff minutes.
12. Arthur William Tedder, *With Prejudice: The War Memoirs of Marshal of the Royal Air Force, Lord Tedder* (Boston: Little, Brown, 1967), 422, 452–53.
13. Headquarters Eighth Air Force, "Summary of Eighth Air Force Heavy Bomber Operations as Called For in Combined Bomber Offensive Plan: September, 3rd Month of Second Phase," 1 October 1943, 168.61-10, AFHRA.
14. OSS, "Bomb Damage Report," 18 September 1943, 1.
15. Mets, *Master of Airpower*, 163–64.
16. Dwight D. Eisenhower, *Crusade in Europe* (Garden City, NY: Doubleday, 1948), 179.
17. Mets, *Master of Airpower*, 164.
18. Eisenhower, *Crusade in Europe*, 161, 247.

19. 109th meeting of the CCS, in Slany et al., *Foreign Relations of the United States, 1943*.
20. Enclosure to CCS 309, 15 August 1943, document 449, in Slany et al., *Foreign Relations of the United States, 1943*.
21. Parton, *Air Force Spoken Here*, 304.
22. CCS 303/3, 17 August 1943, document 451, in Slany et al., *Foreign Relations of the United States, 1943*.
23. Headquarters VIII Bomber Command, "Bomber Command Narrative of Operations, 92nd Operation," 7 September 1943, 145.81-140, AFHRA, 1.
24. Powys-Lybbe, *The Eye of Intelligence,* 190.
25. This inquiry fell under the purview of Charles D. Ellis, chairman of the rocket subcommittee of the Crossbow committee, who formed a team later known as "the Sanders Mission" under Colonel Terence Sanders of the British armament design department. Their purpose was to investigate the heavily constructed Crossbow sites ("problem children") other than the obvious ski and rocket sites after Allied occupation. The committee comprised membership primarily from the British Ministry of Supply, Air Ministry, and War Office. See C. D. Ellis, memorandum for Col. T. R. B. Sanders, in "Report by the Sanders Mission to the Chairman of the Crossbow Committee," October 1944, 505.58-32, appendix F, AFHRA; Col. Terence R. B. Sanders, "Investigation of the 'Heavy' Crossbow Installations in Northern France," in "Report by the Sanders Mission to the Chairman of the Crossbow Committee," 21 February 1945, 6.
26. Sanders, "Investigation of the 'Heavy' Crossbow Installations," appendix C.
27. MEW analysts also noted interest by the German navy to produce hydrogen peroxide–propelled submarines and torpedoes, though they found "no evidence this material was ever used operationally in either weapon." See Foreign Office German Economic Department, "Economic Intelligence Weekly," no. 10, 1 August 1945, 512.611B, AFHRA, 1–3.
28. On 16 December 1943 Eighth Air Force disseminated a classified summary about Crossbow down to each group headquarters, noting with a certain better-late-than-never irony that "the importance of imparting the information . . . to combat crews operating against the installations described therein cannot be overemphasized." Interestingly, the American summary for aircrew contended that a ski site was "nearing completion" at Watten

when it was attacked on 27 August. The Sanders mission contended that "there are no indications that it was to be used for projection of any type of missile." See Col. H. G. Culton, memorandum, Subject: "CROSSBOW," Headquarters Eighth Air Force, 16 December 2017, 520.431A, AFHRA, 1–2; Sanders, "Investigation of the 'Heavy' Crossbow Installations," 6; USSBS, *V-Weapons (Crossbow) Campaign*, 5.

29. Headquarters 3rd Air Division, "Mission 46: Watten (France)," 27 August 1943, 527.332, Primary Target, AFHRA. Also, an official Air Ministry history contends that the chief of staff ordered the 27 August attack because "it was likely that the building would soon be covered with a concrete roof which would make it difficult serious damage by bombing and hide from the reconnaissance camera the activity of the site." See Air Ministry, *Photographic Reconnaissance*, vol. 2, May 1941–August 1945, 161.
30. S-2 306th Bombardment Group, "Teletype Report, Mission 27 August 1943," 27 August 1943, 525.332B, AFHRA, 2.
31. S-2 305th Bombardment Group, "Teletype Report, Mission 27 August 1943," 28 August 1943, 525.332B, AFHRA, 2.
32. CIU, "Interpretation Report No. S.A. 493," 29 August 1943, 527.332, AFHRA, 1.
33. CIU, "Interpretation Report No. S.A. 493."
34. Headquarters 4th Bombardment Wing, "Operations Broadcast, Teletype," 6 September 1943, Additional Briefing Material on Z-782, 527.332, AFHRA.
35. Headquarters VIII Bomber Command, "Report of Operations," in "Mission No. 92–93," 7 September 1943, Summary of Operations, 520.332, AFHRA.
36. Headquarters VIII Bomber Command, "Report of Operations"; VIII Bomber Command, "Bomber Command Narrative of Operations, 92nd Operation," 2.
37. VIII Bomber Command, "Bomber Command Narrative of Operations, 92nd Operation," 4.
38. The desire to reduce aircraft weight to gain performance would not have been unique to the Americans. For example, British Lancaster crews had been caught "dumping their 4,000-lb 'cookies' in the North Sea to gain height and speed." Needless to say, bringing bombs home was not a preferred option for any bomber crew. See Hastings, *Bomber Command*, 219.
39. 4th Bombardment Wing, "Operations Broadcast, Teletype," 6 September 1943, Advance Warning to 4BW Field Order No. 54.

40. John B. Bayer Jr. (S-2), Interrogation Form, Headquarters 4th Bombardment Wing, Group 94, Squadron 410, Crew 14, 7 September 1943, 527.332, AFHRA.
41. S-2 94th Bombardment Group, Telephone Report, Form 102, Headquarters 94th Bombardment Group, 7 September 1943, 527.332, AFHRA, 1.
42. VIII Bomber Command, "Bomber Command Narrative of Operations, 92nd Operation," 7 September 1943, 2; VIII Bomber Command, "Report of Operations, Summary of Operations," 7 September 1943.
43. CIU, "Interpretation Report No. S.A. 538," 8 September 1943, 520.332, AFHRA, 1.
44. CIU, "Negative Damage Report No. S.A. 209," 8 September 1943, 520.332, AFHRA.
45. Eighth Air Force, "Summary of Eighth Air Force Heavy Bomber Operations as Called For in Combined Bomber Offensive Plan: September, 3rd Month of Second Phase," III.
46. The Sanders mission report focused on the aftermath. It was as if the British scientists sought to validate that the bombing had done as well as it could, but the Germans persevered through sheer will and manpower: "Heavy raids in August and September, 1943, caused great damage to [concrete buildings], but by November of that year the site had been cleared up and new and stronger buildings were started. . . . The enemy showed the great importance he attached to it by the tremendous effort he put into it." Sanders, "Investigation of the 'Heavy' Crossbow Installations," appendix C.
47. The bombing may have caused short-term delays at Watten and other V-weapons sites, but it was ultimately the Allied armies on the ground that stopped the missiles. Sanders, "Investigation of the 'Heavy' Crossbow Installations."
48. According to Harrison, Sir Charles Portal interpreted the Pointblank Directive even more broadly than Eighth Air Force and certainly than Arnold's A-2 staff. See Gordon A. Harrison, *Cross-Channel Attack* (Washington, DC: Department of the Army, 1951), 209.
49. VIII Bomber Command, "Bomber Command Narrative of Operations, 92nd Operation."
50. A-2 Eighth Air Force, "Semi-monthly Report of Bombing Results, 16 September through 30 September 1943," ca. 1 October 1943, 520.307, AFHRA, 8; Hansell, *The Air Plan that Defeated Hitler*, 201–2.

51. Brig. Gen. F. L. Anderson, "Report of Operations," 7 September 1943, in "Tactical Mission Report, Brussels/Evere," 10 September 1943, 520.332, AFHRA, 2; Headquarters VIII Bomber Command, "Bombing Data."
52. S-2 306th Bombardment Group, "Teletype Report, Mission 7 September 1943," 8 September 1943, 525.332B, AFHRA, 1.
53. CIU, "Interpretation Report No. S.A. 536," 9 September 1943, 520.332, AFHRA, 1.
54. Headquarters 1st Bombardment Division, "Group Bombing Plot and Report," in "Brussels/Evere Mission," 7 September 1943, 525.332, AFHRA.
55. CIU, "Immediate Interpretation Report K.1710," 8 September 1943, 520.332, AFHRA.
56. CIU, "Immediate Interpretation Report K.1728," 19 September 1943, 520.332, AFHRA.
57. CIU, "Interpretation Report KS.280," AFHRA, 14 January 1944, 520.332, AFHRA, 1.
58. CIU, "Interpretation Report KS.280."
59. CIU, "Interpretation Report KS.280."
60. Babington-Smith, *Air Spy*, 101; Roy M. Stanley, *World War II Photo Intelligence* (New York: Scribner, 1981), 331.
61. Notes on Meeting with General Eaker, 5 April 1943.
62. Assistant Chief of Air Staff (A-2), "An Appraisal of Accomplishments and Potentialities," 10 September 1943.
63. Assistant Chief of Air Staff (A-2), i.
64. Assistant Chief of Air Staff (A-2).
65. Assistant Chief of Air Staff (A-2), ii.
66. Assistant Chief of Air Staff (A-2), 1.
67. Assistant Chief of Air Staff (A-2), 39, 43, 48.
68. Assistant Chief of Air Staff (A-2), ii.
69. Assistant Chief of Air Staff (A-2), 5.
70. Assistant Chief of Air Staff (A-2), 10.
71. Assistant Chief of Air Staff (A-2), 13.
72. Assistant Chief of Air Staff (A-2), signature page.
73. George V. Strong, Memorandum, "Organization of Military Intelligence Division, War Department," 30 August 1943, 203–6v6, AFHRA, 2.
74. Edgar P. Sorensen, Memorandum, "Cooperation with the Office of Assistant Chief of Staff, G-2," 6 September 1943, 203–6v6, AFHRA.

75. Sorensen, "Cooperation with the Office of Assistant Chief of Staff."
76. Assistant Chief of Air Staff (A-2), "An Appraisal of Accomplishments and Potentialities," 26.
77. Assistant Chief of Air Staff (A-2), 27.
78. DeWitt S. Copp, *Forged in Fire: Strategy and Decisions in the Air War over Europe, 1940–45* (Garden City, NY: Doubleday, 1982), 338.
79. McArthur, *Operations Analysis*, 108.
80. Eighth Air Force, "Semi-monthly Report of Bombing Results, 16 September through 30 September 1943," 5.
81. Craven and Cate, *Argument to V-E Day*, 692. Interestingly, an end-of-month report, likely submitted by Eaker's staff, included Emden as an "industrial" target. Eighth Air Force, "Summary of Eighth Air Force Heavy Bomber Operations as Called For in Combined Bomber Offensive Plan: September, 3rd Month of Second Phase, 1 October 1943," II-Report Against Individual Targets.
82. Lt. Col. Carl H. Norcross, "Additional Briefing Material on Target GH 5477, 3rd Bombardment Division," 26 September 1943, 527.332, AFHRA.
83. Headquarters 3rd Bombardment Division, "Field Order No. 66," 26 September 1943, 527.332, AFHRA, 1.
84. An alternate procedure, used by the British in night visual conditions, was to illuminate the target with flares for aiming by subsequent bombers—a technique known as "groundmarking." Harris, *Despatch on War Operations,* 79–81; Hajo Herrmann, *Eagle's Wings* (Stillwater, MN: Motorbooks International, 1991), 202.
85. 3rd Bombardment Division, "Field Order No. 66," 2.
86. Headquarters VIII Bomber Command, "Bomber Command Narrative of Operations, 104th Operation," 27 September 1943, 145.81-140, AFHRA, 1, 5.
87. Headquarters VIII Bomber Command, "Bomber Command Narrative," 2.
88. 410th Bombardment Squadron, "Interrogation Form, Crew No. 427," 27 September 1943, 527.332, AFHRA.
89. 410th Bombardment Squadron, "Interrogation Form, Crew No. 200," 27 September 1943, 527.332, AFHRA.
90. S-2 305th Bombardment Group, "Teletype Report, Mission 27 September 1943," 2.
91. S-2 92nd Bombardment Group, "Teletype Report, Mission 27 September 1943," 27 September 1943, 525.332B, AFHRA, 2.

92. S-2 306th Bombardment Group, "Teletype Report, Mission 27 September 1943," 27 September 1943, 525.332B, AFHRA, 1.
93. 3rd Bombardment Division, "Field Order No. 66," 26 September 1943, 2.
94. S-2 94th Bombardment Group, "Teletype Report, Form 103A Narrative, 3rd Bombardment Division," 27 September 1943, 527.332, AFHRA, 2.
95. Capt. George Welter, "Memorandum to A-2 Section, Headquarters 1st Bombardment Division," 27 September 1943, 525.332, AFHRA.
96. 1st Lt. William F. Sink, "Photo & Bomb Plotting Report, 3rd Bombardment Division," 27 September 1943, 527.332, AFHRA.
97. 1st Lt. William F. Sink, "Mission Camera Report, 3rd Bombardment Division," 27 September 1943, 527.332, AFHRA.
98. CIU, "Interpretation Report No. S.A. 602," 29 September 1943, 525.332B, AFHRA.
99. Headquarters 3rd Bombardment Division, "Annex No. 1 to 3 B. D. Field Order No. 68," 28 September 1943, 527.332, AFHRA.
100. Bomber crews were consistent in their praise for the ability of escorts to persist in the target area for both Emden missions. In this case, a group S-2 recorded the word "magnificent" during crew interrogation and pushed it up in his report. S-2 94th Bombardment Group, "Hand-written notes for Teletype Report," 2 October 1943, 527.332, AFHRA; Perret, *Winged Victory*, 273; Head-quarters 3rd Bombardment Division, "Advance Warning to 3 BD Field Order No. 69," 1 October 1943, 527.332, AFHRA.
101. S-2 306th Bombardment Group, "Teletype Report, War Department," 2 October 1943, 525.332B, AFHRA, 1.
102. 94th Bombardment Group, "Hand-written notes for Teletype Report."
103. It could be that this feedback was passed directly to those responsible for the Pathfinder's flare settings (rather than forwarded further up the chain) or that the remark was screened before sending the S-2 report. In either case, it is clear that the crews appreciated the listening ear of the S-2, and they took the opportunity to vent, whether or not the feedback fell under the responsibility of the S-2. S-2 94th Bombardment Group, "Teletype Report," 2 October 1943, 527.332, AFHRA, 2; S-2 94th Bombardment Group, "Form 103A Narrative," 2 October 1943, 527.332, AFHRA.
104. Headquarters 3rd Bombardment Division, "Annex No. 1 to 3 B.D. Field Order No. 69," 2 October 1943, 527.332, AFHRA; Headquarters 4th

Bombardment Wing, "Annex No. 1 of 4th Combat Wing Field Order No. 36," 2 October 1943, 527.332, AFHRA; Headquarters 3rd Bombardment Division, "Annex No. 2 to 3 B.D. Field Order No. 69," 1 October 1943, 527.332, AFHRA.

105. CIU, "Supplement to Interpretation Report No. K. 1756," 6 October 1943, 527.332, AFHRA; CIU, "Immediate Interpretation Report No. K.1756," 4 October 1943, 527.332, AFHRA.

106. Headquarters VIII Bomber Command, "Flash Report—104 Operation," 27 September 1943, 527.332, AFHRA; Headquarters VIII Bomber Command, "Flash Report—Operation No. 106," 2 October 1943, 527.332, AFHRA.

107. National Security Agency and Central Security Service, *ULTRA*, 87.

108. Office of the Combined Chiefs of Staff, "Sextant Conference, November-December 1943," in *Papers and Minutes of Meetings, Sextant and Eureka Conferences* (Washington, DC: Joint History Office, 2003), 129; Headquarters Eighth Air Force, "Statistical Summary of Eighth Air Force Operations, European Theater, 17 August 1942–8 May 1945," 10 June 1945, 520.308-1, AFHRA, 14.

109. Davis, *Bombing the European Axis Powers*, 182.

110. COA, "Meeting Minutes," 30 September 1943, 118.151-8, AFHRA, 1.

111. Coffey, *Decision over Schweinfurt*, 287–90.

112. Perret, *Winged Victory*, 278–79.

113. Arnold, *American Airpower Comes of Age*, vol. 2, 47.

114. S-2 92nd Bombardment Group, "Teletype Report, Mission 14 October 1943," 16 October 1943, 525.332B, AFHRA, 7.

115. S-2 306th Bombardment Group, "Teletype Report, Mission 14 October 1943," 14 October 1943, 525.332B, AFHRA, 3.

116. CIU, "Interpretation Report No. S.A. 628," in "Attack on Schweinfurt Ball-Bearing Industry on 14.10.43," 16 October 1943, 520.365, AFHRA, 1.

117. Maj. Gen. Ira C. Eaker, letter to Arnold, 15 October 1943, box 16, Eaker Papers, AFHSO collection, Manuscript Division, LOC.

118. CIU, "Immediate Interpretation Report No. K.1785," in "Locality: Schweinfurt," 17 October 1943, 520.365, AFHRA, 1.

119. "Schweinfurt—A Symbol," *Washington Star*, 19 October 1943, in COA, "Damage Assessment, Clippings, Headquarters Army Air Forces," ca. 1 January 1944, 118.952-1, folder 2, AFHRA.

120. Col. Guido R. Perera, Lt. Col. W. B. Leach, and Brig. Gen. Byron E. Gates, "Suggested Bombardment Program in Preparation for Overlord," in "COA History" (Tab 68), 25 October 1943, 118.02v2, AFHRA, 1.
121. Perera, Leach, and Gates, "Suggested Bombardment Program in Preparation for Overlord," 1, 4.
122. Perera, Leach, and Gates, "Suggested Bombardment Program," 6.
123. COA, "Brief Analysis of Target Systems for Maximum Short-Term Effect on Germany's War Effort," in "COA History" (tab A of tab 68), 11 October 1943, 118.02v2, AFHRA.
124. Perera, Leach, and Gates, "Suggested Bombardment Program," 7.
125. Perera, Leach, and Gates, "Suggested Bombardment Program," 8.
126. Perera, Leach, and Gates, "Suggested Bombardment Program."
127. Perera, Leach, and Gates, "Suggested Bombardment Program," 9.
128. COA, "Brief Analysis of Target Systems."
129. Ministry of Economic Warfare, "M.E.W. Intelligence Weekly," 29 February 1944, 512.607A, AFHRA, 16.
130. Hughes' use of passive voice is curiously ambiguous. Ostensibly, he sought to avoid pinning criticism on his revered boss, but the implication was clear. See Hughes, "Memoirs," 38.
131. Office of the Director of Intelligence Eighth Air Force, "Target Priorities of the Eighth Air Force, A Resume of the Bombardment Directives and Concepts Underlying Them," 15 May 1945, 520.323-1, AFHRA, 12.
132. Eaker, letter to Arnold, 15 October 1943.
133. H. H. Arnold, message to Eaker, 16 October 1943, box 324, Spaatz Papers, Manuscript Division, LOC.
134. Arnold, *American Airpower Comes of Age*, vol. 2, 108.
135. The allusion here is to the single piece of prose most representative of the way pilots think. John Gillespie Magee Jr., "High Flight," *All Hands* (April 2003): 7. Of note, the publisher of this version refers to the poem as "an anthem for aviators around the world."
136. Hastings, *Bomber Command*, 215.
137. Rostow, "Rostow Report," 54–55.
138. Rostow, "Rostow Report."
139. Rostow, "Rostow Report," 55.
140. Rostow, "Rostow Report," 54–55.

141. Laurence S. Kuter, memorandum, AC/AS Plans to AC/AS Intelligence, "Subject: Combined Bomber Offensive," 25 October 1943, 145.81-140, AFHRA.
142. Stewart W. Bentley Jr., *The Touch of Greatness: Colonel William C. Bentley Jr., USAAC/USAF, Aviation Pioneer* (Bloomington, IN: AuthorHouse, 2010), xii.
143. Assistant Chief of Air Staff (A-2), "The Strategic Bomber Offensive, Results of Operations to 1 November 1943, Colonel William C. Bentley," 5 November 1943, 145.81-140, AFHRA, 2.
144. A-2, "The Strategic Bomber Offensive," 2–3.
145. A-2, "The Strategic Bomber Offensive," 6, schedule B.
146. A-2, "The Strategic Bomber Offensive," 8.
147. George Catlett Marshall, *The Papers of George Catlett Marshall*, vol. 4, "Aggressive and Determined Leadership, June 1, 1943–December 31, 1944," ed. Larry I. Bland and Sharon Ritenour Stevens (Baltimore: Johns Hopkins University Press, 1996), 191–96. Official records do not reveal deeper insight into Spaatz's nomination to command USSTAF, except that "on his way back from Cairo, Arnold stopped in Tunis to talk with Eisenhower about air command reorganization," and they agreed on Spaatz. See Marshall, *The Papers of George Catlett Marshall*, 202–4.
148. Eisenhower, *Crusade in Europe*, 216.
149. Mets, *Master of Airpower*, 176; Parton, *Air Force Spoken Here*, 341.
150. Combined Chiefs of Staff, "Sextant Conference," 120.
151. Combined Chiefs of Staff, "Sextant Conference," 121.
152. Combined Chiefs of Staff, "Sextant Conference."
153. Combined Chiefs of Staff, "Sextant Conference," 474–75.
154. Maj. Gen. Ira C. Eaker, memorandum to commanding general, ETOUSA, "Plan for Build-up and Employment of the Bomber Offensive," Eighth Air Force, in personal collection of Gen. Henry H. Arnold, part 3 of 6, 18 April 1943, MICFILM 28253, AFHRA.
155. Combined Chiefs of Staff, "Sextant Conference," 476.
156. Combined Chiefs of Staff, "Sextant Conference," 475.
157. Combined Chiefs of Staff, "Sextant Conference."
158. Combined Chiefs of Staff, "Sextant Conference."
159. Word traveled quickly. Arnold's chief of operational plans submitted a memorandum to Arnold's office during the conference suggesting that his

division determine if future bombing plans "are in conformity," after noting, "It is our understanding that General Arnold and Air Chief Marshal Portal are in agreement as to the priority targets of the Combined Bomber Offensive and that General Eaker and Air Marshal Harris are not conforming." Chief of Operational Plans Army Air Forces, memorandum to commanding general from AC/AS Plans, "Subject: Combined Bomber Offensive, Joe L. Loutzenheiser," 4 December 1943, 145.81-140, AFHRA.

160. Craven and Cate, *Torch to Pointblank*, 750.
161. Combined Chiefs of Staff, "Sextant Conference," 475.
162. It is notable that the September report, after specifying the OSS and Economic Warfare Division, stipulated, "Neither this report nor any of its conclusions contained herein should be ascribed to either of these agencies as necessarily representing their views," but the more forceful December report stated, "The report is concurred in and adopted for separate issuance by these agencies with the approval of the AC/AS, Intelligence." It meant that Arnold, ever sensitive to the implied objectivity of outside perspectives, had the OSS backing this negative evaluation. Assistant Chief of Air Staff (A-2), "An Appraisal of Accomplishments and Potentialities," signature page.
163. Arnold, *Global Mission*, 77, 106.
164. Hansell, *The Air Plan that Defeated Hitler*, 65–73.
165. After Bissell took over as the air staff A-2, he paid a visit to AAFAIS in Harrisburg. According to the optimistic viewpoint evident in the school's internally produced history, Bissell expressed pleasure to the faculty in what he had observed there, before he "personally interviewed every member of the academic and administrative staffs." In reality, Bissell was not there for a glad-handing walkabout as a general officer. He understood that the school's problems were much larger than its faculty. Finney, *History of the Air Corps*, 60; *History of AAFAIS*, 16: 14.
166. Arnold had favored Bissell in the complicated and heated battle between Bissell and Claire Chennault over operations in the China air task force. Arnold, *American Airpower Comes of Age: General Henry H. "Hap" Arnold's World War II Diaries*, ed. John W. Huston, vol. 1 (Maxwell AFB, AL: Air University Press, 2001), 446–47, 91.
167. Arnold, *Global Mission*, 419–20; Arnold, *American Airpower Comes of Age*, vol. 1, 447.

168. At the time, air intelligence officers would not have been considered airmen by the Army Air Corps.
169. Assistant Chief of Air Staff (A-2), "An Appraisal of Accomplishments and Potentialities," iv.
170. Assistant Chief of Air Staff (A-2), ii.
171. Clayton Bissell, letter to Eaker, 3 December 1943, 830.289v1, AFHRA.
172. Bissell.
173. Ira Eaker, letter to Bissell, 15 December 1943, 830.289v1, AFHRA.
174. Eaker.
175. Assistant Chief of Air Staff (A-2), "An Appraisal of Accomplishments," 13.
176. Assistant Chief of Air Staff (A-2), 14.
177. Assistant Chief of Air Staff (A-2), foreword.
178. Perera, "History of the Organization and Operations of the Committee of Operations Analysts," 99–100.
179. Though many reports out of Eighth Air Force did not specifically attribute the originating office, the bimonthly reports (titled "semi-monthly" after 1 August 1943—both were produced every two weeks) did. Distribution went directly to General Arnold and General Devers, in addition to copies retained locally. For example, see A-2 Eighth Air Force, "Semi-monthly Report of Bombing Results, 16 August through 31 August 1943," 2 September 1943, 520.307, AFHRA, 17. Semimonthly reports continued as an operational intelligence function after reorganization to USSTAF as well. See Lewis F. Powell Jr., "Notes on Operational Intelligence Division of Directorate of Intelligence, USSTAF, A-2 United States Strategic Air Forces in Europe," ca. May 1945, 519.600, AFHRA, 18.
180. A-2 Eighth Air Force, "Semi-monthly Report of Bombing Results, 1 October through 15 October 1943," 26 October 1943, 520.307, AFHRA, 6.
181. Arnold, *Global Mission*, 502. Plans to move Eaker may well have already been in place prior to Arnold internalizing the December assessment, but it is worth noting that even in James Parton's account, which was shamelessly in Eaker's defense as written by one of his former staffers, the decision was still in the air until the very end of 1943. It is also likely that Arnold was familiar with the substance of the A-2 assessment well prior to placing his signature on the foreword. See Parton, *Air Force Spoken Here*, 333–45.
182. Arnold, *Global Mission*, 333–34.

183. H. H. Arnold, letter to Giles, "Subject: Analysis of Eighth Air Force Heavy Bomber Effort," 5 January 1944, 168.491v1, AFHRA. See also McFarland and Newton, *To Command the Sky*, 147–51.
184. Assistant Chief of Air Staff (A-2), "An Appraisal of Accomplishments and Potentialities," iv.
185. Hansell, *The Air Plan that Defeated Hitler*, 163.
186. Assistant Chief of Air Staff (A-2), "An Appraisal of Accomplishments and Potentialities," 2.
187. Hansell, *The Air Plan that Defeated Hitler*, 177–78. The combined chiefs agreed that Pointblank should remain unchanged at their 133rd meeting on 3 December 1943. See Combined Chiefs of Staff, "Sextant Conference," 463.
188. Craven and Cate, *Torch to Pointblank*, 307.
189. Parton, *Air Force Spoken Here*, 338.

CONCLUSION

1. H. H. Arnold, memorandum for Maj. Gen. Clayton Bissell, Assistant Chief of Staff (G-2), "Subject: Bombing Targets," 8 January 1945, 142.035-8, AFHRA.
2. H. H. Arnold, letter to Spaatz, 14 July 1944, 118.01v2, tab 81, AFHRA.
3. John G. Winant, telegram, "American Embassy, London to Secretary of State, Washington," 26 February 1944, 145.81-144v2, AFHRA.
4. Joseph T. McNarney, memorandum for chief of staff, "Ball Bearings Supplied to Germany from Sweden," 25 November 1943, 145.81-144v2, AFHRA.
5. Henry L. Stimson, personal letter to the secretary of state, 7 December 1943, 145.81-144v2, AFHRA.
6. Charles M. Taylor, memorandum for Colonel Loutzenheiser, 2 December 1943, 145.81-144v2, AFHRA; CG Strategic Air Forces in Europe, telegraph, 16 March 1944, 145.81–144v2, AFHRA.
7. McNarney, memorandum.
8. According to war department records, ball-bearing shipments from Sweden to Germany did not stop until October 1944. See Memorandum for Record, "Ball Bearing Shipments between Sweden and Germany," 11 October 1944, 145.81-144v2, AFHRA.
9. Assistant Chief of Air Staff (A-2), "Results of Combined Bomber Offensive from 1 July 1943 to September 1944," 19 September 1944, 145.81-140, AFHRA,1.

10. Assistant Chief of Air Staff (A-2), 2–3.
11. Assistant Chief of Air Staff (A-2).
12. Rostow, "Rostow Report," 122.
13. Rostow, "Rostow Report," 123.
14. Assistant Chief of Air Staff (A-2), "Strategic Bombing of Axis Europe, January 1943–September 1944; Bomb Damage to Axis Target Systems, Major General James P. Hodges," 1 December 1944, 142.042-8, AFHRA, 1.
15. Assistant Chief of Air Staff (A-2), 15.
16. Assistant Chief of Air Staff (A-2), 19.
17. Assistant Chief of Air Staff (A-2), 2, 21.
18. Assistant Chief of Air Staff (A-2), 19, 21.
19. The same air service officer who had drafted the report condemning Eaker had moved up to become the war department G-2. An airman conquered the Army's intelligence bureaucracy. Herman S. Wolk, *The Struggle for Air Force Independence, 1943–1947* (Washington, DC: AFHSO, 1997), 323; Arnold, memorandum for Bissell, "Bombing Targets."
20. Meilinger, *Ten Propositions Regarding Air Power*, 20, 78.
21. Meilinger, *Ten Propositions Regarding Air Power*.
22. Meilinger, *Ten Propositions Regarding Air Power*, 23.
23. Brig. Gen. Haywood S. Hansell, memorandum to General Gates, "Subject: Evaluation of Strategic Bombardment Against the Western Axis," in COA History (tab 57), 26 February 1944, 118.02v2, AFHRA, 2.
24. Carl von Clausewitz, *On War*, ed. and trans. Michael Howard and Peter Paret (Princeton, NJ: Princeton University Press, 1984), 121.
25. Paula G. Thornhill, *"Over Not Through": The Search for a Strong, Unified Culture for America's Airmen* (Santa Monica, CA: RAND Corporation, 2012), 3, 8–11. Carl Builder argues that airmen possess a "reverence for technology" in addition to a blindness induced by strategic bombing doctrine. Carl H. Builder, *The Masks of War: American Military Styles in Strategy and Analysis* (Baltimore, MD: Johns Hopkins University Press, 1989), 69–73.
26. For example, Russell Weigley claims strategic bombing greatly extended the costs of war onto the Germans, including civilian casualties, in the process of reducing ground losses to the Allies. Russell Frank Weigley, *The American Way of War: A History of United States Military Strategy and Policy* (Bloomington: Indiana University Press, 1977), 359.

27. "U.S. Intelligence Community Budget," https://www.dni.gov/index.php/what-we-do/ic-budget. For comparative value to $80 billion in 2015 dollars, see the White House, "Remarks by the President at the NAACP Conference," news release, 14 July 2015, https://www.whitehouse.gov/the press office/2015/07/14/remarks president naacp conference.
28. Michael DeVine, "Defense Primer: Intelligence Support to Military Operations," IF10574 (Washington, DC: Congressional Research Service, 2018).
29. Jeff Kimmons, Ronald Makuta, and Graham Gilmer, *Remaking Intelligence Processing, Exploitation and Dissemination*, Booz Allen Hamilton Inc., https://governmenttechnologyinsider.com/wp-content/uploads/2018/02/12012017-Intelligence-Processing-Exploitation-and-Dissemination-PED-Thought-Piece.pdf, 4. See also Andy J. Fawkes and Martin Menzel, "The Future Role of Artificial Intelligence: Military Opportunities and Challenges," *Transforming Joint Air Power: The Journal of the JAPCC*, 27 (Autumn/Winter 2018): 75.
30. David E. Johnson, *Fast Tanks and Heavy Bombers: Innovation in the U.S. Army, 1917–1945* (Ithaca, NY: Cornell University Press, 1998), 211.
31. Stephen Peter Rosen, "Competitive Strategies: Theoretical Foundations, Limits, and Extentions," in *Competitive Strategies for the 21st Century: Theory, History, and Practice*, ed. Thomas G. Mahnken (Stanford, CA: Stanford University Press, 2012), 25.

BIBLIOGRAPHY

ARCHIVAL SOURCES

Air Force Historical Research Agency (AFHRA), Maxwell Air Force Base, AL
Clark Special Collections Branch, U.S. Air Force Academy, Colorado Springs, CO
Library of Congress (LOC), Manuscript Division, Washington, DC
National Archives and Records Administration (NARA), Washington, DC
Truman Library, Independence, MO
UK National Archives, London

PRIMARY SOURCES

Armstrong, Brig. Gen. Frank A. "Air Discipline." *Air Force: Official Service Journal of the U.S. Army Air Forces* 28, no. 11 (1943).

Army Air Forces Air Intelligence School. *The Briefing and Interrogation of Bomber Crews.* Harrisburg, PA: United States Army Air Forces, 1942.

———. *Group and Squadron S-2.* Revised ed. Washington, DC: U.S. Government Printing Office, 1943.

———. *Photo Intelligence for Combat Aviation.* Harrisburg, PA: United States Army Air Forces, 1942.

Arnold, Henry Harley. *American Airpower Comes of Age: General Henry H. "Hap" Arnold's World War II Diaries.* Edited by John W. Huston. 2 Vols. Maxwell AFB, AL: Air University Press, 2001.

———. *Global Mission.* Blue Ridge Summit, PA: Tab Books, 1989.

Arnold, Henry Harley, and Ira Eaker. *This Flying Game.* New York: Funk & Wagnalls, 1936 (reprinted 1940).

Arps, Leslie H., et al. *Operations Analysis in the Eighth Air Force, 1942–1945: Four Contemporary Accounts.* Linthicum, MD: INFORMS, 1997.

Babington-Smith, Constance. *Air Spy: The Story of Photo Intelligence in World War II.* New York: Harper, 1957.

Barlow, Jane A., and Clinton C. Gardner. *World War II Remembered.* Hanover, NH: Kendal at Hanover Residents Association, 2012.

Cabell, Charles P., and Charles P. Cabell Jr. *Memoirs of War, Peace, and the CIA.* Colorado Springs, CO: Impavide Publications, 1997.

Combined Chiefs of Staff. "Sextant Conference, November-December 1943." In *Papers and Minutes of Meetings, Sextant and Eureka Conferences*. Washington, DC: Joint History Office, 1943.

Eisenhower, Dwight D. *Crusade in Europe.* Garden City, NY: Doubleday, 1948.

Hansell, Haywood S. *The Air Plan That Defeated Hitler.* Atlanta: Higgins-McArthur/Longino and Porter, 1972.

———. *The Strategic Air War against Germany and Japan: A Memoir.* Washington, DC: Office of Air Force History, 1986.

Harris, Arthur Travers. *Bomber Offensive.* South Yorkshire, UK: Pen & Sword Military Classics, 2005.

———. *Despatch on War Operations, 23rd February 1942 to 8th May 1945.* Portland, OR: F. Cass, 1995.

Marshall, George Catlett. *"Aggressive and Determined Leadership," June 1, 1943–December 31, 1944: The Papers of George Catlett Marshall.* Vol. 4. Edited by Larry I. Bland and Sharon Ritenour Stevens. Baltimore, MD: Johns Hopkins University Press, 1996.

Minneapolis-Honeywell Regulator. "Here's How: Operation of the C-1 Autopilot." Minneapolis, MN: Minneapolis-Honeywell, 1944.

National Security Agency and Central Security Service. *ULTRA: History of U.S. Strategic Air Force Europe vs. German Air Force.* Vol. SRH-013. Washington, DC: Held by Air Force Historical Studies Office, June 1945.

Office of the Director of National Intelligence. "U.S. Intelligence Community Budget." https://www.dni.gov/index.php/what-we-do/ic-budget.

"Robot Nemesis a Woman: WAAF Photo Interpreter First Spotted Bomb 18 Months Ago." *New York Times*. 10 September 1944.

Ruskin, John. *The Seven Lamps of Architecture.* London: Chiswick Press, 1880.

Sedgwick, A. "Ploesti Smashed—300 Tons Rain on Major Gasoline Source of Reich Air Force." *New York Times*. 2 August 1943.

Straubel, James H. "Cross Country." *Air Force: Official Service Journal of the U.S. Army Air Forces* 26, no. 10 (1942).

Tedder, Arthur William. *With Prejudice: The War Memoirs of Marshal of the Royal Air Force, Lord Tedder.* Boston: Little, Brown, 1967.

Trachtenberg, Marc, David Rosenberg, and Stephen Van Evera. "An Interview with Carl Kaysen." MIT Security Studies Program, Massachusetts Institute of Technology, 1988, http://web.mit.edu/ssp/publications/working_papers/Kaysen%20working%20paper.pdf.

United States Congress. Hearings before the United States Joint Committee on the Investigation of the Pearl Harbor Attack, Seventy-Ninth Congress, Second Session, part 14, 1946.

United States Strategic Bombing Survey (USSBS). *Aircraft Division Industry Report.* No. 4. Washington, DC: USSBS, January 1947.

———. *Blohm and Voss Shipyards, Hamburg, Germany.* No. 94. Washington, DC: USSBS, 1947.

———. *Bremer Vulcan, Vegesack, Germany.* No. 100. Washington, DC: USSBS, 1947.

———. *The German Abrasives Industry.* No. 51. Washington, DC: USSBS, 1947.

———. *Huels Synthetic Rubber Plant.* No. 128. Washington, DC: USSBS, 1947.

———. *Messerschmitt Ag Augsburg, Germany, Part B.* No. 11. Washington, DC: USSBS, 1947.

———. *Over-All Report (European War).* Vol. 2. Washington, DC: U.S. Government Printing Office, 30 September 1945.

———. *V-Weapons (Crossbow) Campaign.* No. 60. Washington, DC: USSBS, 1947.

U.S. War Department. *Field Service Regulations, United States Army, 1923.* Washington, DC: War Department, 1924.

———. *Washington Organization.* Edited by Strategic Services Unit History Project. Vol. 1. Washington, DC: U.S. Government Printing Office, July 1949.

von Clausewitz, Carl, *On War.* Edited and Translated by Michael Howard and Peter Paret. Princeton, NJ: Princeton University Press, 1984.

"WAAF Tells of Aid in Saving New York." *New York Times*. 6 October 1945.

Wright, L. B. "Three-Dimension View of the Enemy." *Air Force: Official Journal of the U.S. Army Air Forces* 26, no. 2 (February 1943).

SECONDARY SOURCES

Benady, David. "Marketing Fear." *Marketing* (19 August 2009): 24–25.

Bentley Jr., Stewart W. *The Touch of Greatness: Colonel William C. Bentley Jr., USAAC/USAF; Aviation Pioneer.* Bloomington, IN: AuthorHouse, 2010.

Benton, Jeffrey C. *They Served Here: Thirty-Three Maxwell Men.* Maxwell AFB, AL: Air University Press, 1999.

Biddle, Tami Davis. *Rhetoric and Reality in Air Warfare: The Evolution of British and American Ideas About Strategic Bombing, 1914–1945.* Princeton, NJ: Princeton University Press, 2002.

Blunden, Margaret. "Geoffrey Vickers—An Intellectual Journey." In *The Vickers Papers*, edited by Open Systems Group. London: Harper & Row, 1984.

Boog, Horst, Gerhard Krebs, and Detlef Vogel. *The Strategic Air War in Europe and the War in the West and East Asia 1943–1944/5.* Oxford: Clarendon Press, 2006.

Borneman, Walter R. *The Admirals: Nimitz, Halsey, Leahy, and King—The Five-Star Admirals Who Won the War at Sea.* New York: Little, Brown and Co., 2012.

Boyne, Walter J. *Fw 190 Wurger* 92, 4 (2009): 80.

Brauer, Jurgen, and Hubert P. Van Tuyll. *Castles, Battles, and Bombs: How Economics Explains Military History.* Chicago: University of Chicago Press, 2008.

Brothers, Leroy A. "Operations Analysis in the United States Air Force." *Journal of the Operations Research Society of America* 2, no. 1 (1954): 1–16.

Builder, Carl H. *The Masks of War: American Military Styles in Strategy and Analysis.* Baltimore, MD: Johns Hopkins University Press, 1989.

Carter, Kit C., and Robert Mueller. *U.S. Army Air Forces in World War II: Combat Chronology 1941–1945.* Maxwell AFB, AL: AFHRA, 1991.

Cline, Ray S. *Washington Command Post: The Operations Division.* Washington, DC: Office of the Chief of Military History, Department of the Army, 1951.

"The Clydesdale Horse—Dialogue." *The Farmers' Cabinet and American Herd-Book* V, no. 1 (15 August 1840).

Coffey, Thomas M. *Decision over Schweinfurt: The U.S. 8th Air Force Battle for Daylight Bombing.* New York: Mckay, 1977.

Copp, DeWitt S. *Forged in Fire: Strategy and Decisions in the Air War over Europe, 1940–45.* Garden City, NY: Doubleday, 1982.

Craven, Wesley Frank, and James Lea Cate, eds. *Europe: Argument to V-E Day, January 1944 to May 1945.* Vol. 3 of *The Army Air Forces in World War II.* Washington, DC: Office of Air Force History, 1983.

———. *Europe: Torch to Pointblank, August 1942 to December 1943*. Vol. 2 of *The Army Air Forces in World War II*. Washington, DC: Office of Air Force History, 1983.

———. *Men and Planes*. Vol. 6 of *The Army Air Forces in World War II*. Washington, DC: Office of Air Force History, 1983.

———. *Plans and Early Operations, January 1939 to August 1942*. Vol. 1 of *The Army Air Forces in World War II*. Wash-ington, DC: Office of Air Force History, 1983.

Davies, Peter. "Geoffrey Vickers and Lessons from the Ministry of Economic Warfare for Cold War Defence Intelligence." *Intelligence and National Security* 31, no. 6 (2016): 810–28.

Davis, Richard G. *Bombing the European Axis Powers: A Historical Digest of the Combined Bomber Offensive, 1939–1945.* Maxwell AFB, AL: Air University Press, 2006.

———. *Carl A. Spaatz and the Air War in Europe.* Washington, DC: Department of the Air Force, 1993.

DeVine, Michael R. "Defense Primer: Intelligence Support to Military Operations." Washington, DC: Congressional Research Service, 2018.

Downing, Taylor. *Spies in the Sky: The Secret Battle for Aerial Intelligence During World War II.* London: Little, Brown, 2011.

Fawkes, Andy J., and Martin Menzel. "The Future Role of Artificial Intelligence: Military Opportunities and Challenges." *Transforming Joint Air Power: The Journal of the JAPCC* 27 (Autumn/Winter 2018): 70–77.

Finney, Robert T. *History of the Air Corps Tactical School, 1920–1940.* Washington, DC: Center for Air Force History, 1992.

Fritz, Martin, and Birgit Karlsson. *Skf—A Global Story: 1907–2007.* Stockholm: Informationsförlaget, 2006.

Gilpin, Robert, and Jean M. Gilpin. *Global Political Economy: Understanding the International Economic Order.* Princeton, NJ: Princeton University Press, 2001.

Grandstaff, Mark R. "Muir Fairchild and the Origins of Air University, 1945–46." *Airpower Journal* XI, no. 4 (Winter 1997).

Greer, Thomas H. *The Development of Air Doctrine in the Army Air Arm, 1917–1941.* Washington, DC: Office of Air Force History, 1985.

Griffith, Charles. *The Quest: Haywood Hansell and American Strategic Bombing in World War II.* Maxwell AFB, AL: Air University Press, 1999.

Gropman, Alan L. *Mobilizing U.S. Industry in World War II: Myth and Reality.* Washington, DC: National Defense University Press, 1996.

Gruen, Adam L. *Preemptive Defense: Allied Air Power Versus Hitler's V-Weapons, 1943–1945.* Washington, DC: U.S. Government Printing Office, 1998.

Harrison, Gordon A. *Cross-Channel Attack.* Washington, DC: Department of the Army, 1951.

Harwood, Jeremy. *World War Two from Above: An Aerial View of the Global Conflict.* Wollombi, AUS: Exisle Publishing, 2014.

Hastings, Max. *Bomber Command.* Minneapolis, MN: Zenith Press, 2013.

Herrmann, Hajo. *Eagle's Wings.* Stillwater, MN: Motorbooks International, 1991.

Hohn, Uta. "The Bomber's Baedeker—Target Book for Strategic Bombing in the Economic Warfare against German Towns 1943–45." *GeoJournal* 34, no. 2 (1994): 213–30.

Hoover Medal, Board of Award. "William Loren Batt: Thirteenth Hoover Medalist." New York, 1951.

Johnson, David E. *Fast Tanks and Heavy Bombers: Innovation in the U.S. Army, 1917–1945.* Ithaca, NY: Cornell University Press, 1998.

———. *Modern U.S. Civil-Military Relations: Wielding the Terrible Swift Sword.* Washington, DC: National Defense University Press, 1997.

Jones, R. V. *The Wizard War: British Scientific Intelligence, 1939–1945.* New York: Coward, McCann & Geoghegan, 1978.

Kahn, David. "The Intelligence Failure of Pearl Harbor." *Foreign Affairs* 70, no. 5 (1991): 138.

Kaysen, Carl. "Notes on Strategic Air Intelligence in World War II (ETO)." Santa Monica, CA: Project RAND, October 1949.

Kimmons, Jeff, Ronald Makuta, and Graham Gilmer. *Remaking Intelligence Processing, Exploitation and Dissemination.* Booz Allen Hamilton Inc. https://governmenttechnologyinsider.com/wp-content/uploads/2018/02/12012017-Intelligence-Processing-Exploitation-and-Dissemination-PED-Thought-Piece.pdf.

Knight, Charlotte. "Ask Them Another." *Air Force* 28, no. 8 (1945): 30–31, 34, 60.

Kozak, Warren. *LeMay: The Life and Wars of General Curtis LeMay.* Washington, DC: Regnery, 2009.

Kreis, John F. *Piercing the Fog: Intelligence and Army Air Forces Operations in World War II.* Washington, DC: Air Force History and Museums Program, 1996.

Landauer, Carl. "A Break in Keynes's Theory of Interest." *The American Economic Review* 27, no. 2 (1937): 260–66.

Larrabee, Eric. *Commander in Chief: Franklin Delano Roosevelt, His Lieutenants, and Their War.* New York: Simon & Schuster, 1988.

Levine, Alan J. *The Strategic Bombing of Germany, 1940–1945.* Westport, CT: Praeger, 1992.

"L'heure Bleue." https://www.guerlain.com/us/en-us/fragrance/womens-fragrances/lheure-bleue.

Lockwood, John Hoyt. *Western Massachusetts: A History, 1636–1925.* Vol. 3. New York: Lewis Historical Publishing Co., 1926.

MacPherson, Nelson. *American Intelligence in War-Time London: The Story of the OSS.* Portland, OR: Frank Cass Publishers, 2003.

Magee Jr., John Gillespie. "High Flight." *All Hands* (April 2003): 7.

Matloff, Maurice. *The 90-Division Gamble.* Washington, DC: U.S. Army Center of Military History, 1990.

———, ed. *Strategic Planning for Coalition Warfare*. Washington, DC: U.S. Army Center of Military History, 1994.

———. *Strategic Planning for Coalition Warfare, 1943–1944.* Washington, DC: Office of the Chief of Military History, Department of the Army, 1959.

Maurer, Maurer. *The U.S. Air Service in World War I.* 4 vols. Maxwell AFB, AL: AFHRA, 1978.

McArthur, Charles W. *Operations Analysis in the U.S. Army Eighth Air Force in World War II.* Providence, RI: American Mathematical Society, 1990.

McCloskey, Joseph F. "The Beginnings of Operations Research: 1934–1941." *Operations Research* 35, no. 1 (1987): 143–52.

McFarland, Stephen Lee. *America's Pursuit of Precision Bombing, 1910–1945.* Washington, DC: Smithsonian Institution Press, 1995.

McFarland, Stephen Lee, and Wesley Phillips Newton. *To Command the Sky: The Battle for Air Superiority over Germany, 1942–1944.* Tuscaloosa: University of Alabama Press, 2006.

Meilinger, Phillip S. *Airmen and Air Theory: A Review of the Sources.* Maxwell AFB, AL: Air University Press, 2001.

———. *Ten Propositions Regarding Air Power*. Washington, DC: Air Force History and Museums Program, 1995.

Mets, David R. *Master of Airpower: General Carl A. Spaatz.* Novato, CA: Presidio Press, 1988.

Meyer, John W., and Brian Rowan. "Institutionalized Organizations: Formal Structure as Myth and Ceremony." *American Journal of Sociology* 83, no. 2 (1977): 340–63.

Middlebrook, Martin. *The Schweinfurt-Regensburg Mission.* New York: Scribner, 1983.

Officer, Lawrence H. "Review of *International Monetary Economics, 1870–1960: Between the Classical and the New Classical*, by M. June Flanders." *The Journal of Economic History* 50, no. 3 (1990): 779–81.

Overy, R. J. *The Air War, 1939–1945.* Washington, DC: Potomac Books, Inc., 1980.

Paret, Peter, Gordon Alexander Craig, and Felix Gilbert. *Makers of Modern Strategy: From Machiavelli to the Nuclear Age.* Princeton, NJ: Princeton University Press, 1986.

Parton, James. *Air Force Spoken Here: General Ira Eaker and the Command of the Air.* Bethesda, MD: Adler and Adler Publishers Inc., 1986.

Perret, Geoffrey. *Winged Victory: The Army Air Forces in World War II.* New York: Random House, 1993.

Posen, Barry. *The Sources of Military Doctrine: France, Britain, and Germany Between the World Wars.* Ithaca, NY: Cornell University Press, 1984.

Powaski, Ronald E. *The Cold War: The United States and the Soviet Union, 1917–1991.* New York: Oxford University Press, 1998.

Powys-Lybbe, Ursula. *The Eye of Intelligence.* London: W. Kimber, 1983.

Rast, Vicki J. *The Air University Pantheon of Air, Space, and Cyberspace Power Thinkers.* Maxwell AFB, AL: Air University Press, 2009.

Richards, Denis. *Portal of Hungerford: The Life of Marshal of the Royal Air Force Viscount Portal of Hungerford KG, GCB, OM, DSO, MC.* New York: Holmes and Meier, 1977.

Rigg, Brian Mark. "Half-Jewish Field Marshal Erhard Milch." *World War II* (January 2004): 72–76, 96.

Rosen, Stephen Peter. "Competitive Strategies: Theoretical Foundations, Limits, and Extentions." In *Competitive Strategies for the 21st Century: Theory, History, and Practice*, edited by Thomas G. Mahnken. Stanford, CA: Stanford University Press, 2012.

Rostow, W. W. "Waging Economic Warfare from London." *Studies in Intelligence* 7, no. 1 (1992): 73–79.

Schur, Norman W., Eugene Ehrlich, and Richard Ehrlich. *British English A to Zed: A Definitive Guide to the Queen's English.* New York: Skyhorse, 2013.

Shiner, John F. *Foulois and the U.S. Army Air Corps, 1931–1935*. Washington, DC: Air Force Historical Studies Office, 1984.

Shrader, Charles R. *History of Operations Research in the United States Army*. Washington, DC: U.S. Army Center of Military History, 2006.

Slany, William Z., et al. *Foreign Relations of the United States, 1943*. Washington, DC: Office of the Historian, Department of State, 1970.

Slessor, John Cotesworth. *Air Power and Armies*. Tuscaloosa: University of Alabama Press, 2009.

Stanley, Roy M. *V-Weapons Hunt: Defeating German Secret Weapons*. Barnsley, UK: Pen & Sword Military, 2010.

———. *World War II Photo Intelligence*. New York: Scribner, 1981.

Stewart, Richard W. *American Military History*. Vol. 2. Washington, DC: U.S. Army Center of Military History, 2005.

Thornhill, Paula G. *"Over Not Through": The Search for a Strong, Unified Culture for America's Airmen*. Santa Monica, CA: RAND Corporation, 2012.

Thorpe, Nick, and King of Romania Michael I. "Nobody Lifted a Finger." *Hungarian Review*, 6 (2011): 29–36.

Tsoukas, Haridimos. *New Thinking in Organizational Behaviour: From Social Engineering to Reflective Action*. Oxford: Butterworth-Heinemann, 1994.

Tyson, James L. "The EOU Vs. Hitler's Mini-Missiles." *International Journal of Intelligence and CounterIntelligence* 12, no. 1 (1999): 80–87.

Vaught, Wilma L. "In Defense of America: Women Who Serve." *USA Today* 122, no. 2586 (1994): 86.

Wakelam, Randall T. *The Science of Bombing: Operational Research in RAF Bomber Command*. Toronto: University of Toronto Press, 2009.

Watts, Barry D. *The Foundations of U.S. Air Doctrine: The Problem of Friction in War*. Maxwell AFB, AL: Air University Press, 1985.

Weaver, Michael E. "International Cooperation and Bureaucratic In-Fighting: American and British Economic Intelligence Sharing and the Strategic Bombing of Germany, 1939–41." *Intelligence and National Security* 23, no. 2 (April 2008): 153–75.

Webster, Charles K., and Noble Frankland. *The Strategic Air Offensive against Germany, 1939–1945*. 4 vols. London: Her Majesty's Stationery Office, 1961.

Webster's New Modern English Dictionary. Chicago: Consolidated Book Publishers, 1922.

Weigley, Russell Frank. *The American Way of War: A History of United States Military Strategy and Policy.* Bloomington: Indiana University Press, 1977.

The White House. "Remarks by the President at the NAACP Conference." News release, 14 July 2015. https://www.whitehouse.gov/the-press-office/2015/07/14/remarks-president-naacp-conference.

Williams, Allan. *Operation Crossbow: The Untold Story of Photographic Intelligence and the Search for Hitler's V Weapons.* London: Preface, 2011.

Winton, Harold R., and David R. Mets. *The Challenge of Change: Military Institutions and New Realities, 1918–1941.* Lincoln: University of Nebraska Press, 2000.

Wohlstetter, Roberta. *Pearl Harbor: Warning and Decision.* Stanford, CA: Stanford University Press, 1962.

Wolk, Herman S. "Decision at Casablanca." *Air Force Magazine* 86, no. 1 (2003): 78–82.

———. *The Struggle for Air Force Independence, 1943–1947.* Washington, DC: Air Force Historical Support Office, 1997.

Yenne, Bill. *Big Week: Six Days That Changed the Course of World War II.* New York: Berkley Books, 2013.

INDEX

Note: *p* with page reference indicates photograph